THE RIGHTS OF THE INDIVIDUAL
VERSUS
THE POWER OF THE GOVERNMENT

Should the members of the government be elected by direct vote of the people? Should the central government of the United States be stronger than the individual state governments? Does slavery have any place in a nation dedicated to liberty? Should the government be headed by a single executive, and how powerful should that executive be? Should immigrants be allowed into the United States? Which citizens should have the vote? How should judges be appointed, and what should their role in government be? What human rights should be safe from government infringement? In 1787, these important questions and others were raised as the states debated the merits of the proposed Constitution. Along with *The Federalist Papers*, this invaluable book documents the political context in which the Constitution was born.

D0054405

Ralph Ketcham is Professor of History and Political Science at the Maxwell School of Citizenship and Public Affairs of Syracuse University. He is the author of many books on American History, including *Presidents Above Party: The First American Presidency*; *From Colony to Country: The Revolution in American Thought, 1750–1820*; and *James Madison: A Biography*.

THE
ANTI-FEDERALIST PAPERS
AND
THE CONSTITUTIONAL
CONVENTION DEBATES

EDITED AND WITH AN INTRODUCTION BY

Ralph Ketcham

SIGNET CLASSICS

SIGNET CLASSICS
Published by New American Library, a division of
Penguin Group (USA) Inc., 375 Hudson Street,
New York, New York 10014, USA
Penguin Group (Canada), 90 Eglinton Avenue East, Suite 700, Toronto,
Ontario M4P 2Y3, Canada (a division of Pearson Penguin Canada Inc.)
Penguin Books Ltd., 80 Strand, London WC2R 0RL, England
Penguin Ireland, 25 St. Stephen's Green, Dublin 2,
Ireland (a division of Penguin Books Ltd.)
Penguin Group (Australia), 250 Camberwell Road, Camberwell, Victoria 3124,
Australia (a division of Pearson Australia Group Pty. Ltd.)
Penguin Books India Pvt. Ltd., 11 Community Centre, Panchsheel Park,
New Delhi - 110 017, India
Penguin Group (NZ), 67 Apollo Drive, Rosedale, Auckland 0632,
New Zealand (a division of Pearson New Zealand Ltd.)
Penguin Books (South Africa) (Pty.) Ltd., 24 Sturdee Avenue,
Rosebank, Johannesburg 2196, South Africa

Penguin Books Ltd., Registered Offices:
80 Strand, London WC2R 0RL, England

Published by Signet Classics, an imprint of New American Library, a division of Penguin Group (USA) Inc. Previously published in a Mentor edition.

First Signet Classics Printing, May 2003
40   39   38   37   36   35   34   33   32

The documents in the sections on the ratification contest by "Brutus," "Cato," "Centinel," "Federal Farmer," "John Dewitt," Patrick Henry, Melancton Smith, and the Pennsylvania Minority are reprinted from *The Complete Anti-Federalist* (seven-volume set), edited by Herbert J. Storing with the assistance of Murray Dry, © The University of Chicago, 1981; all rights reserved; vol. II, 116–19, 136–43, 223–34, 363–72, 382–87, 393–400, 413–28, 437–46; vol. III, 146–65; vol. V, 211–29; vol. VI, 149–69, 171–73, with the generous permission of the University of Chicago Press. Some of the documents are also included in *The Anti-Federalist: An Abridgement of the Seven-Volume Set of the Complete Anti-Federalist*, edited by Herbert J. Storing and abridged by Murray Dry, © The University of Chicago, 1981, 1985; all rights reserved.

 REGISTERED TRADEMARK—MARCA REGISTRADA

Printed in the United States of America

Contents

PART I
THE FEDERAL
CONVENTION OF 1787

PART II
RATIFICATION OF THE CONSTITUTION

Introduction

The Revolutionary Background of American Constitutional Thought

For anyone interested in political thought in action, the United States during the 1770s and 1780s is perhaps the most exciting period in the country's history. The discussion of political ideas that accompanied the American Revolution was seminal to the effort in 1787–1788 to draft and ratify a new constitution for the United States. In the years before 1776, as tension increased between Great Britain and her North American dominions, the rapidly maturing colonies were a laboratory of proposals and revised forms of union and confederated government. Each colony was more or less self-governing under its own "constitution," but officials on both sides of the Atlantic probed for a more satisfactory relationship between the colonies and the mother country. The eleven years between the Stamp Act Crisis (1765) and the Declaration of Independence (1776) were years of vigorous, creative political thinking which produced hundreds of pamphlets, newspaper articles, and other writings on questions of representative government and confederation. Writers in Great Britain, too, debated basic political principles and regarded the many proposals for governing the empire as part of the quest for freer, eventually more democratic government.

Political independence, moreover, required new modes of thinking not only about the government but also about national identity. Initially, Britons in America often felt a sharp sense of loss in their repudiation of loyalty to the mother country. Gone or discredited were important parts of the body politic and their undergirding ideas. Revolutionists challenged the House of Lords, military institutions and traditions, and even the monarch himself—symbol and embodiment of the nation. Colonials who still thought of England as "home" regretted, too, the distancing from a cherished land and culture; Salisbury Plain and London, Shakespeare and Milton, the ale house and the parish church remained deep in the consciousness—or subconsciousness—of many transatlantic Britons. Americans were uneasy about giving up this national identity and hence moved slowly and reluctantly toward independence. Many remained "loyalists" because they could not countenance such traumatic loss. Yet, by 1776, the "radical change in the principles, opinions, sentiments, and affections [that] was the real American Revolution," as John Adams put it, had taken place: Americans no longer thought of themselves as members of the British body politic; they were no longer part of what they, and most enlightened European opinion, often regarded as the freest, best-governed nation in the world.

New institutions and new ideas of government were needed, then, to replace the rejected British models. Yet, as the revolutionary tracts showed, and as the debate over the new constitution would demonstrate anew, Americans had very little beyond British ideology and experience with which to fashion a new nationhood. All the best-known writers—Harrington, Locke, Hutcheson, Algernon Sidney, Swift, Trenchard and Gordon, Price, Burgh, and even the works of Voltaire and Montesquieu idealizing British government—focused American attention on English history and thought. Within this thoroughly British pattern, however, American political thinkers began to express vital differences in emphasis. Traditional, Tory ideas had much less weight in America than they had in Britain. Ancient institutions such as the Church, the nobility, and the common law weakened in the New World. The palaces and fortresses of authority could not cross the Atlantic Ocean. On the other hand, "radical Whig" thought, emphasizing openness and freedom, loomed proportionately larger in America. A century and one half of physical separation and relatively isolated development had nurtured what in many ways were distinctive societies. As political leaders sought after 1776 to move from colony to country, they used British concepts and precedents, but they also fashioned anew for a new nation in a New World. To an initial revolution in loyalty which repudiated a nationality, Americans had to add a second revolution in purpose that would form ideas and institutions for a new polity.

Between 1776 and 1787, then, Americans undertook to create a new republic. They had to articulate and establish, perhaps beginning with revised understandings of human nature itself, basic principles and institutions of free government. Following the lead of Tom Paine in *Common Sense* (1776), many dreamed that the overthrow of oppressive, irrational customs and authority might be followed by a paradisiacal age when only the mildest and simplest bonds of self-government would be necessary. A western Massachusetts town resolved in 1776 that "what is the fundamental Constitution of this province, what are the undeniable Rights of the people, the powers of the Rulers, how often to be elected by the people, etc." were matters to be determined explicitly and anew by the people. Though John Adams believed Paine's ideas a "Star of Disaster," and warned that it was "safest to proceed in all established modes to which the people have been familiarized by habit," he still saw in Independence "Rays of Ravishing Light and Glory." Americans would create, as they announced on their great seal, *novus ordo seclorum,* "a new order of the ages." The new government to be fashioned in the United States might become a model for the world.

Beginning with New Hampshire in January 1776, every state drafted at least one constitution before 1787 (Connecticut and Rhode Island, without royal governors before 1776, merely had to remove references to Great Britain from colonial charters). Thus the new states added to the theoretical debates of the Revolutionary era a considerable practical experience in drafting and inaugurating new, constitutional governments. They tried many often novel proposals for legislative, executive, and judicial departments. By 1787, in a famous calculation by Thomas Jefferson, the new states had had eleven times thirteen, or nearly 150, years of experience in republican government. On the whole Jefferson thought the experiments remarkably successful, proving that the people were capable of governing themselves.

Mindful of the oppressions of their last British governors,

most states established legislative supremacy based on the principle of consent in their new constitutions. Pennsylvania gave broad powers to an annually-elected single-house (unicameral) legislature. In Virginia and other states, the legislature elected the governor and often had the power to appoint judges and other officials. In some states, though, notably New York and Massachusetts, the executive had more power and was elected directly by the qualified voters. Maryland chose the upper house by means of an elector college similar to that eventually put into the federal constitution. Bills of rights were drafted and debated in every state. Writing and ratifying the Articles of Confederation led to further discussion of principles and forms of government. By 1787, not only had the theory of self-government been widely debated, but virtually every conceivable device for implementing it had been suggested, if not tried.

As had been true during the long debate over "representation" within the British Empire before 1776, much attention focused on giving voice to the undistorted and uncorrupted will of the people. Small districts, annual elections, rotation in office, versions of referendum and recall, and unicameral legislatures were among the devices tried to tie representatives to that will. Intense rivalries, clash of interests, and manipulation of voters and representatives, though, seemed often to lead legislative governments into biased and unwise measures. Many states with two-house (bicameral) legislatures, and some with frankly aristocratic upper houses, even found that prolonged deliberation and checks on popular will could result in more dispassionate and practical legislation. By 1787 Americans had tried many devices of representative government, and had discussed at length the more sophisticated dilemmas it posed.

The liabilities of executive weakness had by 1787 also become apparent. Jefferson and Madison considered the impotent governorship of Virginia "the worst part of a bad constitution." The governor, elected by the legislature and required to act only with the consent of a council also elected by the legislature, was simply unable to govern. The elections of the governor and council became occasions for intrigue and influence-swapping of the worst sort. As experience with elective rather than hereditary or appointed executives accumulated, furthermore, a new and intriguing possibility emerged: the elective governor might himself become a legitimate part of government by consent when he vetoed laws, made appointments, or commanded the militia. Thus election of the governor by the people was a potentially effective *extension* of popular influence, rather than a checking of it as had normally been the case under a monarchical executive. As James Wilson would put it in 1790, with executives elected by the people and thus drawn from the same source as legislatures, "they who execute and they who administer the laws, are as much the servants, and therefore as much the friends of the people, as those who make them."

The judiciary also came under reconsideration. Experiments with legislative appointment of judges, or even election by the people, undertaken on democratic principles, seemed often to subject judges to political pressures that hindered impartiality and "equal justice." A few years' experience in Virginia with legislature-appointed judges had led, in Madison's opinion, to the sacrifice of "private rights" and the exposure of judges to "all the corruptions of the two other departments." Instead, foreshadowing provisions for the new federal judiciary, Madison favored executive appointment, fixed salaries, and life tenure to shield judges from legislative intrigue and popular sentiment.

In another effort to resist, as Madison put it, "the maxim . . . that the interest of the majority is the political standard of right and wrong," many leaders sought to establish written constitutions, with their bills of rights, clear definitions of procedure, and careful limitations of power, as fundamental law, above legislative or executive authority. Massachusetts and other states elected special conventions to draft constitutions and then held special elections to ratify them to underscore the supremacy and the republican character of constitutional provisions. These solemn, deliberate acts of the people established a "higher law" that a majority of the legislature or even of the people would be forbidden to violate.

American political thought and experience after 1776 in fact highlighted a tension built into the Declaration of Independence which proclaimed in one clause that certain rights were "unalienable," and in another that "Governments . . . derive their just powers from the consent of the governed." Rights to life, liberty, and the pursuit of happiness were not to be submitted to a vote or to depend on the outcome of elections; that is, not even the consent of the governed could legitimately abridge them. But it was nonetheless possible that the people, through their elected representatives, might sanction laws violating "unalienable" rights. Suppose legislatures, state or national, passed laws abridging freedom of the press, or violating liberty of conscience, or permitting default on contracts, as happened in the 1780s. Which principle had priority, that of "consent" or that of "unalienable rights"? Unless it could be assured that all, or at least a majority, of the people would always protect "unalienable rights," which few thought likely, the American Revolutionists seemed committed to propositions not always compatible. The Federal Constitution of 1787 was one effort to contain the tension, and the debate over its ratification often revolved around whether the framers had properly adjusted the balance of the two principles. Virtually all the members of the Federal Convention, and both sides in the ratification struggle, sought to fulfill the purposes of the Declaration of Independence to both protect rights and insure government by consent. The key differences arose over which purpose to emphasize and what mechanisms of government best assured some fulfillment of each. The separation from Great Britain and eleven years of independent state and national government had left Americans with an uncertain national identity, an intriguing republican idealism, and an intricate array of unresolved tensions and practical problems.

Republicanism in the 1780s

As the Federal Convention assembled in May 1787 its members did agree, though, on some basic principles and use of terms. All believed in government by consent, which in eighteenth-century understanding included (1) constitutional monarchy, where the monarch's powers were limited and where the government included an assembly elected by the people; (2) a republic, meaning some form of representative government without a hereditary executive; and (3) democracy, which meant either town-meeting style democracy or simply the direct voice of the people within a government. The Revolutionary struggle against the government of George III left even constitutional monarchy in ill-repute in America. (Many leaders, however, including at times John Adams and Alexander Hamilton, continued to think it theoretically the form most likely to insure freedom and good government.) Equally discredited was "mere democracy" which still meant, as Aristotle had taught, rule by the passionate, ignorant, demagogue-dominated "voice of the people." This was sure to produce first injustice, then anarchy, and finally tyranny. Hence, virtually all shades of opinion reviled monarchy and democracy, and, publicly at least, affirmed republicanism. (This republicanism of the 1780s was not in principle different from what in Britain and America by mid-nineteenth century was generally called representative democracy. The founders would not have been opposed to the modern connotations of the word "democracy," nor would they have used the word "republic" to mark out a distinction from those connotations. In scorning "democracy," eighteenth-century theorists had in mind Aristotle's picture of a heedless, emotional, manipulated populace that would still be denigrated by most modern democratic theorists.)

By 1787, republicanism, then, was positioned between monarchy and "mere democracy." As it benefited from the experience of the years after 1776 and struggled to contain the tension between "unalienable rights" and majority rule, republicanism became both more moderate and more intricate. A broadly based lower house of a legislature continued to be basic to government by consent, but, increasingly, the election of other officials came to be regarded as good republican practice. Also, mindful of colonial experience and following the arguments of Montesquieu, the idea that the legislative, executive, and judicial powers had to be "separated," made to "check and balance" each other in order to prevent tyranny, gained wide acceptance. This often validated devices of government that would restrain or "refine" the will of the majority in order to protect rights, or "higher law."

Thus, while eighteenth-century American republicanism was committed to the sovereignty of the people, it was also a complicated approach to government. It opposed traditional, monarchical tyranny, but was equally hostile to mob rule. It also sought balancing and refining devices that would at once restrain the power of rulers, encourage the better judgment of the people, and enable the union to defend itself in a dangerous world. Edmund Burke stated the problem succinctly: "to make a government requires no great prudence; settle the seat of power, teach obedience, and the work is done. To give freedom is still more easy. It is not necessary to guide; it only requires to let go the rein. But to form a free government, that is, to temper together the opposite elements of liberty and restraint in one conscious work, requires much thought; deep reflection; a sagacious, powerful, and combining mind." Madison's formulation in Federalist No. 51 made the same point: "You must first enable the government to control the governed; and in the next place, oblige it to control itself"—as much a need in a republic as in any other form of government.

In a way, to oblige government to "control itself" was more difficult in the new United States than it was in Europe. There, "balance of power" theorists made use of the essentially different orders of traditional society—king, lords, commons, or first, second, and third estates—to achieve equilibrium in government. Thus British government preserved balanced freedom by giving each of the distinct—separately derived—orders of society a means of self-defense. The monarch, the House of Lords, and the House of Commons each had effective legislative voice. The balance was enduring because the king and the nobility and the commoners were formally and permanently separate. But in the United States, without a hereditary monarch or nobility, and without politically powerful bishops or other privileged elements formally distinct from "the people," how could checks and balances work? What real balance could there be when ultimately, as republican theory required, all legitimate power came from one entity, the people? Could the separation of powers among levels and branches of governments all resting on consent provide checks like those arising from the distinct orders of a hierarchical society? Were, then, the ideas of deriving all just power from the consent of the governed, and genuine balance of powers, mutually exclusive? Yet another complicated problem faced the framers and ratifiers of 1787–1788.

The response, drawn in part from the ideas of David Hume but best elaborated by James Madison, was to try to build into the mechanism of government itself enough variations on election, powers, term of office, and complication of function to *create* separate interests and perspectives. Thus, for example, even though an upper and a lower house of the legislature might each *eventually* derive from the people, different districts, different terms of office, different modes of election, and different definitions of authority would create balances of power. Complex arrangements for appointing and giving power to other officials, and "refinements" of popular will through devices like an electoral college, it was theorized, would become further effective substitutes for the balances inherent in the lasting divisions within traditional societies. Could mere complication of government, together with devices to "refine" the expression of majority will, without departing fundamentally from the principle of consent, protect basic rights both from potential tyrants within government and from popular passions? The intention was to temper idealism with realism, and to substitute complexity for balance of orders. The challenge offered wide scope for political theorists as well as practical strategists as the time approached to revise the Federal Constitution.

Political Currents of the 1780s

These difficult and important theoretical problems existed at the Federal Convention amid a welter of clashing interests, social distinctions, ethnic diversities, religious backgrounds, and disparities of wealth. Differences over geography, commerce, religion, customs, land speculation, slavery, and credit influenced proposals for structures of government and sometimes required compromise of principle as well as of interests. These concerns, especially that of the New England states to regulate commerce by majority vote in Congress, and of Georgia and South Carolina to keep open the slave trade (settled by compromise; see pp. 153–58), had an impact on many decisions. The Constitution also gave implicit sanction to private property (including slaves) and otherwise sustained the planter-yeoman/farmer/mercantile society that had emerged in the thirteen newly independent states. Yet, the Constitution as drafted also reflects the ebb and flow of debate over principles of government. In fact, there are some signs that the various special interests represented at the Convention counteracted and often nullified each other and thus in a way gave scope to discussion of basic constitutional issues. There is little evidence, in any case, that determined factions—creditors, land speculators, merchants, slave owners, or any others—implanted in the draft constitution a self-interested mode of government inconsistent with republican principles.

The principle of consent, furthermore, since it was thought of largely as applying to those with a material stake in society (land, securities, slaves, mercantile property, tax payments, etc.), was less inclusive in the eighteenth century than it would become two hundred years later. Property qualifications for voting and office-holding were common, and women were barred from doing either. Most extreme, black slaves were not regarded as part of the political community and hence were entirely denied participation and protection of rights. Though some advanced thinkers saw the inconsistencies in these limitations (especially of slave owners and slave traders proclaiming the blessings of liberty) and cried out against them, sentiment in 1787 had not generally reached the point where universal suffrage would be on the agenda of constitution framers. Thus the Convention ignored those issues by accepting the guidelines already existing in state constitutions and in the Articles of Confederation. Though this did not advance the causes of enlarged suffrage and abolition of slavery, at the same time, deliberately, there were no explicit barriers in the Constitution to liberalization when sentiment within any state moved in that direction. States were able to abolish slavery, and voting for members of

the lower house in Congress was to carry the same limitations—
or lack of limitation—as for the lower house of the state legislature. The Convention had to find mechanisms of government
that would guarantee the power of the people to decide economic as well as other matters, and protect the "unalienable
rights" gained by the Revolution.

These theoretical and practical concerns persisted as the new
nation struggled to survive, first in war and then in peace. As the
states drafted and revised their constitutions, they also worked
to form a confederal constitution. The *ad hoc* actions of the Continental Congresses, setting aside British authority and fighting
the Revolutionary War, had to be formalized and a permanent
form of government established. Congress approved "Articles of
Confederation" in 1777 that were finally ratified (by all the states)
and became the basis for national government in 1781. They were
the first American constitution. Almost at once, though, complaints arose about their weakness and inefficiency. "National-
ists" such as Robert Morris, Alexander Hamilton, James Madison,
James Wilson, and George Washington agreed that the Articles
were inadequate and made various proposals for strengthening
them. They sought especially to give Congress wider taxing
power, more control over interstate and foreign commerce, and
power to compel state compliance with acts of Congress. Since
the Articles required unanimous consent of the states for amendment, proposals for change were easily blocked. A conference
at Mount Vernon in 1785, though, which settled navigation,
boundary, and other disputes between Maryland and Virginia,
encouraged the idea of a larger meeting to cope with problems
apparently stymied in Congress under the Articles. A convention
at Annapolis in September 1786, asking all the states to discuss
interstate commerce regulation, failed because most states did
not send delegates. It did, however, call for another convention
to meet in May 1787 in Philadelphia. A heightened sense of
futility in Congress and disarray in the nation (Shays' rebellion
flared that winter) led Congress and all states except Rhode Island to endorse that call. Hence, the fifty-five delegates who
came to the Federal Convention of 1787 (others appointed did
not come at all) had in mind generally to strengthen the Articles,

but beyond that there was little agreement on how extensively and in what way to do that.

The Federal Convention of 1787

The debates of the Convention, known to us largely through notes taken by James Madison during its deliberations, flowed through readily discernible stages. The largely favorable reception by the Convention of the "Virginia Plan" (see pp. 7–12), conceived by Madison and agreed to by the Virginia delegation, implied that the Convention intended to frame a new government rather than merely amend the Articles of Confederation, as most delegates had been instructed to do. For two weeks the delegates debated representation, executive powers, state-national relations, and other basic matters. Though the Convention voted down the clause in the Virginia Plan giving Congress the power to "negative" "improper" state laws, in general there was surprising support for provisions to strengthen the national government. On June 13 the Convention accepted nineteen resolves largely following the Virginia Plan. The "small state" forces, however, still opposed bitterly the tentative switch from an equal vote for each state in the national legislature (as under the Articles of Confederation) to representation according to the population.

The Convention entered a new phase on June 15 when William Paterson introduced what became known as the "New Jersey Plan" (see pp. 39–48), retaining the equality of the states and other provisions closer to the Articles. The challenge had been made, and for a month the delegates debated state equality with increased passion and rancor, sought compromises, and struggled to prevent disruption of the Convention. Madison, James Wilson, Rufus King, and other proponents of proportional representation stood firm. Paterson, Luther Martin of Maryland, and other small-state delegates insisted just as strongly on state equality, while the Convention conciliators, mainly Benjamin Franklin and William Samuel Johnson of Connecticut, suggested compromise. A grand committee, appointed to settle the deadlocked issue, reported on July 5 recommending the so-called "Great Compromise." The lower house would have representation according to population, and the states would be equal in the upper house. Though Madison and Wilson opposed the compromise because to them it violated the vital republican principle of majority rule, most of the delegates were ready to accept an accommodation. On July 16, the Convention approved the "Great Compromise."

Having settled this major point, the Convention considered, in ten days of important debate, the powers and election of the executive, the judiciary, the method of ratification, and the powers of Congress. After making some tentative decisions and deferring others, on July 26 the Convention appointed a committee of detail to arrange and systemize what had been done so far and to make proposals on unsettled matters. Its report (see pp. 122–134), made on August 6, was the first document before the Convention to resemble the final constitution. Perhaps most notable, instead of the broad power in the Virginia Plan for Congress "to legislate in all cases to which the separate States are incompetent," the draft enumerated the powers of Congress. Madison and other advocates of broad national power came to favor a more careful definition of congressional power after the adoption of what they regarded as the flawed "Great Compromise." They were unwilling to so generally empower a body where a few states containing a small minority of the population could have a deciding voice. Small-state delegates, on the other hand, assured of an equal voice in the Senate, became increasingly willing to put power in the hands of the central government, a circumstance that led in time to the quick ratification of the Constitution by most of the small states.

For more than a month, August 7–September 10, the Convention debated, clause-by-clause, the articles of the draft constitution. As the delegates thus settled matters of detail and accepted the practical compromise between New England and the deep South states on slavery and commercial regulation (see pp. 153–58), they continued to dispute the powers of the executive department and its relation to the Senate. How to elect the executive, how he might exercise his veto, and how he might be joined with the Senate in appointive and treaty-making powers, continued to vex and divide the delegates. By September 10, after several referrals of unsettled matters to select committees, the Convention felt it had sufficiently resolved all questions to entrust its work to a committee on arrangement and style. The actual draft of the final document seems to have been executed by Gouverneur Morris.

As the Constitution took final shape, however, it was apparent that three delegates still at the Convention, Edmund Randolph and George Mason of Virginia and Elbridge Gerry of Massachusetts, did not approve it. Before and after the committee on arrangement and style did its work, they complained about many particulars, but mainly opposed the scope of powers given to the new federal government. (Their objections, reprinted on pp. 166–71, in fact anticipated many of the arguments anti-federalists would offer in the ratification debates.) Nonetheless thirty-nine delegates approved their work, and after a few changes in detail, moved, with the unanimous consent of all states present, to submit the constitution to the Confederation Congress and to the people of the states.

The Ratification Contest

The ratification struggle began with a clever move by the proponents of the new constitution: since sentiment in the country was hostile to the idea of a national government and preferred a confederation, or federation (the words were synonymous in the eighteenth century), the proponents called themselves "federalists" even though the new document was not, strictly speaking, a federation, a league of governments, as the old Articles were. In fact, the new constitution, as Madison explained carefully in Federalist No. 39, was a "composite," partly national in that some powers impinged directly on the people (most notably the taxing power and the election of the House of Representatives) and partly federal in that the states acted as "units" of the central government (most notably in the election of the Senate). By taking the popular word "federal" to denote the new constitution, its backers gained an important "image" victory for themselves. The word "federal" came eventually to mean the form of government embodied in the new Constitution, just as "confederation" came to mean the more strictly "league of states" idea of the Articles of Confederation and eventually the "Confederacy" of 1861–1865. The foes of ratification, moreover, were left with the negative designation, "anti-federalists." (The term "federalist" here, uncapitalized, refers to the proponents of the new constitution, 1787–1789, and is a different group from the political party formed in the 1790s, called "Federalist," usually capitalized.)

Important backers of the new constitution, most notably Alexander Hamilton and James Madison, returned to New York (where the Articles of Confederation Congress was in session) to organize their campaign for ratification. With Hamilton taking the initiative, he, Madison, and John Jay agreed to write a series of essays for New York newspapers explaining and defending the new Constitution. They used the pseudonym "Publius," the legendary law-giver of the Roman republic extolled by Plutarch, in addressing "the People of the State of New York." Jay's illness during the winter of 1787–1788 limited his contribution to only five of the eighty-five essays. Hamilton wrote fifty-one and Madison twenty-nine (the long dispute over authorship of some essays is now settled; Madison wrote all the essays he designated as his in old age). Anxious to get the systematic argument for the new Constitution before the public, Hamilton and Madison hurried three or four essays a week to the newspapers between October 27, 1787, and April 2, 1788. In general, Hamilton wrote the essays on the need for a more energetic government, on the powers of Congress, and on the executive and judicial departments, while Madison explained the nature of the federal system, the formal and informal checks and balances, and the House of Representatives and the Senate. At the time, however, readers did not know who "Publius" was, and saw the *Federalist* as a comprehensive, single-minded advocacy of the Constitution. At the same time other federalist essays and speeches appeared in the newspapers, and the major anti-federalist series of essays, "Centinel," "Cato," "Brutus," and "The Federal Farmer," came out

initially in Philadelphia and New York newspapers, and were
soon reprinted throughout the country.

As the theoretical arguments developed before the public,
separate ratification struggles took place in each state. Reflect-
ing satisfaction over the state equality in the Senate, and anxious
for protection within a stronger union, conventions in three
small states, Delaware, New Jersey, and Georgia, ratified early
and unanimously. Connecticut was also strongly federalist and
ratified readily (128–40), while the vagaries of Pennsylvania
politics, plus the zeal of James Wilson and other federalists, produced an early federalist victory (46–23) there, too. Thus, when
the closely divided Massachusetts convention met in January
1788, five states had already ratified. After a long, spirited debate, and some clever maneuvering by the federalists, the Massachusetts convention voted on February 16, 1787, 187–168, to
ratify.

This close vote, and the strength of the anti-federalists in the
critical states of Virginia and New York, created an air of uncertainty during the first six months of 1788. The eventual, easy
ratifications by Maryland (63–11) and South Carolina (149–73)
in April and May cheered the federalists; only one more state
would need to ratify to implement the new government. Yet,
awareness that anti-federalists were dominant in New Hampshire, that Rhode Island and North Carolina were hostile, and
that the vital states of Virginia and New York might not ratify,
left the issue in balance as the Virginia convention assembled in
June. There, in the most important of the ratification contests,
Madison, Randolph, and other federalists achieved a debating
victory over George Mason, Patrick Henry, and their anti-federal
allies. Virginia voted to ratify, 89–79, on June 25, and in the
meantime New Hampshire had enough shifted its position to
ratify, 57–47, on June 21. With ten states having ratified, establishment of the new government was certain. Faced with this
circumstance, the New York convention, though its delegates
were elected largely as anti-federalists (46–19), nonetheless after thorough debate voted to ratify, 30–27. The North Carolina
convention voted against ratification, 193–75, while Rhode Island refused even to call a convention. North Carolina ratified

the constitution and joined the union in November 1789, and Rhode Island did so in May 1790.

Federalist Principles

As this political struggle progressed, crucial theoretical differences clarified. The federalists on the whole saw and sought the benefits more effective, energetic government could bring even, perhaps especially, in a republic (see Federalist Nos. 1, 23). Well aware of the tendency of confederations and small, vulnerable republics to be merely provincial, to quarrel among themselves, and to be gobbled up by more united, powerful nations (see Nos. 18–20), the federalists sought the stability and strength that could come from union and from steady, effective government. As James Wilson saw with particular clarity, strong government could as much serve the people when controlled by them as it could injure them when it was hostile to them. Therefore, the need to limit the powers of government so important during the long struggle to end the tyranny of kings was perhaps misguided when the government was not alien or from above, but *of the people* (see No. 70). The goal, then, was not simply the *limitation* of the powers of the executive, or even of the government as a whole, but the insurance of its faithfulness to the people and of the stability and wisdom of its enactments. To Hamilton, Madison, and other federalists, government in the United States, even though more fully republican than any other in the world, had also often been weak, unstable, and foolish. Foreign intrigue, domestic insurrection, bankruptcy, and dismemberment all threatened the new nation, and, in the opinion of the federalists, could only be avoided by a stronger union (see Nos. 2–8).

Despite this sharp critique, the federalists still thought of themselves as heirs to the American Revolution and sincere friends of government by consent. To them the ideals of human rights and rule by the people required not suspicion of government but *use* of it. They were confident that human ingenuity could devise mechanisms that would at once protect liberty, allow effective government, and rest on the consent of the people (see Nos. 10, 37). It was possible both to give sufficient powers to the House of Representatives and to the president, and to guard against the abuse of those powers. It was only prudent to erect barriers against tendencies toward greed, passion, and selfish ambition in any human government, but it was also important to benefit from wise and good rule (see Nos. 51, 78). If good government was impossible when "the people" chose their own rulers, then the very idea of government by consent stood condemned (see No. 57). The federalists believed the new Constitution provided effective resolution of these intricacies.

They also had high hopes that with the stability and energy of the new Constitution the nation might expand and progress rapidly. The federalists sought agricultural and commercial growth that would bring wealth and prosperity to all the people, and they saw the national government as a guide and partner in the westward expansion of the nation (see No. 14). They also supposed that the nation needed vigor and power in order to survive and exert its influence in the dangerous but opportunity-laden international scene. In short, the federalists sought English-style commercial growth, domestic prosperity, and world power, which they thought were compatible with Revolutionary ideals of freedom and self-government. They believed the new Constitution furnished the means for achieving those goals.

Anti-federalist Political Thought

Perceiving these aspirations and purposes, the anti-federalists were at once skeptical and disheartened. They saw in federalist hopes for commercial growth and international prestige only the lust of ambitious men for a "splendid empire" where, in the time-honored way, the people would be burdened with taxes, conscription, and campaigns (see Patrick Henry and "John DeWitt"). Uncertain that any government over so vast a domain as the United States could be controlled by the people, the anti-federalists saw in the enlarged powers of the central government only the familiar threats to the rights and liberties of the people.

The federal judiciary, for example, seemed like simply another magistry removed from the people that would enforce harsh and arbitrary laws (see "Brutus," Nos. 11, 12, 15). The broad power to lay and collect taxes, the president's role as commander-in-chief, Congress' authority to pass any laws "necessary and proper" to carry out its enumerated powers, and the "supreme law" and treaty-making powers, all seemed unbounded and at least potentially tyrannical. A persistent thrust in anti-federal thought, then, was both to withdraw some of the explicit powers given to the national government and to restrain with further checks and balances the exercise of its remaining powers. The anti-federalists were, in a sense, "men of little faith" as both contemporary and modern critics have charged, but this was true only within their fear that centralized power tended to become arbitrary and impersonal. The anti-federalists came to these views more readily, of course, because the Whig rhetoric of eighteenth-century British radicalism and the ideology of the American Revolution were filled with suspicions of power, especially distant, centralized power. These arguments were now handy for use against other advocates of such power.

The anti-federalists also had a positive idealism of their own, a republican vision they thought far closer to the purpose of the American Revolution than the political and commercial ambitions of the federalists. The anti-federalists looked to the Classical idealization of the small, pastoral republic where virtuous, self-reliant citizens managed their own affairs and shunned the power and glory of empire. To them, the victory in the American Revolution meant not so much the big chance to become a wealthy world power, but rather the opportunity to achieve a genuinely republican polity, far from the greed, lust for power, and tyranny that had generally characterized human society. Was it possible, they asked themselves, to found society on other bases and with other aspirations that would nourish the virtue and happiness of all the people? Could they break the self-fulfilling cycle where selfish people needed to be controlled by checks and balances which in turn required and encouraged more and more self-seeking by the people?

To the anti-federalists this meant retaining as much as possible the vitality of local government where rulers and ruled could see, know, and understand each other. Thus they cherished the Revolutionary emphasis on state and local councils and committees, and the Articles of Confederation where the central government rested entirely on the states. The idea of self-government was tied inextricably to something like a town meeting directness or at least to a state legislature of many annually elected representatives who would really know the people of their districts. Each "district," furthermore, would be a town or ward or region conscious of its own particular identity rather than being some amorphous, arbitrary geographic entity (see "John DeWitt"). Only with such intimacy could the trust, goodwill, and deliberation essential to wise and virtuous public life be a reality. Anything else, even though resting in some fashion on the consent of the people, would not really be self-government.

The intense anti-federalist suspicions of corruption, greed, and lust for power were directed generally at those who ruled from on high and without restraint. Corruption and tyranny would be rampant as they always had been when those who exercised power felt little connection with the people. This would be true, moreover, for elected representatives, as well as for kings and nobles and bishops, who lived in a distant capital milieu where power, intrigue, and wealth exerted their baneful influence. The more remote and distantly powerful a government was, the more visions of imperial Rome or Versailles or London came to mind with all their venality, cynicism, corruption, and neglect of the people (see "Cato"). Would some future capital of the United States be as filled with courtiers, courtesans, military heroes, and superfluous officeholders as London or Paris or St. Petersburg? The anti-federalists thought so under a constitution that consolidated power in a central government remote from the people.

On the other hand, legends of the Greek and Roman republics, the maturing ideology of natural rights, and the substantial experience of local self-government in the New World seemed to offer a far more alluring prospect. *If* the basic decency in human nature, most evident among ordinary people at the local level amid family, church, school, and other nourishing institutions, could impinge directly and continuously on government, then perhaps it too might be kept virtuous and worthy of confidence. Then, instead of endless suspicion of and guarding against the evil and corruption of government, it might be possible to trust it and use it for the public benefit. The result might even be a society where honest, hardworking people could enjoy the fruits of their labor, where institutions encouraged and rested on virtue rather than greed, where officials were servants of the people rather than oppressors, and where peace and prosperity came from vigilant self-confidence rather than from conquest and dominion (see Patrick Henry). Anti-federalists saw mild, grassroots, small-scale governments in sharp contrast to the splendid edifice and overweening ambition implicit in the new Constitution—and, indeed, heralded by Publius and its other proponents. The first left citizens free to live their own lives and to cultivate the virtue (private and public) vital to republicanism, while the second soon entailed taxes and drafts and offices and wars damaging to human dignity and thus fatal to self-government.

The anti-federalist ideal emerged most clearly and practically in its understanding of what representation and government by consent could really mean. Instead of seeking to insulate officials from popular influence, as, for example, Publius argued federal judges should be (Federalist No. 78), anti-federalists sought to insure the public good by requiring close association. If legislators, for example, rather than federal judges appointed for life, had the power to interpret the Constitution, they would do so "at their peril"; if the people disapproved the interpretation, they "could remove them" ("Brutus," No. 15). The ideal went beyond a close control of officials by the people. In a truly self-governing society, there would be such dialogue, empathy, and even intimacy that the very distinction between ruler and ruled would tend to disappear. Such a close link between the people and officials would embody the idea of liberty being both security of rights and effective voice in public affairs. The anti-federalists groped for mechanisms that would give reality to this idea: how could it be achieved, in substance as well as in form, in a large nation?

For anti-federalists the bonds between the people and their representatives had to be trustworthy as well as close. Not only, as Melancton Smith put it, should "representatives resemble those they represent," but they should possess especially the virtues most characteristic of ordinary people: they should be temperate, moral, and of restrained ambition. Smith acknowledged that "the same passions and prejudices govern all men," but it was also true that "circumstances . . . give a cast to human character." The wealthy and the powerful, sad to say, were inclined to cheat customers, disdain honest labor, raise armies, put on social airs, and oppress the people. Could they be expected to rule wisely and justly in the interests of all? Rather, it was necessary that people of the "middling sort," average people, perhaps yeoman farmers, themselves take part in government—even be elected to office in large enough numbers to "set the tone" in the capital. Such people, in the daily round of their occupations, Smith observed, had "less temptations, [and] are inclined by habit, and by the company with whom they associate, to set bounds to their passions and appetites." He envisioned, then, a government of popular confidence and respect, vital at the local levels where the virtues of ordinary people could prevail. Though Smith articulated this more forthrightly than most anti-federalists, many others expressed the ideal implicitly (see "John DeWitt," Patrick Henry, and "the Federal Farmer"), and it was consistent with a moral and civic tradition long familiar in the Western world.

This was idealistic, of course, but the anti-federalists thought the goal of the American Revolution was to end the ancient equation of power where arrogant, oppressive, and depraved rulers on one side produced subservience and a gradual erosion of the self-respect, capacities, and virtue of the people on the other side. The result was an increasing corruption and degeneracy in both rulers and ruled. Unless this cycle could be broken, Independence would mean little more than the exchange of one tyranny for another. The aspirations of the federalists for commercial growth, westward expansion, increased national power, and effective world diplomacy were in some ways attractive and worthy, but they also fitted an ominous, all too familiar pattern of "great, splendid, . . . consolidated government" and "Universal Empire" that the American Revolution had been fought to eradicate. Many anti-federalists, inchoately perhaps, were unwilling to abandon this ideal and the hope that the New World might be a different and better place to live.

The ratification contest, then, was at bottom a debate over the future of the nation. Beneath the disputes about detailed clauses were deep differences over what fulfillment of the American Revolution meant. To the federalists, it meant independence, growth in national power, and prosperity, all within a federal system of government retaining the states and deriving its authority from the people, but also competent to all the needs and exigencies of respectable, energetic nationhood. This was an attractive purpose for large numbers of people of all classes and was in their view a legitimate outgrowth of the Revolution. The anti-federalists, on the other hand, sought a society where virtuous, hardworking honest men and women lived simply in their own communities, enjoyed their families and their neighbors, were devoted to the common welfare, and had such churches, schools, trade associations, and local governments as they needed to sustain their values and purposes. Though this intention was seldom fully or clearly articulated, it permeates anti-federalist writing enough to reveal what their positive ideal was. The quick adoption of the Bill of Rights, the ready acceptance of the new constitution by former anti-federalists, and the Jeffersonian triumph of 1801 with its manifold anti-federalist overtones, all attest to the vigor and influence of anti-federalism and its ability to find fulfillment even under the document opposed so vehemently in 1787–1788. Anti-federal ideas have also surfaced again and again in various guises among later generations of Americans. Those ideas, as well as the enticing prospects held out by Publius, are a vital element in the American political tradition and are properly viewed as part of the philosophy of the Constitution.

—RALPH KETCHAM
Syracuse University

Arrangement, Use,
and Editing
of the Documents

This book, along with the Signet Classics edition of *The Federalist Papers,* presents the context of political ideas within which the Federal Constitution of 1787 came into being. The selections from the debates at the Federal Convention of 1787 (almost entirely from Madison's Notes) have been made to emphasize basic expositions, disagreements, and stages of development of the Constitution. Thus, such major representations at the Convention as William Paterson's proposals and speech of June 15, Hamilton's speech of the 18th, and Madison's of June 6 and June 19 are printed in full. Selections from the ratification controversy are not necessarily the best known or most influential contributions to the debate but rather have been chosen for the cogency of their political thought. In most cases, full speeches, exchanges in debate, and essays are printed, rather than excerpts. Largely neglected are explanations of votes on specific issues, the various practical compromises that influenced the shape of the final document, and ratification pieces concentrating on particular economic or regional disputes. There is no effort, then, to explain or document either the Convention of 1787 or the ratification process as political events, though they surely were such and have been described and analyzed often by historians in that way (see bibliography). Readers will find in this volume and in *The Federalist Papers* the most profound and enduring political thought evoked by the drafting and ratification of the world's oldest still-in-use constitution.

Used with the Signet Classics edition of *The Federalist Papers,*

this book gives scholars and students access to the major expositions of and arguments over the Federal Constitution of 1787.
Throughout the general introduction and the notes for particular
documents, cross-references are made to related or contrasting
numbers of *The Federalist Papers.* A table on p. xxxix lists opposing federalist and anti-federalist writings on major topics. The index of ideas in this volume uses the same topics as appear in the
"Index of Ideas" in the Signet Classics editon of *The Federalist
Papers* to facilitate comparisons of thought in the Convention debates, in *The Federalist Papers* and in anti-federalist writings. This
volume is thus designed to be an easy-to-use companion to *The
Federalist Papers* by offering from the other major sources on the
Constitution parallel or equivalent expressions of political thought.

The editor's "long list" of the best *Federalist* papers would
include Numbers 1, 2, 3, 6, 9, 10, 14, 15, 23, 27, 30, 37, 39, 45,
49, 51, 52, 53, 57, 62, 63, 66, 67, 68, 69, 70, 73, 76, 78, and 84.
A shorter list of the most important *Federalist* essays would include only Numbers 1, 2, 6, 10, 14, 23, 39, 45, 51, 57, 62, 70, 78,
and 84. Clinton Rossiter, editor of the Signet Classics *Federalist,*
lists Numbers 1, 2, 6, 9, 10, 14, 15, 16, 23, 37, 39, 47, 48, 49, 51,
62, 63, 70, 78, 84, and 85 as "the cream of the eighty-five papers." Readers wanting to read or teachers having time to assign
only part of *The Federalist Papers* can be guided by these selected lists, or make their own abridgements.

Two documents beyond selections from the Convention debates and anti-federalist writings are included. First, James
Madison's letter to George Washington of April 16, 1787, outlining what would become known as the Virginia Plan, is reprinted as a general introduction to the work of the Federal
Convention. Second, James Wilson's speech of October 6, 1787,
the most complete, visible, and widely commented-on early defense of the Constitution, is reprinted because it was the target,
direct or indirect, of much of the anti-federalist criticism reprinted in this volume. More than *The Federalist Papers* (or any
of its authors, who were unidentified in 1787–1788), Wilson was
the chief public advocate of the Constitution. His speech holds
an especially important place, theoretically and practically, in
the ratification contest.

The selections from the Convention debates are in chronological order with titles added to indicate in general the focus of any particular excerpt. Debate among several Convention delegates is often included when the exchanges reveal opposing arguments on basic points. Editorial apparatus indicates briefly the place of each document in the ratification debate, identifies (where possible) its author, and states the time and place of first delivery and/or printing. The selections from anti-federalist writings are grouped according to their place in the evolution of the fundamental theoretical controversy. That is, documents questioning whether a more energetic central government was needed in 1787 come first (the starting place for the debate over the proposed constitution), those asserting the tyrannical tendencies of the more energetic frame of government come next, and those explicating an emerging anti-federalist idea of government by consent come last. Though this arrangement imposes some order that would perhaps not have been evident in 1787–1788, it is intended to help students understand the most important theoretical issues of the debate. Since the date of first delivery or publication of each selection is indicated, easy reference to them in chronological order is possible (see chronology, pp. xxxvi–xxxviii).

In some cases, punctuation, italics, and spellings likely to confuse twentieth-century readers have been corrected to conform to modern usage. Brackets in the printed sources indicating slight variations in texts have been removed, and most abbreviations have been spelled out, to enhance readability. Ellipses indicate short deletion of words. In general, care has been taken to ensure fidelity to the original text and to remove obstacles to easy reading for modern students.

ACKNOWLEDGMENTS

The editor gratefully acknowledges the support of the John Ben Snow Foundation in preparing the manuscript, and the advice of the staff of the Institute of Early American History and Culture on editorial matters.

List of Plans,
Proposals, and Amendments

Chronology of Documents and Important Events

1781: March 1 - Articles of Confederation become effective
1786: Sept. 14 - Annapolis Convention calls for a Convention of all the states
1787: Feb. 21 - Continental Congress calls a Convention in Philadelphia to revise the Articles of Confederation

April 16 - Letter, Madison to Washington, outlining the "Virginia Plan" (p. 3)

May 25 - Constitutional Convention begins in Philadelphia

May 29 - Randolph presents the "Virginia Plan" (p. 7)

June 15 - Paterson presents the "New Jersey Plan" (p. 39)

June 18 - Hamilton presents plan for national government (p. 48)

July 16 - "Great Compromise" adopted

August 6 - First Draft of Constitution (p. 122)

Sept. 17 - Constitution approved, Convention adjourns (p. 177)

Oct. 5 - "Centinel" No. 1 (p. 232)

Oct. 6 - Speech of James Wilson, supporting the Constitution (p. 181)

Oct. 8 - "Federal Farmer" No. 1 (p. 266)

Oct. 9 - "Federal Farmer" No. 2 (p. 276)

Oct. 18 - "Brutus" No. 1 (p. 281)

Oct. 22 - "John DeWitt" No. 1 (p. 188)

Oct. 27 - "John DeWitt" No. 2 (p. 194); Federalist No. 1

Oct. 31 - Federalist No. 2

Nov. 5 - "John DeWitt" No. 3 (p. 329)

Nov. 14 - Federalist No. 6

Nov. 22 - Federalist No. 10

Nov. 22 - "Cato" No. 5 (p. 336)

Nov. 29 - "Brutus" No. 4 (p. 345)

Nov. 30 - Federalist No. 14

Dec. 7 - Delaware ratifies (30–0)

Dec. 12 - Pennsylvania ratifies (46–23)

Dec. 18 - New Jersey ratifies (39–0); Federalist No. 23; Address of Pennsylvania Minority (p. 243)

Dec. 27 - "Brutus" No. 6 (p. 293)

1788:   Jan. 2 - Georgia ratifies (26–0)

Jan. 3 - "Cato" No. 7 (p. 341)

Jan. 9 - Connecticut ratifies (128–40)

Jan. 16 - Federalist No. 39

Jan. 24 - "Brutus" No. 10 (p. 302)

Jan. 26 - Federalist No. 45

Jan. 31 - "Brutus" No. 11 (p. 308)

Feb. 6 - Federalist No. 51; Massachusetts ratifies (187–168)

Feb. 7 - "Brutus" No. 12 (p. 315); Massachusetts proposed amendments (p. 220)

Feb. 14 - "Brutus" No. 12 (Part II) (p. 319)

Feb. 19 - Federalist No. 57

Feb. 27 - Federalist No. 62

March 15 - Federalist No. 70

March 20 - "Brutus" No. 15 (p. 322)

April 10 - "Brutus" No. 16 (p. 353)

April 26 - Maryland ratifies (63–11)

May 23 - South Carolina ratifies (149–73)

May 28 - Federalist Nos. 78 and 84

June 5 and 7 - Patrick Henry speeches opposing ratification in Virginia (p. 199)

June 21 - New Hampshire ratifies (57–47); the ninth state

June 20–27 - Melancton Smith speeches opposing ratification in New York (p. 358)

June 25 - Virginia ratifies (89–79)

June 27 - Virginia proposes amendments (p. 222)

July 26 - New York ratifies (30–27)

August 4 - North Carolina rejects ratification (193–75)

1789:   March 4 - Constitution takes effect

June 8 - Madison introduces amendments for a Bill of Rights in Congress

Nov. 21 - North Carolina ratifies (195–77)

1790:   May 29 - Rhode Island ratifies (34–32)

1791:   Nov. 3 - Bill of Rights (Amendments 1–10) takes effect

Summary of Opposed Arguments
in Federalist and Anti-federalist Writings

Subject	Anti-federalist Writing	[opposes] Federalist
Need for Stronger Union	John Dewitt # I & II	Federalist # 1–6
Bill of Rights	John Dewitt # II	James Wilson, 10/6/87
		Federalist # 84
Nature and Powers of the Union	Patrick Henry, 6/5/88	Federalist # 1, 14, 15
Responsibility and Checks in Self-government	Centinel # I	Federalist # 10, 51
Extent of Union, States' Rights, Bill of Rights, Taxation	Pennsylvania Minority; Brutus # I	Federalist # 10, 32, 33, 35, 36, 39, 45, 84
Extended Republics, Taxation	Federal Farmer # I & II	Federalist # 8, 10, 14, 35, 36
Broad Construction, Taxing Powers	Brutus # VI	Federalist # 23, 30–34
Defense, Standing Armies	Brutus # X	Federalist # 24–29
The Judiciary	Brutus # XI, XII, XV	Federalist # 78–83
Government Resting on the People	John DeWitt # III	Federalist # 23, 49
Executive Power	Cato # V	Federalist # 67
Regulating Elections	Cato # VII	Federalist # 59
House of Representatives	Brutus # IV	Federalist # 27, 28, 52–54, 57
The Senate	Brutus # XVI	Federalist # 62, 63
Representation in House of Representatives and Senate	Melancton Smith, 6/20–6/27/88	Federalist # 52–57, 62, 63

PART I

THE FEDERAL CONVENTION OF 1787

James Madison
to George Washington
(April 16, 1787)

Even before the final ratification and implementation of the Articles of Confederation on March 1, 1781, many political leaders had challenged them. Those with heavy responsibility for conducting the war against Great Britain, including George Washington, Robert Morris, and Alexander Hamilton, believed the Articles were inadequate to the needs of national government. Many who had long served in the Continental Congress, including James Madison, Thomas Jefferson, and James Wilson, became convinced that that body was ill-conceived to provide effective, republican government. When quarrels among the states, stalemate in Congress, domestic disturbances, foreign intrigue, and commercial disarray clouded public affairs during the 1780s, thoughtful people increasingly advocated a change in the frame of government.

Foremost among such advocates was James Madison, whose service in Congress, 1780–1783, had convinced him that a stronger national government was needed. As a Virginia legislator, 1784–1786, he worked toward that end, and he supported the Mount Vernon meeting of 1785 and the Annapolis Convention of 1786 as steps in the right direction. He also undertook systematic study of "Ancient and Modern Confederacies" to glean ideas for improving the American confederacy. Most pointedly, he examined "The Political System of the United States" to identify its "Vices," as he put it. When it became clear in the winter of 1786–1787 that a new convention of the states would gather in Philadelphia in May 1787, Madison digested his general thoughts into a plan for a new frame of government, for the benefit of his colleagues in the Virginia delegation. He

3

formulated the proposals offered to the convention by Edmund Randolph as the "Virginia Plan," and he wrote to George Washington, on April 16, 1787, explaining the flaws in the Articles of Confederation and the changes that would be needed to give the nation effective government. This letter was first printed in 1840, and is reprinted here from G. Hunt and J. B. Scott, eds., The Debates of the Federal Convention of 1787 (New York, 1920), pp. 592–595.

I have been honoured with your letter of the 31 of March, and find with much pleasure that your views of the reform which ought to be pursued by the Convention, give a sanction to those which I have entertained. Temporising applications will dishonor the Councils which propose them, and may foment the internal malignity of the disease, at the same time that they produce an ostensible palliation of it. Radical attempts, although unsuccessful, will at least justify the authors of them.

Having been lately led to revolve the subject which is to undergo the discussion of the Convention, and formed in my mind *some* outlines of a new system, I take the liberty of submitting them without apology, to your eye.

Conceiving that an individual independence of the States is utterly irreconcilable with their aggregate sovereignty; and that a consolidation of the whole into one simple republic would be as inexpedient as it is unattainable, I have sought for some middle ground, which may at once support a due supremacy of the national authority, and not exclude the local authorities wherever they can be subordinately useful.

I would propose as the ground-work that a change be made in the principle of representation. According to the present form of the Union in which the intervention of the States is in all great cases necessary to effectuate the measures of Congress, an equality of suffrage, does not destroy the inequality of importance, in the several members. No one will deny that Virginia and Massachusetts have more weight and influence both within and without Congress than Delaware or Rhode Island. Under a system which would operate in many essential points without the intervention of the State Legislatures, the ease would be materially altered. A vote in the national Councils from Delaware, would then have the same effect and value as one from the largest State in the Union. I am ready to believe that such a change will not be attended with much difficulty. A majority of the States, and those of greatest influence, will regard it as favorable to them. To the Northern States it will be recommended by their present populousness; to the Southern by their expected advantage in this respect. The lesser States must in every event yield to the predominant will. But the consideration which particularly urges a change in the representation is that it will obviate the principal objections of the larger States to the necessary concessions of power.

I would propose next that in addition to the present federal powers, the national Government should be armed with positive and compleat authority in all cases which require uniformity; such as the regulation of trade, including the right of taxing both exports and imports, the fixing the terms and forms of naturalization, etc. etc.

Over and above this positive power, a negative *in all cases whatsoever* on the legislative acts of the States, as heretofore exercised by the Kingly prerogative, appears to me to be absolutely necessary, and to be the least possible encroachment on the State jurisdictions. Without this defensive power, every positive power that can be given on paper will be evaded and defeated. The States will continue to invade the National jurisdiction to violate treaties and the law of nations and to harass each other with rival and spiteful measures dictated by mistaken views of interest. Another happy effect of this prerogative would be its controul on the internal vicisitudes of State policy, and the aggressions of interested majorities on the rights of minorities and of individuals. The great desideratum which has not yet been found for Republican Governments seems to be some disinterested and dispassionate umpire in disputes between different passions and interests in the State. The majority who alone have the right of decision, have frequently an interest real or supposed in abusing it. In Monarchies the sovereign is more neutral to the interests and views of different parties; but, unfortunately he too often forms interests of his own re-

pugnant to those of the whole. Might not the national prerogative here suggested be found sufficiently disinterested for the
decision of local questions of policy, whilst it would itself be
sufficiently restrained from the pursuit of interests adverse to
those of the whole Society? There has not been any moment
since the peace at which the representatives of the Union would
have given an assent to paper money or any other measure of a
kindred nature.

The national supremacy ought also to be extended as I conceive to the Judiciary departments. If those who are to expound
and apply the laws, are connected by their interests and their
oaths with the particular States wholly, and not with the Union,
the participation of the Union in the making of the laws may be
possibly rendered unavailing. It seems at least necessary that
the oaths of the Judges should include a fidelity to the general
as well as local constitution, and that an appeal should lie to
some National tribunals in all cases to which foreigners or inhabitants of other States may be parties. The admiralty jurisdiction seems to fall entirely within the purview of the national
Government.

The national supremacy in the Executive departments is liable to some difficulty, unless the officers administering them
could be made appointable by the supreme Government. The
Militia ought certainly to be placed in some form or other under
the authority which is entrusted with the general protection and
defence.

A Government composed of such extensive power should be
well organised and balanced. The legislative department might
be divided into two branches; one of them chosen every   years
by the people at large, or by the Legislatures; the other to consist
of fewer members, to hold their places for a longer term, and to
go out in such a rotation as always to leave in office a large
majority of old members. Perhaps the negative on the laws
might be most conveniently exercised by this branch. As a further check, a council of revision including the great ministerial
officers might be super-added.

A National Executive must also be provided. I have scarcely
ventured as yet to form my own opinion either of the manner in

which it ought to be constituted or of the authorities with which it ought to be cloathed.

An article should be inserted expressly guarantying the tranquility of the States against internal as well as external dangers.

In like manner the right of coercion should be expressly declared. With the resources of Commerce in hand, the National administration might always find means of exerting it either by sea or land. But the difficulty and awkwardness of operating by force on the collective will of a State, render it particularly desireable that the necessity of it might be precluded. Perhaps the negative on the laws might create such a mutuality of dependence between the General and particular authorities, as to answer this purpose or perhaps some defined objects of taxation might be submitted along with commerce, to the general authority.

To give a new System its proper validity and energy, a ratification must be obtained from the people, and not merely from the ordinary authority of the Legislatures. This will be the more essential as inroads on the *existing Constitutions* of the States will be unavoidable. . . .

The Virginia Plan
(May 29)

The debates of the Convention began on May 29, when Governor Edmund Randolph of Virginia laid before it the plan of government Madison had outlined to Washington the month before and which the entire Virginia delegation had discussed and agreed to as they waited for other delegates to arrive. The plan embodied Madison's intention to greatly strengthen the national government, and boldly set out to frame an entirely new constitution rather than simply amend the Articles of Confederation as the Convention was formally charged to do. The "Virginia

Plan," as it came to be called, became the agenda for the Convention as its provisions were debated, amended, and voted on in the succeeding weeks. Randolph's introductory remarks and the Virginia Plan follow in full from Madison's notes taken while the Convention was in session and recorded in the third person (all subsequent excerpts from the debates are also from Madison's Notes, unless indicated otherwise). They are reprinted here from the relevant portions of Documents Illustrative of the Formation of the Union of the American States *(Government Printing Office, Washington, DC, 1927), ed. by C. C. Tansill, pp.114–745.*

MR. RANDOLPH expressed his regret, that it should fall to him, rather than those, who were of longer standing in life and political experience, to open the great subject of their mission. But, as the convention had originated from Virginia, and his colleagues supposed that some proposition was expected from them, they had imposed this task on him.

He then commented on the difficulty of the crisis, and the necessity of preventing the fulfillment of the prophecies of the American downfall.

He observed that in revising the federal system we ought to inquire 1) into the properties, which such a government ought to possess, 2) the defects of the confederation, 3) the danger of our situation and 4) the remedy.

1. The Character of such a government ought to secure 1) against foreign invasion: 2) against dissentions between members of the Union, or seditions in particular states: 3) to procure to the several States, various blessings, of which an isolated situation was incapable: 4) to be able to defend itself against incroachment: and 5) to be paramount to the state constitutions.

2. In speaking of the defects of the confederation he professed a high respect for its authors, and considered them, as having done all that patriots could do, in the then infancy of the science, of constitutions, and of confederacies,—when the inefficiency of requisitions was unknown—no commercial discord had arisen among any states—no rebellion had appeared as in Massachusetts—foreign debts had not become urgent—the

havoc of paper money had not been foreseen—treaties had not been violated—and perhaps nothing better could be obtained from the jealousy of the states with regard to their sovereignty.

He then proceeded to enumerate the defects: 1) That the confederation produced no security against foreign invasion; congress not being permitted to prevent a war nor to support it by their own authority—Of this he cited many examples; most of which tended to show, that they could not cause infractions of treaties or of the law of nations, to be punished: that particular states might by their conduct provoke war without control; and that neither militia nor draughts being fit for defence on such occasions, inlistments only could be successful, and these could not be executed without money. 2) That the federal government could not check the quarrels between states, nor a rebellion in any, not having constitutional power nor means to interpose according to the exigency. 3) That there were many advantages, which the U. S. might acquire, which were not attainable under the confederation—such as a productive impost—counteraction of the commercial regulations of other nations—pushing of commerce ad libitum—etc. etc. 4) That the federal government could not defend itself against the incroachments from the states. 5) That it was not even paramount to the state constitutions, ratified, as it was in many of the states.

3. He next reviewed the danger of our situation, appealed to the sense of the best friends of the United States—the prospect of anarchy from the laxity of government everywhere; and to other considerations.

4. He then proceeded to the remedy; the basis of which he said must be the republican principle.

He proposed as conformable to his ideas the following resolutions, which he explained one by one.

Resolutions Proposed by Mr. Randolph in Convention

1. Resolved that the Articles of Confederation ought to be so corrected and enlarged as to accomplish the objects proposed by

their institution; namely, "common defense, security of liberty and general welfare."

2. Resolved therefore that the rights of suffrage in the National Legislature ought to be proportioned to the Quotas of contribution, or to the number of free inhabitants, as the one or the other rule may seem best in different cases.

3. Resolved that the National Legislature ought to consist of two branches.

4. Resolved that the members of the first branch of the National Legislature ought to be elected by the people of the several States every   for the term of   ; to be of the age of   years at least, to receive liberal stipends by which they may be compensated for the devotion of their time to public service; to be ineligible to any office established by a particular State, or under the authority of the United States, except those peculiarly belonging to the functions of the first branch, during the term of service, and for the space of   after its expiration; to be incapable of re-election for the space of   after the expiration of their term of service, and to be subject to recall.

5. Resolved that the members of the second branch of the National Legislature ought to be elected by those of the first, out of a proper number of persons nominated by the individual Legislatures, to be of the age of   years at least; to hold their offices for a term sufficient to ensure their independency; to receive liberal stipends, by which they may be compensated for the devotion of their time to public service; and to be ineligible to any office established by a particular State, or under the authority of the United States, except those peculiarly belonging to the functions of the second branch, during the term of service, and for the space of   after the expiration thereof.

6. Resolved that each branch ought to possess the right of originating Acts; that the National Legislature ought to be impowered to enjoy the Legislative Rights vested in Congress by the Confederation and moreover to legislate in all cases to which the separate States are incompetent, or in which the harmony of the United States may be interrupted by the exercise of individual Legislation; to negative all laws passed by the several States, contravening in the opinion of the National Leg-

islature the articles of Union; and to call forth the force of the Union against any member of the Union failing to fulfill its duty under the articles thereof.

7. Resolved that a National Executive be instituted; to be chosen by the National Legislature for the term of   years to receive punctually at stated times, a fixed compensation for the services rendered, in which no increase or diminution shall be made so as to affect the Magistracy, existing at the time of increase or diminution, and to be ineligible a second time; and that besides a general authority to execute the National laws, it ought to enjoy the Executive rights vested in Congress by the Confederation.

8. Resolved that the Executive and a convenient number of the National Judiciary, ought to compose a Council of revision with authority to examine every act of the National Legislature before it shall operate, and every act of a particular Legislature before a Negative thereon shall be final; and that the dissent of the said Council shall amount to a rejection, unless the Act of the National Legislature be again passed, or that of a particular Legislature be again negatived by   of the members of each branch.

9. Resolved that a National Judiciary be established to consist of one or more supreme tribunals, and of inferior tribunals to be chosen by the National Legislature, to hold their offices during good behaviour; and to receive punctually at stated times fixed compensation for their services, in which no increase or diminution shall be made so as to affect the persons actually in office at the time of such increase or diminution. That the jurisdiction of the inferior tribunals shall be to hear and determine in the first instance, and of the supreme tribunal to hear and determine in the [last] resort, all piracies and felonies on the high seas, captures from an enemy; cases in which foreigners or citizens of other States applying to such jurisdictions may be interested, or which respect the collection of the National revenue; impeachments of any National officers, and questions which may involve the national peace and harmony.

10. Resolved that provision ought to be made for the admission of States lawfully arising within the limits of the United

States, whether from a voluntary junction of Government and Territory or otherwise, with the consent of a number of voices in the National Legislature less than the whole.

11. Resolved that a Republican Government and the territory of each State, except in the instance of a voluntary junction of Government and territory, ought to be guaranteed by the United States to each State.

12. Resolved that provision ought to be made for the continuance of Congress and their authorities and privileges, until a given day after the reform of the articles of Union shall be adopted, and for the completion of all their engagements.

13. Resolved that provision ought to be made for the amendment of the Articles of Union whensoever it shall seem necessary, and that the assent of the National Legislature ought not to be required thereto.

14. Resolved that the Legislative, Executive and Judiciary powers within the several States ought to be bound by oath to support the articles of Union.

15. Resolved that the amendments which shall be offered to the Confederation, by the Convention ought at a proper time, or times, after the approbation of Congress to be submitted to an assembly or assemblies of Representatives, recommended by the several Legislatures to be expressly chosen by the people, to consider and decide thereon.

He concluded with an exhortation, not to suffer the present opportunity of establishing general peace, harmony, happiness and liberty in the U. S. to pass away unimproved.

Debate on Representation
(May 31)

The Convention first took up the clause in the Virginia Plan call-
ing for the members of the House of Representatives to be
elected directly by the people of the several states. The debate
revealed basically divergent attitudes toward rule by the people.

MR. SHERMAN opposed the election by the people, insisting
that it ought to be by the State Legislatures. The people he said,
immediately should have as little to do as may be about the
Government. They want information and are constantly liable to
be misled.

MR. GERRY. The evils we experience flow from the excess of
democracy. The people do not want virtue, but are the dupes of
pretended patriots. In Massachusetts it had been fully confirmed
by experience that they are daily misled into the most baneful
measures and opinions by the false reports circulated by designing men, and which no one on the spot can refute. One principal
evil arises from the want of due provision for those employed in
the administration of Government. It would seem to be a maxim
of democracy to starve the public servants. He mentioned the
popular clamour in Massachusetts for the reduction of salaries
and the attack made on that of the Governor though secured by
the spirit of the Constitution itself. He had he said been too republican heretofore: he was still however republican, but had
been taught by experience the danger of the levolling spirit.

MR. MASON argued strongly for an election of the larger
branch by the people. It was to be the grand depository of the
democratic principle of the government. It was, so to speak, to
be our House of Commons—It ought to know and sympathize
with every part of the community; and ought therefore to be

taken not only from different parts of the whole republic, but also from different districts of the larger members of it, which had in several instances particularly in Virginia different interests and views arising from difference of produce, of habits etc., etc. He admitted that we had been too democratic but was afraid we should incautiously run into the opposite extreme. We ought to attend to the rights of every class of the people. He had often wondered at the indifference of the superior classes of society to this dictate of humanity and policy; considering that however affluent their circumstances, or elevated their situations, might be, the course of a few years, not only might but certainly would, distribute their posterity throughout the lowest classes of Society. Every selfish motive therefore, every family attachment, ought to recommend such a system of policy as would provide no less carefully for the rights and happiness of the lowest than of the highest orders of Citizens.

MR. WILSON contended strenuously for drawing the most numerous branch of the Legislature immediately from the people. He was for raising the federal pyramid to a considerable altitude, and for that reason wished to give it as broad a basis as possible. No government could long subsist without the confidence of the people. In a republican Government this confidence was peculiarly essential. He also thought it wrong to increase the weight of the State Legislatures by making them the electors of the National Legislature. All interference between the general and local governments should be obviated as much as possible. On examination it would be found that the opposition of States to federal measures had preceded much more from the officers of the States, than from the people at large.

MR. MADISON considered the popular election of one branch of the National Legislature as essential to every plan of free Government. He observed that in some of the States one branch of the Legislature was composed of men already removed from the people by an intervening body of electors. That if the first branch of the general legislature should be elected by the State Legislatures, the second branch elected by the first—the Executive by the second together with the first; and other appointments again made for subordinate purposes by the Executive, the people would be lost sight of altogether; and the necessary sympathy between them and their rulers and officers, too little felt. He was an advocate for the policy of refining the popular appointments by successive filtrations, but thought it might be pushed too far. He wished the expedient to be resorted to only in the appointment of the second branch of the Legislature, and in the Executive and judiciary branches of the Government. He thought too that the great fabric to be raised would be more stable and durable, if it should rest on the solid foundation of the people themselves, than if it should stand merely on the pillars of the Legislatures.

MR. GERRY did not like the election by the people. The maxims taken from the British constitution were often fallacious when applied to our situation which was extremely different. Experience he said had shown that the State legislatures drawn immediately from the people did not always possess their confidence. He had no objection however to an election by the people if it were so qualified that men of honor and character might not be unwilling to be joined in the appointments. He seemed to think the people might nominate a certain number out of which the State Legislatures should be bound to choose.

Debate on Executive Power
(June 1)

The Convention next considered the clause providing for a national executive. Since the Articles of Confederation had not provided for executive power, and since revolutionary hostility to the executive power of the British monarchy remained strong, members were unusually hesitant about fashioning such an unprecedented and potentially oppressive office.

MR. PINCKNEY was for a vigorous Executive but was afraid the Executive powers of the existing Congress might extend to peace and war and etc., etc., which would render the Executive a monarchy, of the worst kind, to wit an elective one.

MR. WILSON moved that the Executive consist of a single person. Mr. C. PINCKNEY seconded the motion, so as to read "that a National Executive to consist of a single person, be instituted."

A considerable pause ensuing and the Chairman asking if he should put the question, Dr. FRANKLIN observed that it was a point of great importance and wished that the gentlemen would deliver their sentiments on it before the question was put.

MR. RUTLEDGE animadverted on the shyness of gentlemen on this and other subjects. He said it looked as if they supposed themselves precluded by having frankly disclosed their opinions from afterwards changing them, which he did not take to be at all the case. He said he was for vesting the Executive power in a single person, though he was not for giving him the power of war and peace. A single man would feel the greatest responsibility and administer the public affairs best.

MR. SHERMAN said he considered the Executive magistracy as nothing more than an institution for carrying the will of the Legislature into effect, that the person or persons ought to be appointed by and accountable to the Legislature only, which was the depository of the supreme will of the Society. As they were the best judges of the business which ought to be done by the Executive department, and consequently of the number necessary from time to time for doing it, he wished the number might not be fixed, but that the Legislature should be at liberty to appoint one or more as experience might dictate.

MR. WILSON preferred a single magistrate, as giving most energy dispatch and responsibility to the office. He did not consider the Prerogatives of the British Monarch as a proper guide in defining the Executive powers. Some of these prerogatives were of a Legislative nature. Among others that of war and peace etc., etc. The only powers he conceived strictly Executive were those of executing the laws, and appointing officers, not appertaining to and appointed by the Legislature.

MR. GERRY favored the policy of annexing a Council to the Executive in order to give weight and inspire confidence.

MR. RANDOLPH strenuously opposed a unity in the Executive magistracy. He regarded it as the fetus of monarchy. We had he said no motive to be governed by the British Government as our prototype. He did not mean however to throw censure on that Excellent fabric. If we were in a situation to copy it he did not know that he should be opposed to it; but the fixed genius of the people of America required a different form of Government. He could not see why the great requisites for the Executive department, vigor, despatch and responsibility could not be found in three men, as well as in one man. The Executive ought to be independent. It ought therefore in order to support its independence to consist of more than one.

MR. WILSON said that unity in the Executive instead of being the fetus of monarchy would be the best safeguard against tyranny. He repeated that he was not governed by the British Model which was inapplicable to the situation of this Country; the extent of which was so great, and the manners so republican, that nothing but a great confederated Republic would do for it.

Opposition to Executive Salaries
(June 2)

As the Convention further inconclusively considered the executive department, Benjamin Franklin spoke on behalf of a favorite idea of his: that officers of government should not receive salaries.

It is with reluctance that I rise to express a disapprobation of any one article of the plan for which we are so much obliged to the honorable gentleman who laid it before us. From its first reading I have borne a good will to it, and in general wished it success. In this particular of salaries to the Executive branch I happen to differ; and as my opinion may appear new and chimerical, it is only from a persuasion that it is right, and from a sense of duty that I hazard it. The Committee will judge of my reasons when they have heard them, and their judgment may possibly change mine—I think I see inconveniences in the appointment of salaries; I see none in refusing them, but on the contrary, great advantages.

Sir, there are two passions which have a powerful influence on the affairs of men. These are ambition and avarice; the love of power, and the love of money. Separately each of these has great force in prompting men to action; but when united in view of the same object, they have in many minds the most violent effects. Place before the eyes of such men, a post of *honour* that shall be at the same time a place of *profit,* and they will move heaven and earth to obtain it. The vast number of such places it is that renders the British Government so tempestuous. The struggles for them are the true sources of all those factions which are perpetually dividing the Nation, distracting its Councils, hurrying sometimes into fruitless and mischievous wars, and often compelling a submission to dishonorable terms of peace.

And of what kind are the men that will strive for this profitable pre-eminence, through all the bustle of cabal, the heat of contention, the infinite mutual abuse of parties, tearing to pieces the best of characters? It will not be the wise and moderate; the lovers of peace and good order, the men fittest for the trust. It will be the bold and the violent, the men of strong passions and indefatigable activity in their selfish pursuits. These will thrust themselves into your Government and be your rulers—And these too will be mistaken in the expected happiness of their situation: For their vanquished competitors of the same spirit, and from the same motives will perpetually be endeavouring to distress their administration, thwart their measures, and render them odious to the people.

Besides these evils, Sir, though we may set out in the beginning with moderate salaries, we shall find that such will not be of long continuance. Reasons will never be wanting for proposed augmentations. And there will always be a party for giving more to the rulers, that the rulers may be able in return to give more to them.—Hence as all history informs us, there has been in every State and Kingdom a constant kind of warfare between the governing and governed: the one striving to obtain more for its support, and the other to pay less. And this has alone occasioned great convulsions, actual civil wars, ending either in dethroning of the Princes, or enslaving of the people. Generally indeed the ruling power carries its point, the revenues of princes constantly increasing, and we see that they are never satisfied, but always in want of more. The more the people are discontented with the oppression of taxes; the greater need the prince has of money to distribute among his partizans and pay the troops that are to suppress all resistance, and enable him to plunder at pleasure. There is scarce a king in a hundred who would not, if he could, follow the example of Pharaoh, get first all the people's money, then all their lands, and then make them and their children servants for ever. It will be said, that we don't propose to establish Kings. I know it. But there is a natural inclination in mankind to Kingly Government. It sometimes relieves them from Aristocratic domination. They had rather have one tyrant than five hundred. It gives more of the appearance of equality among Citizens, and that they like. I am apprehensive therefore, perhaps too apprehensive, that the Government of these States, may in future times, end in a Monarchy. But this Catastrophe I think may be long delayed, if in our proposed System we do not sow the seeds of contention, faction and tumult, by making our posts of honor, places of profit. If we do, I fear that though we do employ at first a number, and not a single person, the number will in time be set aside, it will only nourish the fetus of a King, as the honorable gentleman from Virginia very aptly expressed it, and a King will the sooner be set over us.

It may be imagined by some that this is an Utopian Idea, and that we can never find men to serve us in the Executive department, without paying them well for their services. I conceive this to be a mistake. Some existing facts present themselves to me, which incline me to a contrary opinion. The high Sheriff of a County in England is an honorable office, but it is not a profitable one. It is rather expensive and therefore not sought for. But yet, it is executed and well executed, and usually by some of the principal Gentlemen of the County. In France, the office of Counselor or Member of their Judiciary Parliaments is more honorable. It is therefore purchased at a high price: There are indeed fees on the law proceedings, which are divided among them, but these fees do not amount to more than three percent on the sum paid for the place. Therefore as legal interest is there at five percent they in fact pay two percent for being allowed to do the Judiciary business of the Nation, which is at the same time entirely exempt from the burden of paying them any salaries for their services. I do not however mean to recommend this as an eligible mode for our Judiciary department. I only bring the instance to show that the pleasure of doing good and serving their Country and the respect such conduct entitles them to, are sufficient motives with some minds to give up a great portion of their time to the public, without the mean inducement of pecuniary satisfaction.

Another instance is that of a respectable Society who have made the experiment, and practised it with success more than an hundred years. I mean the Quakers. It is an established rule with them, that they are not to go to law; but in their controversies they must apply to their monthly, quarterly and yearly meetings. Committees of these sit with patience to hear the parties, and spend much time in composing their differences. In doing this, they are supported by a sense of duty, and the respect paid to usefulness. It is honorable to be so employed, but it was never made profitable by salaries, fees, or perquisites. And indeed in all cases of public service the less the profit the greater the honor.

To bring the matter nearer home, have we not seen, the great and most important of our offices, that of General of our armies executed for eight years together without the smallest salary, by a Patriot whom I will not now offend by any other praise; and this through fatigues and distresses in common with the other brave men his military friends and companions, and the constant anxieties peculiar to his station? And shall we doubt finding three or four men in all the United States, with public spirit enough to bear sitting in peaceful Council for perhaps an equal term, merely to preside over our civil concerns, and see that our laws are duly executed? Sir, I have a better opinion of our Country. I think we shall never be without a sufficient number of wise and good men to undertake and execute well and faithfully the office in question.

Sir, the saving of the salaries that may at first be proposed is not an object with me. The subsequent mischiefs of proposing them are what I apprehend. And therefore it is, that I move the amendment. If it is not seconded or accepted I must be contented with the satisfaction of having delivered my opinion frankly and done my duty.

The motion was seconded by COLONEL HAMILTON with the view he said merely of bringing so respectable a proposition before the Committee, and which was besides enforced by arguments that had a certain degree of weight. No debate ensued, and the proposition was postponed for the consideration of the members. It was treated with great respect, but rather for the author of it, than from any apparent conviction of its expediency or practicability.

Opposition to a Unitary Executive
(June 4)

Still in an unsettled mood, the Convention again debated the merits of a single vs. a plural executive. George Mason preserved among his papers a copy of a speech opposing a unitary executive. Portions of it are reprinted here from Robert Rutland, ed., The Papers of George Mason *(3 vols., Chapel Hill, NC, 1970), III, pp. 896–898.*

The chief advantages which have been urged in favour of Unity in the Executive, are the Secrecy, the Dispatch, the Vigour and Energy which the Government will derive from it; especially in time of War. That these are great Advantages, I shall most readily allow. They have been strongly insisted on by all monarchical Writers—they have been acknowledged by the ablest and most candid Defenders of Republican Government; and it can not be denied that a Monarchy possesses them in a much greater Degree than a Republic. Yet perhaps a little Reflection may incline us to doubt whether these advantages are not greater in Theory than in Practice—or lead us to enquire whether there is not some prevailing Principle in Republican Government, which sets at Naught, and tramples upon this boasted Superiority—as hath been experienced, to their cost by most Monarchys, which have been imprudent enough to invade or attack their republican Neighbors. This invincible Principle is to be found in the Love the Affection the Attachment of the Citizens to their Laws, to their Freedom, and to their Country. Every Husbandman will be quickly converted into a Soldier, when he knows and feels that he is to fight not in defence of the Rights of a particular Family, or a Prince; but for his own. This is the true Construction of that pro Aris and focis [for altars and firesides] which has, in all Ages, perform'd such Wonders. It was this which, in ancient times, enabled the little Cluster of Grecian Republics to resist, and almost constantly to defeat the Persian Monarch. It was this which supported the States of Holland against a Body of veteran Troops through a Thirty Years War with Spain, then the greatest Monarchy in Europe and finally rendered them victorious. It is this which preserves the Freedom and Independence of the Swiss Cantons, in the midst of the most powerful Nations. And who that reflects seriously upon the Situation of America, in the Beginning of the late War—without Arms—without Soldiers—without Trade, Money, or Credit—in a Manner destitute of all Resources, but must ascribe our Success to this pervading all-powerful Principle?

We have not yet been able to define the Powers of the Executive; and however moderately some Gentlemen may talk or think upon the Subject, I believe there is a general Tendency to a strong Executive and I am inclined to think a strong Executive necessary. If strong and extensive Powers are vested in the Executive, and that Executive consists only of one Person, the Government will of course degenerate, (for I will call it degeneracy) into a Monarchy—A Government so contrary to the Genius of the People, that they will reject even the Appearance of it. I consider the federal Government as in some Measure dissolved by the Meeting of this Convention. Are there no Dangers to be apprehended from procrastinating the time between the breaking up of this Assembly and the adoption of a new System of Government. I dread the Interval. If it should not be brought to an Issue in the Course of the first Year, the Consequences may be fatal. Has not the different Parts of this extensive Government, the several States of which it is composed a Right to expect an equal Participation in the Executive, as the best Means of securing an equal Attention to their Interests. Should an Insurrection, a Rebellion or Invasion happen in New Hampshire when the single supreme Magistrate is a Citizen of Georgia, would not the people of New Hampshire naturally ascribe any Delay in defending them to such a Circumstance and so vice versa. If the Executive is vested in three Persons, one chosen from the northern, one from the middle, and one from the Southern States, will it not contribute to quiet the Minds of the People, & convince them that there will be proper attention paid to their respective Concerns? Will not three Men so chosen bring with them, into Office, a more perfect and extensive Knowledge of the real Interests of this great Union? Will not such a Model of Appointment be the most effectual means of preventing Cabals and Intrigues between the Legislature and the Candidates for this Office, especially with those Candidates who from their local Situation, near the seat of the federal Government, will have the greatest Temptations and the greatest Opportunities. Will it not be the most effectual Means of checking and counteracting the aspiring Views of dangerous and ambitious Men, and consequently the best Security for the Stability and Duration of our Government upon the invaluable Principles of Liberty? These Sir, are some of my Motives for preferring an Executive consisting of three Persons rather than of one.

Electing Representatives
(June 6)

After inconclusive discussions of the judiciary and some minor matters, the Convention resumed consideration of the mode of electing the House of Representatives. It debated a motion that the state legislatures, not the people, ought to elect the Representatives.

MR. GERRY. Much depends on the mode of election. In England, the people will probably lose their liberty from the smallness of the proportion having a right of suffrage. Our danger arises from the opposite extreme; hence in Massachusetts the worst men get into the Legislature. Several members of that Body had lately been convicted of infamous crimes. Men of indigence, ignorance and baseness, spare no pains, however dirty to carry their point against men who are superior to the artifices practised. He was not disposed to run into extremes. He was as much principled as ever against aristocracy and monarchy. It was necessary on the one hand that the people should appoint one branch of the government in order to inspire them with the necessary confidence. But he wished the election on the other to be so modified as to secure more effectually a just preference of merit. His idea was that the people should nominate certain persons in certain districts, out of whom the State Legislatures should make the appointment.

MR. WILSON. He wished for vigor in the government but he wished that vigorous authority to flow immediately from the legitimate source of all authority. The government ought to possess not only first the *force,* but secondly the *mind or sense* of the people at large. The Legislature ought to be the most exact transcript of the whole Society. Representation is made necessary only because it is impossible for the people to act collectively. The opposition was to be expected he said from the *Governments,* not from the Citizens of the States. The latter had parted as was observed [by Mr. King] with all the necessary powers, and it was immaterial to them, by whom they were exercised, if well exercised. The State officers were to be the losers of power. The people he supposed would be rather more attached to the national Government than to the State governments as being more important in itself, and more flattering to their pride. There is no danger of improper elections if made by *large* districts. Bad elections proceed from the smallness of the districts which give an opportunity to bad men to intrigue themselves into office.

MR. SHERMAN. If it were in view to abolish the State governments, the elections ought to be by the people. If the State governments are to be continued, it is necessary in order to preserve harmony between the National and State governments that the elections to the former should be made by the latter. The right of participating in the National Government would be sufficiently secured to the people by their election of the State Legislatures. The objects of the Union, he thought were few. 1. defence against foreign danger. 2. against internal disputes and a resort to force. 3. treaties with foreign nations. 4. regulating foreign commerce, and drawing revenue from it. These and perhaps a few lesser objects alone rendered a Confederation of the States necessary. All other matters civil and criminal would be much better in the hands of the States. The people are more happy in small than large States. States may indeed be too small as Rhode Island, and thereby be too subject to faction. Some others were perhaps too large, the powers of government not being able to pervade them. He was for giving the General government power to legislate and execute within a defined province.

COLONEL MASON. Under the existing Confederacy, congress represents the *States* not the *people* of the States: their acts operate on the *States,* not on the individuals. The case will be changed in the new plan of government. The people will be represented; they ought therefore to choose the Representatives. The requisites in actual representation are that the Representatives should sympathize with their constituents; should think as they think, and feel as they feel; and that for these purposes should even be residents among them. Much he said had been alleged against democratic elections. He admitted that much might be said; but it was to be considered that no Government was free from imperfections and evils; and that improper elections in many instances, were inseparable from Republican Governments. But compare these with the advantage of this Form in favor of the rights of the people, in favor of human nature. He was persuaded there was a better chance for proper elections by the people, if divided into large districts, than by the State Legislatures. Paper money had been issued by the latter when the former were against it. Was it to be supposed that the State Legislatures then would not send to the National Legislature patrons of such projects, if the choice depended on them.

MR. MADISON considered an election of one branch at least of the Legislature by the people immediately, as a clear principle of free government and that this mode under proper regulations had the additional advantage of securing better representatives, as well as of avoiding too great an agency of the State Governments in the General one.—He differed from the member from Connecticut [Mr. Sherman] in thinking the objects mentioned to be all the principal ones that required a National government. Those were certainly important and necessary objects; but he combined with them the necessity of providing more effectually, for the security of private rights, and the steady dispensation of Justice. Interferences with these were evils which had more perhaps than any thing else, produced this convention. Was it to be supposed that republican liberty could long exist under the abuses of it practised in some of the States. The gentleman [Mr. Sherman] had admitted that in a very small State, faction and oppression would prevail. It was to be inferred then that wherever these prevailed the State was too small. Had they not prevailed in the largest as well as the smallest though less than in the smallest; and were we not thence admonished to enlarge the sphere as far as the nature of the government would admit. This was the only defence against the inconveniences of democracy consistent with the democratic form of government. All civilized

Societies would be divided into different Sects, Factions, and interests, as they happened to consist of rich and poor, debtors and creditors, the landed, the manufacturing, the commercial interests, the inhabitants of this district or that district, the followers of this political leader or that political leader, the disciples of this religious Sect or that religious Sect. In all cases where a majority are united by a common interest or passion, the rights of the minority are in danger. What motives are to restrain them? A prudent regard to the maxim that honesty is the best policy is found by experience to be as little regarded by bodies of men as by individuals. Respect for character is always diminished in proportion to the number among whom the blame or praise is to be divided. Conscience, the only remaining tie, is known to be inadequate in individuals: In large numbers, little is to be expected from it. Besides, Religion itself may become a motive to persecution and oppression.—These observations are verified by the Histories of every Country ancient and modern. In Greece and Rome the rich and poor, the creditors and debtors, as well as the patricians and plebeians alternately oppressed each other with equal unmercifulness. What a source of oppression was the relation between the parent cities of Rome, Athens and Carthage, and their respective provinces: the former possessing the power, and the latter being sufficiently distinguished to be separate objects of it? Why was America so justly apprehensive of Parliamentary injustice? Because Great Britain had a separate interest real or supposed, and if her authority had been admitted, could have pursued that interest at our expense. We have seen the mere distinction of colour made in the most enlightened period of time, a ground of the most oppressive dominion ever exercised by man over man. What has been the source of those unjust laws complained of among ourselves? Has it not been the real or supposed interest of the major number? Debtors have defrauded their creditors. The landed interest has borne hard on the mercantile interest. The Holders of one species of property have thrown a disproportion of taxes on the holders of another species. The lesson we are to draw from the whole is that where a majority are united by a common sentiment, and have an opportunity, the rights of the minor party become insecure. In a republican government the Majority if united have always an opportunity. The only remedy is to enlarge the sphere, and thereby divide the community into so great a number of interests and parties, that in the first place a majority will not be likely at the same moment to have a common interest separate from that of the whole or of the minority; and in the second place, that in case they should have such an interest, they may not be apt to unite in the pursuit of it. It was incumbent on us then to try this remedy, and with that view to frame a republican system on such a scale and in such a form as will control all the evils which have been experienced.

MR. DICKINSON considered it as essential that one branch of the Legislature should be drawn immediately from the people; and as expedient that the other should be chosen by the Legislatures of the States. This combination of the State governments with the national government was as politic as it was unavoidable. In the formation of the Senate we ought to carry it through such a refining process as will assimilate it as near as may be to the House of Lords in England. He repeated his warm eulogiums on the British Constitution. He was for a strong National government but for leaving the States a considerable agency in the System. The objection against making the former dependent on the latter might be obviated by giving to the Senate an authority permanent and irrevocable for three, five or seven years. Being thus independent they will speak and decide with becoming freedom.

MR. READ. Too much attachment is betrayed to the State governments. We must look beyond their continuance. A national government must soon of necessity swallow all of them up. They will soon be reduced to the mere office of electing the National Senate. He was against patching up the old federal System: he hoped the idea would be dismissed. It would be like putting new cloth on an old garment. The confederation was founded on temporary principles. It cannot last: it cannot be amended. If we do not establish a good government on new principles, we must either go to ruin, or have the work to do over again. The people at large are wrongly suspected of being averse to a general government. The aversion lies among interested men who possess their confidence.

MR. PIERCE was for an election by the people as to the first branch and by the States as to the second branch; by which means the Citizens of the States would be represented both *individually and collectively.*

Debate on Method of Electing Senators (June 7)

The next day the Convention took up a motion by John Dickinson that the Senate be elected by the state legislatures.

MR. SHERMAN seconded the motion; observing that the particular States would thus become interested in supporting the national government and that a due harmony between the two governments would be maintained. He admitted that the two ought to have separate and distinct jurisdictions, but that they ought to have a mutual interest in supporting each other.

MR. PINCKNEY. If the small States should be allowed one Senator only, the number will be too great, there will be 80 at least.

MR. DICKINSON had two reasons for his motion. 1. because the sense of the States would be better collected through their Governments than immediately from the people at large; 2. because he wished the Senate to consist of the most distinguished characters, distinguished for their rank in life and their weight of property, and bearing as strong a likeness to the British House of Lords as possible; and he thought such characters more likely to be selected by the State Legislatures, than in any other mode. The greatness of the number was no objection with him. He hoped there would be 80 and twice 80 of them. If their number should be small, the popular branch could not be balanced by them. The legislature of a numerous people ought to be a numerous body.

MR. WILLIAMSON preferred a small number of Senators, but wished that each State should have at least one. He suggested 25 as a convenient number. The different modes of representation in the different branches, will serve as a mutual check.

MR. BUTLER was anxious to know the ratio of representation before he gave any opinion.

MR. WILSON. If we are to establish a national Government, that Government ought to flow from the people at large. If one branch of it should be chosen by the Legislatures, and the other by the people, the two branches will rest on different foundations, and dissensions will naturally arise between them. He wished the Senate to be elected by the people as well as the other branch, and the people might be divided into proper districts for the purpose and moved to postpone the motion of Mr. Dickinson, in order to take up one of that import.

MR. MORRIS seconded him.

MR. READ proposed "that the Senate should be appointed by the Executive Magistrate out of a proper number of persons to be nominated by the individual legislatures." He said he thought it his duty, to speak his mind frankly. Gentlemen he hoped would not be alarmed at the idea. Nothing short of this approach towards a proper model of Government would answer the purpose, and he thought it best to come directly to the point at once.—His proposition was not seconded nor supported.

MR. MADISON. If the motion [of Mr. Dickinson] should be agreed to, we must either depart from the doctrine of proportional representation; or admit into the Senate a very large number of members. The first is inadmissible, being evidently unjust. The second is inexpedient. The use of the Senate is to consist in its proceeding with more coolness, with more system, and with more wisdom, than the popular branch. Enlarge their number and you communicate to them the vices which they are meant to correct. He differed from Mr. D. who thought that the additional number would give additional weight to the body. On the contrary it appeared to him that their weight would be in an inverse ratio to their number. The example of the Roman Tribunes was applicable. They lost their influence and power, in proportion as their number was augmented. The reason seemed to be obvious:

They were appointed to take care of the popular interests and pretensions at Rome, because the people by reason of their numbers could not act in concert; were liable to fall into factions among themselves, and to become a prey to their aristocratic adversaries. The more the representatives of the people therefore were multiplied, the more they partook of the infirmities of their constituents, the more liable they became to be divided among themselves either from their own indiscretions or the artifices of the opposite faction, and of course the less capable of fulfilling their trust. When the weight of a set of men depends merely on their personal characters, the greater the number the greater the weight. When it depends on the degree of political authority lodged in them, the smaller the number the greater the weight. These considerations might perhaps be combined in the intended Senate; but the latter was the material one.

MR. GERRY. Four modes of appointing the Senate have been mentioned. 1. By the first branch of the National Legislature. This would create a dependence contrary to the end proposed. 2. By the National Executive. This is a stride towards monarchy that few will think of. 3. By the people. The people have two great interests, the landed interest, and the commercial including the stockholders. To draw both branches from the people will leave no security to the latter interest; the people being chiefly composed of the landed interest, and erroneously supposing, that the other interest are adverse to it. 4. By the Individual Legislatures. The elections being carried through this refinement, will be most likely to provide some check in favor of the commercial interest against the landed; without which oppression will take place, and no free Government can last long where that is the case. He was therefore in favor of this last.

MR. DICKINSON. The preservation of the States in a certain degree of agency is indispensable. It will produce that collision between the different authorities which should be wished for in order to check each other. To attempt to abolish the States altogether, would degrade the Councils of our Country, would be impracticable, would be ruinous. He compared the proposed National System to the Solar System, in which the States were the planets, and ought to be left to move freely in their proper

orbits. The Gentleman from Pennsylvania [Mr. Wilson] wished
he said to extinguish these planets. If the State Governments
were excluded from all agency in the national one, and all power
drawn from the people at large, the consequence would be that
the national government would move in the same direction as
the State governments now do, and would run into all the same
mischiefs. The reform would only unite the 13 small streams
into one great current pursuing the same course without any opposition whatever. He adhered to the opinion that the Senate
ought to be composed of a large number, and that their influence
from family weight and other causes would be increased thereby.
He did not admit that the Tribunes lost their weight in proportion
as their number was augmented and gave a historical sketch of
this institution. If the reasoning of [Mr. Madison] was good it
would prove that the number of the Senate ought to be reduced
below ten, the highest number of the Tribunitial corps.

MR. WILSON. The subject it must be owned is surrounded with
doubts and difficulties. But we must surmount them. The British
government cannot be our model. We have no materials for a
similar one. Our manners, our laws, the abolition of entails and of
primo-geniture, the whole genius of the people, are opposed to it.
He did not see the danger of the States being devoured by the
national government. On the contrary, he wished to keep them
from devouring the national government. He was not however for
extinguishing these planets as was supposed by Mr. D.—neither
did he on the other hand, believe that they would warm or en-
lighten the Sun. Within their proper orbits they must still be suffered to act for subordinate purposes for which their existence is
made essential by the great extent of our Country. He could not
comprehend in what manner the landed interest would be rendered less predominant in the Senate, by an election through the
medium of the Legislatures than by the people themselves. If the
Legislatures, as was now complained, sacrificed the commercial
to the landed interest, what reason was there to expect such a
choice from them as would defeat their own views. He was for an
election by the people in large districts which would be most
likely to obtain men of intelligence and uprightness; subdividing
the districts only for the accommodation of voters.

Mr. MADISON could as little comprehend in what manner family weight, as desired by Mr. D. would be more certainly conveyed into the Senate through elections by the State Legislatures, than in some other modes. The true question was in what mode the best choice would be made? If an election by the people, or through any other channel than the State Legislatures promised as uncorrupt and impartial a preference of merit, there could surely be no necessity for an appointment by those Le_islatures. Nor was it apparent that a more useful check would be derived through that channel than from the people through some other. The great evils complained of were that the State Legislatures run into schemes of paper money etc., etc., whenever solicited by the people, and sometimes without even the sanction of the people. Their influence then, instead of checking a like propensity in the National Legislature, may be expected to promote it. Nothing can be more contradictory than to say that the National Legislature without a proper check, will follow the example of the State Legislatures, and in the same breath, that the State Legislatures are the only proper check.

Mr. SHERMAN opposed elections by the people in districts, as not likely to produce such fit men as elections by the State Legislatures.

Mr. GERRY insisted that the commercial and monied interest would be more secure in the hands of the State Legislatures, than of the people at large. The former have more sense of character, and will be restrained by that from injustice. The people are for paper money when the Legislatures are against it. In Massachusetts the County Conventions had declared a wish for a *depreciating* paper that would sink itself. Besides, in some States there are two Branches in the Legislature, one of which is somewhat aristocratic. There would therefore be so far a better chance of refinement in the choice. There seemed, he thought to be three powerful objections against elections by districts. 1. It is impracticable; the people cannot be brought to one place for the purpose; and whether brought to the same place or not, numberless frauds would be unavoidable. 2. Small States forming part of the same district with a large one, or large part of a large one, would have no chance of gaining an appointment for its citizens of merit. 3. A new source of discord would be opened between different parts of the same district.

MR. PINCKNEY thought the second branch ought to be permanent and independent, and that the members of it would be rendered more so by receiving their appointment from the State Legislatures. This mode would avoid the [rivalries] and discontents incident to the election by districts. He was for dividing the States into three classes according to their respective sizes, and for allowing to the first class three members—to the second two, and to the third one.

Debate on Veto of State Laws
(June 8)

The Convention soon faced directly the most debilitating weakness of the Articles of Confederation: the inability of Congress to control state legislation that violated national laws or treaties. Strong sentiment existed, as the Virginia Plan revealed, for explicit power in Congress to invalidate, or "negative" "improper" state laws. (At the conclusion of the debate, the motion for a Congressional negative on state laws was defeated, 7 states no, 3 states yes, and 1 state divided.)

MR. PINCKNEY moved "that the National Legislature should have authority to negative all laws which they should judge to be improper." He urged that such a universality of the power was indispensably necessary to render it effectual; that the States must be kept in due subordination to the nation; that if the States were left to act of themselves in any case, it would be impossible to defend the national prerogatives, however extensive they might be on paper; that the acts of Congress had been defeated by this means; nor had foreign treaties escaped repeated violations; that this universal negative was in fact the corner stone of an efficient national government; that under the British government the negative of the Crown had been found beneficial, and the *States* are more one nation now, than the *Colonies* were then.

MR. MADISON seconded the motion. He could not but regard an indefinite power to negative legislative acts of the States as absolutely necessary to a perfect system. Experience had evinced a constant tendency in the States to encroach on the federal authority; to violate national Treaties; to infringe the rights and interests of each other; to oppress the weaker party within their respective jurisdictions. A negative was the mildest expedient that could be devised for preventing these mischiefs. The existence of such a check would prevent attempts to commit them. Should no such precaution be engrafted, the only remedy would lie in an appeal to coercion. Was such a remedy eligible? was it practicable? Could the national resources, if exerted to the utmost enforce a national decree against Massachusetts abetted perhaps by several of her neighbours? It would not be possible. A small proportion of the Community, in a compact situation, acting on the defensive, and at one of its extremities might at any time bid defiance to the National authority. Any government for the United States formed on the supposed practicability of using force against the unconstitutional proceedings of the States, would prove as visionary and fallacious as the government of Congress. The negative would render the use of force unnecessary. The States could of themselves then pass no operative act, any more than one branch of a Legislature where there are two branches, can proceed without the other. But in order to give the negative this efficacy, it must extend to all cases. A discrimination would only be a fresh source of contention between the two authorities. In a word, to recur to the illustrations borrowed from the planetary system. This prerogative of the General government is the great pervading principle that must control the centrifugal tendency of the States; which, without it, will continually fly out of their proper orbits and destroy the order and harmony of the political System.

MR. WILLIAMSON was against giving a power that might restrain the States from regulating their internal police.

MR. GERRY could not see the extent of such a power, and was

against every power that was not necessary. He thought a remonstrance against unreasonable acts of the States would reclaim them. If it should not force might be resorted to. He had no objection to authorize a negative to paper money and similar measures. When the confederation was depending before Congress, Massachusetts was then for inserting the power of emitting paper money among the exclusive powers of Congress. He observed that the proposed negative would extend to the regulations of the Militia, a matter on which the existence of a State might depend. The National Legislature with such a power may enslave the States. Such an idea as this will never be acceded to. It has never been suggested or conceived among the people. No speculative projector, and there are enough of that character among us, in politics as well as in other things, has in any pamphlet or newspaper thrown out the idea. The States too have different interests and are ignorant of each other's interests. The negative therefore will be abused. New States too having separate views from the old States will never come into the Union. They may even be under some foreign influence; are they in such case to participate in the negative on the will of the other States?

MR. SHERMAN thought the cases in which the negative ought to be exercised, might be defined. He wished the point might not be decided till a trial at least should be made for that purpose.

MR. WILSON would not say what modifications of the proposed power might be practicable or expedient. But however novel it might appear the principle of it when viewed with a close and steady eye, is right. There is no instance in which the laws say that the individual should be bound in one case, and at liberty to judge whether he will obey or disobey in another. The cases are parallel. Abuses of the power over the individual person may happen as well as over the individual States. Federal liberty is to States, what civil liberty, is to private individuals. And States are not more unwilling to purchase it, by the necessary concession of their political sovereignty, than the savage is to purchase civil liberty by the surrender of his personal sovereignty, which he enjoys in a State of nature. A definition of the cases in which the Negative should be exercised, is impracticable. A discretion must be left on one side or the other? will it not be most safely lodged on the side of the National government? Among the first sentiments expressed in the first Congress one was that Virginia is no more, that Massachusetts is no, that Pennsylvania is no more etc., etc. We are now one nation of brethren. We must bury all local interests and distinctions. This language continued for some time. The tables at length began to turn. No sooner were the State governments formed than their jealousy and ambition began to display themselves. Each endeavoured to cut a slice from the common loaf, to add to its own morsel, till at length the confederation became frittered down to the impotent condition in which it now stands. Review the progress of the articles of Confederation through Congress and compare the first and last draught of it. To correct its vices is the business of this convention. One of its vices is the want of an effectual control in the whole over its parts. What danger is there that the whole will unnecessarily sacrifice a part? But reverse the case, and leave the whole at the mercy of each part, and will not the general interest be continually sacrificed to local interests?

MR. DICKINSON deemed it impossible to draw a line between the cases proper and improper for the exercise of the negative. We must take our choice of two things. We must either subject the States to the danger of being injured by the power of the National government or the latter to the danger of being injured by that of the States. He thought the danger greater from the States. To leave the power doubtful, would be opening another spring of discord, and he was for shutting as many of them as possible.

MR. BEDFORD. In answer to his colleague's question where would be the danger to the States from this power, would refer him to the smallness of his own State which may be injured at pleasure without redress. It was meant he found to strip the small States of their equal right of suffrage. In this case Delaware would have about one ninetieth for its share in the General Councils, whilst Pennsylvania and Virginia would possess one third of the whole. Is there no difference of interests, no rivalship of commerce, of manufactures? Will not these large States crush the small ones whenever they stand in the way of their ambitious or interested views. This shows the impossibility of adopting such a system as that on the table, or any other founded on a change in the principle of representation. And after all, if a State does not obey the law of the new System, must not force be resorted to as the only ultimate remedy, in this as in any other system. It seems as if Pennsylvania and Virginia by the conduct of their deputies wished to provide a system in which they would have an enormous and monstrous influence. Besides, how can it be thought that the proposed negative can be exercised? are the laws of the States to be suspended in the most urgent cases until they can be sent seven or eight hundred miles, and undergo the deliberations of a body who may be incapable of Judging of them? Is the National Legislature too to sit continually in order to revise the laws of the States?

MR. MADISON observed that the difficulties which had been stated were worthy of attention and ought to be answered before the question was put. The case of laws of urgent necessity must be provided for by some emanation of the power from the National government into each State so far as to give a temporary assent at least. This was the practice in Royal Colonies before the Revolution and would not have been inconvenient, if the supreme power of negativing had been faithful to the American interest, and had possessed the necessary information. He supposed that the negative might be very properly lodged in the senate alone, and that the more numerous and expensive branch therefore might not be obliged to sit constantly.—He asked Mr. Bedford what would be the consequence to the small States of a dissolution of the Union which seemed likely to happen if no effectual substitute was made for the defective System existing, and he did not conceive any effectual system could be substituted on any other basis than that of a proportional suffrage? If the large States possessed the avarice and ambition with which they were charged, would the small ones in their neighbourhood, be more secure when all control of a General Government was withdrawn.

MR. BUTLER was vehement against the Negative in the proposed extent, as cutting off all hope of equal justice to the distant States. The people there would not he was sure give it a hearing.

The New Jersey Plan
(June 15)

After three days of increasingly contentious debate and votes on many detailed points, the Convention reported a series of resolves that represented its decisions thus far. Most of the major points of the Virginia Plan had been accepted, but delegates who opposed such marked strengthening of the national government, and especially those from small states who wanted to retain the equal voting power of the states, sought to put forward a plan more to their liking. After a day's adjournment to settle on such a plan, William Paterson of New Jersey offered a series of resolutions embodying the more "purely federal" plan; that is, one maintaining the "league of states" form of the Articles of Confederation.

1. Resolved that the articles of Confederation ought to be so revised, corrected and enlarged, as to render the federal Constitution adequate to the exigencies of Government, and the preservation of the Union.

2. Resolved that in addition to the powers vested in the United States in Congress, by the present existing articles of Confederation, they be authorized to pass acts for raising a revenue, by levying a duty or duties on all goods or merchandizes of foreign growth or manufacture, imported into any part of the United States, by Stamps on paper, vellum or parchment, and by a postage on all letters or packages passing through the general post-office, to be applied to such federal purposes as they shall deem proper and expedient; to make rules and regulations for the collection thereof; and the same from time to time, to alter and amend in such manner as they shall think proper: to pass Acts for the regulation of trade and commerce as well with for-

eign nations as with each other: provided that all punishments, fines, forfeitures and penalties to be incurred for contravening such acts rules and regulations shall be adjudged by the Common law Judiciaries of the State in which any offence contrary to the true intent and meaning of such Acts rules and regulations shall have been committed or perpetrated, with liberty of commencing in the first instance all suits and prosecutions for that purpose in the superior common law Judiciary in such State, subject nevertheless, for the correction of all errors, both in law and fact in rendering Judgment, to an appeal to the Judiciary of the United States.

3. Resolved that whenever requisitions shall be necessary, instead of the rule for making requisitions mentioned in the articles of Confederation, the United States in Congress be authorized to make such requisitions in proportion to the whole number of white and other free citizens and inhabitants of every age sex and condition including those bound to servitude for a term of years and three fifths of all other persons not comprehended in the foregoing description, except Indians not paying taxes; that if such requisitions be not complied with, in the time specified therein, to direct the collection thereof in the non complying States and for that purpose to devise and pass acts directing and authorizing the same; provided that none of the powers hereby vested in the United States in Congress shall be exercised without the consent of at least   States, and in that proportion if the number of Confederated States should hereafter be increased or diminished.

4. Resolved that the United States in Congress be authorized to elect a federal Executive to consist of   persons, to continue in office for the term of   years, to receive punctually at stated times a fixed compensation for their services, in which no increase or diminution shall be made so as to affect the persons composing the Executive at the time of such increase or diminution, to be paid out of the federal treasury; to be incapable of holding any other office or appointment during their time of service and for   years thereafter; to be ineligible a second time, and removeable by Congress on application by a majority of the Executives of the several States; that the Executives be-

sides their general authority to execute the federal acts ought to appoint all federal officers not otherwise provided for, and to direct all military operations; provided that none of the persons composing the federal Executive shall on any occasion take command of any troops, so as personally to conduct any enterprise as General or in other capacity.

5. Resolved that a federal Judiciary be established to consist of a supreme Tribunal the Judges of which to be appointed by the Executive, and to hold their offices during good behaviour, to receive punctually at stated times a fixed compensation for their services in which no increase or diminution shall be made, so as to affect the persons actually in office at the time of such increase or diminution; that the Judiciary so established shall have authority to hear and determine in the first instance on all impeachments of federal officers, and by way of appeal in the [last] resort in all cases touching the rights of Ambassadors, in all cases of captures from an enemy, in all cases of piracies and felonies on the high Seas, in all cases in which foreigners may be interested, in the construction of any treaty or treaties, or which may arise on any of the Acts for regulation of trade, or the collection of the federal Revenue: that none of the Judiciary shall during the time they remain in office be capable of receiving or holding any other office or appointment during their time of service, or for   thereafter.

6. Resolved that all Acts of the United States in Congress made by virtue and in pursuance of the powers hereby and by the articles of Confederation vested in them, and all Treaties made and ratified under the authority of the United States shall be the supreme law of the respective States so far forth as those Acts or Treaties shall relate to the said States or their Citizens, and that the Judiciary of the several States shall be bound thereby in their decisions, any thing in the respective laws of the Individual States to the contrary notwithstanding; and that if any State, or any body of men in any State shall oppose or prevent the carrying into execution such acts or treaties, the federal Executive shall be authorized to call forth the power of the Confederated States, or so much thereof as may be necessary to enforce and compel an obedience to such Acts, or an observance of such Treaties.

7. Resolved that provision be made for the admission of new States into the Union.

8. Resolved the rule for naturalization ought to be the same in every State.

9. Resolved that a Citizen of one State committing an offence in another State of the Union, shall be deemed guilty of the same offence as if it had been committed by a Citizen of the State in which the offence was committed.

Debate of the New Jersey Plan
(June 16)

The next day Paterson spoke in defense of the New Jersey Plan, while James Wilson and Edmund Randolph explained why they still preferred the Virginia Plan.

MR. PATERSON said as he had on former occasion given his sentiments on the plan proposed by Mr. Randolph he would now avoiding repetition as much as possible give his reasons in favor of that proposed by himself. He preferred it because it accorded 1. with the powers of the Convention, 2. with the sentiments of the people. If the confederacy was radically wrong, let us return to our States, and obtain larger powers, not assume them of ourselves. I came here not to speak my own sentiments, but the sentiments of those who sent me. Our object is not such a government as may be best in itself, but such a one as our Constituents have authorized us to prepare, and as they will approve. If we argue the matter on the supposition that no Confederacy at present exists, it can not be denied that all the States stand on the footing of equal sovereignty. All therefore must concur before any can be bound. If a proportional representation be right, why do we not vote so here? If we argue on the fact that a federal compact actually exists, and consult the articles of it we still find an equal Sovereignty to be the basis of it. He reads the fifth article of Confederation giving each State a vote—and the thirteenth declaring that no alteration shall be made without unanimous consent. This is the nature of all treaties. What is unanimously done, must be unanimously undone. It was observed [by Mr. Wilson] that the larger States gave up the point, not because it was right, but because the circumstances of the moment urged the concession. Be it so. Are they for that reason at liberty to take it back. Can the donor resume his gift without the consent of the donee. This doctrine may be convenient, but it is a doctrine that will sacrifice the lesser States. The large States acceded readily to the confederacy. It was the small ones that came in reluctantly and slowly. N. Jersey and Maryland were the two last, the former objecting to the want of power in Congress over trade: both of them to the want of power to appropriate the vacant territory to the benefit of the whole.—If the sovereignty of the States is to be maintained, the Representatives must be drawn immediately from the States, not from the people: and we have no power to vary the idea of equal sovereignty. The only expedient that will cure the difficulty, is that of throwing the States into Hotchpot. To say that this is impracticable, will not make it so. Let it be tried, and we shall see whether the Citizens of Massachusetts, Pennsylvania and Virginia accede to it. It will be objected that Coercion will be impracticable. But will it be more so in one plan than the other? Its efficacy will depend on the quantum of power collected, not on its being drawn from the States, or from the individuals; and according to his plan it may be exerted on individuals as well as according that of Mr. Randolph. A distinct executive and Judiciary also were equally provided by his plan. It is urged that two branches in the Legislature are necessary. Why? for the purpose of a check. But the reason of the precaution is not applicable to this case. Within a particular State, where party heats prevail, such a check may be necessary. In such a body as Congress it is less necessary, and besides, the delegations of the different States are checks on each other. Do the people at large complain of Congress? No, what they wish is that Congress may have more power. If the power now proposed be not enough, the people hereafter will make additions to it. With proper powers Congress will act with more energy and wisdom than the proposed National Legislature; being fewer in number, and more secreted and refined by the mode of election. The plan of Mr. Randolph will also be enormously expensive. Allowing Georgia and Delaware two representatives each in the popular branch the aggregate number of that branch will be 180. Add to it half as many for the other branch and you have 270. Members coming once at least a year from the most distant as well as the most central parts of the republic. In the present deranged state of our finances can so expensive a system be seriously thought of? By enlarging the powers of Congress the greatest part of this expense will be saved, and all purposes will be answered. At least a trial ought to be made.

MR. WILSON entered into a contrast of the principal points of the two plans so far he said as there had been time to examine the one last proposed. These points were 1. in the Virginia plan there are two and in some degree three branches in the Legislature: in the plan from N. J. there is to be a *single* legislature only—2. Representation of the people at large is the basis of the one:— the State Legislatures, the pillars of the other—3. Proportional representation prevails in one:—equality of suffrage in the other—4. A single Executive Magistrate is at the head of the one—a plurality is held out in the other.—5. In the one the majority of the people of the United States must prevail:—in the other a minority may prevail. 6. The National Legislature is to make laws in all cases to which the separate States are incompetent and—in place of this Congress are to have additional power in a few cases only—7. A negative on the laws of the States:—in place of this coercion to be substituted—8. The Executive to be removeable on impeachment and conviction;—in one plan: in the other to be removeable at the instance of majority of the Executives of the States—9. Revision of the laws provided for in one—no such check in the other—10. Inferior national tribunals in one—none such in the other. 11. In the one, jurisdiction of National tribunals to extend etc., etc.—; an appellate jurisdiction only allowed in the other. 12. Here the jurisdiction is to extend to all cases affecting the National peace and harmony:

there, a few cases only are marked out. 13. Finally the ratification is in this to be by the people themselves:—in that by the legislative authorities according to the thirteenth article of Confederation.

With regard to the *power of the Convention,* he conceived himself authorized to *conclude nothing,* but to be at liberty to *propose any thing.* In this particular he felt himself perfectly indifferent to the two plans.

With regard to the *sentiments of the people,* he conceived it difficult to know precisely what they are. Those of the particular circle in which one moved, were commonly mistaken for the general voice. He could not persuade himself that the State Governments and Sovereignties were so much the idols of the people, nor a National Government so obnoxious to them, as some supposed. Why should a National Government be unpopular? Has it less dignity? Will each Citizen enjoy under it less liberty or protection? Will a Citizen of *Delaware* be degraded by becoming a Citizen of the *United States?* Where do the people look at present for relief from the evils of which they complain? Is it from an internal reform of their Governments? No, Sir. It is from the National Councils that relief is expected. For these reasons he did not fear, that the people would not follow us into a national Government and it will be a further recommendation of Mr. Randolph's plan that it is to be submitted to *them,* and not to the *Legislatures,* for ratification.

Proceeding now to the first point on which he had contrasted the two plans, he observed that anxious as he was for some augmentation of the federal powers, it would be with extreme reluctance indeed that he could ever consent to give powers to Congress; he had two reasons either of which was sufficient. 1. Congress, as a Legislative body does not stand on the people. 2. It is a *single* body. He would not repeat the remarks he had formerly made on the principles of Representation. He would only say that an inequality in it, has ever been a poison contaminating every branch of Government. In Great Britain where this poison has had a full operation, the security of private rights is owing entirely to the purity of Her tribunals of Justice, the Judges of which are neither appointed nor paid, by a venal Parliament. The political liberty of that Nation, owing to the inequality of representation is at the mercy of its rulers. He means not to insinuate that there is any parallel between the situation of that Country and ours at present. But it is a lesson we ought not to disregard, that the smallest bodies in Great Britain are notoriously the most corrupt. Every other source of influence must also be stronger in small than large bodies of men. When Lord Chesterfield had told us that one of the Dutch provinces had been seduced into the views of France, he need not have added, that it was not Holland, but one of the *smallest* of them. There are facts among ourselves which are known to all. Passing over others, he will only remark that the *Impost,* so anxiously wished for by the public was defeated not by any of the *larger* States in the Union. 2. *Congress is a single Legislature.* Despotism comes on Mankind in different Shapes, sometimes in an Executive, sometimes in a Military, one. Is there no danger of a Legislative despotism? Theory and practice both proclaim it. If the Legislative authority be not restrained, there can be neither liberty nor stability; and it can only be restrained by dividing it within itself, into distinct and independent branches. In a single House there is no check, but the inadequate one, of the virtue and good sense of those who compose it.

On another great point, the contrast was equally favorable to the plan reported by the Committee of the whole. It vested the Executive powers in a single Magistrate. The plan of New Jersey, vested them in a plurality. In order to control the Legislative authority, you must divide it. In order to control the Executive you must unite it. One man will be more responsible than three. Three will contend among themselves till one becomes the master of his colleagues. In the triumvirates of Rome first Caesar, then Augustus, are witnesses of this truth. The Kings of Sparta, and the Consuls of Rome prove also the factious consequences of dividing the Executive Magistracy. Having already taken up so much time he would not he said proceed to any of the other points. Those on which he had dwelt, are sufficient of themselves: and on a decision of them, the fate of the others will depend. . . .

MR. RANDOLPH was not scrupulous on the point of power. When the salvation of the Republic was at stake, it would be treason to our trust, not to propose what we found necessary. He painted in strong colours, the imbecility of the existing Confederacy, and the danger of delaying a substantial reform. In answer to the objection drawn from the sense of our Constituents as denoted by their acts relating to the Convention and the objects of their deliberation, he observed that as each State acted separately in the case, it would have been indecent for it to have charged the existing Constitution with all the vices which it might have perceived in it. The first State that set on foot this experiment would not have been justified in going so far, ignorant as it was of the opinion of others, and sensible as it must have been of the uncertainty of a successful issue to the experiment. There are certainly seasons of a peculiar nature where the ordinary cautions must be dispensed with; and this is certainly one of them. He would not as far as depended on him leave any thing that seemed necessary, undone. The present moment is favorable, and is probably the last that will offer.

The true question is whether we shall adhere to the federal plan, or introduce the national plan. The insufficiency of the former has been fully displayed by the trial already made. There are but two modes, by which the end of a General Government can be attained: the first is by coercion as proposed by Mister Paterson's plan. 2. By real legislation as proposed by the other plan. Coercion he pronounced to be *impracticable, expensive, cruel to individuals.* It tended also to habituate the instruments of it to shed the blood and riot in the spoils of their fellow Citizens, and consequently trained them up for the service of ambition. We must resort therefore to a National *Legislation over individuals,* for which Congress are unfit. To vest such power in them, would be blending the Legislative with the Executive, contrary to the recorded maxim on this subject: If the Union of these powers heretofore in Congress has been safe, it has been owing to the general impotency of that body. Congress are moreover not elected by the people, but by the Legislatures who retain even a power of recall. They have therefore no will of their own, they are a mere diplomatic body, and are always obsequious to the views of the States, who are always encroaching on the authority of the United States. A provision for harmony

among the States, as in trade, naturalization, etc.—for crushing
rebellion whenever it may rear its crest—and for certain other
general benefits, must be made. The powers for these purposes,
can never be given to a body, inadequate as Congress are in
point of representation, elected in the mode in which they are,
and possessing no more confidence than they do: for notwithstanding what has been said to the contrary, his own experience
satisfied him that a rooted distrust of Congress pretty generally
prevailed. A National Government alone, properly constituted,
will answer the purpose; and he begged it to be considered that
the present is the last moment for establishing one. After this
select experiment, the people will yield to despair.

Plan for National Government
(June 18)

*Sensing that the Convention had been sent into disarray by the
dissension over the Virginia and New Jersey Plans, and thus
might be open to a radically different form of government, Alexander Hamilton made a long speech presenting a plan vastly
strengthening the national government.*

MR. HAMILTON had been hitherto silent on the business before the Convention, partly from respect to others whose superior abilities age and experience rendered him unwilling to bring
forward ideas dissimilar to theirs, and partly from his delicate
situation with respect to his own State, to whose sentiments as
expressed by his Colleagues, he could by no means accede. The
crisis however which now marked our affairs, was too serious to
permit any scruples whatever to prevail over the duty imposed
on every man to contribute his efforts for the public safety and
happiness. He was obliged therefore to declare himself unfriendly to both plans. He was particularly opposed to that from

New Jersey, being fully convinced, that no amendment of the Confederation, leaving the States in possession of their Sovereignty could possibly answer the purpose. On the other hand he confessed he was much discouraged by the amazing extent of the Country in expecting the desired blessings from any general sovereignty that could be substituted.—As to the powers of the Convention, he thought the doubts started on that subject had arisen from distinctions and reasonings too subtle. A *federal* Government he conceived to mean an association of independent Communities into one. Different Confederacies have different powers, and exercise them in different ways. In some instances the powers are exercised over collective bodies; in others over individuals, as in the German Diet—and among ourselves in cases of piracy. Great latitude therefore must be given to the signification of the term. The plan last proposed departs itself from the *federal* idea, as understood by some, since it is to operate eventually on individuals. He agreed moreover with the Honorable gentleman from Virginia [Mr. Randolph] that we owed it to our Country, to do on this emergency whatever we should deem essential to its happiness. The States sent us here to provide for the exigences of the Union. To rely on and propose any plan not adequate to these exigences, merely because it was not clearly within our powers, would be to sacrifice the means to the end. It may be said that the *States* can not *ratify* a plan not within the purview of the article of Confederation providing for alterations and amendments. But may not the States themselves in which no constitutional authority equal to this purpose exists in the Legislatures, have had in view a reference to the people at large. In the Senate of New York, a proviso was moved, that no act of the Convention should be binding untill it should be referred to the people and ratified; and the motion was lost by a single voice only, the reason assigned against it being, that it might possibly be found an inconvenient shackle.

The great question is what provision shall we make for the happiness of our Country? He would first make a comparative examination of the two plans—prove that there were essential defects in both—and point out such changes as might render a *national one,* efficacious.—The great and essential principles necessary for the support of Government are 1. An active and constant interest in supporting it. This principle does not exist in the States in favor of the federal Government. They have evidently in a high degree, the esprit de corps. They constantly pursue internal interests adverse to those of the whole. They have their particular debts—their particular plans of finance etc. All these when opposed to, invariably prevail over the requisitions and plans of Congress. 2. The love of power. Men love power. The same remarks are applicable to this principle. The States have constantly shown a disposition rather to regain the powers delegated by them than to part with more, or to give effect to what they had parted with. The ambition of their demagogues is known to hate the control of the General Government. It may be remarked too that the Citizens have not that anxiety to prevent a dissolution of the General Government as of the particular Governments. A dissolution of the latter would be fatal; of the former would still leave the purposes of Government attainable to a considerable degree. Consider what such a State as Virginia will be in a few years, a few compared with the life of nations. How strongly will it feel its importance and self-sufficiency? 3. An habitual attachment of the people. The whole force of this tie is on the side of the State Government. Its sovereignty is immediately before the eyes of the people: its protection is immediately enjoyed by them. From its hand distributive justice, and all those acts which familiarize and endear Government to a people, are dispensed to them. 4. *Force* by which may be understood a *coertion of laws* or *coertion of arms*. Congress have not the former except in few cases. In particular States, this coercion is nearly sufficient; though he held it in most cases, not entirely so. A certain portion of military force is absolutely necessary in large communities. Massachusetts is now feeling this necessity and making provision for it. But how can this force be exerted on the States collectively. It is impossible. It amounts to a war between the parties. Foreign powers also will not be idle spectators. They will interpose, the confusion will increase, and a dissolution of the Union ensue. 5. *Influence.* He did not mean corruption, but a dispensation of those regular honors and emoluments, which produce an attachment to the Government. Almost all the weight of these is on the side of the States; and must continue so as long as the States continue to exist. All the passions then we see, of avarice, ambition, interest, which govern most individuals, and all public bodies, fall into the current of the States, and do not flow in the stream of the General Government. The former therefore will generally be an overmatch for the General Government and render any confederacy, in its very nature precarious. Theory is in this case fully confirmed by experience. The Amphyctionic Council had it would seem ample powers for general purposes. It had in particular the power of fining and using force against delinquent members. What was the consequence. Their decrees were mere signals of war. The Phocian war is a striking example of it. Philip at length taking advantage of their disunion, and insinuating himself into their Councils, made himself master of their fortunes. The German Confederacy affords another lesson. The authority of Charlemagne seemed to be as great as could be necessary. The great feudal chiefs however, exercising their local sovereignties, soon felt the spirit and found the means of, encroachments, which reduced the imperial authority to a nominal sovereignty. The Diet has succeeded, which though aided by a Prince at its head, of great authority independently of his imperial attributes, is a striking illustration of the weakness of Confederated Governments. Other examples instruct us in the same truth. The Swiss cantons have scarce any Union at all, and have been more than once at war with one another.—How then are all these evils to be avoided? Only by such a compleat sovereignty in the general Government as will turn all the strong principles and passions above mentioned on its side. Does the scheme of New Jersey produce this effect? Does it afford any substantial remedy whatever? On the contrary it labors under great defects, and the defect of some of its provisions will destroy the efficacy of others. It gives a direct revenue to Congress but this will not be sufficient. The balance can only be supplied by requisitions: which experience proves can not be relied on. If States are to deliberate on the mode, they will also deliberate on the object of the supplies, and will grant or not grant as they approve or disapprove of it. The delinquency of one will invite and countenance it in

others. Quotas too must in the nature of things be so unequal as
to produce the same evil. To what standard will you resort? Land
is a fallacious one. Compare Holland with Russia: France or
England with other countries of Europe. Pennsylvania with
North Carolina. Will the relative pecuniary abilities in those instances, correspond with the relative value of land? Take numbers of inhabitants for the rule and make like comparison of
different countries, and you will find it to be equally unjust. The
different degrees of industry and improvement in different
Countries render the first object a precarious measure of wealth.
Much depends too on *situation.* Connecticut, New Jersey and
North Carolina, not being commercial States and contributing to
the wealth of the commercial ones, can never bear quotas as-
sessed by the ordinary rules of proportion. They will and must
fail in their duty, their example will be followed, and the Union
itself be dissolved. Whence then is the national revenue to be
drawn? from Commerce? even from exports which notwithstanding the common opinion are fit objects of moderate taxation, from excise, etc, etc. These though not equal, are less
unequal than quotas. Another destructive ingredient in the plan,
is that equality of suffrage which is so much desired by the small
States. It is not in human nature that Virginia and the large States
should consent to it, or if they did that they should long abide by
it. It shocks too much the ideas of Justice, and every human feeling. Bad principles in a Government though slow are sure in
their operation, and will gradually destroy it. A doubt has been
raised whether Congress at present have a right to keep Ships or
troops in time of peace. He leans to the negative. Mr. Paterson's
plan provides no remedy.—If the powers proposed were adequate, the organization of Congess is such that they could never
be properly and effectually exercised. The members of Congress
being chosen by the States and subject to recall, represent all the
local prejudices. Should the powers be found effectual, they will
from time to time be heaped on them, till a tyrannic sway shall
be established. The general power whatever be its form if it preserves itself, must swallow up the State powers. Otherwise it
will be swallowed up by them. It is against all the principles of
a good Government to vest the requisite powers in such a body

as Congress. Two Sovereignties can not co-exist within the same limits. Giving powers to Congress must eventuate in a bad Government or in no Government. The plan of New Jersey therefore will not do. What then is to be done? Here he was embarrassed. The extent of the Country to be governed, discouraged him. The expense of a general Government was also formidable; unless there were a diminution of expense on the side of the State Government as the case would admit. If they were extinguished, he was persuaded that great economy might be obtained by substituting a general Government. He did not mean however to shock the public opinion by proposing such a measure. On the other hand he saw no *other* necessity for declining it. They are not necessary for any of the great purposes of commerce, revenue, or agriculture. Subordinate authorities he was aware would be necessary. There must be district tribunals: corporations for local purposes. But cui bono, the vast and expensive apparatus now appertaining to the States. The only difficulty of a serious nature which occurred to him, was that of drawing representatives from the extremes to the center of the Community. What inducements can be offered that will suffice? The moderate wages for the first branch would only be a bait to little demagogues. Three dollars or thereabouts he supposed would be the utmost. The Senate he feared from a similar cause, would be filled by certain undertakers who wish for particular offices under the Government. This view of the subject almost led him to despair that a Republican Government could be established over so great an extent. He was sensible at the same time that it would be unwise to propose one of any other form. In his private opinion he had no scruple in declaring, supported as he was by the opinions of so many of the wise and good, that the British Government was the best in the world: and that he doubted much whether any thing short of it would do in America. He hoped Gentlemen of different opinions would bear with him in this, and begged them to recollect the change of opinion on this subject which had taken place and was still going on. It was once thought that the power of Congress was amply sufficient to secure the end of their institution. The error was now seen by every one. The members most tenacious of republicanism, he observed, were as loud as any in declaiming against the vices of democracy. This progress of the public mind led him to anticipate the time, when others as well as himself would join in the praise bestowed by Mr. Neckar on the British Constitution, namely, that it is the only Government in the world "which unites public strength with individual security."—In every community where industry is encouraged, there will be a division of it into the few and the many. Hence separate interests will arise. There will be debtors and creditors etc. Give all power to the many, they will oppress the few. Both therefore ought to have power, that each may defend itself against the other. To the want of this check we owe our paper money, instalment laws etc. To the proper adjustment of it the British owe the excellence of their Constitution. Their house of Lords is a most noble institution. Having nothing to hope for by a change, and a sufficient interest by means of their property, in being faithful to the interest, they form a permanent barrier against every pernicious innovation, whether attempted on the part of the Crown or of the Commons. No temporary Senate will have firmness enough to answer the purpose. The Senate [of Maryland] which seems to be so much appealed to, has not yet been sufficiently tried. Had the people been unanimous and eager, in the late appeal to them on the subject of a paper emission they would have yielded to the torrent. Their acquiescing in such an appeal is a proof of it.—Gentlemen differ in their opinions concerning the necessary checks, from the different estimates they form of the human passions. They suppose seven years a sufficient period to give the senate an adequate firmness, from not duly considering the amazing violence and turbulence of the democratic spirit. When a great object of Government is pursued, which seizes the popular passions, they spread like wild fire, and become irresistable. He appealed to the gentlemen from the New England States whether experience had not there verified the remark.—As to the Executive, it seemed to be admitted that no good could be established on Republican principles. Was not this giving up the merits of the question: for can there be a good Government without a good Executive. The English model was the only good one on this subject. The Hereditary interest of the King was so interwoven with that of the Nation, and his personal emoluments so great, that he was placed above the danger of being corrupted from abroad—and at the same time was both sufficiently independent and sufficiently controled, to answer the purpose of the institution at home. One of the weak sides of Republics was their being liable to foreign influence and corruption. Men of little character, acquiring great power become easily the tools of intermedling Neighbors. Sweden was a striking instance. The French and English had each their parties during the late Revolution which was affected by the predominant influence of the former.—What is the inference from all these observations? That we ought to go as far in order to attain stability and permanency, as republican principles will admit. Let one branch of the Legislature hold their places for life or at least during good behaviour. Let the Executive also be for life. He appealed to the feelings of the members present whether a term of seven years, would induce the sacrifices of private affairs which an acceptance of public trust would require, so as to ensure the services of the best Citizens. On this plan we should have in the Senate a permanent will, a weighty interest, which would answer essential purposes. But is this a Republican Government, it will be asked? Yes if all the magistrates are appointed, and vacancies are filled, by the people, or a process of election originating with the people. He was sensible that an Executive constituted as he proposed would have in fact but little of the power and independence that might be necessary. On the other plan of appointing him for 7 years, he thought the Executive ought to have but little power. He would be ambitious, with the means of making creatures; and as the object of his ambition would be to *prolong* his power, it is probable that in case of a war, he would avail himself of the emergence, to evade or refuse a degradation from his place. An Executive for life has not this motive for forgetting his fidelity, and will therefore be a safer depository of power. It will be objected probably, that such an Executive will be an *elective Monarch,* and will give birth to the tumults which characterize that form of Government. He would reply that *Monarch* is an indefinite term. It marks not either the degree or duration of power. If this Executive Magistrate would be a monarch for life—the other proposed by the Report from the Committee of the whole, would be a monarch for seven years. The circumstance of being elective was also applicable to both. It had been observed by judicious writers that elective monarchies would be the best if they could be guarded against the *tumults* excited by the ambition and intrigues of competitors. He was not sure that tumults were an inseparable evil. He rather thought this character of Elective Monarchies had been taken rather from particular cases than from general principles. The election of Roman Emperors was made by the *Army*. In *Poland* the election is made by great rival *princes* with independent power, and ample means, of raising commotions. In the German Empire, the appointment is made by the Electors and Princes, who have equal motives and means, for exciting cabals and parties. Might not such a mode of election be devised among ourselves as will defend the community against these effects in any dangerous degree? Having made these observations he would read to the Committee a sketch of a plan which he should prefer to either of those under consideration. He was aware that it went beyond the ideas of most members. But will such a plan be adopted out of doors? In return he would ask will the people adopt the other plan? At present they will adopt neither. But he sees the Union dissolving or already dissolved—he sees evils operating in the States which must soon cure the people of their fondness for democracies—he sees that a great progress has been already made and is still going on in the public mind. He thinks therefore that the people will in time be unshackled from their prejudices; and whenever that happens, they will themselves not be satisfied at stopping where the plan of Mr. Randolph would place them, but be ready to go as far at least as he proposes. He did not mean to offer the paper he had sketched as a proposition to the Committee. It was meant only to give a more correct view of his ideas, and to suggest the amendments which he should probably propose to the plan of Mr. Randolph in the proper stages of its future discussion. He read his sketch, in the words following, to wit:

"I. The Supreme Legislative power of the United States of America to be vested in two different bodies of men; the one to be called the Assembly, the other the Senate who together shall form the Legislature of the United States with power to pass all laws whatsoever subject to the Negative hereafter mentioned.

II. The Assembly to consist of persons elected by the people to serve for three years.

III. The Senate to consist of persons elected to serve during good behaviour; their election to be made by electors chosen for that purpose by the people: in order to do this the States to be divided into election districts. On the death, removal or resignation of any Senator his place to be filled out of the district from which he came.

IV. The supreme Executive authority of the United States to be vested in a Governor to be elected to serve during good behaviour—the election to be made by Electors chosen by the people in the Election Districts aforesaid.—The authorities and functions of the Executive to be as follows: to have a negative on all laws about to be passed, and the execution of all laws passed; to have the direction of war when authorized or begun; to have with the advice and approbation of the Senate the power of making all treaties; to have the sole appointment of the heads or chief officers of the departments of Finance, War and Foreign Affairs; to have the nomination of all other officers (Ambassadors to foreign Nations included) subject to the approbation or rejection of the Senate; to have the power of pardoning all offences except Treason; which he shall not pardon without the approbation of the Senate.

V. On the death, resignation or removal of the Governor his authorities to be exercised by the President of the Senate till a Successor be appointed.

VI. The Senate to have the sole power of declaring war, the power of advising and approving all Treaties, the power of approving or rejecting all appointments of officers except the heads or chiefs of the departments of Finance, War and Foreign Affairs.

VII. The supreme Judicial authority to be vested in   Judges to hold their offices during good behaviour with adequate and permanent salaries. This Court to have original jurisdiction in all causes of capture, and an appelative jurisdiction in all causes in which the revenues of the general Government or the Citizens of foreign Nations are concerned.

VIII. The Legislature of the United States to have power to institute Courts in each State for the determination of all matters of general concern.

IX. The Governor Senators and all officers of the United States to be liable to impeachment for mal- and corrupt conduct; and upon conviction to be removed from office, and disqualified for holding any place of trust or profit.—All impeachments to be tried by a Court to consist of the Chief [Justice] or Judge of the superior Court of Law of each State, provided such Judge shall hold his place during good behavior, and have a permanent salary.

X. All laws of the particular States contrary to the Constitution or laws of the United States to be utterly void; and the better to prevent such laws being passed, the Governor or president of each State shall be appointed by the General Government and shall have a negative upon the laws about to be passed in the State of which he is Governor or President.

XI. No State to have any forces land or Naval; and the Militia of all the States to be under the sole and exclusive direction of the United States, the officers of which to be appointed and commissioned by them."

Opposition to the New Jersey Plan
(June 19)

The next day, largely ignoring Hamilton's plan because it seemed so far from the general tenor of the Convention, Madison spoke at length opposing the New Jersey Plan. Immediately after his speech the Convention voted, seven states to three, with one divided, to set aside the New Jersey Plan and instead resume its consideration of the Virginia Plan.

MR. MADISON. Much stress had been laid by some gentlemen on the want of power in the Convention to propose any other than a *federal* plan. To what had been answered by others, he would only add, that neither of the characteristics attached to a *federal* plan would support this objection. One characteristic, was that in a *federal* Government, the power was exercised not on the people individually; but on the people *collectively,* on the *States.* Yet in some instances as in piracies, captures etc. the existing Confederacy, and in many instances, the amendments to it proposed by Mr. Paterson, must operate immediately on individuals. The other characteristic was that a *federal* Government derived its appointments not immediately from the people, but from the States which they respectively composed. Here too were facts on the other side. In two of the States, Connecticut and Rhode Island, the delegates to Congress were chosen, not by the Legislatures, but by the people at large; and the plan of Mr. Paterson intended no change in this particular.

It had been alleged [by Mr. Paterson], that the Confederation having been formed by unanimous consent, could be dissolved by unanimous Consent only. Does this doctrine result from the nature of compacts? Does it arise from any particular stipulation in the articles of Confederation? If we consider the federal union as analogous to the fundamental compact by which individuals compose one Society, and which must in its theoretic origin at least, have been the unanimous act of the component members, it can not be said that no dissolution of the compact can be effected without unanimous consent. A breach of the fundamental principles of the compact by a part of the Society would certainly absolve the other part from their obligations to it. If the breach of *any* article by *any* of the parties, does not set the others at liberty, it is because, the contrary is *implied* in the compact itself, and particularly by that law of it, which gives an indefinite authority to the majority to bind the whole in all cases. This latter circumstance shows that we are not to consider the federal Union as analogous to the social compact of individuals: for if it were so, a Majority would have a right to bind the rest, and even to form a new Constitution for the whole, which the Gentleman from New Jersey would be among the last to admit. If we consider the federal Union as analogous not to the social compacts among individual men: but to the conventions among individual States. What is the doctrine resulting from these conventions? Clearly, according to the Expositors of the law of Nations, that a breach of any one article, by any one party, leaves all the other parties at liberty, to consider the whole convention as dissolved, unless they choose rather to compel the delinquent party to repair the breach. In some treaties indeed it is expressly stipulated that a violation of particular articles shall not have this consequence, and even that particular articles shall remain in force during war, which in general is understood to dissolve all subsisting Treaties. But are there any exceptions of this sort to the Articles of confederation? So far from it that there is not even an express stipulation that force shall be used to compell an offending member of the Union to discharge its duty. He observed that the violations of the federal articles had been numerous and notorious. Among the most notorious was an act of New Jersey herself; by which she *expressly refused* to comply with a constitutional requisition of Congress and yielded no farther to the expostulations of their deputies, than barely to rescind her vote of refusal without passing any positive act of compliance. He did not wish to draw any rigid inferences from these observations. He thought it proper however that the true nature of the existing confederacy should be investigated, and he was not anxious to strengthen the foundations on which it now stands.

Proceeding to the consideration of Mr. Paterson's plan, he stated the object of a proper plan to be twofold. 1. To preserve the Union. 2. To provide a Government that will remedy the evils felt by the States both in their united and individual capacities. Examine Mr. Paterson's plan, and say whether it promises satisfaction in these respects.

1. Will it prevent those violations of the law of nations and of Treaties which if not prevented must involve us in the calamities of foreign wars? The tendency of the States to these violations has been manifested in sundry instances. The files of Congress contain complaints already, from almost every nation with which treaties have been formed. Hitherto indulgence has been

shown to us. This can not be the permanent disposition of foreign nations. A rupture with other powers is among the greatest
of national calamities. It ought therefore to be effectually provided that no part of a nation shall have it in its power to bring
them on the whole. The existing Confederacy does not sufficiently provide against this evil. The proposed amendment to it
does not supply the omission. It leaves the will of the States as
uncontrolled as ever.

2. Will it prevent encroachments on the federal authority? A
tendency to such encroachments has been sufficiently exemplified, among ourselves, as well in every other confederated republic ancient and Modern. By the federal articles, transactions
with the Indians appertain to Congress. Yet in several instances,
the States have entered into treaties and wars with them. In like
manner no two or more States can form among themselves any
treaties etc. without the consent of Congress. Yet Virginia and
Maryland in one instance—Pennsylvania and New Jersey in another, have entered into compacts, without previous application
or subsequent apology. No State again can of right raise troops
in time of peace without the like consent. Of all cases of the
league, this seems to require the most scrupulous observance.
Has not Massachusetts, notwithstanding, the most powerful
member of the Union, already raised a body of troops? Is she not
now augmenting them, without having even deigned to apprise
Congress of Her intention? In fine—have we not seen the public
land dealt out to Connecticut to bribe her acquiscence in the
decree constitutionally awarded against her claim on the territory of Pennsylvania for no other possible motive can account
for the policy of Congress in that measure?—If we recur to the
examples of other confederacies, we shall find in all of them
the same tendency of the parts to encroach on the authority of
the whole. He then reviewed the Amphyctionic and Achæan
confederacies among the ancients, and the Helvetic, Germanic
and Belgic among the moderns, tracing their analogy to the
United States—in the constitution and extent of their federal
authorities—in the tendency of the particular members to usurp
on these authorities; and to bring confusion and ruin on the
whole.—He observed that the plan of Mr. Paterson besides

omitting a control over the States as a general defence of the federal prerogatives was particularly defective in two of its provisions. 1. Its ratification was not to be by the people at large, but by the *legislatures.* It could not therefore render the Acts of Congress in pursuance of their powers, even legally *paramount* to the Acts of the States. 2. It gave to the federal Tribunal an appellate jurisdiction only—even in the criminal cases enumerated. The necessity of any such provision supposed a danger of undue acquittals in the State tribunals. Of what avail could an appellate tribunal be, after an acquittal? Besides in most if not all of the States, the Executives have by their respective *Constitutions* the right of pardoning. How could this be taken from them by a *legislative* ratification only?

3. Will it prevent trespasses of the States on each other? Of these enough has been already seen. He instanced Acts of Virginia and Maryland which give a preference to their own Citizens in cases where the Citizens of other States are entitled to equality of privileges by the Articles of Confederation. He considered the emissions of paper money and other kindred measures as also aggressions. The States relatively to one another being each of them either Debtor or Creditor; the creditor States must suffer unjustly from every emission by the debtor States. We have seen retaliating acts on this subject which threatened danger not to the harmony only, but the tranquility of the Union. The plan of Mr. Paterson, not giving even a negative on the acts of the States, left them as much at liberty as ever to execute their unrighteous projects against each other.

4. Will it secure the internal tranquility of the States themselves? The insurrections in Massachusetts admonished all the States of the danger to which they were exposed. Yet the plan of Mr. Paterson contained no provisions for supplying the defect of the Confederation on this point. According to the Republican theory indeed, Right and power being both vested in the majority, are held to be synonimous. According to fact and experience, a minority may in an appeal to force be an overmatch for the majority. 1. If the minority happen to include all such as possess the skill and habits of military life, with such as possess the great pecuniary resources, one third may conquer the remaining

two thirds. 2. one third of those who participate in the choice of rulers may be rendered a majority by the accession of those whose poverty disqualifies them from a suffrage, and who for obvious reasons may be more ready to join the standard of sedition than that of the established Government. 3. where slavery exists, the Republican Theory becomes still more fallacious.

5. Will it secure a good internal legislation and administration to the particular States? In developing the evils which vitiate the political system of the United States it is proper to take into view those which prevail within the States individually as well as those which affect them collectively: Since the former indirectly affect the whole; and there is great reason to believe that the pressure of them had a full share in the motives which produced the present Convention. Under this head he enumerated and animadverted on 1. the multiplicity of the laws passed by the several States. 2. the mutability of their laws. 3. the injustice of them. 4. the impotence of them: observing that Mr. Paterson's plan contained no remedy for this dreadful class of evils, and could not therefore be received as an adequate provision for the exigencies of the Community.

6. Will it secure the Union against the influence of foreign powers over its members? He pretended not to say that any such influence had yet been tried: but it was naturally to be expected that occasions would produce it. As lessons which claimed particular attention, he cited the intrigues practised among the Amphyctionic Confederates first by the Kings of Persia, and afterwards fatally by Philip of Macedon: among the Achæans, first by Macedon and afterwards no less fatally by Rome: among the Swiss by Austria, France and the lesser neighbouring powers: among the members of the Germanic Body by France, England, Spain and Russia—: and in the Belgic Republic, by all the great neighbouring powers. The plan of Mr. Paterson, not giving to the general Councils any negative on the will of the particular States, left the door open for the like pernicious machinations among ourselves.

7. He begged the smaller States which were most attached to Mr. Paterson's plan to consider the situation in which it would leave them. In the first place they would continue to bear the

whole expence of maintaining their Delegates in Congress. It ought not to be said that if they were willing to bear this burden, no others had a right to complain. As far as it led the small States to forbear keeping up a representation, by which the public business was delayed, it was evidently a matter of common concern. An examination of the minutes of Congress would satisfy every one that the public business had been frequently delayed by this cause; and that the States most frequently unrepresented in Congress were not the larger States. He reminded the convention of another consequence of leaving on a small State the burden of maintaining a Representation in Congress. During a considerable period of the War, one of the Representatives of Delaware, in whom alone before the signing of the Confederation the entire vote of that State and after that event one half of its vote, frequently resided, was a Citizen and Resident of Pennsylvania and held an office in his own State incompatible with an appointment from it to Congress. During another period, the same State was represented by three delegates two of whom were citizens of Pennsylvania and the third a Citizen of New Jersey. These expedients must have been intended to avoid the burden of supporting delegates from their own State. But whatever might have been the cause, was not in effect the vote of one State doubled, and the influence of another increased by it? In the second place the coercion, on which the efficacy of the plan depends, can never be exerted but on themselves. The larger States will be impregnable, the smaller only can feel the vengeance of it. He illustrated the position by the history of the Amphyctionic Confederates: and the ban of the German Empire. It was the cobweb which could entangle the weak, but would be the sport of the strong.

8. He begged them to consider the situation in which they would remain in case their pertinacious adherence to an inadmissible plan, should prevent the adoption of any plan. The contemplation of such an event was painful; but it would be prudent to submit to the task of examining it at a distance, that the means of escaping it might be the more readily embraced. Let the Union of the States be dissolved, and one of two consequences must happen. Either the States must remain individually inde-

pendent and sovereign; or two or more Confederacies must be formed among them. In the first event would the small States be more secure against the ambition and power of their larger neighbours, than they would be under a general Government pervading with equal energy every part of the Empire, and having an equal interest in protecting every part against every other part? In the second, can the smaller expect that their larger neighbours would confederate with them on the principle of the present confederacy, which gives to each member, an equal suffrage; or that they would exact less severe concessions from the smaller States, than are proposed in the scheme of Mr. Randolph?

The great difficulty lies in the affair of Representation; and if this could be adjusted, all others would be surmountable. It was admitted by both the gentlemen from New Jersey [Mr. Brearly and Mr. Paterson], that it would not be *just to allow Virginia* which was 16 times as large as Delaware an equal vote only. Their language was that it would not be *safe for Delaware* to allow Virginia 16 times as many votes. The expedient proposed by them was that all the States should be thrown into one mass and a new partition be made into 13 equal parts. Would such a scheme be practicable? The dissimilarities existing in the rules of property, as well as in the manners, habits and prejudices of the different States, amounted to a prohibition of the attempt. It had been found impossible for the power of one of the most absolute princes in Europe [King of France] directed by the wisdom of one of the most enlightened and patriotic Ministers [Mr. Neckar] that any age has produced to equalize in some points only the different usages and regulations of the different provinces. But admitting a general amalgamation and repartition of the States to be practicable, and the danger apprehended by the smaller States from a proportional representation to be real; would not a particular and voluntary coalition of these with their neighbours, be less inconvenient to the whole community, and equally effectual for their own safety. If New Jersey or Delaware conceived that an advantage would accrue to them from an equalization of the States, in which case they would necessarily form a junction with their neighbours, why might not this end be attained by leaving them at liberty by the Constitution to form such a junction whenever they pleased? And why should they wish to obtrude a like arrangement on all the States, when it was, to say the least, extremely difficult, would be obnoxious to many of the States, and when neither the inconveniency, nor the benefit of the expedient to themselves, would be lessened, by confining it to themselves.—The prospect of many new States to the Westward was another consideration of importance. If they should come into the Union at all, they would come when they contained but few inhabitants. If they should be entitled to vote according to their proportions of inhabitants, all would be right and safe. Let them have an equal vote, and a more objectionable minority than ever might give law to the whole.

Debate on Federalism
(June 21)

As the Convention in plenary session considered one by one the resolves based on the Virginia Plan, most of the debate was on technical and practical matters rather than on points of principle, but occasionally more basic arguments surfaced. William Johnson of Connecticut, Wilson, and Madison exchanged views on the tendencies of the state and national governments to encroach on each other.

DR. JOHNSON. On a comparison of the two plans which had been proposed from Virginia and New Jersey, it appeared that the peculiarity which characterized the latter was its being calculated to preserve the individuality of the States. The plan from Virginia did not profess to destroy this individuality altogether, but was charged with such a tendency. One Gentleman alone (Colonel Hamilton) in his animadversions on the plan of New Jersey, boldly and decisively contended for an abolition of the

State Governments. Mr. Wilson and the gentlemen from Virginia who also were adversaries of the plan of New Jersey held a different language. They wished to leave the States in possession of a considerable, though a subordinate jurisdiction. They had not yet however shown how this could consist with, or be secured against the general sovereignty and jurisdiction, which they proposed to give to the national Government. If this could be shown in such a manner as to satisfy the patrons of the New Jersey propositions, that the individuality of the States would not be endangered, many of their objections would no doubt be removed. If this could not be shown their objections would have their full force. He wished it therefore to be well considered whether in case the States, as was proposed, should retain some portion of sovereignty at least, this portion could be preserved, without allowing them to participate effectually in the General Government, without giving them each a distinct and equal vote for the purpose of defending themselves in the general Councils.

MR. WILSON'S respect for Dr. Johnson, added to the importance of the subject led him to attempt, unprepared as he was, to solve the difficulty which had been started. It was asked how the General Government and individuality of the particular States could be reconciled to each other; and how the latter could be secured against the former? Might it not, on the other side be asked how the former was to be secured against the latter? It was generally admitted that a jealousy and [rivalry] would be felt between the General and particular Governments. As the plan now stood, though indeed contrary to his opinion, one branch of the General Government (the Senate or second branch) was to be appointed by the State Legislatures. The State Legislatures, therefore, by this participation in the General Government would have an opportunity of defending their rights. Ought not a reciprocal opportunity to be given to the General Government of defending itself by having an appointment of some one constituent branch of the State Government. If a security be necessary on one side, it would seem reasonable to demand it on the other. But taking the matter in a more general view, he saw no danger to the States from the General Government. In case a combination should be made by the large ones it would produce a general alarm among the rest; and the project would be frustrated. But there was no temptation to such a project. The States having in general a similar interest, in case of any proposition in the National Legislature to encroach on the State Legislatures, he conceived a general alarm would take place in the National Legislature itself, that it would communicate itself to the State Legislatures, and would finally spread among the people at large. The General Government will be as ready to preserve the rights of the States as the latter are to preserve the rights of individuals; all the members of the former, having a common interest, as representatives of all the people of the latter, to leave the State Governments in possession of what the people wish them to retain. He could not discover, therefore any danger whatever on the side from which it had been apprehended. On the contrary, he conceived that in spite of every precaution the general Government would be in perpetual danger of encroachments from the State Governments.

MR. MADISON was of opinion that there was 1. less danger of encroachment from the General Government than from the State Government. 2. That the mischief from encroachments would be less fatal if made by the former, than if made by the latter. 1. All the examples of other confederacies prove the greater tendency in such systems to anarchy than to tyranny; to a disobedience of the members than to usurpations of the federal head. Our own experience had fully illustrated this tendency.—But it will be said that the proposed change in the principles and form of the Union will vary the tendency; that the General Governments will have real and greater powers, and will be derived in one branch at least from the people, not from the Government of the States. To give full force to this objection, let it be supposed for a moment that indefinite power should be given to the General Legislature, and the States reduced to corporations dependent on the General Legislature; why should it follow that the General Government would take from the States any branch of their power as far as its operation was beneficial, and its continuance desirable to the people? In some of the States, particularly in Connecticut, all the Townships are incorporated, and have a certain limited jurisdiction. Have the Representatives of the people of the Townships in the Legislature of the State ever endeavored to despoil the Townships of any part of their local authority? As far as this local authority is convenient to the people they are attached to it; and their representatives chosen by and amenable to them naturally respect their attachment to this, as much as their attachment to any other right or interest. The relation of a General Government to State Governments is parallel. 2. Guards were more necessary against encroachments of the State Governments on the General Government than of the latter on the former. The great objection made against an abolition of the State Government was that the General Government could not extend its care to all the minute objects which fall under the cognizance of the local jurisdictions. The objection as stated lay not against the probable abuse of the general power, but against the imperfect use that could be made of it throughout so great an extent of country, and over so great a variety of objects. As far as its operation would be practicable it could not in this view be improper; as far as it would be impracticable, the conveniency of the General Government itself would concur with that of the people in the maintenance of subordinate Governments. Were it practicable for the General Government to extend its care to every requisite object without the cooperation of the State Governments the people would not be less free as members of one great Republic than as members of thirteen small ones. A Citizen of Delaware was not more free than a Citizen of Virginia: nor would either be more free than a Citizen of America. Supposing therefore a tendency in the General Government to absorb the State Governments no fatal consequence could result. Taking the reverse of the supposition, that a tendency should be left in the State Governments towards an independence on the General Government and the gloomy consequences need not be pointed out. The imagination of them, must have suggested to the States the experiment we are now making to prevent the calamity, and must have formed the chief motive with those present to undertake the arduous task.

Length of Term
in Office for Senators
(June 26)

*After three days discussing details, the Convention debated the
length of term for Senators. The issue provoked Madison, Roger
Sherman, and Hamilton to open a basic question: were long or
short terms more likely to result in wise decisions that would
protect the interests of the people?*

MR. MADISON. In order to judge of the form to be given to
this institution, it will be proper to take a view of the ends to be
served by it. These were first to protect the people against their
rulers: secondly to protect the people against the transient impressions into which they themselves might be led. A people
deliberating in a temperate moment, and with the experience of
other nations before them, on the plan of Government most
likely to secure their happiness, would first be aware, that those
charged with the public happiness, might betray their trust. An
obvious precaution against this danger would be to divide the
trust between different bodies of men, who might watch and
check each other. In this they would be governed by the same
prudence which has prevailed in organizing the subordinate departments of Government, where all business liable to abuses is
made to pass through separate hands, the one being a check on
the other. It would next occur to such a people, that they themselves were liable to temporary errors, through want of information as to their true interest, and that men chosen for a short
term, and employed but a small portion of that in public affairs,
might err from the same cause. This reflection would naturally
suggest that the Government be so constituted, as that one of its
branches might have an opportunity of acquiring a competent

knowledge of the public interests. Another reflection equally becoming a people on such an occasion, would be that they themselves, as well as a numerous body of Representatives, were liable to err also, from fickleness and passion. A necessary fence against this danger would be to select a portion of enlightened citizens, whose limited number, and firmness might seasonably interpose against impetuous councils. It ought finally to occur to a people deliberating on a Government for themselves, that as different interests necessarily result from the liberty meant to be secured, the major interest might under sudden impulses be tempted to commit injustice on the minority. In all civilized Countries the people fall into different classes having a real or supposed difference of interests. There will be creditors and debtors, farmers, merchants and manufacturers. There will be particularly the distinction of rich and poor. It was true as had been observed [by Mr. Pinckney] we had not among us those hereditary distinctions, of rank which were a great source of the contests in the ancient Governments as well as the modern States of Europe, nor those extremes of wealth or poverty which characterize the latter. We cannot however be regarded even at this time, as one homogeneous mass, in which every thing that affects a part will affect in the same manner the whole. In framing a system which we wish to last for ages, we should not lose sight of the changes which ages will produce. An increase of population will of necessity increase the proportion of those who will labour under all the hardships of life, and secretly sigh for a more equal distribution of its blessings. These may in time outnumber those who are placed above the feelings of indigence. According to the equal laws of suffrage, the power will slide into the hands of the former. No agrarian attempts have yet been made in this Country, but symptoms, of a leveling spirit, as we have understood, have sufficiently appeared in a certain quarters to give notice of the future danger. How is this danger to be guarded against on republican principles? How is the danger in all cases of interested coalitions to oppress the minority to be guarded against? Among other means by the establishment of a body in the Government sufficiently respectable for its wisdom and virtue, to aid on such emergences, the preponderance of justice by throwing its weight into that scale. Such being the objects of the second branch in the proposed Government he thought a considerable duration ought to be given to it. He did not conceive that the term of nine years could threaten any real danger; but in pursuing his particular ideas on the subject, he should require that the long term allowed to the second branch should not commence till such a period of life, as would render a perpetual disqualification to be re-elected little inconvenient either in a public or private view. He observed that as it was more than probable we were now digesting a plan which in its operation would decide for ever the fate of Republican Government we ought not only to provide every guard to liberty that its preservation could require, but be equally careful to supply the defects which our own experience had particularly pointed out.

Mr. Sherman. Government is instituted for those who live under it. It ought therefore to be so constituted as not to be dangerous to their liberties. The more permanency it has the worse if it be a bad Government. Frequent elections are necessary to preserve the good behavior of rulers. They also tend to give permanency to the Government, by preserving that good behavior, because it ensures their re-election. In Connecticut elections have been very frequent, yet great stability and uniformity both as to persons and measures have been experienced from its original establishment to the present time; a period of more than 130 years. He wished to have provision made for steadiness and wisdom in the system to be adopted; but he thought six or four years would be sufficient. He should be content with either.

Mr. Read wished it to be considered by the small States that it was their interest that we should become one people as much as possible; that State attachments should be extinguished as much as possible; that the Senate should be so constituted as to have the feelings of Citizens of the whole.

Mr. Hamilton. He did not mean to enter particularly into the subject. He concurred with Mr. Madison in thinking we were now to decide for ever the fate of Republican Government; and that if we did not give to that form due stability and wisdom, it would be disgraced and lost among ourselves, disgraced and lost to mankind for ever. He acknowledged himself not to think fa-

vorably of Republican Government; but addressed his remarks
to those who did think favorably of it, in order to prevail on them
to tone their Government as high as possible. He professed himself to be as zealous an advocate for liberty as any man whatever, and trusted he should be as willing a martyr to it though he
differed as to the form in which it was most eligible.—He concurred also in the general observations of [Mr. Madison] on the
subject, which might be supported by others if it were necessary.
It was certainly true: that nothing like an equality of property
existed: that an inequality would exist as long as liberty existed,
and that it would unavoidably result from that very liberty itself.
This inequality of property constituted the great and fundamental distinction in Society. When the Tribunitial power had levelled the boundary between the *patricians and plebeians,* what
followed? The distinction between rich and poor was substituted. He meant not however to enlarge on the subject. He rose
principally to remark that [Mr. Sherman] seemed not to recollect
that one branch of the proposed government was so formed, as
to render it particularly the guardians of the poorer orders of
Citizens; nor to have adverted to the true causes of the stability
which had been exemplified in Connecticut. Under the British
system as well as the federal, many of the great powers appertaining to Government particularly all those relating to foreign
Nations were not in the hands of the Government there. Their
internal affairs also were extremely simple, owing to sundry
causes many of which were peculiar to that Country. Of late the
Government had entirely given way to the people, and had in
fact suspended many of its ordinary functions in order to prevent
those turbulent scenes which had appeared elsewhere. He asks
Mr. S. whether the State at this time, dare impose and collect a
tax on the people? To these causes and not to the frequency of
elections, the effect, as far as it existed ought to be chiefly ascribed.

Debate on State Equality
in the Senate
(June 28–July 2)

Debate, though, resumed on the most divisive issue before the Convention: should the states have an equal vote in the upper house of the legislature (the Senate)? Madison, Wilson, and other delegates (mostly from large states) opposed state equality because the states themselves were so unequal in size. Equality in the Senate would thus violate the fundamental republican principle of government according to the equal voices of the people consenting to be governed. A series of increasingly vehement speeches over a five-day period (June 28–July 2) revealed bitter rivalry. Madison, Wilson, Rufus King of Massachusetts, and Gouverneur Morris of Pennsylvania argued against state equality in the Senate, while William Samuel Johnson and Oliver Ellsworth of Connecticut and Gunning Bedford of Delaware advocated such equality. Bedford's speech is from the notes of Robert Yates, and is reprinted from C. C. Tansill, ed., Documents, pp. 834–836.

. . . Mr. Madison. Why are counties of the same states represented in proportion to their numbers? Is it because the representatives are chosen by the people themselves? So will be the representatives in the National Legislature. Is it because the larger have more at stake than the smaller? The case will be the same with the larger and smaller States. Is it because the laws are to operate immediately on their persons and properties? The same is the case in some degree as the articles of confederation stand; the same will be the case in a far greater degree under the plan proposed to be substituted. In the cases of captures, of piracies, and of offences in a federal army; the property and persons of individuals depend on the laws of Congress. By the plan proposed a compleat power of taxation, the highest prerogative of supremacy is proposed to be vested in the National Government. Many other powers are added which assimilate it to the Government of individual States. The negative proposed on the State laws, will make it an essential branch of the State Legislatures and of course will require that it should be exercised by a body established on like principles with the other branches of those Legislatures.—That it is not necessary to secure the small States against the large ones he conceived to be equally obvious: Was a combination of the large ones dreaded? This must arise either from some interest common to Virginia, Massachusetts and Pennsylvania and distinguishing them from the other States or from the mere circumstance of similarity of size. Did any such common interest exist? In point of situation they could not have been more effectually separated from each other by the most jealous citizen of the most jealous State. In point of manners, Religion, and the other circumstances which sometimes beget affection between different communities, they were not more assimilated than the other States.—In point of the staple productions they were as dissimilar as any three other States in the Union. The Staple of Massachusetts was *fish,* of Pennsylvania *flour,* of Virginia *Tobacco.* Was a combination to be apprehended from the mere circumstance of equality of size? Experience suggested no such danger. The journals of Congress did not present any peculiar association of these States in the votes recorded. It had never been seen that different Counties in the same State, conformable in extent, but disagreeing in other circumstances, betrayed a propensity to such combinations. Experience rather taught a contrary lesson. Among individuals of superior eminence and weight in Society, rivalships were much more frequent than coalitions. Among independent nations, pre-eminent over their neighbours, the same remark was verified. Carthage and Rome tore one another to pieces instead of uniting their forces to devour the weaker nations of the Earth. The Houses of Austria and France were hostile as long as they remained the greatest powers of Europe. England and France have succeeded to the pre-eminence and to the enmity. To this principle we owe perhaps our liberty. A coalition between those powers would have been fatal to us. Among the principal members of ancient and Modern confederacies, we find the same effect from the same cause. The contentions, not the Coalitions of Sparta, Athens and Thebes, proved fatal to the smaller members of the Amphyctionic Confederacy. The contentions, not the combinations of Prussia and Austria, have distracted and oppressed the Germanic empire. Were the large States formidable *singly* to their smaller neighbours? On this supposition the latter ought to wish for such a general Government as will operate with equal energy on the former as on themselves. The more lax the band, the more liberty the larger will have to avail themselves of their superior force. Here again Experience was an instructive monitor. What is the situation of the weak compared with the strong in those stages of civilization in which the violence of individuals is least controled by an efficient Government? The Heroic period of Ancient Greece, the feudal licentiousness of the middle ages of Europe, the existing condition of the American Savages, answer this question. What is the situation of the minor sovereigns in the great society of independent nations, in which the more powerful are under no control but the nominal authority of the law of Nations? Is not the danger to the former exactly in proportion to their weakness? But there are cases still more in point. What was the condition of the weaker members of the Amphyctionic Confederacy. Plutarch [life of Themistocles] will inform us that it happened but too often that the strongest cities corrupted and awed the weaker, and that Judgment went in favor of the more powerful party. What is the condition of the lesser states in the German Confederacy? We all know that they are exceedingly trampled upon; and that they owe their safety as far as they enjoy it, partly to their enlisting themselves, under the rival banners of the pre-eminent members, partly to alliances with neighbouring Princes which the Consitution of the Empire does not prohibit. What is the state of things in the lax system of the Dutch Confederacy? Holland contains about one half the people, supplies about one half of the money, and by her influence, silently and indirectly governs the whole republic. In a word, the two extremes before us are a perfect separation and a perfect incorporation, of the 13 States. In the first case they would be independent nations subject to no law, but the law of nations. In the last, they would be mere counties of one entire republic, subject to one common law. In the first case the smaller States would have every thing to fear from the larger. In the last they would have nothing to fear. The true policy of the small States therefore lies in promoting those principles and that form of Government which will most approximate the States to the condition of counties. Another consideration may be added. If the General Government be feeble, the large States distrusting its continuance, and foreseeing that their importance and security may depend on their own size and strength, will never submit to a partition. Give to the General Government sufficient energy and permanency, and you remove the objection. Gradual partitions of the large, and junctions of the small States will be facilitated, and time may effect that equalization, which is wished for by the small States now, but can never be accomplished at once. . . .

DR. JOHNSON. The controversy must be endless whilst Gentlemen differ in the grounds of their arguments: Those on one side considering the States as districts of people composing one political Society; those on the other considering them as so many political societies. The fact is that the States do exist as political Societies, and a Government is to be formed for them in their political capacity, as well as for the individuals composing them. Does it not seem to follow, that if the States as such are to exist they must be armed with some power of self-defence. This is the idea of [Colonel Mason] who appears to have looked to the bottom of this matter. Besides the Aristocratic and other interests, which ought to have the means of defending themselves, the States have their interests as such, and are equally entitled to like means. On the whole he thought that as in some respects the States are to be considered in their political capacity, and in others as districts of individual citizens, the two ideas embraced on different sides, instead of being opposed to each other, ought to be combined; that in *one* branch the *people,* ought to be represented; in the *other* the *States.* . . .

MR. MADISON agreed with Dr. Johnson, that the mixed nature

of the Government ought to be kept in view; but thought too
much stress was laid on the rank of the States as political societies. There was a gradation, he observed, from the smallest corporation, with the most limited powers, to the largest empire with
the most perfect sovereignty. He pointed out the limitations on
the sovereignty of the States, as now confederated their laws in
relation to the paramount law of the Confederacy were analogous
to that of bye laws to the supreme law within a State. Under the
proposed Government the powers of the States will be much farther reduced. According to the views of every member, the General Government will have powers far beyond those exercised by
the British Parliament, when the States were part of the British
Empire. It will in particular have the power, without the consent
of the State Legislatures, to levy money directly on the people
themselves; and therefore not to divest such *unequal* portions of
the people as composed the several States, of an *equal* voice,
would subject the system to the reproaches and evils which have
resulted from the vicious representation in Great Britain.

He entreated the gentlemen representing the small States to
renounce a principle which was confessedly unjust, which could
never be admitted, and if admitted must infuse mortality into a
Constitution which we wished to last forever. He prayed them to
ponder well the consequences of suffering the Confederacy to
go to pieces. It had been said that the want of energy in the large
states would be a security to the small. It was forgotten that this
want of energy proceeded from the supposed security of the
States against all external danger. Let each state depend on itself
for its security, and let apprehensions arise of danger, from distant powers or from neighbouring States, and the languishing
condition of all the States, large as well as small, would soon be
transformed into vigorous and high toned Government. His
great fear was that their Governments would then have too much
energy, that these might not only be formidable in the large to
the small States, but fatal to the internal liberty of all. The same
causes which have rendered the old world the Theatre of inces-
sant wars, and have banished liberty from the face of it, would
soon produce the same effects here. The weakness and jealousy
of the small States would quickly introduce some regular mili-

tary force against sudden danger from their powerful neighbours. The example would be followed by others, and would soon become universal. In time of actual war, great discretionary powers are constantly given to the Executive Magistrate. Constant apprehension of war, has the same tendency to render the head too large for the body. A standing military force, with an overgrown Executive will not long be safe companions to liberty. The means of defence against foreign danger, have been always the instruments of tyranny at home. Among the Romans it was a standing maxim to excite a war, whenever a revolt was apprehended. Throughout all Europe, the armies kept up under the pretext of defending, have enslaved the people. It is perhaps questionable, whether the best concerted system of absolute power in Europe could maintain itself, in a situation, where no alarms of external danger could tame the people to the domestic yoke. The insular situation of Great Britain was the principal cause of her being an exception to the general fate of Europe. It has rendered less defence necessary, and admitted a kind of defence which could not be used for the purpose of oppression.— These consequences he conceived ought to be apprehended whether the States should run into a total separation from each other, or should enter into partial confederacies. Either event would be truly deplorable; and those who might be accessary to either, could never be forgiven by their Country, nor by themselves.

MR. HAMILTON observed that individuals forming political Societies modify their rights differently, with regard to suffrage. Examples of it are found in all the States. In all of them some individuals are deprived of the right altogether, not having the requisite qualification of property. In some of the States the right of suffrage is allowed in some cases and refused in others. To vote for a member in one branch, a certain quantum of property, to vote for a member in another branch of the Legislature, a higher quantum of property is required. In like manner States may modify their right of suffrage differently, the larger exercising a larger, the smaller a smaller share of it. But as States are a collection of individual men which ought we to respect most, the rights of the people composing them, or of the artificial beings resulting from the composition. Nothing could be more preposterous or absurd than to sacrifice the former to the latter. It has been said that if the smaller States renounce their *equality,* they renounce at the same time their *liberty.* The truth is it is a contest for power, not for liberty. Will the men composing the small States be less free than those composing the larger. The State of Delaware having 40,000 souls will *lose power,* if she has one tenth only of the votes allowed to Pennsylvania having 400,000: but will the people of Delaware *be less free,* if each citizen has an equal vote with each citizen of Pennsylvania. He admitted that common residence within the same State would produce a certain degree of attachment; and that this principle might have a certain influence in public affairs. He thought however that this might by some precautions be in a great measure excluded: and that no material inconvenience could result from it, as there could not be any ground for combination among the States whose influence was most dreaded. The only considerable distinction of interests, lay between the carrying and non-carrying States, which divide instead of uniting the largest States. No considerable inconvenience had been found from the division of the State of New York into different districts of different sizes.

Some of the consequences of a dissolution of the Union, and the establishment of partial confederacies, had been pointed out. He would add another of a most serious nature. Alliances will immediately be formed with different rival and hostile nations of Europe, who will foment disturbances among ourselves, and make us parties to all their own quarrels. Foreign Nations having American dominions are and must be jealous of us. Their representatives betray the utmost anxiety for our fate, and for the result of this meeting, which must have an essential influence on it.—It had been said that respectability in the eyes of foreign Nations was not the object at which we aimed; that the proper object of republican Government was domestic tranquility and happiness. This was an ideal distinction. No Government could give us tranquility and happiness at home, which did not possess sufficient stability and strength to make us respectable abroad. This was the critical moment for forming such a Government.

We should run every risk in trusting to future amendments. As yet we retain the habits of union. We are weak and sensible of our weakness. Henceforward the motives will become feebler, and the difficulties greater. It is a miracle that we were now here exercising our tranquil and free deliberations on the subject. It would be madness to trust to future miracles. A thousand causes must obstruct a reproduction of them. . . .

MR. ELLSWORTH moved that the rule of suffrage in the second branch be the same with that established by the articles of confederation. He was not sorry on the whole he said that the vote just passed, had determined against this rule in the first branch. He hoped it would become a ground of compromise with regard to the second branch. We were partly national; partly federal. The proportional representation in the first branch was conformable to the national principle and would secure the large States against the small. An equality of voices was conformable to the federal principle and was necessary to secure the Small States against the large. He trusted that on this middle ground a compromise would take place. He did not see that it could on any other. And if no compromise should take place, our meeting would not only be in vain but worse than in vain. To the Eastward he was sure Massachusetts was the only State that would listen to a proposition for excluding the States as equal political Societies, from an equal voice in both branches. The others would risk every consequence rather than part with so dear a right. An attempt to deprive them of it, was at once cutting the body of America in two, and as he supposed would be the case, somewhere about this part of it. The large States he conceived would notwithstanding the equality of votes, have an influence that would maintain their superiority. Holland, as had been admitted [by Mr. Madison] had, notwithstanding a like equality in the Dutch Confederacy, a prevailing influence in the public measures. The power of self-defence was essential to the small States. Nature had given it to the smallest insect of the creation. He could never admit that there was no danger of combinations among the large States. They will like individuals find out and avail themselves of the advantage to be gained by it. It was true the danger would be greater, if they were contiguous and had a more immediate common interest. A defensive combination of the small States was rendered more difficult by their greater number. He would mention another consideration of great weight. The existing confederation was founded on the equality of the States in the article of suffrage: was it meant to pay no regard to this antecedent plighted faith. Let a strong Executive, a Judiciary and Legislative power be created; but let not too much be attempted; by which all may be lost. He was not in general a half-way man, yet he preferred doing half the good we could, rather than do nothing at all. The other half may be added, when the necessity shall be more fully experienced. . . .

MR. WILSON did not expect such a motion after the establishment of the contrary principle in the first branch; and considering the reasons which would oppose it, even if an equal vote had been allowed in the first branch. The Gentleman from Connecticut [Mr. Ellsworth] had pronounced that if the motion should not be acceded to, of all the States North of Pennsylvania one only would agree to any General Government. He entertained more favorable hopes of Connecticut and of the other Northern States. He hoped the alarms exceeded their cause, and that they would not abandon a Country to which they were bound by so many strong and endearing ties. But should the deplored event happen, it would neither stagger his sentiments nor his duty. If the minority of the people of America refuse to coalesce with the majority on just the proper principles, if a separation must take place, it could never happen on better grounds. The votes of yesterday against the just principle of representation, were as 22 to 90 of the people of America. Taking the opinions to be the same on this point, and he was sure if there was any room for change, it could not be on the side of the majority, the question will be shall less than one quarter of the United States withdraw themselves from the Union; or shall more than three quarters renounce the inherent, indisputable, and unalienable rights of men, in favor of the artificial systems of States. If issue must be joined, it was on this point he would choose to join it. The gentleman from Connecticut in supposing that the preponderancy secured to the majority in the first branch had removed the objections to an equality of votes in the second branch for the security of the minority, narrowed the case extremely. Such an equality will enable the minority to control in all cases whatsoever, the sentiments and interests of the majority. Seven States will control six: Seven States, according to the estimates that had been used, composed twenty-four ninetieths of the whole people. It would be in the power then of less than one third to overrule two thirds whenever a question should happen to divide the States in that manner. Can we forget for whom we are forming a Government? Is it for *men,* or for the imaginary beings called *States?* Will our honest Constituents be satisfied with metaphysical distinctions? Will they, ought they to be satisfied with being told that the one third compose the greater number of States? The rule of suffrage ought on every principle to be the same in the second as in the first branch. If the Government be not laid on this foundation, it can be neither solid nor lasting. Any other principle will be local, confined and temporary. This will expand with the expansion, and grow with the growth of the United States.—Much has been said of an imaginary combination of three States. Sometimes a danger of monarchy, sometimes of aristocracy, has been charged on it. No explanation however of the danger has been vouchsafed. It would be easy to prove both from reason and history that rivalships would be more probable than coalitions; and that there are no coinciding interests that could produce the latter. No answer has yet been given to the observations of [Mr. Madison] on this subject. Should the Executive Magistrate be taken from one of the large States would not the other two be thereby thrown into the scale with the other States? Whence then the danger of monarchy? Are the people of the three large States more aristocratic than those of the small ones? Whence then the danger of aristocracy from their influence? It is all a mere illusion of names. We talk of States, till we forget what they are composed of. Is a real and fair majority, the natural hot-bed of aristocracy? It is a part of the definition of this species of Government or rather of tyranny, that the smaller number governs the greater. It is true that a majority of States in the second branch can not carry a law against a majority of the people in the first. But this removes half only of the objection. Bad Governments are of two sorts. 1. that

which does too little. 2. that which does too much: that which
fails through weakness; and that which destroys through oppression. Under which of these evils do the United States at present
groan? under the weakness and inefficiency of its Government.
To remedy this weakness we have been sent to this Convention.
If the motion should be agreed to, we shall leave the United
States fettered precisely as heretofore; with the additional mortification of seeing the good purposes of the fair representation
of the people in the first branch, defeated in second. Twenty four
will still control sixty six. He lamented that such a disagreement
should prevail on the point of representation, as he did not foresee that it would happen on the other point most contested, the
boundary between the General and the local authorities. He
thought the States necessary and valuable parts of a good system.

MR. ELLSWORTH. The capital objection of Mr. Wilson "that
the minority will rule the majority" is not true. The power is
given to the few to save them from being destroyed by the many.
If an equality of votes had been given to them in both branches,
the objection might have had weight. Is it a novel thing that the
few should have a check on the many? Is it not the case in the
British Constitution the wisdom of which so many gentlemen
have united in applauding? Have not the House of Lords, who
form so small a proportion of the nation a negative on the laws,
as a necessary defence of their peculiar rights against the encroachment of the Commons. No instance of a Confederacy has
existed in which an equality of voices has not been exercised by
the members of it. We are running from one extreme to another.
We are razing the foundations of the building, when we need
only repair the roof. No salutary measure has been lost for want
of *a majority of the States,* to favor it. If security be all that the
great States wish for the first branch secures them. The danger
of combinations among them is not imaginary. Although no particular abuses could be foreseen by him, the possibility of them
would be sufficient to alarm him. But he could easily conceive
cases in which they might result from such combinations. Suppose that in pursuance of some commercial treaty or arrangement, three or four free ports and no more were to be established

would not combinations be formed in favor of Boston, Philadelphia, and some port in Chesapeak? A like concert might be formed in the appointment of the great officers. He appealed again to the obligations of the federal pact which was still in force, and which had been entered into with so much solemnity; persuading himself that some regard would still be paid to the plighted faith under which each State small as well as great, held an equal right of suffrage in the general Councils. His remarks were not the result of partial or local views. The State he represented [Connecticut] held a middle rank.

MR. MADISON did justice to the able and close reasoning of Mr. Ellsworth but must observe that it did not always accord with itself. On another occasion, the large States were described by him as the Aristocratic States, ready to oppress the small. Now the small are the House of Lords requiring a negative to defend them against the more numerous commons. Mr. Ellsworth had also erred in saying that no instance had existed in which confederated States had not retained to themselves a perfect equality of suffrage. Passing over the German system in which the King of Prussia has nine voices, he reminded Mr. Ellsworth of the Lycian confederacy, in which the component members had votes proportioned to their importance, and which Montesquieu recommends as the fittest model for that form of Government. Had the fact been as stated by Mr. Ellsworth it would have been of little avail to him, or rather would have strengthened the arguments against him; the History and fate of the several confederacies modern as well as Ancient, demonstrating some radical vice in their structure. In reply to the appeal of Mr. Ellsworth to the faith plighted in the existing federal compact, he remarked that the party claiming from others an adherence to a common engagement ought at least to be guiltless itself of a violation. Of all the States however Connecticut was perhaps least able to urge this plea. Besides the various omissions to perform the stipulated acts from which no State was free, the Legislature of that State had by a pretty recent vote, *positively, refused* to pass a law for complying with the Requisitions of Congress and had transmitted a copy of the vote to Congress. It was urged, he said, continually that an equality of votes in the second branch was not only necessary to secure the small, but would be perfectly safe to the large ones whose majority in the first branch was an effectual bulwark. But notwithstanding this apparent defence, the majority of States might still injure the majority of people. 1. They could *obstruct* the wishes and interests of the majority. 2. They could *extort* measures repugnant to the wishes and interest of the majority. 3. They could *impose* measures adverse thereto; as the second branch will probly exercise some great powers, in which the first will not participate. He admitted that every peculiar interest whether in any class of citizens, or any description of States, ought to be secured as far as possible. Wherever there is danger of attack there ought to be given a constitutional power of defence. But he contended that the States were divided into different interests not by their difference of size, but by other circumstances; the most material of which resulted partly from climate, but principally from the effects of their having or not having slaves. These two causes concurred in forming the great division of interests in the United States. It did not lie between the large and small States: It lay between the Northern and Southern, and if any defensive power were necessary, it ought to be mutually given to these two interests. He was so strongly impressed with this important truth that he had been casting about in his mind for some expedient that would answer the purpose. The one which had occurred was that instead of proportioning the votes of the States in both branches, to their respective numbers of inhabitants computing the slaves in the ratio of 5 to 3, they should be represented in one branch according to the number of free inhabitants only; and in the other according to the whole number counting the slaves as if free. By this arrangement the Southern Scale would have the advantage in one House, and the Northern in the other. He had been restrained from proposing this expedient by two considerations: one was his unwillingness to urge any diversity of interests on an occasion where it is but too apt to arise of itself—the other was, the inequality of powers that must be vested in the two branches, and which would destroy the equilibrium of interests. . . .

MR. KING observed that the simple question was whether

each State should have an equal vote in the second branch; that it must be apparent to those gentlemen who liked neither the motion for this equality, nor the report as it stood, that the report was as susceptible of melioration as the motion; that a reform would be nugatory and nominal only if we should make another Congress of the proposed Senate: that if the adherence to an equality of votes was fixed and unalterable, there could not be less obstinacy on the other side, and that we were in fact cut asunder already, and it was in vain to shut our eyes against it: that he was however filled with astonishment that if we were convinced that every *man* in America was secured in all his rights, we should be ready to sacrifice this substantial good to the phantom of *State* sovereignty: that his feelings were more harrowed and his fears more agitated for his Country than he could express, that he conceived this to be the last opportunity of providing for its liberty and happiness: that he could not therefore but repeat his amazement that when a just Government founded on a fair representation of the *people* of America was within our reach, we should renounce the blessing, from an attachment to the ideal freedom and importance of *States:* that should this wonderful illusion continue to prevail, his mind was prepared for every event, rather than to sit down under a Government founded in a vicious principle of representation, and which must be as short lived as it would be unjust.

Mr. BEDFORD. That all the states at present are equally sovereign and independent, has been asserted from every quarter of this house. Our deliberations here are a confirmation of the position; and I may add to it, that each of them act from interested, and many from ambitious motives. Look at the votes which have been given on the floor of this house, and it will be found that their numbers, wealth and local views, have actuated their determinations; and that the larger states proceed as if our eyes were already perfectly blinded. Impartiality, with them, is already out of the question—the reported plan is their political creed, and they support it, right or wrong. Even the diminutive state of Georgia has an eye to her future wealth and greatness—South Carolina, puffed up with the possession of her wealth and negroes, and North Carolina, are all, from different views, united with the great states. And these latter, although it is said they can never, from interested views, form a coalition, we find closely united in one scheme of interest and ambition, notwithstanding they endeavor to amuse us with the purity of their principles and the rectitude of their intentions, in asserting that the general government must be drawn from an equal representation of the people. Pretences to support ambition are never wanting. Their cry is, where is the danger? and they insist that altho' the powers of the general government will be increased, yet it will be for the good of the whole; and although the three great states form nearly a majority of the people of America, they never will hurt or injure the lesser states. *I do not, gentlemen, trust you.* If you possess the power, the abuse of it could not be checked; and what then would prevent you from exercising it to our destruction? You gravely alledge that there is no danger of combination, and triumphantly ask, how could combinations be affected? "The larger states," you say, "all differ in productions and commerce; and experience shows that instead of combinations, they would be rivals, and counteract the views of one another." This, I repeat, is language calculated only to amuse us. Yes, sir, the larger states will be rivals, but not against each other—they will be rivals against the *rest of the states.* But it is urged that such a government would suit the people, and that its principles are equitable and just. How often has this argument been refuted, when applied to a *federal* government. The small states never can agree to the Virginia plan; and why then is it still urged? But it is said that it is not expected that the state governments will approve the proposed system, and that this house must directly carry it to THE PEOPLE for their approbation! Is it come to this, then, that *the sword* must decide this controversy, and that the horrors of war must be added to the rest of our misfortunes? But what have the people already said? "We find the confederation defective—go, and give additional powers to the confederation— give to it the imposts, regulation of trade, power to collect the taxes, and the means to discharge our foreign and domestic debts." Can we not then, as their delegates, agree upon these points? As their ambassadors, can we not clearly grant those powers? Why then, when we are met, must entire, distinct, and

new grounds be taken, and a government, of which the people had
no idea, be instituted? And are we to be told, if we won't agree to
it, it is the last moment of our deliberations? I say, it is indeed the
last moment, if we do agree to this assumption of power. The states
will never again be entrapped into a measure like this. The people
will say the *small* states would confederate, and grant further powers to Congress; but you, the *large* states, would not. Then the fault
will be yours, and all the nations of the earth will justify us. But
what is to become of our public debts if we dissolve the union?
Where is your plighted faith? Will you crush the smaller states, or
must they be left unmolested? Sooner than be ruined, there are
foreign powers who will take us by the hand. I say not this to
threaten or intimidate, but that we should reflect seriously before
we act. If we once leave this floor, and solemnly renounce your
new project, what will be the consequence? You will annihilate
your federal government, and ruin must stare you in the face. Let
us then do what is in our power—*amend and enlarge the confederation, but not alter the federal system.* The people expect this,
and no more. We all agree in the necessity of a more efficient
government—and cannot this be done? Although my state is
small, I know and respect its rights, as much, at least, as those who
have the honor to represent any of the larger states.

MR. KING was for preserving the States in a subordinate degree, and as far as they could be necessary for the purposes
stated by Mr. Ellsworth. He did not think a full answer had been
given to those who apprehended a dangerous encroachment on
their jurisdictions. Expedients might be devised as he conceived
that would give them all the security the nature of things would
admit of. In the establishment of Societies the Constitution was
to the Legislature what the laws were to individuals. As the fundamental rights of individuals are secure by express provisions
in the State Constitutions; why may not a like security be provided for the Rights of States in the National Constitution. The
articles of Union between England and Scotland furnish an example of such a provision in favor of sundry rights of Scotland.
When that Union was in agitation, the same language of apprehension which has been heard from the smaller States, was in
the mouths of the Scotch patriots. The articles however have not

been violated and the Scotch have found an increase of prosperity and happiness. He was aware that this will be called a mere *paper security*. He thought it a sufficient answer to say that if fundamental articles of compact, are no sufficient defence against physical power, neither will there be any safety against it if there be no compact. He could not sit down, without taking some notice of the language of the honorable gentleman from Delaware [Mr. Bedford]. It was not he that had uttered a dictatorial language. This intemperance had marked the honorable gentleman himself. It was not he who with a vehemence unprecedented in that House, had declared himself ready to turn his hopes from our common Country, and court the protection of some foreign hand. This too was the language of the Honorable member himself. He was grieved that such a thought had entered into his heart. He was more grieved that such an expression had dropped from his lips. The gentleman could only excuse it to himself on the score of passion. For himself whatever might be his distress, he would never court relief from a foreign power. . . .

MR. GOUVERNEUR MORRIS thought a Committee adviseable as the Convention had been equally divided. He had a stronger reason also. The mode of appointing the second branch tended he was sure to defeat the object of it. What is this object? to check the precipitation, changeableness, and excesses of the first branch. Every man of observation had seen in the democratic branches of the State Legislatures, precipitation—in Congress changeableness, in every department excesses against personal liberty, private property and personal safety. What qualities are necessary to constitute a check in this case? *Abilities* and *virtue,* are equally necessary in both branches. Something more then is now wanted. 1. The checking branch must have a personal interest in checking the other branch, one interest must be opposed to another interest. Vices as they exist, must be turned against each other. 2. It must have great personal property, it must have the aristocratic spirit; it must love to lord it through pride, pride is indeed the great principle that actuates both the poor and the rich. It is this principle which in the former resists, in the latter abuses authority. 3. It should be independent. In Religion the Creature is apt to forget its Creator. That it is otherwise in political affairs, the late debates here are an unhappy proof. The aristocratic body, should be as independent and as firm as the democratic. If the members of it are to revert to a dependence on the democratic choice, the democratic scale will preponderate. All the guards contrived by America have not restrained the Senatorial branches of the Legislatures from a servile complaisance to the democratic. If the second branch is to be dependent we are better without it. To make it independent, it should be for life. It will then do wrong, it will be said. He believed so: He hoped so. The Rich will strive to establish their dominion and enslave the rest. They always did. They always will. The proper security against them is to form them into a separate interest. The two forces will then control each other. Let the rich mix with the poor and in a Commercial Country, they will establish an oligarchy. Take away commerce, and the democracy will triumph. Thus it has been all the world over. So it will be among us. Reason tells us we are but men: and we are not to expect any particular interference of Heaven in our favor. By thus combining and setting apart, the aristocratic interest, the popular interest will be combined against it. There will be a mutual check and mutual security. 4. An independence for life, involves the necessary permanency. If we change our measures no body will trust us: and how avoid a change of measures, but by avoiding a change of men. Ask any man if he confides in Congress, if he confides in the State of Pennsylvania, if he will lend his money or enter into contract? He will tell you no. He sees no stability. He can repose no confidence. If Great Britain were to explain her refusal to treat with us, the same reasoning would be employed.—He disliked the exclusion of the second branch from holding offices. It is dangerous. It is like the imprudent exclusion of the military officers during the war, from civil appointments. It deprives the Executive of the principal source of influence. If danger be apprehended from the Executive what a left-handed way is this of obviating it? If the son, the brother or the friend can be appointed, the danger may be even increased, as the disqualified father etc. can then boast of a disinterestedness which he does not possess. Besides shall the best, the most able, the most virtuous citizens not be permitted to hold offices?

Who then are to hold them? He was also against paying the Senators. They will pay themselves if they can. If they can not they will be rich and can do without it. Of such the second branch ought to consist; and none but such can compose it if they are not to be paid.—He contended that the Executive should appoint the Senate and fill up vacancies. This gets rid of the difficulty in the present question. You may begin with any ratio you please; it will come to the same thing. The members being independent and for life, may be taken as well from one place as from another.—It should be considered too how the scheme could be carried through the States. He hoped there was strength of mind enough in this House to look truth in the face. He did not hesitate therefore to say that loaves and fishes must bribe the Demogogues. They must be made to expect higher offices under the general than the State Government. A Senate for life will be a noble bait. Without such captivating prospects, the popular leaders will oppose and defeat the plan. He perceived that the first branch was to be chosen by the people of the States: the second by those chosen by the people. Is not here a Government by the States. A Government by Compact between Virginia in the first and second branch; Massachusetts in the first and second branch etc. This is going back to mere treaty. It is no Government at all. It is altogether dependent on the States, and will act over again the part which Congress has acted. A firm Government alone can protect our liberties. He fears the influence of the rich. They will have the same effect here as elsewhere if we do not by such a Government keep them within their proper sphere. We should remember that the people never act from reason alone. The Rich will take advantage of their passions and make these the instruments for oppressing them. The Result of the Contest will be a violent aristocracy, or a more violent despotism. The schemes of the Rich will be favored by the extent of the Country. The people in such distant parts can not communicate and act in concert. They will be the dupes of those who have more knowledge and intercourse. The only security against encroachments will be a select and sagacious body of men, instituted to watch against them on all sides. He meant only to hint these observations, without grounding any motion on them.

Majority Rule,
the Basic Republican Principle
(July 5, 13, 14)

*To end the impasse over the composition of the Senate, a grand
Committee was appointed to seek a compromise. It proposed
that representation be according to population in the lower
house, that all money bills originate in that house, and that in
the upper house, "each state shall have an equal vote." Thus the
"Great Compromise" implanted the different basis for the two
houses that became the foundation for the new Constitution.
Madison, however, thought the compromise was neither fair nor
true to republican principles. Eight days later, after tedious debate about details of representation, Wilson made the same point
in even more basic terms. The next day, July 14, as the Convention moved toward approval of the Great Compromise, Madison
and Wilson again stated their objections.*

MR. MADISON . . . conceived that the Convention was reduced to the alternative of either departing from justice in order
to conciliate the smaller States, and the minority of the people
of the United States or of displeasing these by justly gratifying
the larger States and the majority of the people. He could not
himself hesitate as to the option he ought to make. The Convention with justice and the majority of the people on their side, had
nothing to fear. With injustice and the minority on their side they
had every thing to fear. It was in vain to purchase concord in the
Convention on terms which would perpetuate discord among
their Constituents. The Convention ought to pursue a plan which
would bear the test of examination, which would be espoused
and supported by the enlightened and impartial part of America,
and which they could themselves vindicate and urge. It should

be considered that although at first many may judge of the system recommended, by their opinion of the Convention, yet finally all will judge of the Convention by the System. The merits of the System alone can finally and effectually obtain the public suffrage. He was not apprehensive that the people of the small States would obstinately refuse to accede to a Government founded on just principles, and promising them substantial protection. He could not suspect that Delaware would brave the consequences of seeking her fortunes apart from the other States, rather than submit to such a Government much less could he suspect that she would pursue the rash policy of courting foreign support, which the warmth of one of her representatives [Mr. Bedford] had suggested, or if she should that any foreign nation would be so rash as to hearken to the overture. As little could he suspect that the people of New Jersey notwithstanding the decided tone of the gentlemen from that State, would choose rather to stand on their own legs, and bid defiance to events, than to acquiesce under an establishment founded on principles the justice of which they could not dispute, and absolutely necessary to redeem them from the exactions levied on them by the commerce of the neighbouring States. A review of other States would prove that there was as little reason to apprehend an inflexible opposition elsewhere. Harmony in the Convention was no doubt much to be desired. Satisfaction to all the States, in the first instance still more so. But if the principal States comprehending a majority of the people of the U.S. should concur in a just and judicious plan, he had the firmest hopes, that all the other States would by degrees accede to it. . . .

MR. WILSON. If a general declaration would satisfy any gentleman he had no indisposition to declare his sentiments. Conceiving that all men wherever placed have equal rights and are equally entitled to confidence, he viewed without apprehension the period when a few States should contain the superior number of people. The majority of people wherever found ought in all questions to govern the minority. If the interior Country should acquire this majority, it will not only have the right, but will avail themselves of it whether we will or no. This jealousy misled the policy of Great Britain with regard to America. The fatal maxims espoused by her were that the Colonies were growing too fast, and that their growth must be stinted in time. What were the consequences? first, enmity on our part, then actual separation. Like consequences will result on the part of the interior settlements, if like jealousy and policy be pursued on ours. Further, if numbers be not a proper rule, why is not some better rule pointed out. No one has yet ventured to attempt it. Congress have never been able to discover a better. No State as far as he has heard, has suggested any other. In 1783, after elaborate discussion of a measure of wealth all were satisfied then as they are now that the rule of numbers, does not differ much from the combined rule of numbers and wealth. Again he could not agree that property was the sole or the primary object of Government and society. The cultivation and improvement of the human mind was the most noble object. With respect to this object, as well as to other *personal* rights, numbers were surely the natural and precise measure of Representation. And with respect to property, they could not vary much from the precise measure. In no point of view however could the establishment of numbers as the rule of representation in the first branch vary his opinion as to the impropriety of letting a vicious principle into the second branch. . . .

MR. MADISON expressed his apprehensions that if the proper foundation of Government was destroyed, by substituting an equality in place of a proportional Representation, no proper superstructure would be raised. If the small States really wish for a Government armed with the powers necessary to secure their liberties, and to enforce obedience on the larger members as well as on themselves he could not help thinking them extremely mistaken in their means. He reminded them of the consequences of laying the existing confederation on improper principles. All the principal parties to its compilation, joined immediately in mutilating and fettering the Government in such a manner that it has disappointed every hope placed on it. He appealed to the doctrine and arguments used by themselves on a former occasion. It had been very properly observed by [Mr. Paterson] that Representation was an expedient by which the meeting of the people themselves was rendered unnecessary;

and that the representatives ought therefore to bear a proportion to the votes which their constituents if convened, would respectively have. Was not this remark as applicable to one branch of the Representation as to the other? But it had been said that the Government would in its operation be partly federal, partly national; that although in the latter respect the Representatives of the people ought to be in proportion to the people: yet in the former it ought to be according to the number of States. If there was any solidity in this distinction he was ready to abide by it, if there was none it ought to be abandoned. In all cases where the General Government is to act on the people, let the people be represented and the votes be proportional. In all cases where the Government is to act on the States as such, in like manner as Congress now act on them, let the States be represented and the votes be equal. This was the true ground of compromise if there was any ground at all. But he denied that there was any ground. He called for a single instance in which the General Government was not to operate on the people individually. The practicability of making laws, with coercive sanctions, for the States as Political bodies, had been exploded on all hands. He observed that the people of the large States would in some way or other secure to themselves a weight proportioned to the importance accruing from their superior numbers. If they could not effect it by a proportional representation in the Government they would probably accede to no Government which did not in great measure depend for its efficacy on their voluntary cooperation; in which case they would indirectly secure their object. The existing confederacy proved that where the Acts of the General Government were to be executed by the particular Government the latter had a weight in proportion to their importance. No one would say that either in Congress or out of Congress Delaware had equal weight with Pennsylvania. If the latter was to supply ten times as much money as the former, and no compulsion could be used, it was of ten times more importance, that she should voluntarily furnish the supply. In the Dutch confederacy the votes of the Provinces were equal. But Holland which supplies about half the money, governs the whole republic. He enumerated the objections against an equality of votes in the second branch, notwithstanding the proportional representation in the first. 1. The minority could negative the will of the majority of the people. 2. They could extort measures by making them a condition of their assent to other necessary measures. 3. They could obtrude measures on the majority by virtue of the peculiar powers which would be vested in the Senate. 4. The evil instead of being cured by time, would increase with every new State that should be admitted, as they must all be admitted on the principle of eq al- ity. 5. The perpetuity it would give to the preponderance of the Northern against the Southern Scale was a serious consider- ation. It seemed now to be pretty well understood that the real difference of interests lay, not between the large and small but between the Northern and Southern States. The institution of slavery and its consequences formed the line of discrimination. There were 5 States on the South, 8 on the Northern side of this line. Should a proportional representation take place it was true, the Northern side would still outnumber the other; but not in the same degree, at this time; and every day would tend towards an equilibrium.

MR. WILSON would add a few words only. If equality in the second branch was an error that time would correct, he should be less anxious to exclude it being sensible that perfection was unattainable in any plan; but being a fundamental and a perpet- ual error, it ought by all means to be avoided. A vice in the Representation, like an error in the first concoction, must be fol- lowed by disease, convulsions, and finally death itself. The jus- tice of the general principle of proportional representation has not in argument at least been yet contradicted. But it is said that a departure from it so far as to give the States an equal vote in one branch of the Legislature is essential to their preservation. He had considered this position maturely, but could not see its application. That the States ought to be preserved he admitted. But does it follow that an equality of votes is necessary for the purpose? Is there any reason to suppose that if their preservation should depend more on the large than on the small States the security of the States against the General Government would be diminished? Are the large States less attached to their existence, more likely to commit suicide, than the small? An equal vote then is not necessary as far as he can conceive: and is liable among other objections to this insuperable one: The great fault of the existing confederacy is its inactivity. It has never been a complaint against Congress that they governed overmuch. The complaint has been that they have governed too little. To remedy this defect we were sent here. Shall we effect the cure by establishing an equality of votes as is proposed? no: this very equality carries us directly to Congress: to the system which it is our duty to rectify. The small States cannot indeed act, by virtue of this equality, but they may control the Government as they have done in Congress. This very measure is here prosecuted by a minority of the people of America. Is then the object of the Convention likely to be accomplished in this way? Will not our Constituents say we sent you to form an efficient Government and you have given us one more complex indeed, but having all the weakness of the former Government? He was anxious for uniting all the States under one Government. He knew there were some respectable men who preferred three confederacies, united by offensive and defensive alliances. Many things may be plausibly said, some things may be justly said, in favor of such a project. He could not however concur in it himself; but he thought nothing so pernicious as bad first principles.

Election and Term of Office of the National Executive
(July 17, 19)

The Convention next took up the long postponed and largely unsettled questions of the composition, election, and powers of the national executive. After deciding unanimously that it should be "a single person," the Convention debated a motion that it be chosen by the Congress. Many delegates took part in the resulting inconclusive discussion. Two days later Gouverneur Morris,

Madison, and Elbridge Gerry debated whether the executive should be eligible for reelection. Still, little was settled.

MR. GOUVERNEUR MORRIS was pointedly against his being so chosen. He will be the mere creature of the Legislative: if appointed and impeachable by that body. He ought to be elected by the people at large, by the freeholders of the Country. That difficulties attend this mode, he admits. But they have been found superable in New York and in Connecticut and would he believed be found so, in the case of an Executive for the United States. If the people should elect, they will never fail to prefer some man of distinguished character, or services; some man, if he might so speak, of continental reputation.—If the Legislature elect, it will be the work of intrigue, of cabal, and of faction; it will be like the election of a pope by a conclave of cardinals; real merit will rarely be the title to the appointment. He moved to strike out "National Legislature" and insert "citizens of United States."

MR. SHERMAN thought that the sense of the Nation would be better expressed by the Legislature, than by the people at large. The latter will never be sufficiently informed of characters, and besides will never give a majority of votes to any one man. They will generally vote for some man in their own State, and the largest State will have the best chance for the appointment. If the choice be made by the Legislature, a majority of voices may be made necessary to constitute an election.

MR. WILSON. Two arguments have been urged against an election of the Executive Magistrate by the people. 1. The example of Poland where an Election of the supreme Magistrate is attended with the most dangerous commotions. The cases he observed were totally dissimilar. The Polish nobles have resources and dependents which enable them to appear in force, and to threaten the Republic as well as each other. In the next place the electors all assemble in one place: which would not be the case with us. The second argument is that a *majority* of the people would never concur. It might be answered that the concurrence of a majority of people is not a necessary principle of election, nor required as such in any of the States. But allowing the objection all its force, it may be obviated by the expedient used in Massachusetts where the Legislature by majority of voices, decide in case a majority of people do not concur in favor of one of the candidates. This would restrain the choice to a good nomination at least, and prevent in a great degree intrigue and cabal. A particular objection with him against an absolute election by the Legislature was that the Executive in that case would be too dependent to stand the mediator between the intrigues and sinister views of the Representatives and the general liberties and interests of the people.

MR. PINCKNEY did not expect this question would again have been brought forward; an Election by the people being liable to the most obvious and striking objections. They will be led by a few active and designing men. The most populous States by combining in favor of the same individual will be able to carry their points. The National Legislature being most immediately interested in the laws made by themselves, will be most attentive to the choice of a fit man to carry them properly into execution.

MR. GOUVERNEUR MORRIS. It is said that in case of an election by the people the populous States will combine and elect whom they please. Just the reverse. The people of such States cannot combine. If there be any combination it must be among their representatives in the Legislature. It is said the people will be led by a few designing men. This might happen in a small district. It can never happen throughout the continent. In the election of a Governor of New York, it sometimes is the case in particular spots, that the activity and intrigues of little partizans are successful, but the general voice of the State is never influenced by such artifices. It is said the multitude will be uninformed. It is true they would be uninformed of what passed in the Legislative Conclave, if the election were to be made there; but they will not be uninformed of those great and illustrious characters which have merited their esteem and confidence. If the Executive be chosen by the National Legislature, he will not be independent of it; and if not independent, usurpation and tyranny on the part of the Legislature will be the consequence. This was the case in England in the last Century. It has been the case in Holland, where their Senates have engrossed all power. It has been the case every where. He was surprised that an election by the people at large should ever have been likened to the Polish election of the first Magistrate. An election by the Legislature will bear a real likeness to the election by the Diet of Poland. The great must be the electors in both cases, and the corruption and cabal which are known to characterise the one would soon find their way into the other. Appointments made by numerous bodies, are always worse than those made by single responsible individuals, or by the people at large.

COLONEL MASON. It is curious to remark the different language held at different times. At one moment we are told that the Legislature is entitled to thorough confidence, and to indefinite power. At another, that it will be governed by intrigue and corruption, and cannot be trusted at all. But not to dwell on this inconsistency he would observe that a Government which is to last ought at least to be practicable. Would this be the case if the proposed election should be left to the people at large. He conceived it would be as unnatural to refer the choice of a proper character for chief Magistrate to the people, as it would, to refer a trial of colours to a blind man. The extent of the Country renders it impossible that the people can have the requisite capacity to judge of the respective pretensions of the Candidates.

MR. WILSON could not see the [contradiction] stated [by Colonel Mason]. The Legislature might deserve confidence in some respects, and distrust in others. In acts which were to affect them and their Constituents precisely alike confidence was due. In others jealousy was warranted. The appointment to great offices, where the Legislature might feel many motives not common to the public, confidence was surely misplaced. This branch of business it was notorious was most corruptly managed of any that had been committed to legislative bodies. . . .

MR. GOUVERNEUR MORRIS. It is necessary to take into one view all that relates to the establishment of the Executive; on the due formation of which must depend the efficacy and utility of the Union among the present and future States. It has been a maxim in Political Science that Republican Government is not adapted to a large extent of Country, because the energy of the Executive Magistracy can not reach the extreme parts of it. Our

Country is an extensive one. We must either then renounce the blessings of the Union, or provide an Executive with sufficient vigor to pervade every part of it. This subject was of so much importance that he hoped to be indulged in an extensive view of it. One great object of the Executive is to control the Legislature. The Legislature will continually seek to aggrandize and perpetuate themselves; and will seize those critical moments produced by war, invasion or convulsion for that purpose. It is necessary then that the Executive Magistrate should be the guardian of the people, even of the lower classes, against Legislative tyranny, against the Great and the wealthy who in the course of things will necessarily compose the Legislative body. Wealth tends to corrupt the mind and to nourish its love of power, and to stimulate it to oppression. History proves this to be the spirit of the opulent. The check provided in the second branch was not meant as a check on Legislative usurpations of power, but on the abuse of lawful powers, on the propensity in the first branch to legislate too much to run into projects of paper money and similar expedients. It is no check on Legislative tyranny. On the contrary it may favor it, and if the first branch can be seduced may find the means of success. The Executive therefore ought to be so constituted as to be the great protector of the Mass of the people.—It is the duty of the Executive to appoint the officers and to command the forces of the Republic: to appoint 1. ministerial officers for the administration of public affairs 2. officers for the dispensation of Justice. Who will be the best Judges whether these appointments be well made? The people at large, who will know, will see, will feel the effects of them. Again who can judge so well of the discharge of military duties for the protection and security of the people, as the people themselves who are to be protected and secured?—He finds too that the Executive is not to be re-eligible. What effect will this have? 1. It will destroy the great incitement to merit public esteem by taking away the hope of being rewarded with a reappointment. It may give a dangerous turn to one of the strongest passions in the human breast. The love of fame is the great spring to noble and illustrious actions. Shut the Civil road to Glory and he may be compelled to seek it by the sword. 2. It will tempt him to make the most of the short space of time allotted him, to accumulate wealth and provide for his friends. 3. It will produce violations of the very constitution it is meant to secure. In moments of pressing danger the tried abilities and established character of a favorite Magistrate will prevail over respect for the forms of the Constitution. The Executive is also to be impeachable. This is a dangerous part of the plan. It will hold him in such dependence that he will be no check on the Legislature, will not be a firm guardian of the people and of the public interest. He will be the tool of a faction, of some leading demagogue in the Legislature. These then are the faults of the Executive establishment as now proposed. Can no better establishment be devised? If he is to be the Guardian of the people let him be appointed by the people. If he is to be a check on the Legislature let him not be impeachable. Let him be of short duration, that he may with propriety be re-eligible. It has been said that the candidates for this office will not be known to the people. If they be known to the Legislature, they must have such a notoriety and eminence of Character, that they cannot possibly be unknown to the people at large. It cannot be possible that a man shall have sufficiently distinguished himself to merit this high trust without having his character proclaimed by fame throughout the Empire. As to the danger from an unimpeachable magistrate he could not regard it as formidable. There must be certain great officers of State; a minister of finance, of war, of foreign affairs etc. These he presumes will exercise their functions in subordination to the Executive, and will be amenable by impeachment to the public Justice. Without these ministers the Executive can do nothing of consequence. He suggested a biennial election of the Executive at the time of electing the first branch, and the Executive to hold over, so as to prevent any interregnum in the administration. An election by the people at large throughout so great an extent of country could not be influenced, by those little combinations and those momentary lies which often decide popular elections within a narrow sphere. It will probably be objected that the election will be influenced by the members of the Legislature; particularly of the first branch, and that it will be nearly the same thing with an election by the Legislature itself. It could not be denied that such an influence would exist. But it might be answered that as the Legislature or the candidates for it would be divided, the enmity of one part would counteract the friendship of another: that if the administration of the Executive were good, it would be unpopular to oppose his re-election, if bad it ought to be opposed and a reappointment prevented; and lastly that in every view this indirect dependence on the favor of the Legislature could not be so mischievous as a direct dependence for his appointment. He saw no alternative for making the Executive independent of the Legislature but either to give him his office for life, or make him eligible by the people.—Again, it might be objected that two years would be too short a duration. But he believes that as long as he should behave himself well, he would be continued in his place. The extent of the Country would secure his reelection against the factions and discontents of particular States. It deserved consideration also that such an ingredient in the plan would render it extremely palatable to the people. These were the general ideas which occurred to him on the subject, and which led him to wish and move that the whole constitution of the Executive might undergo reconsideration. . . .

Mr. Madison. If it be a fundamental principle of free Government that the Legislative, Executive and Judiciary powers should be *separately* exercised, it is equally so that they be *independently* exercised. There is the same and perhaps greater reason why the Executive should be independent of the Legislature, than why the Judiciary should: A coalition of the two former powers would be more immediately and certainly dangerous to public liberty. It is essential then that the appointment of the Executive should either be drawn from some source, or held by some tenure, that will give him a free agency with regard to the Legislature. This could not be if he was to be appointable from time to time by the Legislature. It was not clear that an appointment in the first instance even with an ineligibility afterwards would not establish an improper connection between the two departments. Certain it was that the appointment would be attended with intrigues and contentions that ought not to be unnecessarily admitted. He was disposed for these reasons to refer the appointment to some other source. The people at large was in his opinion the fittest in itself. It would be as likely as any that could be devised to produce an Executive Magistrate of distinguished Character. The people generally could only know and vote for some Citizen whose merits had rendered him an object of general attention and esteem. There was one difficulty however of a serious nature attending an immediate choice by the people. The right of suffrage was much more diffusive in the Northern than the Southern States; and the latter could have no influence in the election on the score of the Negroes. The substitution of electors obviated this difficulty and seemed on the whole to be liable to fewest objections.

MR. GERRY. If the Executive is to be elected by the Legislature he certainly ought not to be re-eligible: This would make him absolutely dependent. He was against a popular election. The people are uninformed, and would be misled by a few designing men. He urged the expediency of an appointment of the Executive by Electors to be chosen by the State Executives. The people of the States will then choose the first branch: The legislatures of the States the second branch of the National Legislature, and the Executives of the States, the National Executive. This he thought would form a strong attachment in the States to the National System. The popular mode of electing the chief Magistrate would certainly be the worst of all. If he should be so elected and should do his duty, he will be turned out for it like Governor Bowdoin in Massachusetts and President Sullivan in New Hampshire.

The Judiciary, the Veto,
and Separation of Powers
(July 21)

The Convention also considered the veto power of the executive. A motion that "the national judiciary should be associated with the executive" in this power led to a general discussion of separation of powers, especially the character and role of the judiciary.

MR. WILSON. This proposition had been before made and failed: but he was so confirmed by reflection in the opinion of its utility, that he thought it incumbent on him to make another effort: The Judiciary ought to have an opportunity of remonstrating against projected encroachments on the people as well as on themselves. It had been said that the Judges, as expositors of the Laws would have an opportunity of defending their constitutional rights. There was weight in this observation; but this power of the Judges did not go far enough. Laws may be unjust, may be unwise, may be dangerous, may be destructive; and yet may not be so unconstitutional as to justify the Judges in refusing to give them effect. Let them have a share in the Revisionary power, and they will have an opportunity of taking notice of these characters of a law, and of counteracting, by the weight of their opinions the improper views of the Legislature.

MR. MADISON seconded the motion.

MR. GORHAM did not see the advantage of employing the Judges in this way. As Judges they are not to be presumed to possess any peculiar knowledge of the mere policy of public measures. Nor can it be necessary as a security for their constitutional rights. The Judges in England have no such additional provision for their defence, yet their jurisdiction is not invaded.

He thought it would be best to let the Executive alone be responsible, and at most to authorize him to call on Judges for their opinions.

MR. ELLSWORTH approved heartily of the motion. The aid of the Judges will give more wisdom and firmness to the Executive. They will possess a systematic and accurate knowledge of the Laws, which the Executive can not be expected always to possess. The law of Nations also will frequently come into question. Of this the Judges alone will have competent information.

MR. MADISON considered the object of the motion as of great importance to the meditated Constitution. It would be useful to the Judiciary department by giving it an additional opportunity of defending itself against Legislative encroachments: It would be useful to the Executive, by inspiring additional confidence and firmness in exerting the revisionary power: It would be useful to the Legislature by the valuable assistance it would give in preserving a consistency, conciseness, perspicuity and technical propriety in the laws, qualities peculiarly necessary; and yet shamefully wanting in our republican Codes. It would moreover be useful to the Community at large as an additional check against a pursuit of those unwise and unjust measures which constituted so great a portion of our calamities. If any solid objection could be urged against the motion, it must be on the supposition that it tended to give too much strength either to the Executive or Judiciary. He did not think there was the least ground for this apprehension. It was much more to be apprehended that notwithstanding this co-operation of the two departments, the Legislature would still be an overmatch for them. Experience in all the States had evinced a powerful tendency in the Legislature to absorb all power into its vortex. This was the real source of danger to the American Constitutions; and suggested the necessity of giving every defensive authority to the other departments that was consistent with republican principles.

MR. MASON said he had always been a friend to this provision. It would give a confidence to the Executive, which he would not otherwise have, and without which the Revisionary power would be of little avail.

MR. GERRY did not expect to see this point which had under-
gone full discussion, again revived. The object he conceived of
the Revisionary power was merely to secure the Executive department against legislative encroachment. The Executive therefore who will best know and be ready to defend his rights ought
alone to have the defence of them. The motion was liable to
strong objections. It was combining and mixing together the
Legislative and the other departments. It was establishing an
improper coalition between the Executive and Judiciary departments. It was making Statesmen of the Judges; and setting them
up as the guardians of the Rights of the people. He relied for his
part on the Representatives of the people as the guardians of
their Rights and interests. It was making the Expositors of the
Laws, the Legislators which ought never to be done. A better
expedient for correcting the laws, would be to appoint as had
been done in Pennsylvania a person or persons of proper skill,
to draw bills for the Legislature.

MR. STRONG thought with Mr. Gerry that the power of making ought to be kept distinct from that of expounding, the laws.
No maxim was better established. The Judges in exercising the
function of expositors might be influenced by the part they had
taken, in framing the laws.

MR. GOUVERNEUR MORRIS. Some check being necessary on
the Legislature, the question is in what hands it should be
lodged. On one side it was contended that the Executive alone
ought to exercise it. He did not think that an Executive appointed
for 6 years, and impeachable whilst in office would be a very
effectual check. On the other side it was urged that he ought to
be reinforced by the Judiciary department. Against this it was
objected that Expositors of laws ought to have no hand in making them, and arguments in favor of this had been drawn from
England. What weight was due to them might be easily determined by an attention to facts. The truth was that the Judges in
England had a great share in the Legislation. They are consulted
in difficult and doubtful cases. They may be and some of them
are members of the Legislature. They are or may be members of
the privy Council, and can there advise the Executive as they
will do with us if the motion succeeds. The influence of English

Judges may have in the latter capacity in strengthening the Executive check can not be ascertained, as the King by his influence in a manner dictates the laws. There is one difference in the two Cases however which disconcerts all reasoning from the British to our proposed Constitution. The British Executive has so great an interest in his prerogatives and such powerful means of defending them that he will never yield any part of them. The interest of our Executive is so inconsiderable and so transitory, and his means of defending it so feeble, that there is the justest ground to fear his want of firmness in resisting incroachments. He was extremely apprehensive that the auxiliary firmness and weight of the Judiciary would not supply the deficiency. He concurred in thinking the public liberty in greater danger from Legislative usurpations than from any other source. It had been said that the Legislature ought to be relied on as the proper Guardians of liberty. The answer was short and conclusive. Either bad laws will be pushed or not. On the latter supposition no check will be wanted. On the former a strong check will be necessary: And this is the proper supposition. Emissions of paper money, largesses to the people—a remission of debts and similar measures, will at some times be popular, and will be pushed for that reason. At other times such measures will coincide with the interests of the Legislature themselves, and that will be a reason not less cogent for pushing them. It may be thought that the people will not be deluded and misled in the latter case. But experience teaches another lesson. The press is indeed a great means of diminishing the evil, yet it is found to be unable to prevent it altogether.

Mr. L. Martin considered the association of the Judges with the Executive as a dangerous innovation; as well as one which could not produce the particular advantage expected from it. A knowledge of Mankind, and of Legislative affairs cannot be presumed to belong in a higher degree to the Judges than to the Legislature. And as to the Constitutionality of laws, that point will come before the Judges in their proper official character. In this character they have a negative on the laws. Join them with the Executive in the Revision and they will have a double negative. It is necessary that the Supreme Judiciary should have the confidence of the people. This will soon be lost, if they are employed in the task of remonstrating against popular measures of the Legislature. Besides in what mode and proportion are they to vote in the Council of Revision?

MR. MADISON could not discover in the proposed association of the Judges with the Executive in the Revisionary check on the Legislature any violation of the maxim which requires the great departments of power to be kept separate and distinct. On the contrary he thought it an auxiliary precaution in favor of the maxim. If a Constitutional discrimination of the departments on paper were a sufficient security to each against encroachments of the others, all further provisions would indeed be superfluous. But experience had taught us a distrust of that security; and that it is necessary to introduce such a balance of powers and interests, as will guarantee the provisions on paper. Instead therefore of contenting ourselves with laying down the Theory in the Constitution that each department ought to be separate and distinct, it was proposed to add a defensive power to each which should maintain the Theory in practice. In so doing we did not blend the departments together. We erected effectual barriers for keeping them separate. The most regular example of this theory was in the British Constitution. Yet it was not only the practice there to admit the Judges to a seat in the legislature, and in the Executive Councils, and to submit to their previous examination all laws of a certain description, but it was a part of their Constitution that the Executive might negative any law whatever; a part of *their* Constitution which had been universally regarded as calculated for the preservation of the whole. The objection against a union of the Judiciary and Executive branches in the revision of the laws, had either no foundation or was not carried far enough. If such a Union was an improper mixture of powers, or such a Judiciary check on the laws, was inconsistent with the Theory of a free Constitution, it was equally so to admit the Executive to any participation in the making of laws; and the revisionary plan ought to be discarded altogether.

COLONEL MASON observed that the defence of the Executive was not the sole object of the Revisionary power. He expected even greater advantages from it. Notwithstanding the precautions taken in the Constitution of the Legislature, it would still so much resemble that of the individual States, that it must be expected frequently to pass unjust and pernicious laws. This restraining power was therefore essentially necessary. It would have the effect not only of hindering the final passage of such laws; but would discourage demagogues from attempting to get them passed. It had been said [by Mr. L. Martin] that if the Judges were joined in this check on the laws, they would have a double negative, since in their expository capacity of Judges they would have one negative. He would reply that in this capacity they could impede in one case only, the operation of laws. They could declare an unconstitutional law void. But with regard to every law however unjust oppressive or pernicious, which did not come plainly under this description, they would be under the necessity as Judges to give it a free course. He wished the further use to be made of the Judges, of giving aid in preventing every improper law. Their aid will be the more valuable as they are in the habit and practice of considering laws in their true principles, and in all their consequences.

Appointment of Judges
(July 21)

Later that day Madison proposed that the national judiciary be appointed by the executive unless disagreed to by two thirds of the Senate. Discussion resumed of the same issues raised earlier in the day.

Mr. Madison stated as his reasons for the motion. 1. that it secured the responsibility of the Executive who would in general be more capable and likely to select fit characters than the Legislature, or even the second branch of it, who might hide their selfish motives under the number concerned in the appointment—. 2. that in case of any flagrant partiality or error, in the nomination it might be fairly presumed that two thirds of the second branch would join in putting a negative on it. 3. that as the second branch was very differently constituted when the appointment of the Judges was formerly referred to it, and was now to be composed of equal votes from all the States, the principle of compromise which had prevailed in other instances required in this that there should be a concurrence of two authorities, in one of which the people, in the other the States, should be represented. The Executive Magistrate would be considered as a national officer, acting for and equally sympathising with every part of the United States. If the second branch alone should have this power, the Judges might be appointed by a minority of the people, though by a majority, of the States, which could not be justified on any principle as their proceedings were to relate to the people, rather than to the States: and as it would moreover throw the appointments entirely into the hands of the Northern States, a perpetual ground of jealousy and discontent would be furnished to the Southern States.

Mr. PINCKNEY was for placing the appointment in the second branch exclusively. The Executive will possess neither the requisite knowledge of characters, nor confidence of the people for so high a trust.

Mr. RANDOLPH would have preferred the mode of appointment proposed formerly by Mr. Gorham, as adopted in the Constitution of Massachusetts but thought the motion depending so great an improvement of the clause as it stands, that he anxiously wished it success. He laid great stress on the responsibility of the Executive as a security for fit appointments. Appointments by the Legislatures have generally resulted from cabal, from personal regard, or some other consideration than a title derived from the proper qualifications. The same inconveniencies will proportionally prevail, if the appointments be referred to either branch of the Legislature or to any other authority administered by a number of individuals.

Mr. ELLSWORTH would prefer a negative in the Executive on a nomination by the second branch, the negative to be overruled

by a concurrence of two thirds of the second branch to the mode
proposed by the motion; but preferred an absolute appointment
by the second branch to either. The Executive will be regarded
by the people with a jealous eye. Every power for augmenting
unnecessarily his influence will be disliked. As he will be sta-
tionary it was not to be supposed he could have a better knowledge of characters. He will be more open to caresses and
intrigues than the Senate. The right to supersede his nomination
will be ideal only. A nomination under such circumstances will
be equivalent to an appointment.

MR. GOUVERNEUR MORRIS supported the motion. 1. The
States in their corporate capacity will frequently have an interest staked on the determination of the Judges. As in the Senate
the States are to vote the Judges ought not to be appointed by
the Senate. Next to the impropriety of being Judge in one's own
cause, is the appointment of the Judge. 2. It had been said the
Executive would be uninformed of characters. The reverse was
the truth. The Senate will be so. They must take the character
of candidates from the flattering pictures drawn by their friends.
The Executive in the necessary intercourse with every part of the
United States required by the nature of his administration, will or
may have the best possible information. 3. It had been said that a
jealousy would be entertained of the Executive. If the Executive
can be safely trusted with the command of the army, there cannot
surely be any reasonable ground of Jealousy in the present case.
He added that if the objections against an appointment of the
Executive by the Legislature, had the weight that had been allowed there must be some weight in the objection to an appointment of the Judges by the Legislature or by any part of it.

MR. GERRY. The appointment of the Judges like every other
part of the Constitution should be so modelled as to give satisfaction both to the people and to the States. The mode under
consideration will give satisfaction to neither. He could not conceive that the Executive could be as well informed of characters
throughout the Union, as the Senate. It appeared to him also a
strong objection that two thirds of the Senate were required to
reject a nomination of the Executive. The Senate would be con-

stituted in the same manner as Congress. And the appointments of Congress have been generally good.

MR. MADISON observed that he was not anxious that two thirds should be necessary to disagree to a nomination. He had given this form to his motion chiefly to vary it the more clearly from one which had just been rejected. He was content to obviate the objection last made, and accordingly so varied the motion as to let a majority reject.

COLONEL MASON found it his duty to differ from his colleagues in their opinions and reasonings on this subject. Notwithstanding the form of the proposition by which the appointment seemed to be divided between the Executive and Senate, the appointment was substantially vested in the former alone. The false complaisance which usually prevails in such cases will prevent a disagreement to the first nominations. He considered the appointment by the Executive as a dangerous prerogative. It might even give him an influence over the Judiciary department itself. He did not think the difference of interest between the Northern and Southern States could be properly brought into this argument. It would operate and require some precautions in the case of regulating navigation, commerce and imposts; but he could not see that it had any connection with the Judiciary department.

Method of Ratification
(July 23)

Taking a respite from the unsettled question of the executive department, the Convention considered how the proposed Constitution might be ratified. Oliver Ellsworth of Connecticut supported ratification by the state legislatures, while Mason and Madison of Virginia favored electing special conventions in each state for that purpose.

COLONEL MASON considered a reference of the plan to the authority of the people as one of the most important and essential of the Resolutions. The Legislatures have no power to ratify it. They are the mere creatures of the State Constitutions, and can not be greater than their creators. And he knew of no power in any of the Constitutions, he knew there was no power in some of them, that could be competent to this object. Whither then must we resort? To the people with whom all power remains that has not been given up in the Constitutions derived from them. It was of great moment he observed that this doctrine should be cherished as the basis of free Government. Another strong reason was that admitting the legislatures to have a competent authority, it would be wrong to refer the plan to them, because succeeding Legislatures having equal authority could undo the acts of their predecessors; and the National Government would stand in each State on the weak and tottering foundation of an Act of Assembly. There was a remaining consideration of some weight. In some of the States the Governments were not derived from the clear and undisputed authority of the people. This was the case in Virginia. Some of the best and wisest citizens considered the Constitution as established by an assumed authority. A National Constitution derived from such a source would be exposed to the severest criticisms. . . .

MR. ELLSWORTH. If there be any Legislatures who should find themselves incompetent to the ratification, he should be content to let them advise with their constituents and pursue such a mode as would be competent. He thought more was to be expected from the Legislatures than from the people. The prevailing wish of the people in the Eastern States is to get rid of the public debt; and the idea of strengthening the National Government carries with it that of strengthening the public debt. It was said by Colonel Mason 1. that the Legislatures have no authority in this case 2. that their successors having equal authority could rescind their acts. As to the second point he could not admit it to be well founded. An Act to which the States by their Legislatures, make themselves parties, becomes a compact from which no one of the parties can recede of itself. As to the first point, he observed that a new set of ideas seemed

to have crept in since the articles of Confederation were established. Conventions of the people, or with power derived expressly from the people, were not then thought of. The Legislatures
were considered as competent. Their ratification has been acquiesced in without complaint. To whom have Congress applied on subsequent occasions for further powers? To the
Legislatures; not to the people. The fact is that we exist at present, and we need not enquire how, as a federal Society, united
by a charter one article of which is that alterations therein may
be made by the Legislative authority of the States. It has been
said that if the confederation is to be observed, the States must
unanimously concur in the proposed innovations. He would answer that if such were the urgency and necessity of our situation
as to warrant a new compact among a part of the States, founded
on the consent of the people; the same pleas would be equally
valid in favor of a partial compact, founded on the consent of
the Legislatures. . . .

MR. MADISON thought it clear that the Legislatures were incompetent to the proposed changes. These changes would make
essential inroads on the State Constitutions, and it would be a
novel and dangerous doctrine that a Legislature could change
the constitution under which it held its existence. There might
indeed be some Constitutions within the Union, which had given
a power to the Legislature to concur in alterations of the federal
Compact. But there were certainly some which had not; and in
the case of these, a ratification must of necessity be obtained
from the people. He considered the difference between a system
founded on the Legislatures only, and one founded on the people, to be the true difference between a *league* or *treaty,* and a
Constitution. The former in point of *moral obligation* might be
as inviolable as the latter. In point of *political operation,* there
were two important distinctions in favor of the latter. 1. A law
violating a treaty ratified by a pre-existing law, might be respected by the Judges as a law, though an unwise or perfidious
one. A law violating a constitution established by the people
themselves, would be considered by the Judges as null and void.
2. The doctrine laid down by the law of Nations in the case of
treaties is that a breach of any one article by any of the parties,

frees the other parties from their engagements. In the case of a union of people under one Constitution, the nature of the pact has always been understood to exclude such an interpretation. Comparing the two modes in point of expediency he thought all the considerations which recommended this Convention in preference to Congress for proposing the reform were in favor of State Conventions in preference to the Legislatures for examining and adopting it.

Election of the Executive
(July 24, 25)

Further discussion of the executive followed: first, a motion that the Congress elect the executive (agreed to), and second, that he be ineligible for reelection. The next day Madison summarized the debate and identified the dilemmas and choices before the Convention.

MR. GERRY. The election of the Executive Magistrate will be considered as of vast importance and will excite great earnestness. The best men, the Governors of the States will not hold it derogatory from their character to be the electors. If the motion should be agreed to, it will be necessary to make the Executive ineligible a second time, in order to render him independent of the Legislature; which was an idea extremely repugnant to his way of thinking.

MR. STRONG supposed that there would be no necessity, if the Executive should be appointed by the Legislature, to make him ineligible a second time; as new elections of the Legislature will have intervened; and he will not depend for his second appointment on the same set of men as his first was received from. It had been suggested that *gratitude* for his past appointment would produce the same effect as dependence for his future appointment. He thought very differently. Besides this objection would lie against the Electors who would be objects of gratitude as well as the Legislature. It was of great importance not to make the Government too complex which would be the case if a new set of men like the Electors should be introduced into it. He thought also that the first characters in the States would not feel sufficient motives to undertake the office of Electors.

MR. WILLIAMSON was for going back to the original ground; to elect the Executive for 7 years and render him ineligible a second time. The proposed Electors would certainly not be men of the first nor even of the second grade in the States. These would all prefer a seat either in the Senate or the other branch of the Legislature. He did not like the Unity in the Executive. He had wished the Executive power to be lodged in three men taken from three districts into which the States should be divided. As the Executive is to have a kind of veto on the laws, and there is an essential difference of interests between the Northern and Southern States, particularly in the carrying trade, the power will be dangerous, if the Executive is to be taken from part of the Union, to the part from which he is not taken. The case is different here from what it is in England; where there is a sameness of interests throughout the Kingdom. Another objection against a single Magistrate is that he will be an elective King, and will feel the spirit of one. He will spare no pains to keep himself in for life, and will then lay a train for the succession of his children. It was pretty certain he thought that we should at some time or other have a King; but he wished no precaution to be omitted that might postpone the event as long as possible.—Ineligibility a second time appeared to him to be the best precaution. With this precaution he had no objection to a longer term than 7 years. He would go as far as 10 or 12 years. . . .

MR. L. MARTIN and MR. GERRY moved to re-instate the ineligibility of the Executive a second time.

MR. ELLSWORTH. With many this appears a natural consequence of his being elected by the Legislature. It was not the case with him. The Executive he thought should be re-elected if his conduct proved him worthy of it. And he will be more likely to render himself worthy of it if he be rewardable with it. The most eminent characters also will be more willing to accept the trust under this condition, than if they foresee a necessary degradation at a fixed period. . . .

MR. WILSON. The difficulties and perplexities into which the House is thrown proceed from the election by the Legislature which he was sorry had been reinstated. The inconveniency of this mode was such that he would agree to almost any length of time in order to get rid of the dependence which must result from it. He was persuaded that the longest term would not be equivalent to a proper mode of election; unless indeed it should be during good behaviour. It seemed to be supposed that at a certain advance of life, a continuance in office would cease to be agreeable to the officer, as well as desireable to the public. Experience had shewn in a variety of instances that both a capacity and inclination for public service existed—in very advanced stages. He mentioned the instance of a Doge of Venice who was elected after he was 80 years of age. The popes have generally been elected at very advanced periods, and yet in no case had a more steady or a better concerted policy been pursued than in the Court of Rome. If the Executive should come into office at 35 years of age, which he presumes may happen and his continuance should be fixed at 15 years, at the age of 50 in the very prime of life, and with all the aid of experience, he must be cast aside like a useless hulk. What an irreparable loss would the British Jurisprudence have sustained, had the age of 50 been fixed there as the ultimate limit of capacity or readiness to serve the public. The great luminary [Lord Mansfield] held his seat for thirty years after his arrival at that age. Notwithstanding what had been done he could not but hope that a better mode of election would yet be adopted; and one that would be more agreeable to the general sense of the House. . . .

MR. MADISON. There are objections against every mode that has been, or perhaps can be proposed. The election must be made either by some existing authority under the National or State Constitutions—or by some special authority derived from the people—or by the people themselves.—The two Existing authorities under the National Constitution would be the Legislative and Judiciary. The latter he presumed was out of the question. The former was in his Judgment liable to insuperable objections. Besides the general influence of that mode on the independence of the Executive: 1. The election of the Chief Magistrate would agitate and divide the legislature so much that the public interest would materially suffer by it. Public bodies are always apt to be thrown into contentions, but into more violent ones by such occasions than by any others. 2. The candidate would intrigue with the Legislature, would derive his appointment from the predominant faction, and be apt to render his administration subservient to its views. 3. The Ministers of foreign powers would have and make use of, the opportunity to mix their intrigues and influence with the Election. Limited as the powers of the Executive are, it will be an object of great moment with the great rival powers of Europe who have American possessions, to have at the head of our Government a man attached to their respective politics and interests. No pains, nor perhaps expence, will be spared, to gain from the Legislature an appointment favorable to their wishes. Germany and Poland are witnesses of this danger. In the former, the election of the Head of the Empire, till it became in a manner hereditary, interested all Europe, and was much influenced by foreign interference. In the latter, although the elective Magistrate has very little real power, his election has at all times produced the most eager interference of foreign princes, and has in fact at length slid entirely into foreign hands. The existing authorities in the States are the Legislative, Executive and Judiciary. The appointment of the National Executive by the first, was objectionable in many points of view, some of which had been already mentioned. He would mention one which of itself would decide his opinion. The Legislatures of the States had betrayed a strong propensity to a variety of pernicious measures. One object of the National Legislature was to control this propensity. One object of the National Executive, so far as it would have a negative on the laws, was to control the National Legislature, so far as it might be infected with a similar propensity. Refer the appointment of the National Executive to the State Legislatures, and this controling purpose may be defeated. The Legislatures can and will act with some kind of regular plan, and will promote the appointment of a man who will not oppose himself to a favorite object. Should a majority of the Legislatures at the time of election have the same object, or different objects of the same kind, the National Executive would be rendered subservient to them.—An appointment by the State Executives, was liable among other objections to this insuperable one, that being standing bodies, they could and would be courted, and intrigued with by the Candidates, by their partizans, and by the Ministers of foreign powers. The State Judiciarys had not and he presumed would not be proposed as a proper source of appointment. The option before us then lay between an appointment by Electors chosen by the people—and an immediate appointment by the people. He thought the former mode free from many of the objections which had been urged against it, and greatly preferable to an appointment by the National Legislature. As the electors would be chosen for the occasion, would meet at once, and proceed immediately to an appointment, there would be very little opportunity for cabal, or corruption. As a farther precaution, it might be required that they should meet at some place, distinct from the seat of Government and even that no person within a certain distance of the place at the time should be eligible. This Mode however had been rejected so recently and by so great a majority that it probably would not be proposed anew. The remaining mode was an election by the people or rather by the qualified part of them, at large: With all its imperfections he liked this best. He would not repeat either the general argument for or the objections against this mode. He would only take notice of two difficulties which he admitted to have weight. The first arose from the disposition in the people to prefer a Citizen of their own State, and the disadvantage this would throw on the smaller States. Great as this objection might be he did not think it equal to such as lay against every other mode which had been proposed. He thought too that some expedient might be hit upon that would obviate it. The second difficulty arose from the disproportion of qualified voters in the Northern and Southern States, and the disadvantages which this mode would throw on the latter. The answer to this objection was 1. that this disproportion would be continually decreasing under the influence of the Republican laws introduced in the Southern States, and the more rapid increase of their population. 2. that local considerations must give way to the general interest. As an individual from the S. States he was willing to make the sacrifice.

First Draft of the Constitution (August 6)

On July 26, with many decisions made, but with important questions about the executive, the judiciary, and the powers of Congress still unresolved, the Convention designated a committee on detail to arrange and systematize what had been decided, and to offer proposals on unsettled matters. It then adjourned for ten days while the committee worked. On August 6, the Convention re-assembled and received the following draft constitution from the committee. Consideration of its clauses, to be accepted, amended, or rejected, occupied the Convention until September 10.

"We the people of the States of New Hampshire, Massachusetts, Rhode Island and Providence Plantations, Connecticut, New York, New Jersey, Pennsylvania, Delaware, Maryland, Virginia, North Carolina, South Carolina, and Georgia, do ordain, declare, and establish the following Constitution for the Government of Ourselves and our Posterity.

ARTICLE I

The stile of the Government shall be, "The United States of America."

II

The Government shall consist of supreme legislative, executive, and judicial powers.

III

The legislative power shall be vested in a Congress, to consist of two separate and distinct bodies of men, a House of Representatives and a Senate; each of which shall in all cases have a negative on the other. The Legislature shall meet on the first Monday in December every year.

IV

Sect. 1. The members of the House of Representatives shall be chosen every second year, by the people of the several States comprehended within this Union. The qualifications of the electors shall be the same, from time to time, as those of the electors in the several States, of the most numerous branch of their own legislatures.

Sect. 2. Every member of the House of Representatives shall be of the age of twenty five years at least; shall have been a citizen in the United States for at least three years before his election; and shall be, at the time of his election, a resident of the State in which he shall be chosen.

Sect. 3. The House of Representatives shall, at its first formation, and until the number of citizens and inhabitants shall be taken in the manner herein after described, consist of sixty five Members, of whom three shall be chosen in New Hampshire, eight in Massachusetts, one in Rhode Island and Providence Plantations, five in Connecticut, six in New York, four in New Jersey, eight in Pennsylvania, one in Delaware, six in Maryland, ten in Virginia, five in North Carolina, five in South Carolina, and three in Georgia.

Sect. 4. As the proportions of numbers in different States will alter from time to time; as some of the States may hereafter be divided; as others may be enlarged by addition of territory; as two or more States may be united; as new States will be erected within the limits of the United States, the Legislature shall, in each of these cases, regulate the number of representatives by the number of inhabitants, according to the provisions herein after made, at the rate of one for every forty thousand.

Sect. 5. All bills for raising or appropriating money, and for fixing the salaries of the officers of Government, shall originate in the House of Representatives, and shall not be altered or amended by the Senate. No money shall be drawn from the Public Treasury, but in pursuance of appropriations that shall originate in the House of Representatives.

Sect. 6. The House of Representatives shall have the sole power of impeachment. It shall choose its Speaker and other officers.

Sect. 7. Vacancies in the House of Representatives shall be supplied by writs of election from the executive authority of the State, in the representation from which it shall happen.

V

Sect. 1. The Senate of the United States shall be chosen by the Legislatures of the several States. Each Legislature shall chuse two members. Vacancies may be supplied by the Executive until the next meeting of the legislature. Each member shall have one vote.

Sect. 2. The Senators shall be chosen for six years; but immediately after the first election they shall be divided, by lot, into three classes, as nearly as may be, numbered one, two and three. The seats of the members of the first class shall be vacated at the expiration of the second year, of the second class at the expiration of the fourth year, of the third class at the expiration of the sixth year, so that a third part of the members may be chosen every second year.

Sect. 3. Every member of the Senate shall be of the age of thirty years at least; shall have been a citizen in the United States for at least four years before his election; and shall be, at the time of his election, a resident of the State for which he shall be chosen.

Sect. 4. The Senate shall chuse its own President and other officers.

VI

Sect 1. The times and places and manner of holding the elections of the members of each House shall be prescribed by the Legislature of each State; but their provisions concerning them may, at any time, be altered by the Legislature of the United States.

Sect. 2. The Legislature of the United States shall have authority to establish such uniform qualifications of the members of each House, with regard to property, as to the said Legislature shall seem expedient.

Sect. 3. In each House a majority of the members shall constitute a quorum to do business; but a smaller number may adjourn from day to day.

Sect. 4. Each House shall be the judge of the elections, returns and qualifications of its own members.

Sect. 5. Freedom of speech and debate in the Legislature shall not be impeached or questioned in any Court or place out of the Legislature; and the members of each House shall, in all cases, except treason felony and breach of the peace, be privileged from arrest during their attendance at Congress, and in going to and returning from it.

Sect. 6. Each House may determine the rules of its proceedings; may punish its members for disorderly behaviour; and may expel a member.

Sect. 7. The House of Representatives, and the Senate, when it shall be acting in a legislative capacity, shall keep a journal of their proceedings, and shall, from time to time, publish them: and the yeas and nays of the members of each House, on any question, shall at the desire of one-fifth part of the members present, be entered on the journal.

Sect. 8. Neither House, without the consent of the other, shall adjourn for more than three days, nor to any other place than that at which the two Houses are sitting. But this regulation shall not extend to the Senate, when it shall exercise the powers mentioned in the   article.

Sect. 9. The members of each House shall be ineligible to, and incapable of holding any office under the authority of the United States, during the time for which they shall respectively be elected: and the members of the Senate shall be ineligible to, and incapable of holding any such office for one year afterwards.

Sect. 10. The members of each House shall receive a compensation for their services, to be ascertained and paid by the State, in which they shall be chosen.

Sect. 11. The enacting stile of the laws of the United States shall be: "Be it enacted by the Senate and Representatives in Congress assembled."

Sect. 12. Each House shall possess the right of originating bills, except in the cases beforementioned.

Sect. 13. Every bill, which shall have passed the House of Representatives and the Senate, shall, before it become a law; be presented to the President of the United States for his revision: if, upon such revision, he approve of it, he shall signify his approbation by signing it: But if, upon such revision, it shall appear to him improper for being passed into a law, he shall return it, together with his objections against it, to that House in which it shall have originated, who shall enter the objections at large on their journal and proceed to reconsider the bill. But if after such reconsideration, two thirds of that House shall, notwithstanding the objections of the President, agree to pass it, it shall together with his objections, be sent to the other House, by which it shall likewise be reconsidered, and if approved by two thirds of the other House also, it shall become a law. But in all such cases, the votes of both Houses shall be determined by yeas and nays; and the names of the persons voting for or against the bill shall be entered on the journal of each House respectively. If any bill shall not be returned by the President within seven days after it shall have been presented to him, it shall be a law, unless the legislature, by their adjournment, prevent its return; in which case it shall not be a law.

VII

Sect. 1. The Legislature of the United States shall have the power to lay and collect taxes, duties, imposts and excises;

To regulate commerce with foreign nations, and among the several States;

To establish an uniform rule of naturalization throughout the United States;

To coin money;

To regulate the value of foreign coin;

To fix the standard of weights and measures;

To establish Post-offices;

To borrow money, and emit bills on the credit of the United States;

To appoint a Treasurer by ballot;

To constitute tribunals inferior to the Supreme Court;

To make rules concerning captures on land and water;

To declare the law and punishment of piracies and felonies committed on the high seas, and the punishment of counterfeiting the coin of the United States, and of offences against the law of nations;

To subdue a rebellion in any State, on the application of its legislature;

To make war;

To raise armies;

To build and equip fleets;

To call forth the aid of the militia, in order to execute the laws of the Union, enforce treaties, suppress insurrections, and repel invasions:

And to make all laws that shall be necessary and proper for carrying into execution the foregoing powers, and all other powers vested, by this Constitution, in the government of the United States, or in any department or officer thereof.

Sect. 2. Treason against the United States shall consist only in levying war against the United States, or any of them; and in adhering to the enemies of the United States, or any of them. The Legislature of the United States shall have power to declare the punishment of treason. No person shall be convicted of treason, unless on the testimony of two witnesses. No attainder of treason shall work corruption of blood, nor forfeiture, except during the life of the person attainted.

Sect. 3. The proportions of direct taxation shall be regulated by the whole number of white and other free citizens and inhabitants, of every age, sex and condition, including those bound to servitude for a term of years, and three fifths of all other persons not comprehended in the foregoing description (except Indians not paying taxes) which number shall, within six years after the first meeting of the Legislature, and within the term of every ten years afterwards, be taken in such manner as the said Legislature shall direct.

Sect. 4. No tax or duty shall be laid by the Legislature on articles exported from any State; nor on the migration or importation of such persons as the several States shall think proper to admit; nor shall such migration or importation be prohibited.

Sect. 5. No capitation tax shall be laid, unless in proportion to the Census hereinbefore directed to be taken.

Sect. 6. No navigation act shall be passed without the assent of two thirds of the members present in each House.

Sect. 7. The United States shall not grant any title of Nobility.

VIII

The Acts of the Legislature of the United States made in pursuance of this Constitution, and all treaties made under the authority of the United States shall be the supreme law of the several States, and of their citizens and inhabitants; and the judges in the several States shall be bound thereby in their decisions; any thing in the Constitutions or laws of the several States to the contrary notwithstanding.

IX

Sect. 1. The Senate of the United States shall have power to make treaties, and to appoint Ambassadors, and Judges of the Supreme Court.

Sect. 2. In all disputes and controversies now subsisting, or that may hereafter subsist between two or more States, respecting jurisdiction or territory, the Senate shall possess the following powers. Whenever the Legislature, or the Executive authority, or lawful agent of any State, in controversy with another, shall by memorial to the Senate, state the matter in question, and apply for a hearing; notice of such memorial and application shall be given by order of the Senate, to the Legislature or the Executive authority of the other State in Controversy. The Senate shall also assign a day for the appearance of the parties, by their agents, before the House. The Agents shall be directed to appoint, by joint consent, commissioners or judges to constitute a Court for hearing and determining the matter in question. But if the Agents cannot agree, the Senate shall name three persons out of each of the several States; and from the list of such persons each party shall alternately strike out one, until the number shall be reduced to thirteen; and from that number not less than seven nor more than nine names, as the Senate shall direct, shall in their presence, be drawn out by lot; and the persons whose names shall be so drawn, or any five of them shall be commissioners or Judges to hear and finally determine the controversy; provided a majority of the Judges, who shall hear the cause, agree in the determination. If either party shall neglect to attend at the day assigned, without showing sufficient reasons for not attending, or being present shall refuse to strike, the Senate shall proceed to nominate three persons out of each State, and the Clerk of the Senate shall strike in behalf of the party absent or refusing. If any of the parties shall refuse to submit to the authority of such Court; or shall not appear to prosecute or defend their claim or cause, the Court shall nevertheless proceed to pronounce judgment. The judgment shall be final and conclusive. The proceedings shall be transmitted to the President of the Senate, and shall be lodged among the public records, for the security of the parties concerned. Every Commissioner shall, before he sit in judgment, take an oath, to be administred by one of the Judges of the Supreme or Superior Court of the State where the cause shall be tried, "well and truly to hear and determine the matter in question according to the best of his judgment, without favor, affection, or hope of reward."

Sect. 3. All controversies concerning lands claimed under different grants of two or more States, whose jurisdiction, as they respect such lands shall have been decided or adjusted subsequent to such grants, or any of them, shall, on application to the Senate, be finally determined, as near as may be, in the same manner as is before prescribed for deciding controversies between different States.

X

Sect. 1. The Executive Power of the United States shall be vested in a single person. His stile shall be, "The President of the United States of America;" and his title shall be, "His Excellency." He shall be elected by ballot by the Legislature. He shall hold his office during the term of seven years; but shall not be elected a second time.

Sect. 2. He shall, from time to time, give information to the Legislature, of the state of the Union; he may recommend to their consideration such measures as he shall judge necessary, and expedient: he may convene them on extraordinary occasions. In case of disagreement between the two Houses, with regard to the time of adjournment, he may adjourn them to such time as he thinks proper: he shall take care that the laws of the United States be duly and faithfully executed: he shall commission all the officers of the United States; and shall appoint officers in all cases not otherwise provided for by this Constitution. He shall receive Ambassadors, and may correspond with the supreme Executives of the several States. He shall have power to grant reprieves and pardons; but his pardon shall not be pleadable in bar of an impeachment. He shall be commander in chief of the Army and Navy of the United States, and of the Militia of the several States. He shall, at stated times, receive for his services, a compensation, which shall neither be increased nor diminished during his continuance in office. Before he shall enter on the duties of his department, he shall take the following oath or affirmation, "I —— solemnly swear, (or affirm) that I will faithfully execute the office of President of the United States of America." He shall be removed from his office on impeachment by the House of Representatives, and conviction in the Supreme Court, of treason, bribery, or corruption. In case of his removal as aforesaid, death, resignation, or disability to discharge the powers and duties of his office, the President of the Senate shall exercise those powers and duties, until another President of the United States be chosen, or until the disability of the President be removed.

XI

Sect. 1. The Judicial Power of the United States shall be vested in one Supreme Court, and in such inferior Courts as shall, when necessary, from time to time, be constituted by the Legislature of the United States.

Sect. 2. The Judges of the Supreme Court, and of the Inferior Courts, shall hold their offices during good behaviour. They shall, at stated times, receive for their services, a compensation, which shall not be diminished during their continuance in office.

Sect. 3. The Jurisdiction of the Supreme Court shall extend to all cases arising under laws passed by the Legislature of the United States; to all cases affecting Ambassadors, other Public Ministers and Consuls; to the trial of impeachments of officers of the United States; to all cases of Admiralty and maritime jurisdiction; to controversies between two or more States (except such as shall regard Territory or Jurisdiction), between a State and Citizens of another State, between Citizens of different States, and between a State or the Citizens thereof and foreign States, citizens or subjects. In cases of impeachment, cases affecting Ambassadors, other Public Ministers and Consuls, and those in which a State shall be party, this jurisdiction shall be original. In all the other cases beforementioned, it shall be appellate, with such exceptions and under such regulations as the Legislature shall make. The Legislature may assign any part of the jurisdiction abovementioned (except the trial of the President of the United States) in the manner, and under the limitations which it shall think proper, to such Inferior Courts, as it shall constitute from time to time.

Sect. 4. The trial of all criminal offences (except in cases of impeachments) shall be in the State where they shall be committed; and shall be by Jury.

Sect. 5. Judgment, in cases of Impeachment, shall not extend further than to removal from office, and disqualification to hold and enjoy any office of honour, trust or profit, under the United States. But the party convicted shall, nevertheless be liable and subject to indictment, trial, judgment and punishment according to law.

XII

No State shall coin money; nor grant letters of marque and reprisal; nor enter into any Treaty, alliance, or confederation; nor grant any title of Nobility.

XIII

No State, without the consent of the Legislature of the United States, shall emit bills of credit, or make any thing but specie a tender in payment of debts; nor lay imposts or duties on imports; nor keep troops or ships of war in time of peace; nor enter into any agreement or compact with another State, or with any foreign power; nor engage in any war, unless it shall be actually invaded by enemies, or the danger of invasion be so imminent, as not to admit of delay, until the Legislature of the United States can be consulted.

XIV

The Citizens of each State shall be entitled to all privileges and immunities of citizens in the several States.

XV

Any person charged with treason, felony or high misdemeanor in any State, who shall flee from justice, and shall be found in any other State, shall, on demand of the Executive power of the State from which he fled, be delivered up and removed to the State having jurisdiction of the offence.

XVI

Full faith shall be given in each State to the acts of the Legislatures, and to the records and judicial proceedings of the Courts and magistrates of every other State.

XVII

New States lawfully constituted or established within the limits of the United States may be admitted, by the Legislature, into this Government; but to such admission the consent of two thirds of the members present in each House shall be necessary. If a new State shall arise within the limits of any of the present States, the consent of the Legislatures of such States shall be also necessary to its admission. If the admission be consented to, the new States shall be admitted on the same terms with the original States. But the Legislature may make conditions with the new States, concerning the public debt which shall be then subsisting.

XVIII

The United States shall guaranty to each State a Republican form of Government; and shall protect each State against foreign invasions, and, on the application of its Legislature, against domestic violence.

XIX

On the application of the Legislatures of two thirds of the States in the Union, for an amendment of this Constitution, the Legislature of the United States shall call a Convention for that purpose.

XX

The members of the Legislatures, and the Executive and Judicial officers of the United States, and of the several States, shall be bound by oath to support this Constitution.

XXI

The ratifications of the Conventions of States shall be sufficient for organizing this Constitution.

XXII

This Constitution shall be laid before the United States in Congress assembled, for their approbation; and it is the opinion of this Convention, that it should be afterwards submitted to a Convention chosen, under the recommendation of its legislature, in order to receive the ratification of such Convention.

XXIII

To introduce this government, it is the opinion of this Convention, that each assenting Convention should notify its assent and ratification to the United States in Congress assembled; that Congress, after receiving the assent and ratification of the Conventions of   States, should appoint and publish a day, as early as may be, and appoint a place for commencing proceedings under this Constitution; that after such publication, the Legislatures of the several States should elect members of the Senate, and direct the election of members of the House of Representatives; and that the members of the Legislature should meet at the time and place assigned by Congress, and should, as soon as may be, after their meeting, choose the President of the United States, and proceed to execute this Constitution."

Qualifications for Suffrage
(August 7, 10)

When the Convention convened on August 7, it began a clause-by-clause consideration of the reported draft constitution. Most of the time and energy of the Convention went to decide detailed matters of wording, limiting provisos, alteration of dates and numbers, and so on, but occasionally basic issues surfaced. Important structural changes were made in the powers of the Senate, and in the powers, mode of election, and term of the executive, now called "the president." On the 7th, the provision that the qualifications for voting for members of the House of Representatives be the same in each state as for the voters for the "most numerous branch" of its legislature provoked a spirited exchange. Gouverneur Morris moved to delete this provision in order to substitute a clause that would "restrain the right of suffrage to freeholders." The motion was defeated, 7 to 1 (1 divided and 1 absent).

MR. WILSON. This part of the Report was well considered by the Committee, and he did not think it could be changed for the better. It was difficult to form any uniform rule of qualifications for all the States. Unnecessary innovations he thought too should be avoided. It would be very hard and disagreeable for the same persons at the same time, to vote for representatives in the State Legislature and to be excluded from a vote for those in the National Legislature.

MR. GOUVERNEUR MORRIS. Such a hardship would be neither great nor novel. The people are accustomed to it and not dissatisfied with it, in several of the States. In some the qualifications are different for the choice of the Governor and Representatives; in others for different Houses of the Legislature.

Another objection against the clause as it stands is that it makes the qualifications of the National Legislature depend on the will of the States, which he thought not proper.

MR. ELLSWORTH thought the qualifications of the electors stood on the most proper footing. The right of suffrage was a tender point, and strongly guarded by most of the State Constitutions. The people will not readily subscribe to the National Constitution if it should subject them to be disfranchised. The States are the best Judges of the circumstances and temper of their own people.

COLONEL MASON. The force of habit is certainly not attended to by those gentlemen who wish for innovations on this point. Eight or nine States have extended the right of suffrage beyond the freeholders, what will the people there say, if they should be disfranchised. A power to alter the qualifications would be a dangerous power in the hands of the Legislature.

MR. BUTLER. There is no right of which the people are more jealous than that of suffrage. Abridgments of it tend to the same revolution as in Holland where they have at length thrown all power into the hands of the Senates, who fill up vacancies themselves, and form a rank aristocracy.

MR. DICKINSON had a very different idea of the tendency of vesting the right of suffrage in the freeholders of the Country. He considered them as the best guardians of liberty; and the restriction of the right to them as a necessary defence against the dangerous influence of those multitudes without property and without principle with which our Country like all others, will in time abound. As to the unpopularity of the innovation it was in his opinion chimerical. The great mass of our Citizens is composed at this time of freeholders, and will be pleased with it.

MR. ELLSWORTH. How shall the freehold be defined? Ought not every man who pays a tax, to vote for the representative who is to levy and dispose of his money? Shall the wealthy merchants and manufacturers, who will bear a full share of the public burdens be not allowed a voice in the imposition of them—taxation and representation ought to go together.

MR. GOUVERNEUR MORRIS. He had long learned not to be the dupe of words. The sound of Aristocracy therefore had no effect on him. It was the thing, not the name, to which he was opposed, and one of his principal objections to the Constitution as it is now before us, is that it threatens this Country with an Aristocracy. The aristocracy will grow out of the House of Representatives. Give the votes to people who have no property, and they will sell them to the rich who will be able to buy them. We should not confine our attention to the present moment. The time is not distant when this Country will abound with mechanics and manufacturers who will receive their bread from their employers. Will such men be the secure and faithful Guardians of liberty? Will they be the impregnable barrier against aristocracy?—He was as little duped by the association of the words "taxation and Representation." The man who does not give his vote freely is not represented. It is the man who dictates the vote. Children do not vote. Why? because they want prudence, because they have no will of their own. The ignorant and the dependent can be as little trusted with the public interest. He did not conceive the difficulty of defining "freeholders" to be insuperable. Still less that the restriction could be unpopular. Nine-tenths of the people are at present freeholders and these will certainly be pleased with it. As to Merchants, etc., if they have wealth and value the right they can acquire it. If not they don't deserve it.

COLONEL MASON. We all feel too strongly the remains of ancient prejudices, and view things too much through a British medium. A Freehold is the qualification in England, and hence it is imagined to be the only proper one. The true idea in his opinion was that every man having evidence of attachment to and permanent common interest with the Society ought to share in all its rights and privileges. Was this qualification restrained to freeholders? Does no other kind of property but land evidence a common interest in the proprietor? Does nothing besides property mark a permanent attachment? Ought the merchant, the monied man, the parent of a number of children whose fortunes are to be pursued in his own Country, to be viewed as suspicious characters, and unworthy to be trusted with the common rights of their fellow Citizens.

MR. MADISON. The right of suffrage is certainly one of the fundamental articles of republican Government, and ought not to be left to be regulated by the Legislature. A gradual abridgment of this right has been the mode in which Aristocracies have been built on the ruins of popular forms. Whether the Constitutional qualification ought to be a freehold, would with him depend much on the probable reception such a change would meet with in States where the right was now exercised by every description of people. In several of the States a freehold was now the qualification. Viewing the subject in its merits alone, the freeholders of the Country would be the safest depositories of Republican liberty. In future times a great majority of the people will not only be without landed, but any other sort of, property. These will either combine under the influence of their common situation; in which case, the rights of property and the public liberty, will not be secure in their hands: or which is more probable, they will become the tools of opulence and ambition, in which case there will be equal danger on another side. The example of England had been misconceived [by Colonel Mason]. A very small proportion of the Representatives are there chosen by freeholders. The greatest part are chosen by the Cities and boroughs, in many of which the qualification of suffrage is as low as it is in any one of the United States and it was in the boroughs and Cities rather than the Counties, that bribery most prevailed, and the influence of the Crown on elections was most dangerously exerted.

DR. FRANKLIN. It is of great consequence that we should not depress the virtue and public spirit of our common people; of which they displayed a great deal during the war, and which contributed principally to the favorable issue of it. He related the honorable refusal of the American seamen who were carried in great numbers into the British Prisons during the war, to redeem themselves from misery or to seek their fortunes, by entering on board the Ships of the Enemies to their Country; contrasting their patriotism with a contemporary instance in which the British seamen made prisoners by the Americans, readily entered on the ships of the latter on being promised a share of the prizes that might be made out of their own Country. This proceeded he said from the different manner in which the common people were treated in America and Great Britain. He did not think that the elected had any right in any case to narrow the privileges of the electors. He quoted as arbitrary the British Statute setting forth the danger of tumultuous meetings, and under that pretext narrowing the right of suffrage to persons having freeholds of a certain value; observing that this Statute was soon followed by another under the succeeding Parliament subjecting the people who had no votes to peculiar labors and hardships. He was persuaded also that such a restriction as was proposed would give great uneasiness in the populous States. The sons of a substantial farmer, not being themselves freeholders, would not be pleased at being disfranchised, and there are a great many persons of that description.

MR. MERCER. The Constitution is objectionable in many points, but in none more than the present. He objected to the footing on which the qualification was put, but particularly to the *mode of election* by the people. The people can not know and judge of the characters of Candidates. The worse possible choice will be made. He quoted the case of the Senate in Virginia as an example in point. The people in Towns can unite their votes in favor of one favorite; and by that means always prevail over the people of the Country, who being dispersed will scatter their votes among a variety of candidates.

MR. RUTLEDGE thought the idea of restraining the right of suffrage to the freeholders a very unadvised one. It would create division among the people and make enemies of all those who should be excluded.

The issue of property qualifications came up again three days later in connection with standards for officeholders.

MR. PINCKNEY. The Committee as he had conceived were instructed to report the proper qualifications of property for the members of the National Legislature; instead of which they have referred the task to the National Legislature itself. Should it be left on this footing, the first Legislature will meet without any particular qualifications of property: and if it should happen to consist of rich men they might fix such such qualifications as may be too favorable to the rich; if of poor men, an opposite extreme might be run into. He was opposed to the establishment of an undue aristocratic influence in the Constitution but he thought it essential that the members of the Legislature, the Executive, and the Judges, should be possessed of competent property to make them independent and respectable. It was prudent when such great powers were to be trusted to connect the tie of property with that of reputation in securing a faithful administration. The Legislature would have the fate of the Nation put into their hands. The President would also have a very great influence on it. The Judges would have not only important causes between Citizen and Citizen but also, where foreigners are concerned. They will even be the Umpires between the United States and individual States as well as between one State and another. Were he to fix the quantum of property which should be required, he should not think of less than one hundred thousand dollars for the President, half of that sum for each of the Judges, and in like proportion for the members of the National Legislature. He would however leave the sums blank. His motion was that the President of the United States, the Judges, and members of the Legislature should be required to swear that they were respectively possessed of a cleared unincumbered Estate to the amount of   in the case of the President etc., etc.

MR. RUTLEDGE seconded the motion; observing that the Committee had reported no qualifications because they could not agree on any among themselves, being embarrassed by the danger on one side of displeasing the people by making them high, and on the other of rendering them nugatory by making them low.

MR. ELLSWORTH. The different circumstances of different parts of the U.S. and the probable difference between the present and future circumstances of the whole, render it improper to have either *uniform* or *fixed* qualifications. Make them so high as to be useful in the Southern States, and they will be inapplicable to the Eastern States. Suit them to the latter, and they will serve no purpose in the former. In like manner what may be accommodated to the existing State of things among us, may be very inconvenient in some future state of them. He thought for these reasons that it was better to leave this matter to the Legislative discretion than to attempt a provision for it in the Constitution.

DR. FRANKLIN expressed his dislike of every thing that tended to debase the spirit of the common people. If honesty was often the companion of wealth, and if poverty was exposed to peculiar temptation, it was not less true that the possession of property increased the desire of more property. Some of the greatest rogues he was ever acquainted with, were the richest rogues. We should remember the character which the Scripture requires in Rulers, that they should be men hating covetousness. This Constitution will be much read and attended to in Europe, and if it should betray a great partiality to the rich, will not only hurt us in the esteem of the most liberal and enlightened men there, but discourage the common people from removing into this Country. . . .

When arranging his notes for the debates of the Convention of 1787 in old age, Madison observed that his comments on suffrage did not convey his "full and matured view of the subject." He thus appended two notes, a short one probably written on August 7, 1787, and a longer one probably written in the 1820s.

NO. 1. IN CONVENTION
OF 1787, AUGUST 7TH

As appointments for the General Government here contemplated will, in part, be made by the State Governments, all the Citizens in States where the right of suffrage is not limited to the holders of property, will have an indirect share of representation in the General Government. But this does not satisfy the fundamental principle that men can not be justly bound by laws in making which they have no part. Persons and property being both essential objects of Government, the most that either can claim, is such a structure of it, as will leave a reasonable security for the other. And the most obvious provision, of this double character, seems to be that of confining to the holders of property the object deemed least secure in popular Governments, the right of suffrage for one of the two Legislative branches. This is not without example among us, as well as other constitutional modifications, favoring the influence of property in the Government. But the U.S. have not reached the Stage of Society in which conflicting feelings of the class with, and the class without property, have the operation natural to them in Countries fully peopled. The most difficult of all political arrangements is that of so adjusting the claims of the two classes as to give security to each, and to promote the welfare of all. The federal principle—which enlarges the sphere of power without departing from the elective bases of and controls in various ways the propensity in small republics to rash measures and the facility of forming and executing them, will be found the best expedient yet tried for solving the problem.

No. 2 [1821–1829?]

The right of suffrage is a fundamental Article in Republican Constitutions. The regulation of it is, at the same time, a task of peculiar delicacy. Allow the right exclusively to property, and the rights of persons may be oppressed. The feudal polity alone sufficiently proves it. Extend it equally to all, and the rights of property or the claims of justice may be overruled by a majority without property, or interested in measures of injustice. Of this abundant proof is afforded by other popular Governments and is not without examples in our own, particularly in the laws impairing the obligation of contracts.

In civilized communities, property as well as personal rights is an essential object of the laws, which encourage industry by securing the enjoyment of its fruits: that industry from which property results, and that enjoyment which consists not merely in its immediate use, but in its posthumous destination to objects of choice and of kindred affection.

In a just and a free Government, therefore, the rights both of property and of persons ought to be effectually guarded. Will the former be so in case of a universal and equal suffrage? Will the latter be so in case of a suffrage confined to the holders of property?

As the holders of property have at stake all the other rights

common to those without property, they may be the more restrained from infringing, as well as the less tempted to infringe
the rights of the latter. It is nevertheless certain, that there are
various ways in which the rich may oppress the poor; in which
property may oppress liberty; and that the world is filled with
examples. It is necessary that the poor should have a defence
against the danger.

On the other hand, the danger to the holders of property can
not be disguised, if they be undefended against a majority without property. Bodies of men are not less swayed by interest than
individuals, and are less controlled by the dread of reproach and
the other motives felt by individuals. Hence the liability of the
rights of property, and of the impartiality of laws affecting it, to
be violated by Legislative majorities having an interest real or
supposed in the injustice: Hence agrarian laws, and other leveling schemes: Hence the cancelling or evading of debts, and
other violations of contracts. We must not shut our eyes to the
nature of man, nor to the light of experience. Who would rely on
a fair decision from three individuals if two had an interest in the
case opposed to the rights of the third? Make the number as
great as you please, the impartiality will not be increased, nor
any further security against injustice be obtained, than what may
result from the greater difficulty of uniting the wills of a greater
number.

In all Government there is a power which is capable of oppressive exercise. In Monarchies and Aristocracies oppression
proceeds from a want of sympathy and responsibility in the
Government towards the people. In popular Governments the
danger lies in an undue sympathy among individuals composing
a majority, and a want of responsibility in the majority of the
minority. The characteristic excellence of the political System
of the U.S. arises from a distribution and organization of its
powers which at the same time that they secure the dependence
of the Government on the will of the nation, provides better
guards than are found in any other popular Government against
interested combinations of a Majority against the rights of a Minority.

The United States have a precious advantage also in the actual distribution of property particularly the landed property; and in the universal hope of acquiring property. This latter peculiarity is among the happiest contrasts in their situation to that of the old world, where no anticipated change in this respect, can generally inspire a like sympathy with the rights of property. There may be at present, a Majority of the Nation, who are even freeholders, or the heirs, or aspirants to Freeholds. And the day may not be very near when such will cease to make up a Majority of the community. But they can not always so continue. With every admissible subdivision of the Arable lands, a populousness not greater than that of England or France, will reduce the holders to a Minority. And whenever the Majority shall be without landed or other equivalent property and without the means or hope of acquiring it, what is to secure the rights of property against the danger from an equality and universality of suffrage, vesting compleat power over property in hands without a share in it: not to speak of a danger in the mean time from a dependence of an increasing number on the wealth of a few? In other Countries this dependence results in some from the relations between Landlords and Tenants in others both from that source, and from the relations between wealthy capitalists and indigent labourers. In the U.S. the occurrence must happen from the last source; from the connection between the great Capitalists in Manufacturers and Commerce and the numbers employed by them. Nor will accumulations of Capital for a certain time be precluded by our laws of descent and of distribution; such being the enterprize inspired by free Institutions, that great wealth in the hands of individuals and associations, may not be infrequent. But it may be observed, that the opportunities, may be diminished, and the permanency defeated by the equalizing tendency of the laws.

No free Country has ever been without parties, which are a natural offspring of Freedom. An obvious and permanent division of every people is into the owners of the Soil, and the other inhabitants. In a certain sense the Country may be said to belong to the former. If each landholder has an exclusive property in his share, the Body of Landholders have an exclusive property in the whole. As the Soil becomes subdivided, and actually cultivated by the owners, this view of the subject derives force from the principle of natural law, which vests in individuals an exclusive right to the portions of ground with which they have incorporated their labour and improvements. Whatever may be the rights of others derived from their birth in the Country, from their interest in the high ways and other parcels left open for common use, as well as in the national Edifices and monuments; from their share in the public defence, and from their concurrent support of the Government it would seem unreasonable to extend the right so far as to give them when become the majority, a power of Legislation over the landed property without the consent of the proprietors. Some shield against the invasion of their rights would not be out of place in a just and provident System of Government. The principle of such an arrangement has prevailed in all Governments where peculiar privileges or interests held by a part were to be secured against violation, and in the various associations where pecuniary or other property forms the stake. In the former case a defensive right has been allowed; and if the arrangement be wrong, it is not in the defense, but in the kind of privilege to be defended. In the latter case, the shares of suffrage, allotted to individuals have been with acknowledged justice apportioned more or less to their respective interests in the Common Stock.

These reflections suggest the expediency of such a modification of Government as would give security to the part of the Society having most at stake and being most exposed to danger. Three modifications present themselves.

1. *Confining* the right of suffrage to freeholders, and to such as hold an equivalent property, convertible of course into freeholds. The objection to this regulation is obvious. It violates the vital principle of free Government that those who are to be bound by laws, ought to have a voice in making them. And the violation would be more strikingly unjust as the lawmakers become the minority: The regulation would be as unpropitious also as it would be unjust. It would engage the numerical and physical force in a constant struggle against the public authority; unless kept down by a standing army fatal to all parties.

2. Confining the right of suffrage for one Branch to the

holders of property, and for the other Branch to those without property. This arrangement which would give a mutual defence, where there might be mutual danger of encroachment, has an aspect of equality and fairness. But it would not be in fact either equal or fair, because the rights to be defended would be unequal, being on one side those of property as well as of persons, and on the other those of persons only. The temptation also to encroach though in a certain degree mutual, would be felt more strongly on one side than on the other. It would be more likely to beget an abuse of the Legislative Negative in extorting concessions at the expence of property, than the reverse: the division of the State into the two Classes, with distinct and independent Organs of power, and without any intermingled Agency whatever, might lead to contests and antipathies not dissimilar to those between the Patricians and Plebeians at Rome.

3. Confining the right of electing one Branch of the Legislature to freeholders, and admitting all others to a common right with holders of property, in electing the other Branch. This would give a defensive power to holders of property, and to the class also without property when becoming a majority of electors, without depriving them in the mean time of a participation in the public Councils. If the holders of property would thus have a twofold share of representation, they would have at the same time a twofold stake in it, the rights of property as well as of persons the twofold object of political institutions. And if no exact and safe equilibrium can be introduced, it is more reasonable that a preponderating weight should be allowed to the greater interest than to the lesser. Experience alone can decide how far the practice in this case would accord with the Theory. Such a distribution of the right of suffrage was tried in New York and has been abandoned whether from experienced evils or party calculations, may possibly be a question. It is still on trial in N. Carolina, with what practical indications is not known. It is certain that the trial, to be satisfactory ought to be continued for no inconsiderable period; untill in fact the non freeholders should be the majority.

4. Should Experience or public opinion require an equal and

universal suffrage for each branch of the Government such as prevails generally in the U.S. a resource favorable to the rights of landed and other property, when its possessors become the Minority, may be found in an enlargement of the Election Districts for one branch of the Legislature and a prolongation of its period of service. Large districts are manifestly favorable to the election of persons of general respectability, and of probable attachment to the rights of property, over competitors depending on the personal solicitations practicable on a contracted theatre. And although an ambitious candidate, of personal distinction, might occasionally recommend himself to popular choice by espousing a popular though unjust object, it might rarely happen to many districts at the same time. The tendency of a longer period of service would be, to render the Body more stable in its policy, and more capable of stemming popular currents taking a wrong direction, till reason and justice could regain their ascendancy.

5. Should even such a modification as the last be deemed inadmissible, and universal suffrage and very short periods of elections within contracted spheres be required for each branch of the Government, the security for the holders of property when the minority, can only be derived from the ordinary influence possessed by property, and the superior information incident to its holders; from the popular sense of justice enlightened and enlarged by a diffusive education; and from the difficulty of combining and effectuating unjust purposes throughout an extensive country; a difficulty essentially distinguishing the U.S. and even most of the individual States, from the small communities where a mistaken interest or contagious passion, could readily unite a majority of the whole under a factious leader, in trampling on the rights of the Minor party.

Under every view of the subject, it seems indispensable that the Mass of Citizens should not be without a voice, in making the laws which they are to obey, and in choosing the Magistrates, who are to administer them, and if the only alternative be between an equal and universal right of suffrage for each branch of the Government and a confinement of the *entire* right to a part of the Citizens, it is better that those having the greater interest at stake namely that of property and persons both, should be deprived of half their share in the Government; than, that those having the lesser interest, that of personal rights only, should be deprived of the whole.

Citizenship for Immigrants
(August 9)

A motion to require persons to be a United States citizen for at least 14 years before being eligible to be a member of the Senate led to a lively debate about immigration and its place in the new nation.

MR. GOUVERNEUR MORRIS moved to insert 14 instead of 4 years citizenship as a qualification for Senators: urging the danger of admitting strangers into our public Councils. MR. PINCKNEY seconded him.

MR. ELLSWORTH was opposed to the motion as discouraging meritorious aliens from emigrating to this Country.

MR. PINCKNEY. As the Senate is to have the power of making treaties and managing our foreign affairs, there is peculiar danger and impropriety in opening its door to those who have foreign attachments. He quoted the jealousy of the Athenians on this subject who made it death for any stranger to intrude his voice into their Legislative proceedings.

COLONEL MASON highly approved of the policy of the motion. Were it not that many not natives of this Country had acquired great merit during the revolution, he should be for restraining the eligibility into the Senate, to natives.

MR. MADISON was not averse to some restrictions on this subject; but could never agree to the proposed amendment. He thought any restriction however in the *Constitution* unnecessary, and improper; unnecessary because the National Legislature is to have the right of regulating naturalization, and can by virtue thereof fix different periods of residence as conditions of enjoying different privileges of Citizenship: Improper because it will give a tincture of illiberality to the Constitution: because it will put it out of the power of the National Legislature even by special acts of naturalization to confer the full rank of Citizens on meritorious strangers and because it will discourage the most desireable class of people from emigrating to the United States. Should the proposed Constitution have the intended effect of giving stability and reputation to our Governments great numbers of respectable Europeans: men who love liberty and wish to partake its blessings, will be ready to transfer their fortunes hither. All such would feel the mortification of being marked with suspicious incapacitations though they should not covet the public honors. He was not apprehensive that any dangerous number of strangers would be appointed by the State Legislatures, if they were left at liberty to do so: nor that foreign powers would make use of strangers as instruments for their purposes. Their bribes would be expended on men whose circumstances would rather stifle than excite jealousy and watchfulness in the public.

MR. BUTLER was decidedly opposed to the admission of foreigners without a long residence in the Country. They bring with them, not only attachments to other Countries; but ideas of Government so distinct from ours that in every point of view they are dangerous. He acknowledged that if he himself had been called into public life within a short time after his coming to America, his foreign habits, opinions, and attachments would have rendered him an improper agent in public affairs. He mentioned the great strictness observed in Great Britain on this subject.

DR. FRANKLIN was not against a reasonable time, but should be very sorry to see any thing like illiberality inserted in the Constitution. The people in Europe are friendly to this Country. Even in the Country with which we have been lately at war, we have now and had during the war, a great many friends not only among the people at large but in both houses of Parliament. In every other Country in Europe all the people are our friends. We found in the course of the Revolution that many strangers served us faithfully—and that many natives took part against their Country. When foreigners after looking about for some other Country in which they can obtain more happiness, give a preference to ours, it is a proof of attachment which ought to excite our confidence and affection.

MR. RANDOLPH did not know but it might be problematical whether emigrations to this Country were on the whole useful or not: but he could never agree to the motion for disabling them for 14 years to participate in the public honours. He reminded the Convention of the language held by our patriots during the Revolution, and the principles laid down in all our American Constitutions. Many foreigners may have fixed their fortunes among us under the faith of these invitations. All persons under this description, with all others who would be affected by such a regulation, would enlist themselves under the banners of hostility to the proposed System. He would go as far as seven years, but no farther.

MR. WILSON said he rose with feelings which were perhaps peculiar; mentioning the circumstance of his not being a native, and the possibility, if the ideas of some gentlemen should be pursued, of his being incapacitated from holding a place under the very Constitution, which he had shared in the trust of making. He remarked the illiberal complexion which the motion would give to the System, and the effect which a good system would have in inviting meritorious foreigners among us, and the discouragement and mortification they must feel from the degrading discrimination, now proposed. He had himself experienced this mortification. On his removal into Maryland, he found himself, from defect of residence, under certain legal incapacities which never ceased to produce chagrin, though he assuredly did not desire and would not have accepted the offices to which they related. To be appointed to a place may be a matter of indifference. To be incapable of being appointed, is a circumstance grating and mortifying.

MR. GOUVERNEUR MORRIS. The lesson we are taught is that we should be governed as much by our reason, and as little by our feelings as possible. What is the language of Reason on this subject? That we should not be polite at the expence of prudence. There was a moderation in all things. It is said that some tribes of Indians, carried their hospitality so far as to offer to strangers their wives and daughters. Was this a proper model for us? He would admit them to his house, he would invite them to his table, would provide for them comfortable lodgings; but would not carry the complaisance so far as, to bed them with his wife. He would let them worship at the same altar, but did not choose to make Priests of them. He ran over the privileges which emigrants would enjoy among us, though they should be deprived of that of being eligible to the great offices of Government; observing that they exceeded the privileges allowed to foreigners in any part of the world; and that as every Society from a great nation down to a club had the right of declaring the conditions on which new members should be admitted, there could be no room for complaint. As to those philosophical gentlemen, those citizens of the World as they call themselves, he owned he did not wish to see any of them in our public Councils. He would not trust them. The men who can shake off their attachments to their own Country can never love any other. These attachments are the wholesome prejudices which uphold all Governments. Admit a Frenchman into your Senate, and he will study to increase the commerce of France: an Englishman, he will feel an equal bias in favor of that of England. It has been said that the Legislatures will not choose foreigners, at least improper ones. There was no knowing what Legislatures would do. Some appointments made by them, proved that every thing ought to be apprehended from the cabals practised on such occasions. He mentioned the case of a foreigner who left this State in disgrace, and worked himself into an appointment from another to Congress.

Executive Veto Power
(August 15)

Discussion of the veto power led to a probe of the nature of the executive department.

MR. GOUVERNEUR MORRIS suggested the expedient of an absolute negative in the Executive. He could not agree that the Judiciary which was part of the Executive, should be bound to say that a direct violation of the Constitution was law. A control over the legislature might have its inconveniences. But view the danger on the other side. The most virtuous Citizens will often as members of a legislative body concur in measures which afterwards in their private capacity they will be ashamed of. Encroachments of the popular branch of the Government ought to be guarded against. The Ephori at Sparta became in the end absolute. The Report of the Council of Censors in Pennsylvania points out the many invasions of the legislative department on the Executive numerous as the latter is, within the short term of seven years, and in a State where a strong party is opposed to the Constitution, and watching every occasion of turning the public resentments against it. If the Executive be overturned by the popular branch, as happened in England, the tyranny of one man will ensue. In Rome where the Aristocracy overturned the throne, the consequence was different. He enlarged on the tendency of the legislative Authority to usurp on the Executive and wished the section to be postponed, in order to consider of some more effectual check than requiring two thirds only to overrule the negative of the Executive.

MR. SHERMAN. Can one man be trusted better than all the others if they all agree? This was neither wise nor safe. He disapproved of Judges meddling in politics and parties. We have gone far enough in forming the negative as it now stands. . . .

MR. WILSON, after viewing the subject with all the coolness and attention possible was most apprehensive of a dissolution of the Government from the legislature swallowing up all the other powers. He remarked that the prejudices against the Executive resulted from a misapplication of the adage that the parliament was the palladium of liberty. Where the Executive was really formidable, *King* and *Tyrant,* were naturally associated in the minds of people; not *legislature* and *tyranny.* But where the Executive was not formidable, the two last were most properly associated. After the destruction of the King in Great Britain, a more pure and unmixed tyranny sprang up in the parliament than had been exercised by the monarch. He insisted that we had not guarded against the danger on this side by a sufficient self-defensive power either to the Executive or Judiciary department.

Slavery and the Constitution (August 21, 22)

The Convention was finally compelled to discuss the potentially devisive issue of regulation of the slave trade. The draft constitution forbade either a prohibition or tax on "the migration or importation of such persons as the several states shall think proper to admit."

MR. L. MARTIN proposed to vary the Sect: 4. art. VII. so as to allow a prohibition or tax on the importation of slaves. 1. as five slaves are to be counted as 3 free men in the apportionment of Representatives; such a clause would leave an encouragement to this trafic. 2. slaves weakened one part of the Union which the other parts were bound to protect: the privilege of importing them was therefore unreasonable. 3. it was inconsistent with the principles of the revolution and dishonorable to the American character to have such a feature in the Constitution.

MR. RUTLEDGE did not see how the importation of slaves could be encouraged by this Section. He was not apprehensive of insurrections and would readily exempt the other States from the obligation to protect the Southern against them.—Religion and humanity had nothing to do with this question. Interest alone is the governing principle with nations. The true question at present is whether the Southern States shall or shall not be parties to the Union. If the Northern States consult their interest, they will not oppose the increase of Slaves which will increase the commodities of which they will become the carriers.

MR. ELLSWORTH was for leaving the clause as it stands. Let every State import what it pleases. The morality or wisdom of slavery are considerations belonging to the States themselves. What enriches a part enriches the whole, and the States are the best judges of their particular interest. The old confederation had not meddled with this point, and he did not see any greater necessity for bringing it within the policy of the new one. . . .

MR. PINCKNEY. South Carolina can never receive the plan if it prohibits the slave trade. In every proposed extension of the powers of the Congress, that State has expressly and watchfully excepted that of meddling with the importation of negroes. If the States be all left at liberty on this subject, S. Carolina may perhaps by degrees do of herself what is wished, as Virginia and Maryland have already done.

MR. SHERMAN was for leaving the clause as it stands. He disapproved of the slave trade; yet as the States were now possessed of the right to import slaves, as the public good did not require it to be taken from them, and as it was expedient to have as few objections as possible to the proposed scheme of Government, he thought it best to leave the matter as we find it. He observed that the abolition of Slavery seemed to be going on in the United States and that the good sense of the several States would probably by degrees compleat it. He urged on the Convention the necessity of despatching its business.

COLONEL MASON. This infernal traffic originated in the avarice of British Merchants. The British Government constantly checked the attempts of Virginia to put a stop to it. The present question concerns not the importing States alone but the whole Union. The evil of having slaves was experienced during the late war. Had slaves been treated as they might have been by the Enemy, they would have proved dangerous instruments in their hands. But their folly dealt by the slaves, as it did by the Tories. He mentioned the dangerous insurrections of the slaves in Greece and Sicily; and the instructions given by Cromwell to the Commissioners sent to Virginia, to arm the servants and slaves, in case other means of obtaining its submission should fail. Maryland and Virginia he said had already prohibited the importation of slaves expressly. North Carolina had done the same in substance. All this would be in vain if South Carolina and Georgia be at liberty to import. The Western people are already calling out for slaves for their new lands, and will fill that Country with slaves if they can be got through South Carolina and Georgia. Slavery discourages arts and manufactures. The poor despise labor when performed by slaves. They prevent the immigration of Whites, who really enrich and strengthen a Country. They produce the most pernicious effect on manners. Every master of slaves is born a petty tyrant. They bring the judgment of heaven on a Country. As nations can not be rewarded or punished in the next world they must be in this. By an inevitable chain of causes and effects providence punishes national sins, by national calamities. He lamented that some of our Eastern brethren had from a lust of gain embarked in this nefarious traffic. As to the States being in possession of the Right to import, this was the case with many other rights, now to be properly given up. He held it essential in every point of view that the General Government should have power to prevent the increase of slavery.

MR. ELLSWORTH. As he had never owned a slave, he could not judge of the effects of slavery on character: He said however that if it was to be considered in a moral light we ought to go farther and free those already in the Country.—As slaves also multiply so fast in Virginia and Maryland that it is cheaper to raise than import them, whilst in the sickly rice swamps foreign supplies are necessary, if we go no farther than is urged, we shall be unjust towards South Carolina and Georgia. Let us not inter-meddle. As population increases poor laborers will be so plenty as to render slaves useless. Slavery in time will not be a speck in our Country. Provision is already made in Connecticut for abolishing it. And the abolition has already taken place in Massachussets. As to the danger of insurrections from foreign influence, that will become a motive to kind treatment of the slaves.

MR. PINCKNEY. If slavery be wrong, it is justified by the example of all the world. He cited the case of Greece, Rome and other ancient States; the sanction given by France, England, Holland and other modern States. In all ages one half of mankind have been slaves. If the Southern States were let alone they will probably of themselves stop importations. He would himself as a Citizen of South Carolina vote for it. An attempt to take away the right as proposed will produce serious objections to the Constitution which he wished to see adopted.

GENERAL PINCKNEY declared it to be his firm opinion that if himself and all his colleagues were to sign the Constitution and use their personal influence, it would be of no avail towards obtaining the assent of their Constituents. South Carolina and Georgia cannot do without slaves. As to Virginia she will gain by stopping the importations. Her slaves will rise in value, and she has more than she wants. It would be unequal to require South Carolina and Georgia to confederate on such unequal terms. He said the Royal assent before the Revolution had never been refused to South Carolina as to Virginia. He contended that the importation of slaves would be for the interest of the whole Union. The more slaves, the more produce to employ the carrying trade; the more consumption also, and the more of this, the more of revenue for the common treasury. He admitted it to be reasonable that slaves should be dutied like other imports, but should consider a rejection of the clause as an exclusion of South Carolina from the Union.

MR. BALDWIN had conceived national objects alone to be before the Convention, not such as like the present were of a local nature. Georgia was decided on this point. That State has always hitherto supposed a General Government to be the pursuit of the central States who wished to have a vortex for every thing—that her distance would preclude her from equal advantage—and that she could not prudently purchase it by yielding national powers. From this it might be understood in what light she would view an attempt to abridge one of her favorite prerogatives. If left to herself, she may probably put a stop to the evil. As one ground for this conjecture, he took notice of the sect of   which he said was a respectable class of people, who carried their ethics beyond the mere *equality of men,* extending their humanity to the claims of the whole animal creation.

MR. WILSON observed that if South Carolina and Georgia were themselves disposed to get rid of the importation of slaves in a short time as had been suggested, they would never refuse to Unite because the importation might be prohibited. As the Section now stands all articles imported are to be taxed. Slaves alone are exempt. This is in fact a bounty on that article.

MR. GERRY thought we had nothing to do with the conduct of the States as to Slaves, but ought to be careful not to give any sanction to it.

MR. DICKINSON considered it as inadmissible on every principle of honor and safety that the importation of slaves should be authorised to the States by the Constitution. The true question was whether the national happiness would be promoted or impeded by the importation, and this question ought to be left to the National Government not to the States particularly interested. If England and France permit slavery, slaves are at the same time excluded from both those Kingdoms. Greece and Rome were made unhappy by their slaves. He could not believe that the Southern States would refuse to confederate on the account apprehended; especially as the power was not likely to be immediately exercised by the General Government.

MR. WILLIAMSON stated the law of North Carolina on the subject, to wit that it did not directly prohibit the importation of slaves. It imposed a duty of £5 on each slave imported from Africa, £10 on each from elsewhere, and £50 on each from a State licensing manumission. He thought the Southern States could not be members of the Union if the clause should be rejected, and that it was wrong to force any thing down, not absolutely necessary, and which any State must disagree to.

MR. KING thought the subject should be considered in a political light only. If two States will not agree to the Constitution as stated on one side, he could affirm with equal belief on the other, that great and equal opposition would be experienced from the other States. He remarked on the exemption of slaves from duty whilst every other import was subjected to it, as an inequality that could not fail to strike the commercial sagacity of the Northern and middle States.

MR. LANGDON was strenuous for giving the power to the General Government. He could not with a good conscience leave it with the States who could then go on with the traffic, without being restrained by the opinions here given that they will themselves cease to import slaves.

GENERAL PINCKNEY thought himself bound to declare candidly that he did not think South Carolina would stop her importations of slaves in any short time, but only stop them occasionally as she now does. He moved to commit the clause that slaves might be made liable to an equal tax with other imports which he thought right and which would remove one difficulty that had been started.

MR. RUTLEDGE. If the Convention thinks that North Carolina, South Carolina and Georgia will ever agree to the plan, unless their right to import slaves be untouched, the expectation is vain. The people of those States will never be such fools as to give up so important an interest. . . .

Debate on this issue, and a concurrent one on the requirement of a two-thirds vote in Congress to pass laws regulating foreign commerce, soon made clear that a trade-off had been agreed to between Georgia and South Carolina determined to keep open the slave trade, and the New England states anxious to remove the two-thirds restriction on commercial regulation: New England would not vote to prohibit the slave trade if Georgia and South Carolina would not insist on the two-thirds vote on commercial laws. This compromise resolved the last major conflict of interest facing the Convention.

Election and Powers
of the President
(September 4, 5, 6)

By early September the Convention had gone through the draft constitution clause by clause, largely approving its provisions, but also making some important changes. The Senate was empowered to amend (but not originate) money bills, property qualifications for officers of government were discarded, the powers of Congress were enlarged, and the requirement that a two-thirds vote be required to pass navigation laws was dropped. The Convention, though, proved unwilling to accept the articles about the election and powers of the president, and the nature of the powers shared with the Senate. On September 4, a committee appointed to resolve these matters returned a report that contained many provisions closer to those in the present Constitution: the electoral college, four-year terms for president and vice president, impeachment by the House of Representatives and trial by the Senate, and appointment and treaty-making powers given to the president, with the advice and consent of the Senate. The committee report, however, proposed that the Senate choose the president in case of a tie in the electoral college, or a failure of any candidate to receive a majority of the votes. Serious debate began with Gouverneur Morris's explanation of the committee proposals.

MR. GOUVERNEUR MORRIS said he would give the reasons of the Committee and his own. The First was the danger of intrigue and faction if the appointment should be made by the Legislature. 2. The inconveniency of an ineligibility required by that mode in order to lessen its evils. 3. The difficulty of establishing a Court of Impeachments, other than the Senate which would not be so proper for the trial nor the other branch for the impeachment of the President, if appointed by the Legislature. 4. No body had appeared to be satisfied with an appointment by the Legislature. 5. Many were anxious even for an immediate choice by the people. 6. The indispensible necessity of making the Executive independent of the Legislature.—As the Electors would vote at the same time throughout the U.S. and at so great a distance from each other, the great evil of cabal was avoided. It would be impossible also to corrupt them. A conclusive reason for making the Senate instead of the Supreme Court the Judge of impeachments, was that the latter was to try the President after the trial of the impeachment.

COLONEL MASON confessed that the plan of the Committee had removed some capital objections, particularly the danger of cabal and corruption. It was liable however to this strong objection, that nineteen times in twenty the President would be chosen by the Senate, an improper body for the purpose.

MR. BUTLER thought the mode not free from objections, but much more so than an election by the Legislature, where as in elective monarchies, cabal faction and violence would be sure to prevail.

MR. PINCKNEY stated as objections to the mode 1. that it threw the whole appointment in fact into the hands of the Senate. 2. The Electors will be strangers to the several candidates and of course unable to decide on their comparative merits. 3. It makes the Executive re-eligible which will endanger the public liberty. 4. It makes the same body of men which will in fact elect the President his Judges in case of an impeachment.

MR. WILLIAMSON had great doubts whether the advantage of re-eligibility would balance the objection to such a dependence of the President on the Senate for his reappointment. He thought at least the Senate ought to be restrained to the *two* highest on the list.

MR. GOUVERNEUR MORRIS said the principal advantage aimed at was that of taking away the opportunity for cabal. The President may be made if thought necessary ineligible on this as well as on any other mode of election. Other inconveniences may be no less redressed on this plan than any other.

MR. BALDWIN thought the plan not so objectionable when well considered, as at first view. The increasing intercourse among the people of the States, would render important characters less and less unknown; and the Senate would consequently be less and less likely to have the eventual appointment thrown into their hands.

MR. WILSON. This subject has greatly divided the House, and will also divide people out of doors. It is in truth the most difficult of all on which we have had to decide. He had never made up an opinion on it entirely to his own satisfaction. He thought the plan on the whole a valuable improvement on the former. It gets rid of one great evil, that of cabal and corruption; and Continental Characters will multiply as we more and more coalesce, so as to enable the electors in every part of the Union to know and judge of them. It clears the way also for a discussion of the question of re-eligibility on its own merits, which the former mode of election seemed to forbid. He thought it might be better however to refer the eventual appointment to the Legislature than to the Senate, and to confine it to a smaller number than five of the Candidates. The eventual election by the Legislature would not open cabal anew, as it would be restrained to certain designated objects of choice, and as these must have had the previous sanction of a number of the States: and if the election be made as it ought as soon as the votes of the electors are opened and it is known that no one has a majority of the whole, there can be little danger of corruption. Another reason for preferring the Legislature to the Senate in this business, was that the House of Representatives will be so often changed as to be free from the influence and faction to which the permanence of the Senate may subject that branch.

MR. RANDOLPH preferred the former mode of constituting the Executive, but if the change was to be made, he wished to know why the eventual election was referred to the *Senate* and not to the *Legislature?* He saw no necessity for this and many objections to it. He was apprehensive also that the advantage of the eventual appointment would fall into the hands of the States near the Seat of Government.

MR. GOUVERNEUR MORRIS said the *Senate* was preferred

because fewer could then, say to the President, you owe your appointment to us. He thought the President would not depend so much on the Senate for his re-appointment as on his general good conduct. . . .

Debate on the executive department resumed on September 5 and 6. At its conclusion the delegates accepted the provisions found in the final draft of the Constitution.

The Report made yesterday as to the appointment of the Executive being taken up. MR. PINCKNEY renewed his opposition to the mode, arguing 1. that the electors will not have sufficient knowledge of the fittest men, and will be swayed by an attachment to the eminent men of their respective States. Hence secondly the dispersion of the votes would leave the appointment with the Senate, and as the President's reappointment will thus depend on the Senate he will be the mere creature of that body. 3. He will combine with the Senate against the House of Representatives. 4. This change in the mode of election was meant to get rid of the ineligibility of the President a second time, whereby he will become fixed for life under the auspices of the Senate. . . .

COLONEL MASON admitted that there were objections to an appointment by the Legislature as originally planned. He had not yet made up his mind, but would state his objections to the mode proposed by the Committee. 1. It puts the appointment in fact into the hands of the Senate, as it will rarely happen that a majority of the whole votes will fall on any one candidate: and as the Existing President will always be one of the five highest, his re-appointment will of course depend on the Senate. 2. Considering the powers of the President and those of the Senate, if a coalition should be established between these two branches, they will be able to subvert the Constitution.—The great objection with him would be removed by depriving the Senate of the eventual election. He accordingly moved to strike out the words "if such number be a majority of that of the electors."

MR. WILLIAMSON seconded the motion. He could not agree to the clause without some such modification. He preferred making the highest though not having a majority of the votes, President, to a reference of the matter to the Senate. Referring the appointment to the Senate lays a certain foundation for corruption and aristocracy.

MR. GOUVERNEUR MORRIS thought the point of less consequence than it was supposed on both sides. It is probable that a majority of votes will fall on the same man. As each elector is to give two votes, more than one quarter will give a majority. Besides as one vote is to be given to a man out of the State, and as this vote will not be thrown away, one half of the votes will fall on characters eminent and generally known. Again if the President shall have given satisfaction, the votes will turn on him of course, and a majority of them will reappoint him, without resort to the Senate: If he should be disliked, all disliking him, would take care to unite their votes so as to ensure his being supplanted. . . .

MR. WILSON said that he had weighed carefully the report of the Committee for remodelling the constitution of the Executive; and on combining it with other parts of the plan, he was obliged to consider the whole as having a dangerous tendency to aristocracy; as throwing a dangerous power into the hands of the Senate. They will have in fact, the appointment of the President, and through his dependence on them, the virtual appointment to offices; among others the offices of the Judiciary Department. They are to make Treaties; and they are to try all impeachments. In allowing them thus to make the Executive and Judiciary appointments, to be the Court of impeachments, and to make Treaties which are to be laws of the land, the Legislative, Executive and Judiciary powers are all blended in one branch of the Government. The power of making Treaties involves the case of subsidies, and here as an additional evil, foreign influence is to be dreaded. According to the plan as it now stands, the President will not be the man of the people as he ought to be, but the Minion of the Senate. He cannot even appoint a tide-waiter without the Senate. He had always thought the Senate too numerous a body for making appointments to office. The Senate, will moreover in all probability be in constant Session. They will have high salaries. And with all those powers, and the President in their interest, they will depress the other branch of the Legislature, and aggrandize themselves in proportion. Add to all this, that the Senate sitting in conclave, can by holding up to their respective States various and improbable candidates, contrive so to scatter their votes, as to bring the appointment of the President ultimately before themselves. Upon the whole, he thought the new mode of appointing the President, with some amendments, a valuable improvement; but he could never agree to purchase it at the price of the ensuing parts of the Report, nor befriend a system of which they make a part.

MR. GOUVERNEUR MORRIS expressed his wonder at the observations of Mr. Wilson so far as they preferred the plan in the printed Report to the new modification of it before the House, and entered into a comparative view of the two, with an eye to the nature of Mr. Wilson's objections to the last. By the first the Senate he observed had a voice in appointing the President out of all the Citizens of the United States; by this they were limited to five candidates previously nominated to them, with a probability of being barred altogether by the successful ballot of the Electors. Here surely was no increase of power. They are now to appoint Judges nominated to them by the President. Before they had the appointment without any agency whatever of the President. Here again was surely no additional power. If they are to make Treaties as the plan now stands, the power was the same in the printed plan. If they are to try impeachments, the Judges must have been triable by them before. Wherein then lay the dangerous tendency of the innovations to establish an aristocracy in the Senate? As to the appointment of officers, the weight of sentiment in the House, was opposed to the exercise of it by the President alone; though it was not the case with himself. If the Senate would act as was suspected, in misleading the States into a fallacious disposition of their votes for a President, they would, if the appointment were withdrawn wholly from them, make such representations in their several States where they have influence, as would favor the object of their partiality.

MR. WILLIAMSON replying to Mr. Morris: observed that the aristocratic complexion proceeds from the change in the mode of appointing the President which makes him dependent on the Senate.

MR. CLYMER said that the aristocratic part to which he could never accede was that in the printed plan, which gave the Senate the power of appointing to offices.

MR. HAMILTON said that he had been restrained from entering into the discussions by his dislike of the Scheme of Government in General; but as he meant to support the plan to be recommended, as better than nothing, he wished in this place to offer a few remarks. He liked the new modification, on the whole, better than that in the printed Report. In this the President was a Monster elected for seven years, and ineligible afterwards; having great powers, in appointments to office, and continually tempted by this constitutional disqualification to abuse them in order to subvert the Government. Although he should be made re-eligible, still if appointed by the Legislature, he would be tempted to make use of corrupt influence to be continued in office. It seemed peculiarly desireable therefore that some other mode of election should be devised. Considering the different views of different States, and the different districts, Northern, Middle, and Southern, he concurred with those who thought that the votes would not be concentered, and that the appointment would consequently in the present mode devolve on the Senate. The nomination to offices will give great weight to the President. Here then is a mutual connection and influence, that will perpetuate the President, and aggrandize both him and the Senate. What is to be the remedy? He saw none better than to let the highest number of ballots, whether a majority or not, appoint the President. What was the objection to this? Merely that too small a number might appoint. But as the plan stands, the Senate may take the candidate having the smallest number of votes, and make him President.

Opposition to the Constitution
(September 7, 10, 15)

Though the Constitution was largely agreed on and most of the delegates were anxious to go home, three delegates, Gerry of Massachusetts and Randolph and Mason of Virginia, objected to basic provisions and declared their intention not to sign the document as it seemed to be shaping up. A speech by Mason on September 7, proposing a Privy Council for the president, one by Randolph on the 10th, speeches by all three on the 15th, and a statement of objections apparently drafted by Mason on the 15th summarized the arguments of the three delegates in opposition. Mason's statement of objections is reprinted from Rutland, ed., The Papers of George Mason, *III, pp. 991–993.*

COLONEL MASON thought the office of vice president an encroachment on the rights of the Senate; and that it mixed too much the Legislative and Executive, which as well as the Judiciary departments, ought to be kept as separate as possible. He took occasion to express his dislike of any reference whatever of the power to make appointments to either branch of the Legislature. On the other hand he was averse to vest so dangerous a power in the President alone. As a method for avoiding both, he suggested that, a privy Council of six members to the president should be established; to be chosen for six years by the Senate, two out of the Eastern, two out of the middle, and two out of the Southern quarters of the Union, and to go out in rotation two every second year; the concurrence of the Senate to be required only in the appointment of Ambassadors, and in making treaties, which are more of a legislative nature. This would prevent the constant sitting of the Senate which he thought dangerous, as well as keep the departments separate and distinct. It would also save the expence of constant sessions of the Senate. He had he said always considered the Senate as too unwieldy and expensive for appointing officers, especially the smallest, such as tide waiters etc. He had not reduced his idea to writing, but it could be easily done if it should be found acceptable. . . .

MR. RANDOLPH took this opportunity to state his objections to the System. They turned on the Senate's being made the Court of Impeachment for trying the Executive—on the necessity of three quarters instead of two thirds of each house to overrule the negative of the President—on the smallness of the number of the Representative branch—on the want of limitation to a standing army—on the general clause concerning necessary and proper laws—on the want of some particular restraint on navigation acts—on the power to lay duties on exports—on the Authority of the General Legislature to interpose on the application of the *Executives* of the States—on the want of a more definite boundary between the General and State Legislatures—and between the General and State Judiciaries—on the unqualified power of the President to pardon treasons—on the want of some limit to the power of the Legislature in regulating their own compensations. With these difficulties in his mind, what course he asked was he to pursue? Was he to promote the establishment of a plan which he verily believed would end in Tyranny? He was unwilling he said to impede the wishes and Judgment of the Convention, but he must keep himself free, in case he should be honored with a seat in the Convention of his State, to act according to the dictates of his judgment. The only mode in which his embarrassments could be removed, was that of submitting the plan to Congress to go from them to the State Legislatures, and from these to State Conventions having power to adopt, reject or amend; the process to close with another General Convention with full power to adopt or reject the alterations proposed by the State Conventions, and to establish finally the Government. . . .

MR. RANDOLPH [commenting] on the indefinite and dangerous power given by the Constitution to Congress, expressing the pain he felt at differing from the body of the Convention, on the close of the great and awful subject of their labours, and anxiously wishing for some accommodating expedient which would relieve him from his embarrassments, made a motion importing "that amendments to the plan might be offered by the State Conventions, which should be submitted to and finally decided on by another general Convention." Should this proposition be disregarded, it would he said be impossible for him to put his name to the instrument. Whether he should oppose it afterwards he would not then decide but he would not deprive himself of the freedom to do so in his own State, if that course should be prescribed by his final judgment.

COLONEL MASON seconded and followed Mr. Randolph in animadversions on the dangerous power and structure of the Government, concluding that it would end either in monarchy, or a tyrannical aristocracy; which, he was in doubt, but one or other, he was sure. This Constitution had been formed without the knowledge or idea of the people. A second Convention will know more of the sense of the people, and be able to provide a system more consonant to it. It was improper to say to the people, take this or nothing. As the Constitution now stands, he could neither give it his support or vote in Virginia; and he could not sign here what he could not support there. With the expedient of another Convention as proposed, he could sign. . . .

MR. GERRY stated the objections which determined him to withhold his name from the Constitution. 1. The duration and re-eligibility of the Senate. 2. The power of the House of Representatives to conceal their journals. 3. The power of Congress over the places of election. 4. The unlimited power of Congress over their own compensations. 5. Massachusetts has not a due share of Representatives allotted to her. 6. Three fifths of the Blacks are to be represented as if they were freemen. 7. Under the power over commerce, monopolies may be established. 8. The vice president being made head of the Senate. He could however he said get over all these, if the rights of the Citizens were not rendered insecure 1. By the general power of the Legislature to make what laws they may please to call necessary and proper. 2. Raise armies and money without limit. 3. To establish a tribunal without juries, which will be a Star-chamber as to Civil cases. Under such a view of the Constitution, the best that could be done he conceived was to provide for a second general Convention.

[Mason's] Objections to
This Constitution of Government

There is no Declaration of Rights, and the laws of the general government being paramount to the laws and constitution of the several States, the Declarations of Rights in the separate States are no security. Nor are the people secured even in the enjoyment of the benefit of the common law.

In the House of Representatives there is not the substance but the shadow only of representation; which can never produce proper information in the legislature, or inspire confidence in the people; the laws will therefore be generally made by men little concerned in, and unacquainted with their effects and consequences.

The Senate have the power of altering all money bills, and of originating appropriations of money, and the salaries of the officers of their own appointment, in conjunction with the president of the United States, although they are not the representatives of the people or amenable to them.

These with their other great powers, viz.: their power in the appointment of ambassadors and all public officers, in making treaties, and in trying all impeachments, their influence upon and connection with the supreme Executive from these causes, their duration of office and their being a constantly existing body, almost continually sitting, joined with their being one complete branch of the legislature, will destroy any balance in the government, and enable them to accomplish what usurpations they please upon the rights and liberties of the people.

The Judiciary of the United States is so constructed and extended, as to absorb and destroy the judiciaries of the several States; thereby rendering law as tedious, intricate and expensive, and justice as unattainable, by a great part of the community, as in England, and enabling the rich to oppress and ruin the poor.

The President of the United States has no Constitutional Council, a thing unknown in any safe and regular government. He will therefore be unsupported by proper information and advice, and will generally be directed by minions and favorites; or he will become a tool to the Senate—or a Council of State will grow out of the principal officers of the great departments; the worst and most dangerous of all ingredients for such a council in a free country: From this fatal defect has arisen the improper power of the Senate in the appointment of public officers, and the alarming dependence and connection between that branch of the legislature and the supreme Executive.

Hence also sprung that unnecessary officer the vice president, who for want of other employment is made president of the Senate, thereby dangerously blending the executive and legislative powers, besides always giving to some one of the States an unnecessary and unjust pre-eminence over the others.

The President of the United States has the unrestrained power of granting pardons for treason, which may be sometimes exercised to screen from punishment those whom he had secretly instigated to commit the crime, and thereby prevent a discovery of his own guilt.

By declaring all treaties supreme laws of the land, the Executive and the Senate have, in many cases, an exclusive power of legislation; which might have been avoided by proper distinctions with respect to treaties, and requiring the assent of the House of Representatives, where it could be done with safety.

By requiring only a majority to make all commercial and navigation laws, the five Southern States, whose produce and circumstances are totally different from that of the eight Northern and Eastern States, may be ruined, for such rigid and premature regulations may be made as will enable the merchants of the Northern and Eastern States not only to demand an exhorbitant freight, but to monopolize the purchase of the commodities at their own price, for many years, to the great injury of the landed interest, and impoverishment of the people; and the danger is the greater as the gain on one side will be in proportion to the loss on the other. Whereas requiring two-thirds of the members present in both Houses would have produced mutual moderation, promoted the general interest, and removed an insuperable objection to the adoption of this government.

Under their own construction of the general clause, at the end of the enumerated powers, the Congress may grant monopolies in trade and commerce, constitute new crimes, inflict unusual and severe punishments, and extend their powers as far as they shall think proper; so that the State legislatures have no security for the powers now presumed to remain to them, or the people for their rights.

There is no declaration of any kind, for preserving the liberty of the press, or the trial by jury in civil causes; nor against the danger of standing armies in time of peace.

The State legislatures are restrained from laying export duties on their own produce.

Both the general legislature and the State legislature are expressly prohibited making *ex post facto* laws; though there never was nor can be a legislature but must and will make such laws, when necessity and the public safety require them; which will hereafter be a breach of all the constitutions in the Union, and afford precedents for other innovations.

This government will set out a moderate aristocracy: it is at present impossible to foresee whether it will, in its operation, produce a monarchy, or a corrupt, tyrannical aristocracy; it will most probably vibrate some years between the two, and then terminate in the one or the other.

The general legislature is restrained from prohibiting the further importation of slaves for twenty odd years; though such importations render the United States weaker, more vulnerable, and less capable of defence.

Signing the Constitution
(September 17)

On the last day of the Convention Franklin made a graceful speech pleading with all his colleagues, despite their objections to some parts of the Constitution, to sign it as on the whole probably the best that could be done by any convention of fallible human beings. A discussion followed, revealing some of the hopes and fears of the delegates as they finished their work.

Mr. President: I confess that there are several parts of this constitution which I do not at present approve, but I am not sure I shall never approve them. For having lived long, I have experienced many instances of being obliged by better information, or fuller consideration, to change opinions even on important subjects, which I once thought right, but found to be otherwise. It is therefore that the older I grow, the more apt I am to doubt my own judgment, and to pay more respect to the judgment of others. Most men indeed as well as most sects in Religion, think themselves in possession of all truth, and that wherever others differ from them it is so far error. Steele, a Protestant, in a Dedication tells the Pope, that the only difference between our Churches in their opinions of the certainty of their doctrines is, the Church of Rome is infallible and the Church of England is never in the wrong. But though many private persons think almost as highly of their own infallibility as of that of their sect, few express it so naturally as a certain French lady, who in a dispute with her sister, said "I don't know how it happens, Sister, but I meet with no body but myself, that's always in the right— *Il n'y a que moi qui a toujours raison.*"

In these sentiments, Sir, I agree to this Constitution with all

its faults, if they are such; because I think a general Government
necessary for us, and there is no form of Government but what
may be a blessing to the people if well administered, and believe
farther that this is likely to be well administered for a course of
years, and can only end in Despotism, as other forms have done
before it, when the people shall become so corrupted as to need
despotic Government, being incapable of any other. I doubt too
whether any other Convention we can obtain, may be able to
make a better Constitution. For when you assemble a number of
men to have the advantage of their joint wisdom, you inevitably
assemble with those men, all their prejudices, their passions,
their errors of opinion, their local interests, and their selfish
views. From such an assembly can a perfect production be expected? It therefore astonishes me, Sir, to find this system approaching so near to perfection as it does; and I think it will
astonish our enemies, who are waiting with confidence to hear
that our councils are confounded like those of the Builders of
Babel; and that our States are on the point of separation, only to
meet hereafter for the purpose of cutting one another's throats.
Thus I consent, Sir, to this Constitution because I expect no better, and because I am not sure, that it is not the best. The opinions I have had of its errors, I sacrifice to the public good. I have
never whispered a syllable of them abroad. Within these walls
they were born, and here they shall die. If every one of us in
returning to our Constituents were to report the objections he
has had to it, and endeavor to gain partizans in support of them,
we might prevent its being generally received, and thereby lose
all the salutary effects and great advantages resulting naturally
in our favor among foreign Nations as well as among ourselves,
from our real or apparent unanimity. Much of the strength and
efficiency of any Government in procuring and securing happiness to the people, depends, on opinion, on the general opinion
of the goodness of the Government, as well as of the wisdom
and integrity of its Governors. I hope therefore that for our own
sakes as a part of the people, and for the sake of posterity, we
shall act heartily and unanimously in recommending this constitution (if approved by Congress and confirmed by the Conventions) wherever our influence may extend, and turn our future

thoughts and endeavors to the means of having it well administered.

On the whole, Sir, I can not help expressing a wish that every member of the convention who may still have objections to it, would with me, on this occasion doubt a little of his own infallibility, and to make manifest our unanimity, put his name to this instrument.—

He then moved that the Constitution be signed by the members and offered the following as a convenient form viz. "Done in Convention by the unanimous consent of *the States* present the seventeenth of September etc.—In Witness whereof we have hereunto subscribed our names."

This ambiguous form had been drawn up by Mr. G. Morris in order to gain the dissenting members, and put into the hands of Dr. Franklin that it might have the better chance of success.

MR. GORHAM said if it was not too late he could wish, for the purpose of lessening objections to the Constitution, that the clause declaring "the number of Representatives shall not exceed one for every forty thousand" which had produced so much discussion, might be yet reconsidered, in order to strike out 40,000 and insert "thirty thousand." This would not he remarked establish that as an absolute rule, but only give Congress a greater latitude which could not be thought unreasonable.

MR. KING and Mr. CARROL seconded and supported the ideas of Mr. Gorham.

When the PRESIDENT [Washington] rose, for the purpose of putting the question, he said that although his situation had hitherto restrained him from offering his sentiments on questions depending in the House, and it might be thought, ought now to impose silence on him, yet he could not forbear expressing his wish that the alteration proposed might take place. It was much to be desired that the objections to the plan recommended might be made as few as possible. The smallness of the proportion of Representatives had been considered by many members of the Convention an insufficient security for the right and interests of the people. He acknowledged that it had always appeared to himself among the exceptionable parts of the plan, and late as the present moment was for admitting amendments, he thought this of so much consequence that it would give much satisfaction to see it adopted.*

No opposition was made to the proposition of Mr. Gorham and it was agreed to unanimously.

On the question to agree to the Constitution enrolled in order to be signed. It was agreed to all the States answering ay.

MR. RANDOLPH then rose and with an allusion to the observations of Dr. Franklin apologized for his refusing to sign the constitution notwithstanding the vast majority and venerable names that would give sanction to its wisdom and its worth. He said however that he did not mean by this refusal to decide that he should oppose the Constitution without doors. He meant only to keep himself free to be governed by his duty as it should be prescribed by his future judgment. He refused to sign, because he thought the object of the Convention would be frustrated by the alternative which it presented to the people. Nine States will fail to ratify the plan and confusion must ensue. With such a view of the subject he ought not, he could not, by pledging himself to support the plan, restrain himself from taking such steps as might appear to him most consistent with the public good.

MR. GOUVERNEUR MORRIS said that he too had objections, but considering the present plan as the best that was to be attained, he should take it with all its faults. The majority had determined in its favor and by that determination he should abide. The moment this plan goes forth all other considerations will be laid aside, and the great question will be, shall there be a national Government or not? and this must take place or a general anarchy will be the alternative. He remarked that the signing in the form proposed related only to the fact that the *States* present were unanimous.

MR. WILLIAMSON suggested that the signing should be confined to the letter accompanying the Constitution to Congress, which might perhaps do nearly as well, and would he found be satisfactory to some members who disliked the constitution. For

---

*This was the only occasion on which the president entered at all into the discussions of the Convention.

himself he did not think a better plan was to be expected and had no scruples against putting his name to it.

MR. HAMILTON expressed his anxiety that every member should sign. A few characters of consequence, by opposing or even refusing to sign the Constitution, might do infinite mischief by kindling the latent sparks which lurk under an enthusiasm in favor of the Convention which may soon subside. No man's ideas were more remote from the plan than his were known to be; but is it possible to deliberate between anarchy and Convulsion on one side, and the chance of good to be expected from the plan on the other.

MR. BLOUNT said he had declared that he would not sign, so as to pledge himself in support of the plan, but he was relieved by the form proposed and would without committing himself attest the fact that the plan was the unanimous act of the States in Convention.

DR. FRANKLIN expressed his fears from what Mr. Randolph had said, that he thought himself alluded to in the remarks offered this morning to the House. He declared that when drawing up that paper he did not know that any particular member would refuse to sign his name to the instrument, and hoped to be so understood. He professed a high sense of obligation to Mr. Randolph for having brought forward the plan in the first instance, and for the assistance he had given in its progress, and hoped that he would yet lay aside his objections, and by concurring with his brethren, prevent the great mischief which the refusal of his name might produce.

MR. RANDOLPH could not but regard the signing in the proposed form, as the same with signing the Constitution. The change of form therefore could make no difference with him. He repeated that in refusing to sign the Constitution, he took a step which might be the most awful of his life, but it was dictated by his conscience, and it was not possible for him to hesitate, much less, to change. He repeated also his persuasion, that the holding out this plan with a final alternative to the people, of accepting or rejecting it in toto, would really produce the anarchy and civil convulsions which were apprehended from the refusal of individuals to sign it.

MR. GERRY described the painful feelings of his situation, and the embarrassment under which he rose to offer any further observations on the subject which had been finally decided. Whilst the plan was depending, he had treated it with all the freedom he thought it deserved. He now felt himself bound as he was disposed to treat it with the respect due to the Act of the Convention. He hoped he should not violate that respect in declaring on this occasion his fears that a Civil war may result from the present crisis of the U.S. In Massachusetts, particularly he saw the danger of this calamitous event.—In that State there are two parties, one devoted to Democracy, the worst he thought of all political evils, the other as violent in the opposite extreme. From the collision of these in opposing and resisting the Constitution, confusion was greatly to be feared. He had thought it necessary, for this and other reasons that the plan should have been proposed in a more mediating shape, in order to abate the heat and opposition of parties. As it has been passed by the Convention, he was persuaded it would have a contrary effect. He could not therefore by signing the Constitution pledge himself to abide by it at all events. The proposed form made no difference with him. But if it were not otherwise apparent, the refusals to sign should never be known from him. Alluding to the remarks of Dr. Franklin, he could not he said but view them as levelled at himself and the other gentlemen who meant not to sign. . . .

The members then proceeded to sign the instruments.

Whilst the last members were signing it DR. FRANKLIN looking towards the President's Chair, at the back of which a rising sun happened to be painted, observed to a few members near him, that Painters had found it difficult to distinguish in their art a rising from a setting sun. I have said he, often and often in the course of the Session, and the vicisitudes of my hopes and fears as to its issue, looked at that behind the President without being able to tell whether it was rising or setting: But now at length I have the happiness to know that it is a rising and not a setting Sun.

The Constitution being signed by all the members except Mr. Randolph, Mr. Mason, and Mr. Gerry who declined giving it the sanction of their names, the Convention dissolved itself by an Adjournment sine die—

PART II

RATIFICATION OF THE CONSTITUTION

Speech of James Wilson
(October 6, 1787)

*After the Federal Convention had adjourned and the Continental
Congress referred the new Constitution to the states for possible
ratification, proponents of the Constitution, calling themselves
"federalists," began campaigns to arouse public support and to
elect delegates favorable to it to the state ratification conventions. Because the Pennsylvania legislature was in session when
the new Constitution was referred to the state, and zealous federalists, led by James Wilson, engineered an immediate call for
elections to the state convention, the campaign began early and
intensely there. Wilson was a key figure because he had been a
leading member of the Federal Convention, was well-known as
a vigorous advocate of the new Constitution, and had long been
a prominent, controversial political figure in the state. A large
public meeting on October 6 in the State House (Independence
Hall) yard to nominate delegates to the next Pennsylvania legislature became as well a forum for discussion of the new federal
Constitution. Wilson was asked to speak to the gathering, to explain the new Constitution, and to answer some of the criticisms
that had already been leveled at it. He delivered a "long and
eloquent speech upon the principles of the federal constitution
as proposed by the late convention," as one Philadelphia newspaper described it. This speech, printed in the* Pennsylvania
Packet *on October 10, 1787, soon became one of the most
widely reprinted defenses of the new Constitution, appearing in
newspapers throughout the states, and marked Wilson as its
leading public advocate. It is reprinted here from J. B. McMas-
ter and F. Stone,* Pennsylvania and the Federal Constitution
(Lancaster, PA, 1888), pp. 142–150.

Mr. Chairman and Fellow Citizens: Having received the honor of an appointment to represent you in the late convention, it is perhaps my duty to comply with the request of many gentlemen whose characters and judgments I sincerely respect, and who have urged that this would be a proper occasion to lay before you any information which will serve to explain and elucidate the principles and arrangements of the constitution that has been submitted to the consideration of the United States. . . .

It will be proper . . . to mark the leading discrimination between the State constitutions and the constitution of the United States. When the people established the powers of legislation under their separate governments, they invested their representatives with every right and authority which they did not in explicit terms reserve; and therefore upon every question respecting the jurisdiction of the House of Assembly, if the frame of government is silent, the jurisdiction is efficient and complete. But in delegating federal powers, another criterion was necessarily introduced, and the congressional power is to be collected, not from tacit implication, but from the positive grant expressed in the instrument of the union. Hence, it is evident, that in the former case everything which is not reserved is given; but in the latter the reverse of the proposition prevails, and everything which is not given is reserved.

This distinction being recognized, will furnish an answer to those who think the omission of a bill of rights a defect in the proposed constitution; for it would have been superfluous and absurd to have stipulated with a federal body of our own creation, that we should enjoy those privileges of which we are not divested, either by the intention or the act that has brought the body into existence. For instance, the liberty of the press, which has been a copious source of declamation and opposition—what control can proceed from the Federal government to shackle or destroy that sacred palladium of national freedom? If, indeed, a power similar to that which has been granted for the regulation of commerce had been granted to regulate literary publications, it would have been as necessary to stipulate that the liberty of the press should be preserved inviolate, as that the impost should be general in its operation. With respect likewise to the particular district of ten miles, which is to be made the seat of federal government, it will undoubtedly be proper to observe this salutary precaution, as there the legislative power will be exclusively lodged in the President, Senate, and House of Representatives of the United States. But this could not be an object with the Convention, for it must naturally depend upon a future compact, to which the citizens immediately interested will, and ought to be, parties; and there is no reason to suspect that so popular a privilege will in that case be neglected. In truth, then, the proposed system possesses no influence whatever upon the press, and it would have been merely nugatory to have introduced a formal declaration upon the subject—nay, that very declaration might have been construed to imply that some degree of power was given, since we undertook to define its extent.

Another objection that has been fabricated against the new constitution, is expressed in this disingenious form—"The trial by jury is abolished in civil cases." I must be excused, my fellow citizens, if upon this point I take advantage of my professional experience to detect the futility of the assertion. Let it be remembered then, that the business of the Federal Convention was not local, but general—not limited to the views and establishments of a single State, but co-extensive with the continent, and comprehending the views and establishments of thirteen independent sovereignties. When, therefore, this subject was in discussion, we were involved in difficulties which pressed on all sides, and no precedent could be discovered to direct our course. The cases open to a trial by jury differed in the different States. It was therefore impracticable, on that ground, to have made a general rule. The want of uniformity would have rendered any reference to the practice of the States idle and useless; and it could not with any propriety be said that, "The trial by jury shall be as heretofore," since there has never existed any federal system of jurisprudence, to which the declaration could relate. Besides, it is not in all cases that the trial by jury is adopted in civil questions; for cases depending in courts of admiralty, such as relate to maritime captures, and such as are agitated in courts of equity, do not require the intervention of that tribunal. How, then was the line of discrimination to be drawn? The Convention found the task too difficult for them, and they left the business as it stands, in the fullest confidence that no danger could possibly ensue, since the proceedings of the Supreme Court are to be regulated by the Congress, which is a faithful representation of the people; and the oppression of government is effectually barred, by declaring that in all criminal cases the trial by jury shall be preserved.

This constitution, it has been further urged, is of a pernicious tendency, because it tolerates a standing army in the time of peace. This has always been a topic of popular declamation; and yet I do not know a nation in the world which has not found it necessary and useful to maintain the appearance of strength in a season of the most profound tranquility. Nor is it a novelty with us; for under the present articles of confederation, Congress certainly possesses this reprobated power, and the exercise of that power is proved at this moment by her cantonments along the banks of the Ohio. But what would be our national situation were it otherwise? Every principle of policy must be subverted, and the government must declare war, before they are prepared to carry it on. Whatever may be the provocation, however important the object in view, and however necessary dispatch and secrecy may be, still the declaration must precede the preparation, and the enemy will be informed of your intention, not only before you are equipped for an attack, but even before you are fortified for a defence. The consequence is too obvious to require any further delineation, and no man who regards the dignity and safety of his country can deny the necessity of a military force, under the control and with the restrictions which the new constitution provides.

Perhaps there never was a charge made with less reasons than that which predicts the institution of a baneful aristocracy in the federal Senate. This body branches into two characters, the one legislative and the other executive. In its legislative character it can effect no purpose, without the co-operation of the House of Representatives, and in its executive character it can accomplish no object without the concurrence of the President. Thus fettered, I do not know any act which the Senate can of itself perform, and such dependence necessarily precludes every idea of influence and superiority. But I will confess that in the organization of this body a compromise between contending interests is descernible; and when we reflect how various are the laws, commerce, habits, population and extent of the confederated States, this evidence of mutual concession and accommodation ought rather to command a generous applause, than to excite jealousy and reproach. For my part, my admiration can only be equalled by my astonishment in beholding so perfect a system formed from such heterogeneous materials.

The next accusation I shall consider is that which represents the federal constitution, as not only calculated, but designedly framed, to reduce the State governments to mere corporations, and eventually to annihilate them. Those who have employed the term corporation upon this occasion are not perhaps aware of its extent. In common parlance, indeed, it is generally applied to petty associations for the ease and convenience of a few individuals; but in its enlarged sense, it will comprehend the government of Pennsylvania, the existing union of the States, and even this projected system is nothing more than a formal act of incorporation. But upon what pretence can it be alleged that it was designed to annihilate the State governments? For I will undertake to prove that upon their existence depends the existence of the Federal plan. For this purpose, permit me to call your attention to the manner in which the President, Senate and House of Representatives are proposed to be appointed. The President is to be chosen by electors, nominated in such manner as the legislature of each State may direct; so that if there is no legislature there can be no electors, and consequently the office of President cannot be supplied.

The Senate is to be composed of two Senators from each State, chosen by the Legislature; and, therefore, if there is no Legislature, there can be no Senate. The House of Representatives is to be composed of members chosen every second year by the people of the several States, and the electors in each State shall have the qualifications requisite for electors of the most numerous branch of the State Legislature; unless, therefore, there is a State Legislature, that qualification cannot be ascertained, and the popular branch of the federal constitution must be extinct. From this view, then, it is evidently absurd to suppose that the annihilation of the separate governments will result from their union; or, that having that intention, the authors of the new system would have bound their connection with such indissoluble ties. Let me here advert to an arrangement highly advantageous, for you will perceive, without prejudice to the powers of the Legislature in the election of Senators, the people at large will acquire an additional privilege in returning members to the House of Representatives; whereas, by the present confederation, it is the Legislature alone that appoints the delegates to Congress.

The power of direct taxation has likewise been treated as an improper delegation to the federal government; but when we consider it as the duty of that body to provide for the national safety, to support the dignity of the union, and to discharge the debts contracted upon the collected faith of the States for their common benefit, it must be acknowledged that those upon whom such important obligations are imposed, ought in justice and in policy to possess every means requisite for a faithful performance of their trust. But why should we be alarmed with visionary evils? I will venture to predict that the great revenue of the United States must, and always will, be raised by impost, for, being at once less obnoxious and more productive, the interest of the government will be best promoted by the accommodation of the people. Still, however, the objects of direct taxation should be within reach in all cases of emergency; and there is no more reason to apprehend oppression in the mode of collecting a revenue from this resource, than in the form of an impost, which, by universal assent, is left to the authority of the federal government. In either case, the force of civil institutions will be adequate to the purpose; and the dread of military violence, which has been assiduously disseminated, must eventually prove the mere effusion of a wild imagination or a factious spirit. But the salutary consequences that must flow from thus enabling the government to receive and support the credit of the union, will afford another answer to the objections upon this ground. The State of Pennsylvania particularly, which has encumbered itself with the assumption of a great proportion of the public debt, will derive considerable relief and advantage; for, as it was the imbecility of the present confederation which gave rise to the funding law, that law must naturally expire, when a competent and energetic federal system shall be substituted— the State will then be discharged from an extraordinary burthen, and the national creditor will find it to be his interest to return to his original security.

After all, my fellow-citizens, it is neither extraordinary or un-expected that the constitution offered to your consideration should meet with opposition. It is the nature of man to pursue his own interest in preference to the public good, and I do not mean to make any personal reflection when I add that it is the interest of a very numerous, powerful and respectable body to counteract and destroy the excellent work produced by the late convention. All the officers of government and all the appointments for the administration of justice and the collection of the public revenue, which are transferred from the individual to the aggregate sover-eignty of the States, will necessarily turn the stream of influence and emolument into a new channel. Every person, therefore, who enjoys or expects to enjoy a place of profit under the present es-tablishment, will object to the proposed innovation; not, in truth, because it is injurious to the liberties of his country, but because it affects his schemes of wealth and consequence. I will confess, indeed, that I am not a blind admirer of this plan of government, and that there are some parts of it which, if my wish had pre-vailed, would certainly have been altered. But, when I reflect how widely men differ in their opinions, and that every man (and the observation applies likewise to every State) has an equal preten-sion to assert his own, I am satisfied that anything nearer to per-fection could not have been accomplished. If there are errors, it should be remembered that the seeds of reformation are sown in the work itself, and the concurrence of two-thirds of the Con-gress may at any time introduce alterations and amendments. Regarding it, then, in every point of view, with a candid and disinterested mind, I am bold to assert that it is the best form of government which has ever been offered to the world.

THE NEED FOR ENERGY IN GOVERNMENT

Explained in Federalist Numbers 1–8, 15–32, 34–36, 73–77 (Nos. 1, 3, 6, 15, 23, 27, 30, 73, and 76 are most important).

   The debate over the new Constitution began positively for its advocates with earnest arguments to establish the need in the United States for a more powerful, or to use the favorite word of the day, "energetic," central government. Publius began, in eight letters (1–8) written by Hamilton and John Jay, by explaining the serious, sure-to-be-fatal consequences, at home and abroad, of continuing under the weak Articles of Confederation. In twenty-one more letters (15–32, 34–36) Publius first elaborated on specific weaknesses of the Articles and then explained how similar flaws had ruined other confederations. Next he justified the specific powers, especially over defense and taxation, given to Congress in the new Constitution. The argument for more energy resumed in Publius' defense of the executive department, especially numbers 73–77. These essays in The Federalist Papers provided the arguments the anti-federalists had to meet if they were to resist successfully the movement to ratify the "more energetic" Constitution.

"John DeWitt," Essays I and II
(October 22 and 27, 1787)

The most effective early anti-federalist argument denying the need for a more energetic central government came from an unidentified Massachusetts anti-federalist who used the pseudonym "John DeWitt," the Dutch patriot of the seventeenth century who had defended the liberties of the people against an oppressive central government. "DeWitt's" five essays appeared in the Boston American Herald, *October–December 1787. The essays reprinted below, numbers I and II, appeared on October 22 and 27, 1787, respectively.*

*To the Free Citizens
of the Commonwealth of Massachusetts.*

I

Whoever attentively examines the history of America, and compares it with that of other nations, will find its commencement, its growth, and its present situation, without a precedent.

It must ever prove a source of pleasure to the Philosopher, who ranges the explored parts of this inhabitable globe, and takes a comparative view, as well of the rise and fall of those nations, which have been and are gone, as of the growth and present existence of those which are now in being, to close his prospect with this Western world. In proportion as he loves his fellow creatures, he must here admire and approve; for while they have severally laid their foundations in the blood and slaughter of three, four, and sometimes, ten successive generations, from their passions have experience, every misery to which human nature is subject, and at this day present striking features of usurped power, unequal justice, and despotic tyranny. America stands completely systemised without any of these misfortunes.—On the contrary, from the first settlement of the country, the necessity of civil associations, founded upon equality, consent, and proportionate justice have ever been universally acknowledged.—The means of education always attended to, and the fountains of science brought within the reach of poverty.—Hitherto we have commenced society, and advanced in all respects resembling a family, without partial affections, or even a domestic bickering: And if we consider her as an individual, instead of an undue proportion of violent passions and bad habits, we must set her down possessed of reason, genius and virtue.—I premise these few observations because there are too many among us of narrow minds, who live in the practice of blasting the reputation of their own country.—They hold it as a maxim, that virtues cannot grow in their own soil.—They will appreciate those of a man, they know nothing about, because he is an exotic; while they are sure to depreciate those much more brilliant in their neighbours, because they are really acquainted with and know them.

Civil society is a blessing.—It is here universally known as such.—The education of every child in this country tends to promote it.—There is scarcely a citizen in America who does not wish to bring it, consistent with our situation and circumstances, to its highest state of improvement.—Nay, I may say further, that the people in general aim to effect this point, in a peaceable, laudable, and rational way. These assertions are proved by stubborn facts, and I need only resort to that moment, when, in contest with a powerful enemy, they paid such an unprecedented attention to civilization, as to select from among themselves their different conventions, and form their several constitutions, which, for their beautiful theoretical structure, caught the admiration of our enemies, and secured to us the applause of the world.—We at this day feel the effects of this disposition, and now live under a government of our own choice, constructed by ourselves, upon unequivocal principles, and requires but to be well administered to make us as happy under it as generally falls to the lot of humanity. The disturbances in the course of the year past cannot be placed as an objection to the principle I advance.—They took their rise in idleness, extravagance and misinformation, a want of knowledge of our several finances, a universal delusion at the close of the war, and in consequence thereof, a pressure of embarrassments, which checked, and in many cases, destroyed that disposition of forbearance, which ought to be exercised towards each other. These were added to the accursed practice of letting money at usury, and some few real difficulties and grievances, which our late situation unavoidably brought upon us. The issue of them, however, rather proves the position for, a very few irreclaimables excepted, we find even an anxiety to hearken to reason pervading all classes—industry and frugality increasing, and the advantages arising from good, wholesome laws, confessed by every one.—Let who will gain say it. I am confident we are in a much better situation, in all respects, than we were at this period the last year; and as fast as can be expected, consistent with the passions and habits of a free people, of men who will think for themselves, coalescing, as a correspondent observes in a late paper, under a firm, wise and efficient government. The powers vested in Congress have hitherto been found inadequate.— Who are those that have been against investing them? The people of this Commonwealth have very generally supposed it expedient, and the farmer equally with the merchant have taken steps to effect it.—A Convention from the different States for that sole purpose hath been appointed of their most respectable citizens—respectable indeed I may say for their equity, for their literature, and for their love of their country.—Their proceedings are now before us for our approbation.—The eagerness with which they have been received by certain classes of our fellow citizens, naturally forces upon us this question: Are we to adopt this Government, without an examination?—Some there are, who, literally speaking, are for pressing it upon us at all events. The name of the man who but lisps a sentiment in objection to it, is to be handed to the printer, by the printer to the public, and by the public he is to be led to execution. They are themselves stabbing its reputation. For my part, I am a stranger to the necessity for all this haste! Is it not a subject of some small importance? Certainly it is.—Are not your lives, your liberties and properties intimately involved in it?—Certainly they are. Is it a government for a moment, a day, or a year? By no means—but for ages—. Altered it may possibly be, but it is easier to correct before it is adopted.—Is it for a family, a state, or a small number of people? It is for a number no less respectable than three millions. Are the enemy at our gates, and have we not time to consider it? Certainly we have. Is it so simple in its form as to be comprehended instantly?—Every letter, if I may be allowed the expression, is an idea. Does it consist of but few additions to our present confederation, and those which have been from time to time described among us, and known to be necessary?—Far otherwise. It is a compleat system of government, and armed with every power, that a people in any circumstances ought to bestow. It is a path newly struck out, and a new set of ideas are introduced that have neither occurred or been digested.—A government for national purposes, preserving our constitution entire, hath been the only plan hitherto agitated. I do not pretend to say, but it is in theory the most unexceptionable, and in practice will be the most conducive to our happiness of any possible to be adopted:—But it ought to undergo a candid and strict examination. It is the duty of every one in the Commonwealth to communicate his sentiments to his neighbour, divested of passion, and equally so of prejudices. If they are honest and he is a real friend to his country, he will do it and embrace every opportunity to do it. If thoroughly looked into before it is adopted, the people will be more apt to approve of it in practice, and every man is a TRAITOR to himself and his posterity, who shall ratify it with his signature, without first endeavouring to understand it.—We are but yet in infancy; and we had better proceed slow than too fast.—It is much easier to dispense powers, than recall them.—The present generation will not be drawn into any system; they are too enlightened; they have not forfeited their right to a share in government, and they ought to enjoy it.

Some are heard to say, "When we consider the men who made it, we ought to take it for sterling, and without hesitation—that they were the collected wisdom of the States, and had no object but the general good."—I do not doubt all this, but facts ought not to be winked out of sight:—They were delegated from different States, and nearly equally represented, though vastly disproportionate both in wealth and numbers. They had local prejudices to combat, and in many instances, totally opposite interests to consult. Their situations, their habits, their extent, and their particular interest, varied each from the other. The gentlemen themselves acknowledge that they have been less rigid upon some points, in consequence of those difficulties than they otherwise should have been.—Others again tell you that the Convention is or will be dissolved; that we must take their proceedings in whole or reject them.—But this surely cannot be a reason for their speedy adoption; it rather works the other way. If evils are acknowledged in the composition, we ought, at least, to see whose shoulders are to bear the most; to compare ours with those of other States, and take care that we are not saddled with more than our proportion: That the citizens of Philadelphia are running mad after it, can be no argument for us to do the like:— Their situation is almost contrasted with ours; they suppose themselves a central State; they expect the perpetual residence of Congress, which of itself alone will ensure their aggrandizement: We, on the contrary, are sure to be near one of the extremes; neither the loaves or fishes will be so plenty with us, or shall we be so handy to procure them.

We are told by some people, that upon the adopting this New Government, we are to become every thing in a moment:—Our foreign and domestic debts will be as a feather; our ports will be crowded with the ships of all the world, soliciting our commerce and our produce: Our manufactures will increase and multiply; and, in short, if we STAND STILL, our country, notwithstanding, will be like the blessed Canaan, a land flowing with milk and honey. Let us not deceive ourselves; the only excellency of any government is in exact proportion to the administration of it:— Idleness and luxury will be as much a bane as ever; our passions will be equally at war with us then as now; and if we have men among us trying with all their ability to undermine our present Constitution, these very persons will direct their force to sap the vitals of the new one.—

Upon the whole, my fellow countrymen, I am as much a federal man as any person: In a federal union lies our political salvation.—To preserve that union, and make it respectable to foreign opticks, the National Government ought to be armed with all necessary powers; but the subject I conceive of infinite delicacy, and requires both ability and reflection. In discussing points of such moment, America has nothing to do with passions or hard words; every citizen has an undoubted right to examine for himself, neither ought he to be ill treated and abused, because he does not think at the same moment exactly as we do. It is true, that many of us have but our liberties to lose, but they are dearly bought, and are not the least precious in estimation:—In the mean time, is it not of infinite consequence, that we pursue inflexibly that path, which I feel persuaded we are now approaching, wherein we shall discourage all foreign importations; shall see the necessity of greater economy and industry; shall smile upon the husbandman, and reward the industrious mechanic; shall promote the growth of our own country, and wear the produce of our own farms; and, finally, shall support measures in proportion to their honesty and wisdom, without any respect to men. Nothing more is wanted to make us happy at home, and respectable abroad.

John DeWitt.

II

In my last address upon the proceedings of the Federal Convention, I endeavored to convince you of the importance of the subject, that it required a cool, dispassionate examination, and a thorough investigation, previous to its adoption—that it was not a mere revision and amendment of our first Confederation, but a compleat System for the future government of the United States, and I may now add in preference to, and in exclusion of, all others heretofore adopted.—It is not TEMPORARY, but in its nature, PERPETUAL.—It is not designed that you shall be annually called, either to revise, correct, or renew it; but, that your posterity shall grow up under, and be governed by it, as well as ourselves.—It is not so capable of alterations as you would at the first reading suppose; and I venture to assert, it never can be, unless by force of arms. The fifth article in the proceedings, it is true, expressly provides for an alteration under certain conditions, whenever "it shall be ratified by the Legislatures of three fourths of the several States, or by Conventions in three fourths thereof, as the one or the other mode of ratification may be proposed by Congress."—Notwithstanding which, such are the *"heterogeneous materials from which this System was formed,"* such is the difference of interest, different manners, and different local prejudices, in the different parts of the United States, that to obtain that majority of three fourths to any one single alteration, essentially affecting this or any other State, amounts to an absolute impossibility. The conduct of the Delegates in dissolving the Convention, plainly speaks this language, and no other.—Their sentiments in their Letter to his Excellency the President of Congress are—that this Constitution was the result of a spirit of amity—that the parties came together disposed to concede as much as possible each to the other—that mutual concessions and compromises did, in fact, take place, and all those which could, consistent with the peculiarity of their political situation. Their dissolution enforces the same sentiment, by confining you to the alternative of taking or refusing their doings in the gross. In this view, who is there to be found among us, who can seriously assert, that this Constitution, after ratification and being practised upon, will be so easy of alteration? Where is the probability that a future Convention, in any future day, will be found possessed of a greater spirit of amity and mutual concession than the present? Where is the probability that three fourths of the States in that Convention, or three fourths of the Legislatures of the different States, whose interests differ scarcely in nothing short of every thing, will be so very ready or willing materially to change any part of this System, which shall be to the emolument of an individual State only? No, my fellow-citizens, as you are now obliged to take it in the whole, so you must hereafter administer it in whole, without the prospect of change, unless by again reverting to a state of Nature, which will be ever opposed with success by those who approve of the Government in being.

That the want of a Bill of Rights to accompany this proposed System, is a solid objection to it, provided there is nothing exceptionable in the System itself, I do not assert.—If, however, there is at any time, a propriety in having one, it would not have been amiss here. A people, entering into society, surrender such a part of their natural rights, as shall be necessary for the existence of that society. They are so precious in themselves, that they would never be parted with, did not the preservation of the remainder require it. They are entrusted in the hands of those, who are very willing to receive them, who are naturally fond of exercising of them, and whose passions are always striving to make a bad use of them.—They are conveyed by a written compact, expressing those which are given up, and the mode in which those reserved shall be secured. Language is so easy of explanation, and so difficult is it by words to convey exact ideas, that the party to be governed cannot be too explicit. The line cannot be drawn with too much precision and accuracy. The necessity of this accuracy and this precision encreases in proportion to the greatness of the sacrifice and the numbers who make it.—That a Constitution for the United States does not require a

Bill of Rights, when it is considered, that a Constitution for an individual State would, I cannot conceive.—The difference between them is only in the numbers of the parties concerned; they are both a compact between the Governors and Governed, the letter of which must be adhered to in discussing their powers. That which is not expressly granted, is of course retained.

The Compact itself is a recital upon paper of that proportion of the subject's natural rights, intended to be parted with, for the benefit of adverting to it in case of dispute. Miserable indeed would be the situation of those individual States who have not prefixed to their Constitutions a Bill of Rights, if, as a very respectable, learned Gentleman at the Southward observes, "the People, when they established the powers of legislation under their separate Governments, invested their Representatives with every right and authority which they did not, in explicit terms, reserve; and therefore upon every question, respecting the jurisdiction of the House of Assembly, if the Frame of Government is silent, the jurisdiction of the House of Assembly, if the Frame of Government is silent, the jurisdiction is efficient and complete." [From James Wilson's speech of Ocober 6, 1787; see above.] In other words, those powers which the people by their Constitutions expressly give them, they enjoy by positive grant, and those remaining ones, which they never meant to give them, and which the Constitutions say nothing about, they enjoy by tacit implication, so that by one means and by the other, they became possessed of the whole.—This doctrine is but poorly calculated for the meridian of America, where the nature of compact, the mode of construing them, and the principles upon which society is founded, are so accurately known and universally diffused. That insatiable thirst for unconditional controul over our fellow-creatures, and the facility of sounds to convey essentially different ideas, produced the first Bill of Rights ever prefixed to a Frame of Government. The people, although fully sensible that they reserved every tittle of power they did not expressly grant away, yet afraid that the words made use of, to express those rights so granted might convey more than they originally intended, they chose at the same moment to express in different language those rights which the agreement did not include, and which they never designed to part with, endeavoring thereby to prevent any cause for future altercation and the intrusion into society of that doctrine of tacit implication which has been the favorite theme of every tyrant from the origin of all governments to the present day.

The proceedings of the Convention are now handed to you by your Legislature, and the second Wednesday in January is appointed for your final answer. To enable you to give that with propriety; that your future reflections may produce peace, however opposed the present issue of your present conduct may be to your present expectations, you must determine, that, in order to support with dignity the Federal Union, it is proper and fit, that the present Confederation shall be annihilated:—That the future Congress of the United States shall be armed with the powers of Legislation, Judgment and Execution.—That annual elections in this Congress shall not be known, and the most powerful body, the Senate, in which a due proportion of representation is not preserved, and in which the smallest State has equal weight with the largest, be the longest in duration:—That it is not necessary for the public good, that persons habituated to the exercise of power should ever be reminded from whence they derive it, by a return to the station of private citizens, but that they shall at all times at the expiration of the term for which they were elected to an office, be capable of immediate re-election to that same office:—That you will hereafter risk the probability of having the Chief Executive Branch chosen from among you; and that it is wholly indifferent, both to you and your children after you, whether this future Government shall be administered within the territories of your own State, or at the distance of four thousand miles from them.—You must also determine, that they shall have the exclusive power of imposts and the duties on imports and exports, the power of laying excises and other duties, and the additional power of laying internal taxes upon your lands, your goods, your chattels, as well as your persons at their sovereign pleasure:—That the produce of these several funds shall be appropriated to the use of the United States, and collected by their own officers, armed with a military force, if a civil aid should not prove sufficient:—That the power of organizing, arming and disciplining the militia shall be lodged in them, and this through fear that they shall not be sufficiently attentive to keeping so respectable a body of men as the yeomanry of this Commonwealth, compleatly armed, organized and disciplined; they shall have also the power of raising, supporting and establishing a standing army in time of peace in your several towns, and I see not why in your several houses:—That should an insurrection or an invasion, however small, take place, in Georgia, the extremity of the Continent, it is highly expedient they should have the power of suspending the writ of Habeas Corpus in Massachusetts, and as long as they shall judge the public safety requires it:—You must also say, that your present Supreme Judicial Court shall be an Inferior Court to a Continental Court, which is to be inferior to the Supreme Court of the United States:—That from an undue bias which they are supposed to have for the citizens of their own States, they shall not be competent to determine title to your real estate, disputes which may arise upon a protested Bill of Exchange, a simple note of hand, or book debt, wherein your citizens shall be unfortunately involved with disputes of such or any other kind, with citizens either of other States or foreign States: In all such cases they shall have a right to carry their causes to the Supreme Court of the United States, whether for delay only or vexation; however distant from the place of your abode, or inconsistent with your circumstances:—That such appeals shall be extended to matters of fact as well as law, and a trial of the cause by jury you shall not have a right to insist upon.—In short, my fellow-citizens, previous to a capacity of giving a compleat answer to these proceedings, you must determine that the Constitution of your Commonwealth, which is instructive, beautiful and consistent in practice, which has been justly admired in Europe, as a model of perfection, and which the present Convention have affected to imitate, a Constitution which is especially calculated for your territory, and is made conformable to your genius, your habits, the mode of holding your estates, and your particular interests, shall be reduced in its powers to those of a City Corporation:—The skeleton of it may remain, but its vital principle shall be transferred to the new Government: Nay, you must go still further, and agree to invest the new Congress with powers, which you have yet thought proper to withhold from your own present Government.—All these, and more, which are contained in the proceedings of the Federal Convention, may be highly proper and necessary.—In this overturn of all individual governments, in this new-fashioned set of ideas, and in this total dereliction of those sentiments which animated us in 1775, the Political Salvation of the United States may be very deeply interested, but BE CAUTIOUS.

John DeWitt

Speeches of Patrick Henry
(June 5 and 7, 1788)

The most moving, eloquent denial by the anti-federalists of the need for a more energetic government came from Patrick Henry in speeches before the Virginia Ratifying Convention, early in its deliberations. They were first printed in a 1788–1789 Petersburg, Virginia, edition of the Debates and Other Proceedings . . . of the Virginia Convention of 1788.

5 June 1788

Mr. Chairman . . . I rose yesterday to ask a question, which arose in my own mind. When I asked the question, I thought the meaning of my interrogation was obvious: The fate of this question and America may depend on this: Have they said, we the States? Have they made a proposal of a compact between States? If they had, this would be a confederation: It is otherwise most clearly a consolidated government. The question turns, Sir, on that poor little thing—the expression, *We, the people,* instead of the States of America. I need not take much pains to show, that the principles of this system, are extremely pernicious, impolitic, and dangerous. Is this a Monarchy, like England—a compact between Prince and people; with checks on the former, to secure the liberty of the latter? Is this a Confederacy, like Holland—an association of a number of independent States, each of which retain its individual sovereignty? It is not a democracy, wherein the people retain all their rights securely. Had these principles been adhered to, we should not have been brought to this alarming transition, from a Confederacy to a consolidated Government. We have no detail of those great considerations which, in my opinion, ought to have abounded before we should recur to a government of this kind. Here is a revolution as radical as that which separated us from Great Britain. It is as radical, if in this transition our rights and privileges are endangered, and the sovereignty of the States be relinquished: And cannot we plainly see, that this is actually the case? The rights of conscience, trial by jury, liberty of the press, all your immunities and franchises, all pretensions to human rights and privileges, are rendered insecure, if not lost, by this change so loudly talked of by some, and inconsiderately by others. Is this same relinquishment of rights worthy of freemen? Is it worthy of that manly fortitude that ought to characterize republicans: It is said eight States have adopted this plan. I declare that if twelve States and an half had adopted it, I would with manly firmness, and in spite of an erring world, reject it. You are not to inquire how your trade may be increased, nor how you are to become a great and powerful people, but how your liberties can be secured; for liberty ought to be the direct end of your Government. Having premised these things, I shall, with the aid of my judgment and information, which I confess are not extensive, go into the discussion of this system more minutely. Is it necessary for your liberty, that you should abandon those great rights by the adoption of this system? Is the relinquishment of the trial by jury, and the liberty of the press, necessary for your liberty? Will the abandonment of your most sacred rights tend to the security of your liberty? Liberty, the greatest of all earthly blessings—give us that precious jewel, and you may take every thing else: But I am fearful I have lived long enough to become an old fashioned fellow: Perhaps an invincible attachment to the dearest rights of man, may, in these refined enlightened days, be deemed *old fashioned:* If so, I am contended to be so: I say, the time has been, when every pore of my heart beat for American liberty, and which, I believe, had a counterpart in the breast of every true American: But suspicions have gone forth—suspicions of my integrity—publicly reported that my professions are not real—23 years ago was I supposed a traitor to my country; I was then said to be a bane of sedition, because I supported the rights of my country: I may be thought suspicious when I say our privileges and rights are in danger: But, Sir, a number of the people of this country are weak enough to think these things are too true: I am happy to find that the Honorable Gentleman on the other side, declares they are groundless: But, Sir, suspicion is a virtue, as long as its object is the preservation of the public good, and as long as it stays within proper bounds: Should it fall on me, I am contented: Conscious rectitude is a powerful consolation: I trust, there are many who think my professions for the public good to be real. Let your suspicion look to both sides: There are many on the other side, who, possibly may have been persuaded of the necessity of these measures, which I conceive to be dangerous to your liberty. Guard with jealous attention the public liberty. Suspect every one who approaches that jewel. Unfortunately, nothing will preserve it, but downright force: Whenever you give up that force, you are inevitably ruined. I am answered by Gentlemen, that though I might speak of terrors, yet the fact was, that we were surrounded by none of the dangers apprehended. I conceive this new Government to be one of those dangers: It has produced those horrors, which distress many of our best citizens. We are come hither to preserve the poor Commonwealth of Virginia, if it can be possibly done: Something must be done to preserve your liberty and mine: The Confederation; this same despised Government, merits, in my opinion, the highest encomium: It carried us through a long and dangerous war: It rendered us victorious in that bloody conflict with a powerful nation: It has secured us a territory greater than any European Monarch possesses: And shall a Government which has been thus strong and vigorous, be accused of imbecility and abandoned for want of energy? Consider what you are about to do before you part with this Government. Take longer time in reckoning things: Revolutions like this have happened in almost every country in Europe: Similar examples are to be found in ancient Greece and ancient Rome: Instances of the people losing their liberty by their own carelessness and the ambition of a few. We are cautioned by the Honorable Gentleman who presides, against faction and turbulence: I acknowledge that licentiousness is dangerous, and that it ought to be provided against: I acknowledge also the new form of Government may effectually prevent it: Yet, there is another thing it will as effectually do: it will oppress and ruin the people. There are sufficient guards placed against sedition and licentiousness: For when power is given to this Government to suppress these, or, for any other purpose, the language it assumes is clear, express, and unequivocal, but when this Constitution speaks of privileges, there is an ambiguity, Sir, a fatal ambiguity;—an ambiguity which is very astonishing: In the clause under consideration, there is the strangest that I can conceive, I mean, when it says, that there shall not be more Representatives, than one for every 30,000. Now, Sir, how easy is it to evade this privilege? "The number shall not exceed one for every 30,000." This may be satisfied by one Representative from each State. Let our numbers be ever so great, this immence continent, may, by this artful expression, be reduced to have but 13 Representatives: I confess this construction is not natural; but the ambiguity of the expression lays a good ground for a quarrel. Why was it not clearly and unequivocally expressed, that they *should* be entitled, to have one for every 30,000? This would have obviated all disputes; and was this difficult to be done? What is the inference? When population increases, and a State shall send Representatives in this proportion, Congress *may* remand them, because the right of having one for every 30,000 is not clearly expressed: this possibility of reducing the number to one for each State, approximates to probability by that other expression, "but each State shall at least have one Representative." Now is it not clear that from the first expression, the number might be reduced so much, that some States should have no Representative at all, were it not for the insertion of this last expression?

And as this is the only restriction upon them, we may fairly conclude that they *may* restrain the number to one from each State: Perhaps the same horrors may hang over my mind again. I shall be told I am continually afraid: But, Sir, I have strong cause of apprehension: In some parts of the plan before you, the great rights of freemen are endangered, in other parts absolutely taken away. How does your trial by jury stand? In civil cases gone—not sufficiently secured in criminal—this best privilege is gone: But we are told that we need not fear, because those in power being our Representatives, will not abuse the powers we put in their hands: I am not well versed in history, but I will submit to your recollection, whether liberty has been destroyed most often by the licentiousness of the people, or by the tyranny of rulers? I imagine, Sir, you will find the balance on the side of tyranny: Happy will you be if you miss the fate of those nations, who, omitting to resist their oppressors, or negligently suffering their liberty to be wrested from them, have groaned under intolerable despotism. Most of the human race are now in this deplorable condition: And those nations who have gone in search of grandeur, power and splendor, have also fallen a sacrifice, and been the victims of their own folly: While they acquired those visionary blessings, they lost their freedom. My great objection to this Government is, that it does not leave us the means of defending our rights; or, of waging war against tyrants: It is urged by some Gentlemen, that this new plan will bring us an acquisition of strength, an army, and the militia of the States: This is an idea extremely ridiculous: Gentlemen cannot be in earnest. This acquisition will trample on your fallen liberty: Let my beloved Americans guard against that fatal lethargy that has pervaded the universe: Have we the means of resisting disciplined armies, when our only defence, the militia is put into the hands of Congress? The Honorable Gentleman said, that great danger would ensue if the Convention rose without adopting this system: I ask, where is that danger? I see none: Other Gentlemen have told us within these walls, that the Union is gone—or, that the Union will be gone: Is not this trifling with the judgment of their fellow-citizens? Till they tell us the ground of their fears, I will consider them as imaginary: I rose to make enquiry where those dangers were; they could make no answer: I believe I never shall have that answer: Is there a disposition in the people of this country to revolt against the dominion of laws? Has there been a single tumult in Virginia? Have not the people of Virginia, when labouring under the severest pressure of accumulated distresses, manifested the most cordial acquiescence in the execution of the laws? What could be more awful than their unanimous acquiescence under general distresses? Is there any revolution in Virginia? Whither is the spirit of America gone? Whither is the genius of America fled? It was but yesterday, when our enemies marched in triumph through our country: Yet the people of this country could not be appalled by their pompous armaments: They stopped their career, and victoriously captured them: Where is the peril now compared to that? Some minds are agitated by foreign alarms: Happily for us, there is no real danger from Europe: that country is engaged in more arduous business; from that quarter there is no cause of fear: You may sleep in safety forever for them. Where is the danger? If, Sir, there was any, I would recur to the American spirit to defend us;—that spirit which has enabled us to surmount the greatest difficulties: To that illustrious spirit I address my most fervent prayer, to prevent our adopting a system destructive to liberty. Let not Gentlemen be told, that it is not safe to reject this Government. Wherefore is it not safe? We are told there are dangers; but those dangers are ideal; they cannot be demonstrated: To encourage us to adopt it, they tell us, that there is a plain easy way of getting amendments: When I come to contemplate this part, I suppose that I am mad, or, that my countrymen are so: The way to amendment, is, in my conception, shut. Let us consider this plain easy way: "The Congress, whenever two-thirds of both Houses shall deem it necessary, shall propose amendments to this Constitution, or, on the application of the Legislatures of two-thirds of the several States, shall call a Convention for proposing amendments, which, in either case, shall be valid to all intents and purposes, as part of this Constitution, when ratified by the Legislatures of three-fourths of the several States, or by Conventions in three-fourths thereof, as the one or the other mode of ratification may be proposed by the Congress.

Provided, that no amendment which may be made prior to the year 1808, shall in any manner affect the first and fourth clauses in the ninth section of the first article; and that no State, without its consent, shall be deprived of its equal suffrage in the Senate." Hence it appears that three-fourths of the States must ultimately agree to any amendments that may be necessary. Let us consider the consequences of this: However uncharitable it may appear, yet I must tell my opinion, that the most unworthy characters may get into power and prevent the introduction of amendments: Let us suppose (for the case is supposeable, possible, and probable) that you happen to deal these powers to unworthy hands; will they relinquish powers already in their possession, or, agree to amendments? Two-thirds of the Congress, or, of the State Legislatures, are necessary even to propose amendments: If one-third of these be unworthy men, they may prevent the application for amendments; but what is destructive and mischievous is, that three-fourths of the State Legislatures, or of State Conventions, must concur in the amendments when proposed: In such numerous bodies, there must necessarily be some designing bad men: To suppose that so large a number as three-fourths of the States will concur, is to suppose that they will possess genius, intelligence, and integrity, approaching to miraculous. It would indeed be miraculous that they should concur in the same amendments, or, even in such as would bear some likeness to one another. For four of the smallest States, that do not collectively contain one-tenth part of the population of the United States, may obstruct the most salutary and necessary amendments: Nay, in these four States, six tenths of the people may reject these amendments; and suppose, that amendments shall be opposed to amendments (which is highly probable) is it possible, that three-fourths can ever agree to the same amendments? A bare majority in these four small States may hinder the adoption of amendments; so that we may fairly and justly conclude, that one-twentieth part of the American people, may prevent the removal of the most grievous inconveniences and oppression, by refusing to accede to amendments. A trifling minority may reject the most salutary amendments. Is this an easy mode of securing the public liberty? It is, Sir, a most fearful situation, when the most contemptible minority can prevent the alteration of the most oppressive Government; for it may in many respects prove to be such: Is this the spirit of republicanism? What, Sir, is the genius of democracy? Let me read that clause of the Bill of Rights of Virginia, which relates to this: third clause. "That Government is or ought to be instituted for the common benefit, protection, and security of the people, nation, or community: Of all the various modes and forms of Government, that is best which is capable of producing the greatest degree of happiness and safety, and is most effectually secured against the danger of mal-administration, and *that whenever any Government shall be found inadequate, or contrary to these purposes, a majority of the community hath, an undubitable, unalienable and indefeasible right to reform, alter, or abolish it, in such manner as shall be judged most conducive to the public weal.*" This, Sir, is the language of democracy; that a majority of the community have a right to alter their Government when found to be oppressive: But how different is the genius of your new Constitution from this? How different from the sentiments of freemen, that a contemptible minority can prevent the good of the majority? If then Gentlemen standing on this ground, are come to that point, that they are willing to bind themselves and their posterity to be oppressed, I am amazed and inexpressibly astonished. If this be the opinion of the majority, I must submit; but to me, Sir, it appears perilous and destructive: I cannot help thinking so: Perhaps it may be the result of my age; these may be feelings natural to a man of my years, when the American spirit has left him, and his mental powers, like the members of the body, are decayed. If, Sir, amendments are left to the twentieth or the tenth part of the people of America, your liberty is gone forever. We have heard that there is a great deal of bribery practiced in the House of Commons in England; and that many of the members raised themselves to preferments, by selling the rights of the people: But, Sir, the tenth part of that body cannot continue oppressions on the rest of the people. English liberty is in this case, on a firmer foundation than American liberty. It will be easily contrived to procure the opposition of one tenth of the people to any alteration, however judicious. The Honorable

Gentleman who presides, told us, that to prevent abuses in our Government, we will assemble in Convention, recall our delegated powers, and punish our servants for abusing the trust reposed in them. Oh, Sir, we should have fine times indeed, if to punish tyrants, it were only sufficient to assemble the people. Your arms wherewith you could defend yourselves, are gone; and have no longer a aristocratical; no longer democratical spirit. Did you ever read of any revolution in any nation, brought about by the punishment of those in power, inflicted by those who had no power at all? You read of a riot act in a country which is called one of the freest in the world, where a few neighbours cannot assemble without the risk of being shot by a hired soldiery, the engines of despotism. We may see such an act in America. A standing army we shall have also, to execute the execrable commands of tyranny: And how are you to punish them? Will you order them to be punished? Who shall obey these orders? Will your Mace-bearer be a match for a disciplined regiment? In what situation are we to be? The clause before you gives a power of direct taxation, unbounded and unlimitted: Exclusive power of Legislation in all cases whatsoever, for ten miles square; and over all places purchased for the erection of forts, magazines, arsenals, dock-yards, etc. What resistance could be made? The attempt would be madness. You will find all the strength of this country in the hands of your enemies: Those garrisons will naturally be the strongest places in the country. Your militia is given up to Congress also in another part of this plan: They will therefore act as they think proper: All power will be in their own possession: You cannot force them to receive their punishment: Of what service would militia be to you, when most probably you will not have a single musket in the State; for as arms are to be provided by Congress, they may or may not furnish them. Let me here call your attention to that part which gives the Congress power, "To provide for organizing, arming, and disciplining the militia, and for governing such part of them as may be employed in the service of the United States, reserving to the States respectively, the appointment of the officers, and the authority of training the militia, according to the discipline prescribed by Congress." By this, Sir, you see that their

control over our last and best defence, is unlimitted. If they neglect or refuse to discipline or arm our militia, they will be useless: The States can do neither, this power being exclusively
given to Congress: The power of appointing officers over men
not disciplined or armed, is ridiculous: So that this pretended
little remains of power left to the States, may, at the pleasure of
Congress, be rendered nugatory. Our situation will be deplorable indeed: Nor can we ever expect to get this government
amended, since I have already shewn, that a very small minority
may prevent it; and that small minority interested in the continuance of the oppression: Will the oppressor let go the oppressed? Was there ever an instance? Can the annals of mankind
exhibit one single example, where rulers overcharged with
power, willingly let go the oppressed, though solicited and requested most earnestly? The application for amendments will
therefore be fruitless. Sometimes the oppressed have got loose
by one of those bloody struggles that desolate a country. A willing relinquishment of power is one of those things which human
nature never was, nor ever will be capable of: The Honorable
Gentleman's observations respecting the people's right of being
the agents in the formation of this Government, are not accurate
in my humble conception. The distinction between a National
Government and a Confederacy is not sufficiently discerned.
Had the delegates who were sent to Philadelphia a power to
propose a Consolidated Government instead of a Confederacy?
Were they not deputed by States, and not by the people? The
assent of the people in their collective capacity is not necessary
to the formation of a Federal Government. The people have no
right to enter into leagues, alliances, or confederations: They are
not the proper agents for this purpose: States and sovereign powers are the only proper agents for this kind of Government: Shew
me an instance where the people have exercised this business:
Has it not always gone through the Legislatures? I refer you to
the treaties with France, Holland, and other nations: How were
they made? Were they not made by the States? Are the people
therefore in their aggregate capacity, the proper persons to form
a Confederacy? This, therefore, ought to depend on the consent
of the Legislatures; the people having never sent delegates to

make any proposition of changing the Government. Yet I must say, at the same time, that it was made on grounds the most pure, and perhaps I might have been brought to consent to it so far as to the change of Government; but there is one thing in it which I never would acquiesce in. I mean the changing it into a Consolidated Government; which is so abhorent to my mind. The Honorable Gentleman then went on to the figure we make with foreign nations; the contemptible one we make in France and Holland; which, according to the system of my notes, he attributes to the present feeble Government. An opinion has gone forth, we find, that we are a contemptible people: The time has been when we were thought otherwise: Under this same despised Government, we commanded the respect of all Europe: Wherefore are we now reckoned otherwise? The American spirit has fled from hence: It has gone to regions, where it has never been expected: It has gone to the people of France in search of a splendid Government—a strong energetic Government. Shall we imitate the example of those nations who have gone from a simple to a splendid Government? Are those nations more worthy of our imitation? What can make an adequate satisfaction to them for the loss they suffered in attaining such a Government for the loss of their liberty? If we admit this Consolidated Government it will be because we like a great splendid one. Some way or other we must be a great and mighty empire; we must have an army, and a navy, and a number of things: When the American spirit was in its youth, the language of America was different: Liberty, Sir, was then the primary object. We are descended from a people whose Government was founded on liberty: Our glorious forefathers of Great-Britain, made liberty the foundation of every thing. That country is become a great, mighty, and splendid nation; not because their Government is strong and energetic; but, Sir, because liberty is its direct end and foundation: We drew the spirit of liberty from our British ancestors; by that spirit we have triumphed over every difficulty: But now, Sir, the American spirit, assisted by the ropes and chains of consolidation, is about to convert this country to a powerful and mighty empire: If you make the citizens of this country agree to become the subjects of one great consolidated

empire of America, your Government will not have sufficent
energy to keep them together: Such a Government is incompatible with the genius of republicanism: There will be no checks,
no real balances, in this Government: What can avail your specious imaginary balances, your rope-dancing, chain-rattling,
ridiculous ideal checks and contrivances? But, Sir, we are not
feared by foreigners: we do not make nations tremble: Would
this, Sir, constitute happiness, or secure liberty? I trust, Sir, our
political hemisphere will ever direct their operations to the security of those objects. Consider our situation, Sir: Go to the
poor man, ask him what he does; he will inform you, that he
enjoys the fruits of his labour, under his own fig-tree, with his
wife and children around him, in peace and security. Go to every
other member of the society, you will find the same tranquil ease
and content; you will find no alarms or disturbances: Why then
tell us of dangers to terrify us into an adoption of this new Government? And yet who knows the dangers that this new system
may produce; they are out of the sight of the common people:
They cannot foresee latent consequences: I dread the operation
of it on the middling and lower class of people: It is for them I
fear the adoption of this system. I fear I tire the patience of the
Committee, but I beg to be indulged with a few more observations: When I thus profess myself an advocate for the liberty of
the people, I shall be told, I am a designing man, that I am to be
a great man, that I am to be a demagogue; and many similar illiberal insinuations will be thrown out; but, Sir, conscious rectitude, out-weighs these things with me: I see great jeopardy in
this new Government. I see none from our present one: I hope
some Gentleman or other will bring forth, in full array, those
dangers, if there be any, that we may see and touch them.

7 June

I have thought, and still think, that a full investigation of the
actual situation of America, ought to precede any decision on
this great and important question. That Government is no more
than a choice among evils, is acknowledged by the most intel-

ligent among mankind, and has been a standing maxim for ages. If it be demonstrated that the adoption of the new plan is a little or a trifling evil, then, Sir, I acknowledge that adoption ought to follow: But, Sir, if this be a truth that its adoption may entail misery on the free people of this country, I then insist, that rejection ought to follow. Gentlemen strongly urge its adoption will be a mighty benefit to us: But, Sir, I am made of such incredulous materials that assertions and declarations, do not satisfy me. I must be convinced, Sir. I shall retain my infidelity on that subject, till I see our liberties secured in a manner perfectly satisfactory to my understanding. . . .

You are told [by Governor Randolph] there is no peace, although you fondly flatter yourselves that all is peace—No peace—a general cry and alarm in the country—Commerce, riches, and wealth vanished—Citizens going to seek comforts in other parts of the world—Laws insulted—Many instances of tyrannical legislation. These things, Sir, are new to me. He has made the discovery—As to the administration of justice, I believe that failures in commerce, etc. cannot be attributed to it. My age enables me to recollect its progress under the old Government. I can justify it by saying, that it continues in the same manner in this State, as it did under former Government. As to other parts of the Continent, I refer that to other Gentlemen. As to the ability of those who administer it, I believe they would not suffer by a comparison with those who administered it under the royal authority. Where is the cause of complaint if the wealthy go away? Is this added to the other circumstances, of such enormity, and does it bring such danger over this Commonwealth as to warrant so important, and so awful a change in so precipitate a manner? As to insults offered to the laws, I know of none. In this respect I believe this Commonwealth would not suffer by a comparison with the former Government. The laws are as well executed, and as patiently acquiesced in, as they were under the royal administration. Compare the situation of the country— Compare that of our citizens to what they were then, and decide whether persons and property are not as safe and secure as they were at that time. Is there a man in this Commonwealth, whose person can be insulted with impunity? Cannot redress be had here for personal insults or injuries, as well as in any part of the world—as well as in those countries where Aristocrats and Monarchs triumph and reign? Is not the protection of property in full operation here? The contrary cannot with truth be charged on this Commonwealth. Those severe charges which are exhibited against it, appear to me totally groundless. On a fair investigation, we shall be found to be surrounded by no real dangers. We have the animating fortitude and persevering alacrity of republican men, to carry us through misfortunes and calamities. 'Tis the fortune of a republic to be able to withstand the stormy ocean of human vicissitudes. I know of no danger awaiting us. Public and private security are to be found here in the highest degree. Sir, it is the fortune of a free people, not to be intimidated by imaginary dangers. Fear is the passion of slaves. Our political and natural hemisphere are now equally tranquil. Let us recollect the awful magnitude of the subject of our deliberation. Let us consider the latent consequences of an erroneous decision—and let not our minds be led away by unfair misrepresentations and uncandid suggestions. There have been many instances of uncommon lenity and temperance used in the exercise of power in this Commonwealth. I could call your recollection to many that happened during the war and since—But every Gentleman here must be apprized of them.

. . . I have said that I thought this a Consolidated Government: I will now prove it. Will the great rights of the people be secured by this Government? Suppose it should prove oppressive, how can it be altered? Our Bill of Rights declares, "That a majority of the community hath an *undubitable, unalienable,* and *indefeasible right* to reform, alter, or abolish it, in such manner as shall be judged most conducive to the public weal." I have just proved that one tenth, or less, of the people of America, a most despicable minority may prevent this reform or alteration. Suppose the people of Virginia should wish to alter their Government, can a majority of them do it? No, because they are connected with other men; or, in other words, consolidated with other States: When the people of Virginia at a future day shall wish to alter their Government, though they should be unanimous in this desire, yet they may be prevented therefrom by a despicable minority at the extremity of the United States: The founders of your own Constitution made your Government changeable: But the power of changing it is gone from you! Whither is it gone? It is placed in the same hands that hold the rights of twelve other States; and those who hold those rights, have right and power to keep them: It is not the particular Government of Virginia: One of the leading features of that Government is, that a majority can alter it, when necessary for the public good. This Government is not a Virginian but an American Government. Is it not therefore a Consolidated Government? The sixth clause of your Bill of Rights tells you, "That elections of members to serve as Representatives of the people in Assembly, ought to be free, and that all men having sufficient evidence of permanent common interest with, and attachment to the community, have the right of suffrage, and *cannot be taxed* or *deprived* of *their property* for public uses, without their own consent, or that of their Representatives so elected, nor bound by any law to which they have not in like manner assented for the public good." But what does this Constitution say? The clause under consideration gives an unlimited and unbounded power of taxation: Suppose every delegate from Virginia opposes a law laying a tax, what will it avail? They are opposed by a majority: Eleven members can destroy their efforts: Those feeble ten cannot prevent the passing the most oppressive tax law. So that in direct opposition to the spirit and express language of your Declaration of Rights, you are taxed not by your own consent, but by people who have no connection with you. The next clause of the Bill of Rights tells you, "That all power of suspending law, or the execution of laws, by any authority without the consent of the Representatives of the people, is injurious to their rights, and ought not to be exercised." This tells us that there can be no suspension of Government, or laws without our own consent: Yet this Constitution can counteract and suspend any of our laws, that contravene its oppressive operation; for they have the power of direct taxation; which suspends our Bill of Rights; and it is expressly provided, that they can make all laws necessary for carrying their powers into execution; and it is declared paramount to the laws and constitutions of the States. Consider how the only remaining defence we have left is destroyed in this manner: Besides the expences of maintaining the Senate and other House in as much splendor as they please, there is to be a great and mighty President, with very extensive powers; the powers of a King: He is to be supported in extravagant magnificence: So that the whole of our property may be taken by this American Government, by laying what taxes they please, giving themselves what salaries they please, and suspending our laws at their pleasure: I might be thought too inquisitive, but I believe I should take up but very little of your time in enumerating the little power that is left to the Government of Virginia; for this power is reduced to little or nothing: Their garrisons, magazines, arsenals, and forts, which will be situated in the strongest places within the States: Their ten miles square, with all the fine ornaments of human life, added to their powers, and taken from the States, will reduce the power of the latter to nothing. The voice of tradition, I trust, will inform posterity of our struggles for freedom: If our descendants be worthy the name of Americans, they will preserve and hand down to their latest posterity, the transactions of the present times; and though, I confess, my exclamations are not worthy the hearing, they will see that I have done my utmost to preserve their liberty: For I never will give up the power of direct taxation, but for a scourge: I am willing to give it conditionally; that is, after non-compliance with requisitions: I will do more, Sir, and what I hope will convince the most sceptical man, that I am a lover of the American Union, that in case Virginia shall not make punctual payment, the control of our custom houses, and the whole regulation of trade, shall be given to Congress, and that Virginia shall depend on Congress even for passports, till Virginia shall have paid the last farthing; and furnished the last soldier: Nay, Sir, there is another alternative to which I would consent: Even that they should strike us out of the Union, and take away from us all federal privileges till we comply with federal requisitions; but let it depend upon our own pleasure to pay our money in the most easy manner for our people. Were all the States, more terrible than the mother country, to join against us, I hope Virginia could defend herself; but, Sir, the dissolution of the Union is most abhorrent to my mind: The first thing I have at heart is American *liberty;* the second thing is American Union; and I hope the people of Virginia will endeavor to preserve that Union: The increasing population of the southern States, is far greater than that of New England: Consequently, in a short time, they will be far more numerous than the people of that country: Consider this, and you will find this State more particularly interested to support American liberty, and not bind our posterity by an improvident relinquishment of our rights. I would give the best security for a punctual compliance with requisitions; but I beseech Gentlemen, at all hazards, not to give up this unlimited power of taxation: The Honorable Gentleman has told us these powers given to Congress, are accompanied by a Judiciary which will connect all: On examination you will find this very Judiciary oppressively constructed; your jury trial destroyed, and the Judges dependent on Congress. In this scheme of energetic Government, the people will find two sets of tax-gatherers—the State and the Federal Sheriffs. This it seems to me will produce such dreadful oppression, as the people cannot possibly bear: The Federal Sheriff may commit what oppression, make what distresses he pleases, and ruin you with impunity: For how are you to tie his hands? Have you any sufficient decided means of preventing him from sucking your blood by speculations, commissions and fees? Thus thousands of your people will be most shamefully robbed: Our State Sheriffs, those unfeeling blood-suckers, have, under the watchful eye of our Legislature, committed the most horrid and barbarous ravages on our people: It has required the most constant vigilance of the Legislature to keep them from totally ruining the people: A repeated succession of laws has been made to suppress their inequitous speculations and cruel extortions; and as often have their nefarious ingenuity devised methods of evading the force of those laws: In the struggle they have generally triumphed over the Legislature. It is fact that lands have sold for five shillings, which were worth one hundred pounds: If Sheriffs thus immediately under the eye of our State Legislature and Judiciary, have dared to commit these outrages, what would they not have done if their masters had been at Philadelphia or New

York? If they perpetrate the most unwarrantable outrage on your persons or property, you cannot get redress on this side of Philadelphia or New York: and how can you get it there? If your domestic avocations could permit you to go thither, there you must appeal to Judges sworn to support this Constitution, in opposition to that of any State, and who may also be inclined to favor their own officers: When these harpies are aided by excise men, who may search at any time your houses and most secret recesses, will the people bear it? If you think so you differ from me: Where I thought there was a possibility of such mischiefs, I would grant power with a niggardly hand; and here there is strong probability that these oppressions shall actually happen. I may be told, that it is safe to err on that side; because such regulations *may* be made by Congress, as shall restrain these officers, and because laws are made by our Representatives, and judged by righteous Judges: But, Sir, as these regulations may be made, so they may not; and many reasons there are to induce a belief that they will not: I shall therefore be an infidel on that point till the day of my death.

This Constitution is said to have beautiful features; but when I come to examine these features, Sir, they appear to me horridly frightful: Among other deformities, it has an awful squinting; it squints towards monarchy: And does not this raise indignation in the breast of every American? Your President may easily become King: Your Senate is so imperfectly constructed that your dearest rights may be sacrificed by what may be a small minority; and a very small minority may continue forever unchangeably this Government, although horridly defective: Where are your checks in this Government? Your strong holds will be in the hands of your enemies: It is on a supposition that our American Governors shall be honest, that all the good qualities of this Government are founded: But its defective, and imperfect construction, puts it in their power to perpetrate the worst of mischiefs, should they be bad men: And, Sir, would not all the world, from the Eastern to the Western hemisphere, blame our distracted folly in resting our rights upon the contingency of our rulers being good or bad. Shew me that age and country where the rights and liberties of the people were placed on the sole chance of their rulers being good men, without a consequent loss of liberty? I say that the loss of that dearest privilege has ever followed with absolute certainty, every such mad attempt. If your American chief, be a man of ambition, and abilities, how easy is it for him to render himself absolute: The army is in his hands, and, if he be a man of address, it will be attached to him; and it will be the subject of long meditation with him to seize the first auspicious moment to accomplish his design; and, Sir, will the American spirit solely relieve you when this happens? I would rather infinitely, and I am sure most of this Convention are of the same opinion, have a King, Lords, and Commons, than a Government so replete with such insupportable evils. If we make a King, we may prescribe the rules by which he shall rule his people, and interpose such checks as shall prevent him from infringing them: But the President, in the field, at the head of his army, can prescribe the terms on which he shall reign master, so far that it will puzzle any American ever to get his neck from under the galling yoke. I cannot with patience, think of this idea. If ever he violates the laws, one of two things will happen: He shall come to the head of his army to carry every thing before him; or, he will give bail, or do what Mr. Chief Justice will order him. If he be guilty, will not the recollection of his crimes teach him to make one bold push for the American throne? Will not the immense difference between being master of every thing, and being ignominiously tried and punished, powerfully excite him to make this bold push? But, Sir, where is the existing force to punish him? Can he not at the head of his army beat down every opposition? Away with your President, we shall have a King: The army will salute him Monarch; your militia will leave you and assist in making him King, and fight against you: And what have you to oppose this force? What will then become of you and your rights? Will not absolute despotism ensue? [Here Mr. Henry strongly and pathetically expatiated on the probability of the president's enslaving America and the horrible consequences that must result.]

What can be more defective than the clause concerning the elections?—The control given to Congress over the time, place, and manner of holding elections, will totally destroy the end of suffrage. The elections may be held at one place, and the most inconvenient in the State; or they may be at remote distances from those who have a right of suffrage: Hence nine out of ten must either not vote at all, or vote for strangers: For the most influential characters will be applied to, to know who are the most proper to be chosen. I repeat that the control of Congress over the *manner,* etc. of electing, well warrants this idea. The natural consequence will be, that this democratic branch, will possess none of the public confidence: The people will be prejudiced against Representatives chosen in such an injudicious manner. The proceedings in the northern conclave will be hidden from the yeomanry of this country: We are told that the yeas and nays shall be taken and entered on the journals: This, Sir, will avail nothing: It may be locked up in their chests, and concealed forever from the people; for they are not to publish what parts they think require secrecy: They *may* think, and *will think,* the whole requires it. Another beautiful feature of this Constitution is the publication from time to time of the receipts and expenditures of the public money. This expression, from time to time, is very indefinite and indeterminate: It may extend to a century. Grant that any of them are wicked, they may squander the public money so as to ruin you, and yet this expression will give you no redress. I say, they may ruin you;—for where, Sir, is the responsibility? The yeas and nays will shew you nothing, unless they be fools as well as knaves: For after having wickedly trampled on the rights of the people, they would act like fools indeed, were they to publish and devulge their iniquity, when they have it equally in their power to suppress and conceal it.— Where is the responsibility—that leading principle in the British government? In that government a punishment, certain and inevitable, is provided: But in this, there is no real actual punishment for the grossest maladministration. They may go without punishment, though they commit the most outrageous violation on our immunities. That paper may tell me they will be punished. I ask, by what law? They must make the law—for there is no existing law to do it. What—will they make a law to punish themselves? This, Sir, is my great objection to the Constitution, that there is no true responsibility—and that the preservation of our liberty depends on the single chance of men being virtuous enough to make laws to punish themselves. In the country from which we are descended, they have real, and not imaginary, responsibility—for there, maladministration has cost their heads, to some of the most saucy geniuses that ever were. The Senate, by making treaties may destroy your liberty and laws for want of responsibility. Two-thirds of those that shall happen to be present, can, with the President, make treaties, that shall be the supreme law of the land: They may make the most ruinous treaties; and yet there is no punishment for them. Whoever shows me a punishment provided for them, will oblige me. So, Sir, notwithstanding there are eight pillars, they want another. Where will they make another? I trust, Sir, the exclusion of the evils wherewith this system is replete, in its present form, will be made a condition, precedent to its adoption, by this or any other State. The transition from a general unqualified admission to offices, to a consolidation of government, seems easy; for though the American States are dissimilar in their structure, this will assimilate them: this, Sir, is itself a strong consolidating feature, and is not one of the least dangerous in that system. Nine States are sufficient to establish this government over those nine: Imagine that nine have come into it. Virginia has certain scruples. Suppose she will consequently, refuse to join with those States:—May not they still continue in friendship and union with her? If she sends her annual requisitions in dollars, do you think their stomachs will be so squeamish that they will refuse her dollars? Will they not accept her regiments? They would intimidate you into an inconsiderate adoption, and frighten you with ideal evils, and that the Union shall be dissolved. 'Tis a bugbear, Sir:—The fact is, Sir, that the eight adopting States can hardly stand on their own legs. Public fame tells us, that the adopting States have already heart-burnings and animosity, and repent their precipitate hurry: This, Sir, may occasion exceeding great mischief. When I reflect on these and many other circumstances, I must think those States will be fond to be in confederacy with us. If we pay our quota of money annually, and furnish our rateable number of men, when necessary, I can see no danger from a rejection. . . .

Amendments Proposed
by the Anti-federalists

As the debate over the new Constitution progressed, anti-federalist objections to the powers granted the federal government began to crystallize in specific proposals for amendments that would limit those powers. In some state conventions, especially where sentiment was closely divided, proposals were made for amendments to be insisted upon prior to ratification, while others were offered in hopes that a second convention might consider them for inclusion in a revised constitution. The Massachusetts convention, which narrowly ratified the Constitution in February 1788, proposed a relatively short list of amendments, while Virginia in June 1788 put forth a much longer list, in large measure duplicated by the North Carolina and New York conventions later in the year. Some of the proposals were similar to those later included in the federal Bill of Rights and thus were matters largely agreed to by both sides, while other amendments would have greatly altered the powers of the new government. The proposals, widely reprinted and circulated in 1788, are reprinted here from Documentary History of the Constitution *(Washington, DC, 1894), pp. 93–96, and from Jonathan Elliot, ed.,* The Debates of the Several State Conventions . . . *(5 vols., Philadelphia, 2nd ed., 1896), III, pp. 657–663. A further, even more radical list of amendments was proposed by a Rhode Island convention on March 6, 1790, before that state ratified the Constitution. Some of these proposed amendments are reprinted here from an original broadside at the John Carter Brown Library, with the kind permission of the library.*

Amendments Proposed by the Massachusetts Convention (February 7, 1788)

. . . As it is the opinion of this Convention that certain amendments and alterations in the said constitution would remove the *fears* and quiet the apprehensions of many of the good people of this Commonwealth and more effectually guard against an undue administration of the Federal Government, The Convention do therefore recommend that the following alterations and provisions be introduced into the said Constitution.

First, That it be explicitly declared that all Powers not expressly delegated by the aforesaid Constitution are reserved to the several States to be by them exercised.

Secondly, That there shall be one representative to every thirty thousand persons according to the Census mentioned in the Constitution until the whole number of the Representatives amounts to Two hundred.

Thirdly, That Congress do not exercise the powers vested in them by the fourth Section of the first article, but in cases when a State shall neglect or refuse to make the regulations therein mentioned or shall make regulations subversive of the rights of the People to a free and equal representation in Congress agreeably to the Constitution.

Fourthly, That Congress do not lay direct Taxes but when the Monies arising from the Impost and Excise are insufficient for the public exigencies nor then until Congress shall have first made a requisition upon the States to assess levy and pay their respective proportions of such Requisition agreeably to the Census fixed in the said Constitution; in such way and manner as the Legislature of the States shall think best, and in such case if any State shall neglect or refuse to pay its proportion pursuant to such requisition then Congress may assess and levy such State's proportion together with interest thereon at the rate of Six per cent per annum from the time of payment prescribed in such requisition.

Fifthly, That Congress erect no Company of Merchants with exclusive advantages of commerce.

Sixthly, That no person shall be tried for any Crime by which he may incur an infamous punishment or loss of life until he be first indicted by a Grand Jury, except in such cases as may arise in the Government and regulation of the Land and Naval forces.

Seventhly, The Supreme Judicial Federal Court shall have no jurisdiction of Causes between Citizens of different States unless the matter in dispute whether it concerns the realty or personalty be of the value of Three thousand dollars at the least nor shall the Federal Judicial Powers extend to any actions between Citizens of different States where the matter in dispute whether it concerns the Realty or personalty is not of the value of Fifteen hundred dollars at the least.

Eighthly, In civil actions between Citizens of different States every issue of fact arising in Actions at common law shall be tried by a Jury if the parties or either of them request it.

Ninthly, Congress shall at no time consent that any person holding an office of trust or profit under the United States shall accept of a title of Nobility or any other title or office from any King, prince or Foreign State.

And the Convention do in the name and in behalf of the People of this Commonwealth enjoin it upon their Representatives in Congress at all times until the alterations and provisions aforesaid have been considered agreeably to the Fifth article of the said Constitution to exert all their influence and use all reasonable and legal methods to obtain a ratification of the said alterations and provisions in such manner as is provided in the said Article.

Additions Proposed by the Virginia Convention: A Proposed Bill of Rights (June 27, 1788)

. . . That there be a declaration or bill of rights asserting, and securing from encroachment, the essential and unalienable rights of the people, in some such manner as the following:—

1st. That there are certain natural rights, of which men, when they form a social compact, cannot deprive or divest their posterity; among which are the enjoyment of life and liberty, with the means of acquiring, possessing, and protecting property, and pursuing and obtaining happiness and safety.

2d. That all power is naturally invested in, and consequently derived from, the people; that magistrates therefore are their *trustees* and *agents,* at all times amenable to them.

3d. That government ought to be instituted for the common benefit, protection, and security of the people; and that the doctrine of non-resistance against arbitrary power and oppression is absurd, slavish, and destructive to the good and happiness of mankind.

4th. That no man or set of men are entitled to separate or exclusive public emoluments or privileges from the community, but in consideration of public services, which not being descendible, neither ought the offices of magistrate, legislator, or judge, or any other public office, to be hereditary.

5th. That the legislative, executive, and judicial powers of government should be separate and distinct; and, that the members of the two first may be restrained from oppression by feeling and participating the public burdens, they should, at fixed periods, be reduced to a private station, return into the mass of the people, and the vacancies be supplied by certain and regular elections, in which all or any part of the former members to be eligible or ineligible, as the rules of the Constitution of government, and the laws, shall direct.

6th. That the elections of representatives in the legislature ought to be free and frequent, and all men having sufficient evidence of permanent common interest with, and attachment to, the community, ought to have the right of suffrage; and no aid, charge, tax, or fee, can be set, rated or levied, upon the people without their own consent, or that of their representatives, so elected; nor can they be bound by any law to which they have not, in like manner, assented, for the public good.

7th. That all power of suspending laws, or the execution of laws, by any authority, without the consent of the representatives of the people in the legislature, is injurious to their rights, and ought not to be exercised.

8th. That, in all criminal and capital prosecutions, a man hath a right to demand the cause and nature of his accusation, to be confronted with the accusers and witnesses, to call for evidence, and be allowed counsel in his favor, and to a fair and speedy trial by an impartial jury of his vicinage, without whose unanimous consent he cannot be found guilty (except in the government of the land and naval forces), nor can he be compelled to give evidence against himself.

9th. That no freeman ought to be taken, imprisoned, or disseized of his freehold, liberties, privileges, or franchises, or outlawed, or exiled, or in any manner destroyed or deprived of his life, liberty, or property, but by the law of the land.

10th. That every freeman restrained of his liberty is entitled to a remedy, to inquire into the lawfulness thereof, and to remove the same, if unlawful, and that such remedy ought not to be denied nor delayed.

11th. That, in controversies respecting property, and in suits between man and man, the ancient trial by jury is one of the greatest securities to the rights of the people, and to remain sacred and inviolable.

12th. That every freeman ought to find a certain remedy, by recourse to the laws, for all injuries and wrongs he may receive in his person, property, or character. He ought to obtain right and justice freely, without sale, completely and without denial, promptly and without delay; and that all establishments or regulations contravening these rights are oppressive and unjust.

13th. That excessive bail ought not to be required, nor excessive fines imposed, nor cruel and unusual punishments inflicted.

14th. That every freeman has a right to be secure from all unreasonable searches and seizures of his person, his papers, and property; all warrants, therefore, to search suspected places, or seize any freeman, his papers, or property, without information on oath (or affirmation of a person religiously scrupulous of taking an oath) of legal and sufficient cause, are grievous and oppressive; and all general warrants to search suspected places, or to apprehend any suspected person, without specially naming or describing the place or person, are dangerous, and ought not to be granted.

15th. That the people have a right peaceably to assemble together to consult for the common good, or to instruct their representatives; and that every freeman has a right to petition or apply to the legislature for redress of grievances.

16th. That the people have a right to freedom of speech, and of writing and publishing their sentiments; that the freedom of the press is one of the greatest bulwarks of liberty, and ought not to be violated.

17th. That the people have a right to keep and bear arms; that a well-regulated militia, composed of the body of the people trained to arms, is the proper, natural, and safe defence of a free state; that standing armies, in time of peace, are dangerous to liberty, and therefore ought to be avoided, as far as the circumstances and protection of the community will admit; and that, in all cases, the military should be under strict subordination to, and governed by, the civil power.

18th. That no soldier in time of peace ought to be quartered in any house without the consent of the owner, and in time of war in such manner only as the law directs.

19th. That any person religiously scrupulous of bearing arms ought to be exempted, upon payment of an equivalent to employ another to bear arms in his stead.

20th. That religion, or the duty which we owe to our Creator, and the manner of discharging it, can be directed only by reason and conviction, not by force or violence; and therefore all men have an equal, natural, and unalienable right to the free exercise of religion, according to the dictates of conscience, and that no particular religious sect or society ought to be favored or established, by law, in preference to others.

Amendments to the Constitution
(June 27, 1788)

1st. That each state in the Union shall respectively retain every power, jurisdiction, and right, which is not by this Constitution delegated to the Congress of the United States, or to the departments of the federal government.

2nd. That there shall be one representative for every thirty thousand according to the enumeration or census mentioned in the Constitution, until the whole number of representatives amounts to two hundred: after which, that number shall be continued or increased, as Congress shall direct, upon the principles fixed in the Constitution, by apportioning the representatives of each state to some greater number of people, from time to time, as population increases.

3d. When the Congress shall lay direct taxes or excises, they shall immediately inform the executive power of each state, of the quota of such state, according to the census herein directed, which is proposed to be thereby raised; and if the legislature of any state shall pass a law which shall be effectual for raising such quota at the time required by Congress, the taxes and excises laid by Congress shall not be collected in such state.

4th. That the members of the Senate and House of Representatives shall be ineligible to and incapable of holding, any civil office under the authority of the United States during the time for which they shall respectively be elected.

5th. That the journals of the proceedings of the Senate and House of Representatives shall be published at least once in every year, except such parts thereof, relating to treaties, alliances, or military operations, as, in their judgment, require secrecy.

6th. That a regular statement and account of the receipts and expenditures of public money shall be published at least once a year.

7th. That no commercial treaty shall be ratified without the concurrence of two thirds of the whole number of the members of the Senate; and no treaty ceding, contracting, restraining, or suspending, the territorial rights or claims of the United States, or any of them, or their, or any of their rights or claims to fishing in the American seas, or navigating the American rivers, shall be made, but in cases of the most urgent and extreme necessity; nor shall any such treaty be ratified without the concurrence of three fourths of the whole number of the members of both houses respectively.

8th. That no navigation law, or law regulating commerce, shall be passed without the consent of two thirds of the members present, in both houses.

9th. That no standing army, or regular troops, shall be raised, or kept up, in time of peace, without the consent of two thirds of the members present, in both houses.

10th. That no soldier shall be enlisted for any longer term than four years, except in time of war, and then for no longer term than the continuance of the war.

11th. That each state respectively shall have the power to provide for organizing, arming, and disciplining its own militia, whensoever Congress shall omit or neglect to provide for the same. That the militia shall not be subject to martial law, except when in actual service, in time of war, invasion, or rebellion; and when not in the actual service of the United States, shall be subject only to such fines, penalties, and punishments, as shall be directed or inflicted by the laws of its own state.

12th. That the exclusive power of legislation given to Congress over the federal town and its adjacent district, and other places, purchased or to be purchased by Congress of any of the states, shall extend only to such regulations as respect the police and good government thereof.

13th. That no person shall be capable of being President of the United States for more than eight years in any term of sixteen years.

14th. That the judicial power of the United States shall be

vested in one Supreme Court, and in such courts of admiralty as Congress may from time to time ordain and establish in any of the different states. The judicial power shall extend to all cases in law and equity arising under treaties made, or which shall be made, under the authority of the United States; to all cases affecting ambassadors, other foreign ministers, and consuls; to all cases of admiralty and maritime jurisdiction; to controversies to which the United States shall be a party; to controversies between two or more states, and between parties claiming lands under the grants of different states. In all cases affecting ambassadors, other foreign ministers, and consuls, and those in which a state shall be a party, the Supreme Court shall have original jurisdiction; in all other cases before mentioned, the Supreme Court shall have appellate jurisdiction, as to matters of law only, except in cases of equity, and of admiralty, and maritime jurisdiction, in which the Supreme Court shall have appellate jurisdiction both as to law and fact, with such exceptions and under such regulations as the Congress shall make: but the judicial power of the United States shall extend to no case where the cause of action shall have originated before the ratification of the Constitution, except in disputes between states about their territory, disputes between persons claiming lands under the grants of different states, and suits for debts due to the United States.

15th. That, in criminal prosecutions, no man shall be restrained in the exercise of the usual and accustomed right of challenging or excepting to the jury.

16th. That Congress shall not alter, modify, or interfere in the times, places, or manner of holding elections for senators and representatives, or either of them, except when the legislature of any state shall neglect, refuse, or be disabled, by invasion or rebellion, to prescribe the same.

17th. That those clauses which declare that Congress shall not exercise certain powers, be not interpreted, in any manner whatsoever, to extend the powers of Congress; but that they be construed either as making exceptions to the specified powers where this shall be the case, or otherwise, as inserted merely for greater caution.

18th. That the laws ascertaining the compensation of senators and representatives for their services, be postponed, in their operation, until after the election of representatives immediately succeeding the passing thereof; that excepted which shall first be passed on the subject.

19th. That some tribunal other than the Senate be provided for trying impeachments of senators.

20th. That the salary of a judge shall not be increased or diminished during his continuance in office, otherwise than by general regulations of salary, which may take place on a revision of the subject at stated periods of not less than seven years, to commence from the time such salaries shall be first ascertained by Congress.

Amendments Proposed by the Rhode Island Convention (March 6, 1790)

The most important amendments proposed by the Rhode Island convention were the following seven.

3. That the powers of government may be reassumed by the people, whensoever it shall become necessary to their happiness:— That the rights of the States respectively to nominate and appoint all State officers, and every other power, jurisdiction and right, which is not by the said Constitution clearly delegated to the Congress of the United States, or to the departments of government thereof, remain to the people of the several States, or their respective State governments, to whom they may have granted the same;—and that those clauses in the said Constitution, which declare that Congress shall not have or exercise certain powers, do not imply, that Congress is entitled to any powers not given by the said Constitution;—but such clauses are to be con-

strued, either as exceptions to certain specified powers, or as inserted merely for greater caution.

6. That elections of Representatives in the Legislature ought to be free and frequent—and all men, having sufficient evidence of permanent common interest with and attachment to the community, ought to have the right of suffrage: And no aid, charge, tax or fee, can be set, rated or levied upon the people, without their own consent, or that of their representatives, so elected;—nor can they be bound by any law, to which they have not, in like manner, assented for the public good.

8. In cases of direct taxes, Congress shall first make requisitions on the several States, to assess, levy and pay, their respective proportions of such requisitions, in such way and manner as the Legislatures of the several States shall judge best. And in case any State shall neglect or refuse to pay its proportion, pursuant to such requisition, then Congress may assess and levy such State's proportion, together with interest at the rate of six per cent, per annum, from the time prescribed in such requisition.

12. As standing armies in time of peace are dangerous to liberty and ought not to be kept up, except in cases of necessity; and as at all times the military should be under strict subordination to the civil power—that therefore no standing army, or regular troops, shall be raised or kept up in time of peace.

13. That no monies be borrowed on the credit of the United States, without the assent of two-thirds of the Senators and Representatives present in each House.

14. That the Congress shall not declare war, without the concurrence of two-thirds of the Senators and Representatives present in each House.

17. As a traffic tending to establish or continue the slavery of any part of the human species, is disgraceful to the cause of liberty and humanity—that Congress shall, as soon as may be, promote

and establish such laws and regulations as may effectually prevent the importation of slaves of every description into the United States.

PREVENTING TYRANNY
UNDER THE NEW CONSTITUTION

Explained in Federalist Numbers 9–14, 33, 37–51, 78–85 (Nos. 10, 14, 37, 39, 45, 49, 51, 78, and 84 are most important).

As the anti-federalists pressed their charges that the powers given to the central government under the new Constitution would be tyrannical, the federalists had increasingly to deny any oppressive tendencies in it. Publius undertook, in Numbers 9–14, to invert the argument that large, united nations threatened liberty. On the contrary, he insisted, it was weakness, fragmentation, and pettiness that led to the cycle of quarrels, war, and despotism. Most sophisticatedly, in the to-be-famous Number 10, Publius (Madison) explained how an enlarged republic, by containing a multitude of counteracting factions, actually prevented the dominion (tyranny) of any one. Then, in a long series of articles on the nature of the federal system (Numbers 37–51), Publius showed that the new Constitution was both faithfully republican and faithfully federal; that is, it depended ultimately on the consent of the people, and the states remained in "co-sovereign" existence as counterweights to the central government. Checks and balances among the departments of the central government completed the pattern of limited power preventing tyranny. A concluding set of articles (Numbers 78–85) explaining the judiciary and the legitimate absence of a bill of rights completed Publius' defense of the liberty-preserving nature of the new Constitution.

The documents in this section by "Brutus," "Centinel," "Federal Farmer," and the Pennsylvania Minority are reprinted from The Complete Anti-Federalist *(7 vols.), edited by Herbert J. Storing with the assistance of Murray Dry, and published by the University of Chicago Press (1981): vol. II, pp. 136–143, 223–234, 363–372, 393–400, 413–428, 437–442, and vol. III, pp. 146–165.*

"Centinel," Number I
(October 5, 1787)

The anti-federalists, faced with the elaborated denial that the new Constitution would be tyrannical, moved themselves to a closer analysis of how and why it would endanger freedom and the reality of government by consent. In a fundamental attack on the whole idea that the intricate checks and balances of the new Constitution would protect liberty, a Pennsylvania anti-federalist, "Centinel," argued that, rather, such intricacy prevented the people from detecting corruption and tyranny in their rulers. A simple, responsive government would be better. Written by Samuel Bryan, "Centinel" set forth a basic anti-federalist argument about the nature of free government (though by no means one they all agreed to). Eighteen "Centinel" articles were printed in the Philadelphia Independent Gazetteer *and the Philadelphia* Freeman's Journal *between October 5, 1787, and April 9, 1788. Only the first "Centinel," itself widely reprinted in newspapers and broadsides at the time, is included here. Centinel's argument that clearly responsible government is best can be read as a refutation of Publius' famous arguments in Federalist Numbers 10 and 51 about the virtues of checks and balances.*

To the Freemen of Pennsylvania.

I

Friends, Countrymen and Fellow Citizens,

Permit one of yourselves to put you in mind of certain *liberties* and *privileges* secured to you by the constitution of this commonwealth, and to beg your serious attention to his uninterested opinion upon the plan of federal government submitted to your consideration, before you surrender these great and valuable privileges up forever. Your present frame of government, secures to you a right to hold yourselves, houses, papers and possessions free from search and seizure, and therefore warrants granted without oaths or affirmations first made, affording sufficient foundation for them, whereby any officer or messenger may be commanded or required to search your houses or seize your persons or property, not particularly described in such warrant, shall not be granted. Your constitution further provides "that in controversies respecting property, and in suits between man and man, the parties have a right *to trial by jury, which ought to be held sacred.*" It also provides and declares, "*that the people have a right of* FREEDOM OF SPEECH, *and of* WRITING *and* PUBLISHING *their sentiments, therefore* THE FREEDOM OF THE PRESS OUGHT NOT TO BE RESTRAINED." The constitution of Pennsylvania is *yet* in existence, *as yet* you have the right to *freedom of speech,* and of *publishing your sentiments.* How long those rights will appertain to you, you yourselves are called upon to say, whether your *houses* shall continue to be your *castles;* whether your *papers,* your *persons* and your *property,* are to be held sacred and free from *general warrants,* you are now to determine. Whether the *trial by jury* is to continue as your birth-right, the freemen of Pennsylvania, nay, of all America, are now called upon to declare.

Without presuming upon my own judgment, I cannot think it an unwarrantable presumption to offer my private opinion, and call upon others for theirs; and if I use my pen with the boldness of a freeman, it is because I know that *the liberty of the press yet remains unviolated,* and *juries yet are judges.*

The late convention have submitted to your consideration a plan of a new federal government.—The subject is highly interesting to your future welfare.—Whether it be calculated to promote the great ends of civil society, viz. the happiness and prosperity of the community; it behoves you well to consider, uninfluenced by the authority of names. Instead of that frenzy of enthusiasm, that has actuated the citizens of Philadelphia, in their approbation of the proposed plan, before it was possible that it could be the result of a rational investigation into its principles; it ought to be dispassionately and deliberately examined, and its own intrinsic merit the only criterion of your patronage. If ever free and unbiased discussion was proper or necessary, it is on such an occasion.—All the blessings of liberty and the dearest privileges of freemen, are now at stake and dependent on your present conduct. Those who are competent to the task of developing the principles of government, ought to be encouraged to come forward, and thereby the better enable the people to make a proper judgment; for the science of government is so abstruse, that few are able to judge for themselves: without such assistance the people are too apt to yield an implicit assent to the opinions of those characters, whose abilities are held in the highest esteem, and to those in whose integrity and patriotism they can confide: not considering that the love of domination is generally in proportion to talents, abilities, and superior acquirements; and that the men of the greatest purity of intention may be made instruments of despotism in the hands of the *artful and designing*. If it were not for the stability and attachment which time and habit gives to forms of government, it would be in the power of the enlightened and aspiring few, if they should combine, at any time to destroy the best establishments, and even make the people the instruments of their own subjugation.

The late revolution having effaced in a great measure all former habits, and the present institutions are so recent, that there exists not that great reluctance to innovation, so remarkable in old communities, and which accords with reason, for the most comprehensive mind cannot foresee the full operation of material changes on civil polity; it is the genius of the common law to resist innovation.

The wealthy and ambitious, who in every community think they have a right to lord it over their fellow creatures, have availed themselves, very successfully, of this favorable disposition; for the people thus unsettled in their sentiments, have been prepared to accede to any extreme of government; all the distresses and difficulties they experience, proceeding from various causes, have been ascribed to the impotency of the present confederation, and thence they have been led to expect full relief from the adoption of the proposed system of government; and in the other event, immediately ruin and annihilation as a nation. These characters flatter themselves that they have lulled all distrust and jealousy of their new plan, by gaining the concurrence of the two men in whom America has the highest confidence, and now triumphantly exult in the completion of their long meditated schemes of power and aggrandisement. I would be very far from insinuating that the two illustrious personages alluded to, have not the welfare of their country at heart; but that the unsuspecting goodness and zeal of the one, has been imposed on, in a subject of which he must be necessarily inexperienced, from his other arduous engagements; and that the weakness and indecision attendant on old age, has been practised on in the other.

I am fearful that the principles of government inculcated in Mr. Adams's treatise, and enforced in the numerous essays and paragraphs in the newspapers, have misled some well designing members of the late Convention.—But it will appear in the sequel, that the construction of the proposed plan of government is infinitely more extravagant.

I have been anxiously expecting that some enlightened patriot would, ere this, have taken up the pen to expose the futility, and counteract the baneful tendency of such principles. Mr. Adams's *sine qua non* of a good government is three balancing powers, whose repelling qualities are to produce an equilibrium of interests, and thereby promote the happiness of the whole community. He asserts that the administrators of every government, will ever be actuated by views of private interest and ambition, to the prejudice of the public good; that therefore the only effectual method to secure the rights of the people and promote their welfare, is to create an opposition of interests between the members of two distinct bodies, in the exercise of the powers of government, and balanced by those of a third. This hypothesis supposes human wisdom competent to the task of instituting three co-equal orders in government, and a corresponding weight in the community to enable them respectively to exercise their several parts, and whose views and interests should be so distinct as to prevent a coalition of any two of them for the destruction of the third. Mr. Adams, although he has traced the constitution of every form of government that ever existed, as far as history affords materials, has not been able to adduce a single instance of such a government; he indeed says that the British constitution is such in theory, but this is rather a confirmation that his principles are chimerical and not to be reduced to practice. If such an organization of power were practicable, how long would it continue? not a day—for there is so great a disparity in the talents, wisdom and industry of mankind, that the scale would presently preponderate to one or the other body, and with every accession of power the means of further increase would be greatly extended. The state of society in England is much more favorable to such a scheme of government than that of America. There they have a powerful hereditary nobility, and real distinctions of rank and interests; but even there, for want of that perfect equallity of power and distinction of interests, in the three orders of government, they exist but in name; the only operative and efficient check, upon the conduct of administration, is the sense of the people at large.

Suppose a government could be formed and supported on such principles, would it answer the great purposes of civil society; if the administrators of every government are actuated by views of private interest and ambition, how is the welfare and happiness of the community to be the result of such jarring adverse interests?

Therefore, as different orders in government will not produce the good of the whole, we must recur to other principles. I believe it will be found that the form of government, which holds those entrusted with power, in the greatest responsibility to their constitutents, the best calculated for freemen. A republican, or free government, can only exist where the body of the people are virtuous, and where property is pretty equally divided; in such a government the people are the sovereign and their sense or opinion is the criterion of every public measure; for when this ceases to be the case, the nature of the government is changed, and an aristocracy, monarchy or despotism will rise on its ruin. The highest responsibility is to be attained, in a simple structure of government, for the great body of the people never steadily attend to the operations of government, and for want of due information are liable to be imposed on.—If you complicate the plan by various orders, the people will be perplexed and divided in their sentiments about the source of abuses or misconduct, some will impute it to the senate, others to the house of representatives, and so on, that the interposition of the people may be rendered imperfect or perhaps wholly abortive. But if, imitating the constitution of Pennsylvania, you vest all the legislative power in one body of men (separating the executive and judicial) elected for a short period, and necessarily excluded by rotation from permanency, and guarded from precipitancy and surprise by delays imposed on its proceedings, you will create the most perfect responsibility for then, whenever the people feel a grievance they cannot mistake the authors, and will apply the remedy with certainty and effect, discarding them at the next election. This tie of responsibility will obviate all the dangers apprehended from a single legislature, and will best secure the rights of the people.

Having premised this much, I shall now proceed to the examination of the proposed plan of government, and I trust, shall make it appear to the meanest capacity, that it has none of the essential requisites of a free government; that it is neither founded on those balancing restraining powers, recommended by Mr. Adams and attempted in the British constitution, or possessed of that responsibility to its constituents, which, in my opinion, is the only effectual security for the liberties and happiness of the people; but on the contrary, that it is a most daring attempt to establish a despotic aristocracy among freemen, that the world has ever witnessed.

I shall previously consider the extent of the powers intended to be vested in Congress, before I examine the construction of the general government.

It will not be controverted that the legislative is the highest delegated power in government, and that all others are subordinate to it. The celebrated *Montesquieu* establishes it as a maxim, that legislation necessarily follows the power of taxation. By sect. 8, of the first article of the proposed plan of government, "the Congress are to have power to lay and collect taxes, duties, imposts and excises, to pay the debts and provide for the common défence and *general welfare* of the United States; but all duties, imposts and excises, shall be uniform throughout the United States." Now what can be more comprehensive than these words; not content by other sections of this plan, to grant all the great executive powers of a confederation, and a STANDING ARMY IN TIME OF PEACE, that grand engine of oppression, and moreover the absolute control over the commerce of the United States and all external objects of revenue, such as unlimited imposts upon imports, etc.—they are to be vested with every species of *internal* taxation;—whatever taxes, duties and excises that they may deem requisite for the *general welfare,* may be imposed on the citizens of these states, levied by the officers of Congress, distributed through every district in America; and the collection would be enforced by the standing army, however grievous or improper they may be. The Congress may construe every purpose for which the state legislatures now lay taxes, to be for the *general welfare,* and thereby seize upon every object of revenue.

The judicial power by 1st sect. of article 3 "shall extend to all cases, in law and equity, arising under this constitution, the laws of the United States, and treaties made or which shall be made under their authority; to all cases affecting ambassadors, other public ministers and consuls; to all cases of admirality and maritime jurisdiction, to controversies to which the United States shall be a party, to controversies between two or more states, between a state and citizens of another state, between citizens of different states, between citizens of the same state claiming lands under grants of different states, and between a state, or the citizens thereof, and foreign states, citizens or subjects."

The judicial power to be vested in one Supreme Court, and in such Inferior Courts as the Congress may from time to time ordain and establish.

The objects of jurisdiction recited above, are so numerous, and the shades of distinction between civil causes are oftentimes so slight, that it is more than probable that the state judicatories would be wholly superceded; for in contests about jurisdiction, the federal court, as the most powerful, would ever prevail. Every person acquainted with the history of the courts in England, knows by what ingenious sophisms they have, at different periods, extended the sphere of their jurisdiction over objects out of the line of their institution, and contrary to their very nature; courts of a criminal jurisdiction obtaining cognizance in civil causes.

To put the omnipotency of Congress over the state government and judicatories out of all doubt, the 6th article ordains that "this constitution and the laws of the United States which shall be made in pursuance thereof, and all treaties made, or which shall be made under the authority of the United States, shall be the *supreme law of the land,* and the judges in every state shall be bound thereby, any thing in the constitution or laws of any state to the contrary notwithstanding."

By these sections the all-prevailing power of taxation, and such extensive legislative and judicial powers are vested in the general government, as must in their operation, necessarily absorb the state legislatures and judicatories; and that such was in the contemplation of the framers of it, will appear from the provision made for such event, in another part of it (but that, fearful of alarming the people by so great an innovation, they have suffered the forms of the separate governments to remain, as a blind). By sect. 4th of the 1st article, "the times, places and manner of holding elections for senators and representatives, shall be prescribed in each state by the legislature thereof; *but the Congress may at any time, by law, make or alter such regulations, except as to the place of chusing senators.*" The plain construction of which is, that when the state legislatures drop out of sight, from the necessary operation of this government, then Congress are to provide for the election and appointment of representatives and senators.

If the foregoing be a just comment—if the United States are to be melted down into one empire, it becomes you to consider, whether such a government, however constructed, would be eligible in so extended a territory; and whether it would be practicable, consistent with freedom? It is the opinion of the greatest writers, that a very extensive country cannot be governed on democratical principles, on any other plan, than a confederation of a number of small republics, possessing all the powers of internal government, but united in the management of their foreign and general concerns.

It would not be difficult to prove, that any thing short of despotism, could not bind so great a country under one government; and that whatever plan you might, at the first setting out, establish, it would issue in a despotism.

If one general government could be instituted and maintained on principles of freedom, it would not be so competent to attend to the various local concerns and wants, of every particular district, as well as the peculiar governments, who are nearer the scene, and possessed of superior means of information; besides, if the business of the *whole* union is to be managed by one government, there would not be time. Do we not already see, that the inhabitants in a number of larger states, who are remote from the seat of government, are loudly complaining of the inconveniencies and disadvantages they are subjected to on this account, and that, to enjoy the comforts of local government, they are separating into smaller divisions.

Having taken a review of the powers, I shall now examine the construction of the proposed general government.

Art. I. Sect. I. "All legislative powers herein granted shall be vested in a Congress of the United States, which shall consist of a senate and house of representatives." By another section, the president (the principal executive officer) has a conditional control over their proceedings.

Sect. 2. "The house of representatives shall be composed of members chosen every second year, by the people of the several states. The number of representatives shall not exceed one for every 30,000 inhabitants."

The senate, the other constituent branch of the legislature, is formed by the legislature of each state appointing two senators, for the term of six years.

The executive power by Art. 2, Sect. 1. is to be vested in a president of the United States of America, elected for four years: Sect. 2. gives him "power, by and with the consent of the senate to make treaties, provided two thirds of the senators present concur; and he shall nominate, and by and with the advice and consent of the senate, shall appoint ambassadors, other public ministers and consuls, judges of the Supreme Court, and all other officers of the United States, whose appointments are not herein otherwise provided for, and which shall be established by law," etc. And by another section he has the absolute power of granting reprieves and pardons for treason and all other high crimes and misdemeanors, except in case of impeachment.

The foregoing are the outlines of the plan.

Thus we see, the house of representatives, are on the part of the people to balance the senate, who I suppose will be composed of the *better sort,* the *well born,* etc. The number of the representatives (being only one for every 30,000 inhabitants) appears to be too few, either to communicate the requisite information, of the wants, local circumstances and sentiments of so extensive an empire, or to prevent corruption and undue influence, in the exercise of such great powers; the term for which they are to be chosen, too long to preserve a due dependence and accountability to their constituents; and the mode and places of their election not sufficiently ascertained, for as Congress have the control over both, they may govern the choice, by ordering the *representatives* of a *whole* state, to be *elected* in *one* place, and that too may be the most *inconvenient.*

The senate, the great efficient body in this plan of government, is constituted on the most unequal principles. The smallest state in the union has equal weight with the great states of Virginia, Massachusetts, or Pennsylvania.—The Senate, besides its legislative functions, has a very considerable share in the Executive; none of the principal appointments to office can be made without its advice and consent. The term and mode of its appointment, will lead to permanency; the members are chosen for six years, the mode is under the control of Congress, and as there is no exclusion by rotation, they may be continued for life, which, from their extensive means of influence, would follow of course. The President, who would be a mere pageant of state, unless he coincides with the views of the Senate, would either become the head of the aristocratic junto in that body, or its minion; besides, their influence being the most predominant, could the best secure his re-election to office. And from his power of granting pardons, he might skreen from punishment the most treasonable attempts on the liberties of the people, when instigated by the Senate.

From this investigation into the organization of this government, it appears that it is devoid of all responsibility or accountability to the great body of the people, and that so far from being a regular balanced government, it would be in practice a *permanent* ARISTOCRACY.

The framers of it, actuated by the true spirit of such a government, which ever abominates and suppresses all free enquiry and discussion, have made no provision for the *liberty of the press,* that grand *palladium of freedom,* and *scourge of tyrants;* but observed a total silence on that head. It is the opinion of some great writers, that if the liberty of the press, by an institution of religion, or otherwise, could be rendered *sacred,* even in *Turkey,* that despotism would fly before it. And it is worthy of remark, that there is no declaration of personal rights, premised in most free constitutions; and that trial by *jury* in *civil* cases is taken away; for what other construction can be put on the following, viz. Article III. Sect. 2d. "In all cases affecting ambassadors, other public ministers and consuls, and those in which a State shall be party, the Supreme Court shall have *original* jurisdiction. In all the other cases above mentioned, the Supreme Court shall have *appellate* jurisdiction, both as to *law and fact*"? It would be a novelty in jurisprudence, as well as evidently improper to allow an appeal from the verdict of a jury, on the matter of fact; therefore, it implies and allows of a dismission of the jury in civil cases, and especially when it is considered, that jury trial in criminal cases is expressly stipulated for, but not in civil cases.

But our situation is represented to be so *critically* dreadful, that, however reprehensible and exceptionable the proposed plan of government may be, there is no alternative, between the adoption of it and absolute ruin.—My fellow citizens, things are not at that crisis, it is the argument of tyrants; the present distracted state of Europe secures us from injury on that quarter, and as to domestic dissentions, we have not so much to fear from them, as to precipitate us into this form of government, without it is a safe and a proper one. For remember, of all *possible* evils, that of *despotism* is the *worst* and the most to be *dreaded*.

Besides, it cannot be supposed, that the first essay on so difficult a subject, is so well digested, as it ought to be,—if the proposed plan, after a mature deliberation, should meet the approbation of the respective States, the matter will end; but if it should be found to be fraught with dangers and inconveniencies, a future general Convention being in possession of the objections, will be the better enabled to plan a suitable government.

> *Who's here so base, that would a bondman be?*
> *If any, speak; for him have I offended.*
> *Who's here so vile, that will not love his country?*
> *If any, speak; for him have I offended.*
> [*Julius Caesar,* Act 3, Scene 2]

Centinel.

The Address and Reasons of Dissent of the Minority of the Convention of Pennsylvania to their Constituents (December 18, 1787)

After the Pennsylvania convention ratified the new Constitution on December 12, 1787, by a vote of 46 to 23, twenty-one members of the minority signed a dissenting address that appeared in the Pennsylvania Packet and Daily Advertiser *on December 18, 1787. The address was subsequently reprinted often in Pennsylvania and other states, becoming in some way a semi-official statement of anti-federalist objections to the new Constitution. The author of the address was probably the same as the author of "Centinel," Samuel Bryan; at least there are notable simi-*

*larities between the two works, and Bryan later claimed author-
ship in letters to Jefferson and to Albert Gallatin.*

It was not until after the termination of the late glorious contest,
which made the people of the United States, an independent
nation, that any defect was discovered in the present confederation. It was formed by some of the ablest patriots in America. It
carried us successfully through the war; and the virtue and patriotism of the people, with their disposition to promote the
common cause, supplied the want of power in Congress. . . .

It was [after the Peace Treaty of 1783] that the want of an
efficient federal government was first complained of, and that
the powers vested in Congress were found to be inadequate to
the procuring of the benefits that should result from the union. The
impost was granted by most of the states, but many refused the
supplementary funds; the annual requisitions were set at nought
by some of the states, while others complied with them by legislative acts, but were tardy in their payments, and Congress
found themselves incapable of complying with their engagements, and supporting the federal government. It was found that
our national character was sinking in the opinion of foreign nations. The Congress could make treaties of commerce, but could
not enforce the observance of them. We were suffering from the
restrictions of foreign nations, who had shackled our commerce,
while we were unable to retaliate: and all now agreed that it
would be advantageous to the union to enlarge the powers of
Congress; that they should be enabled in the amplest manner to
regulate commerce, and to lay and collect duties on the imports
throughout the United States. With this view a convention was
first proposed by Virginia, and finally recommended by Congress for the different states to appoint deputies to meet in convention, "for the purposes of revising and amending the present
articles of confederation, so as to make them adequate to the
exigencies of the union." This recommendation the legislatures
of twelve states complied with so hastily as not to consult their
constituents on the subject; and though the different legislatures
had no authority from their constituents for the purpose, they
probably apprehended the necessity would justify the measure;

and none of them extended their ideas at that time further than "revising and amending the present articles of confederation." Pennsylvania by the act appointing deputies expressly confined their powers to this object; and though it is probable that some of the members of the assembly of this state had at that time in contemplation to annihilate the present confederation, as well as the constitution of Pennsylvania, yet the plan was not sufficiently matured to communicate it to the public. . . .

The Continental convention met in the city of Philadelphia at the time appointed. It was composed of some men of excellent characters; of others who were more remarkable for their ambition and cunning, than their patriotism; and of some who had been opponents to the independence of the United States. The delegates from Pennsylvania were, six of them, uniform and decided opponents to the constitution of this commonwealth. The convention sat upwards of four months. The doors were kept shut, and the members brought under the most solemn engagements of secrecy. Some of those who opposed their going so far beyond their powers, retired, hopeless, from the convention, others had the firmness to refuse signing the plan altogether; and many who did sign it, did it not as a system they wholly approved, but as the best that could be then obtained, and notwithstanding the time spent on this subject, it is agreed on all hands to be a work of haste and accommodation.

Whilst the gilded chains were forging in the secret conclave, the meaner instruments of despotism without, were busily employed in alarming the fears of the people with dangers which did not exist, and exciting their hopes of greater advantages from the expected plan than even the best government on earth could produce. . . .

[After explaining the events leading to the ratifying convention, the minority delegates determined to explain themselves to their constituents.] We entered on the examination of the proposed system of government, and found it to be such as we could not adopt, without, as we conceived, surrendering up your dearest rights. We offered our objections to the convention, and opposed those parts of the plan, which, in our opinion, would be injurious to you, in the best manner we were able; and closed our arguments by offering the following propositions to the convention.

1. The right of conscience shall be held inviolable; and neither the legislative, executive nor judicial powers of the United States shall have authority to alter, abrogate, or infringe any part of the constitution of the several states, which provide for the preservation of liberty in matters of religion.

2. That in controversies respecting property, and in suits between man and man, trial by jury shall remain as heretofore, as well in the federal courts, as in those of the several states.

3. That in all capital and criminal prosecutions, a man has a right to demand the cause and nature of his accusation, as well in the federal courts, as in those of the several states; to be heard by himself and his counsel; to be confronted with the accusers and witnesses; to call for evidence in his favor, and a speedy trial by an impartial jury of his vicinage, without whose unanimous consent, he cannot be found guilty, nor can he be compelled to give evidence against himself; and that no man be deprived of his liberty, except by the law of the land or the judgment of his peers.

4. That excessive bail ought not to be required, nor excessive fines imposed, nor cruel nor unusual punishments inflicted.

5. That warrants unsupported by evidence, whereby any officer or messenger may be commanded or required to search suspected places, or to seize any person or persons, his or their property, not particularly described, are grievous and oppressive, and shall not be granted either by the magistrates of the federal government or others.

6. That the people have a right to the freedom of speech, of writing and publishing their sentiments, therefore, the freedom of the press shall not be restrained by any law of the United States.

7. That the people have a right to bear arms for the defence of themselves and their own state, or the United States, or for the purpose of killing game; and no law shall be passed for disarming the people or any of them, unless for crimes committed, or real danger of public injury from individuals; and as standing armies in the time of peace are dangerous to liberty, they ought

not to be kept up: and that the military shall be kept under strict subordination to and be governed by the civil powers.

8. The inhabitants of the several states shall have liberty to fowl and hunt in seasonable times, on the lands they hold, and on all other lands in the United States not inclosed, and in like manner to fish in all navigable waters, and others not private property, without being restrained therein by any laws to be passed by the legislature of the United States.

9. That no law shall be passed to restrain the legislatures of the several states from enacting laws for imposing taxes, except imposts and duties upon goods imported or exported, and postage on letters shall be levied by the authority of Congress.

10. That the house of representatives be properly increased in number; that elections shall remain free; that the several states shall have power to regulate the elections for senators and representatives, without being controled either directly or indirectly by any interference on the part of the Congress; and that elections of representatives be annual.

11. That the power of organizing, arming and disciplining the militia (the manner of disciplining the militia to be prescribed by Congress) remain with the individual states, and that Congress shall not have authority to call or march any of the militia out of their own state, without the consent of such state, and for such length of time only as such state shall agree.

That the sovereignty, freedom and independency of the several states shall be retained, and every power, jurisdiction and right which is not by this constitution expressly delegated to the United States in Congress assembled.

12. That the legislative, executive, and judicial powers be kept separate; and to this end that a constitutional council be appointed, to advise and assist the president, who shall be responsible for the advice they give, hereby the senators would be relieved from almost constant attendance; and also that the judges be made completely independent.

13. That no treaty which shall be directly opposed to the existing laws of the United States in Congress assembled, shall be valid until such laws shall be repealed, or made conformable to such treaty; neither shall any treaties be valid which are in con-

tradiction to the constitution of the United States, or the constitutions of the several states.

14. That the judiciary power of the United States shall be confined to cases affecting ambassadors, other public ministers and consuls; to cases of admiralty and maritime jurisdiction; to controversies to which the United States shall be a party; to controversies between two or more states—between a state and citizens of different states—between citizens claiming lands under grants of different states; and between a state or the citizen thereof and foreign states, and in criminal cases, to such only as are expressly enumerated in the constitution, and that the United States in Congress assembled, shall not have power to enact laws, which shall alter the laws of descents and distribution of the effects of deceased persons, the titles of lands or goods, or the regulation of contracts in the individual states.

After reading these propositions, we declared our willingness to agree to the plan, provided it was so amended as to meet these propositions, or something similar to them: and finally moved the convention to adjourn, to give the people of Pennsylvania time to consider the subject, and determine for themselves; but these were all rejected, and the final vote was taken, when our duty to you induced us to vote against the proposed plan, and to decline signing the ratification of the same.

During the discussion we met with many insults, and some personal abuse; we were not even treated with decency, during the sitting of the convention, by the persons in the gallery of the house; however, we flatter ourselves that in contending for the preservation of those invaluable rights you have thought proper to commit to our charge, we acted with a spirit becoming freemen, and being desirous that you might know the principles which actuated our conduct, and being prohibited from inserting our reasons of dissent on the minutes of the convention, we have subjoined them for your consideration, as to you alone we are accountable. It remains with you whether you will think those inestimable privileges, which you have so ably contended for, should be sacrificed at the shrine of despotism, or whether you mean to contend for them with the same spirit that has so often baffled the attempts of an aristocratic faction, to rivet the shackles of slavery on you and your unborn posterity.

Our objections are comprised under three general heads of dissent, viz.

We dissent, first, because it is the opinion of the most celebrated writers on government, and confirmed by uniform experience, that a very extensive territory cannot be governed on the principles of freedom, otherwise than by a confederation of republics, possessing all the powers of internal government; but united in the management of their general, and foreign concerns.

If any doubt could have been entertained of the truth of the foregoing principle, it has been fully removed by the concession of *Mr. Wilson,* one of the majority on this question; and who was one of the deputies in the late general convention. In justice to him, we will give his own words; they are as follows, viz., "The extent of country for which the new constitution was required, produced another difficulty in the business of the federal convention. It is the opinion of some celebrated writers, that to a small territory, the democratical; to a middling territory (as Montesquieu has termed it) the monarchial; and to an extensive territory, the despotic form of government is best adapted. Regarding then the wide and almost unbounded jurisdiction of the United States, at first view, the hand of despotism seemed necessary to control, connect, and protect it; and hence the chief embarrassment rose. For, we know that, although our constituents would chearfully submit to the legislative restraints of a free government, they would spurn at every attempt to shackle them with despotic power."—And again in another part of his speech he continues.—"Is it probable that the dissolution of the state governments, and the establishment of one *consolidated empire* would be eligible in its nature, and satisfactory to the people in its administration? I think not, as I have given reasons to show that so extensive a territory could not be governed, connected, and preserved, but by the *supremacy of despotic power.* All the exertions of the most potent emperors of Rome were not capable of keeping that empire together, which in extent was far inferior to the dominion of America."

We dissent, secondly, because the powers vested in Congress by this constitution, must necessarily annihilate and absorb the legislative, executive, and judicial powers of the several states, and produce from their ruins one consolidated government, which from the nature of things will be *an iron handed despotism,* as nothing short of the supremacy of despotic sway could connect and govern these United States under one government.

As the truth of this position is of such decisive importance, it ought to be fully investigated, and if it is founded to be clearly ascertained; for, should it be demonstrated, that the powers vested by this constitution in Congress, will have such an effect as necessarily to produce one consolidated government, the question then will be reduced to this short issue, viz., whether satiated with the blessings of liberty; whether repenting of the folly of so recently asserting their unalienable rights, against foreign despots at the expence of so much blood and treasure, and such painful and arduous struggles, the people of America are not willing to resign every privilege of freemen, and submit to the dominion of an absolute government, that will embrace all America in one chain of despotism; or whether they will with virtuous indignation, spurn at the shackles prepared for them, and confirm their liberties by a conduct becoming freemen.

That the new government will not be a confederacy of states, as it ought, but one consolidated government, founded upon the destruction of the several governments of the states, we shall now shew.

The powers of Congress under the new constitution, are complete and unlimited over the *purse* and the *sword,* and are perfectly independent of, and supreme over, the state governments; whose intervention in these great points is entirely destroyed. By virtue of their power of taxation, Congress may command the whole, or any part of the property of the people. They may impose what imposts upon commerce; they may impose what land taxes, poll taxes, excises, duties on all written instruments, and duties on every other article that they may judge proper; in short, every species of taxation, whether of an external or internal nature is comprised in section the 8th, of article the 1st, viz., "The Congress shall have power to lay and collect taxes, duties, imposts, and excises, to pay the debts, and provide for the common defence and general welfare of the United States."

As there is no one article of taxation reserved to the state governments, the Congress may monopolise every source of revenue, and thus indirectly demolish the state governments, for without funds they could not exist; the taxes, duties and excises imposed by Congress may be so high as to render it impracticable to levy further sums on the same articles; but whether this should be the case or not, if the state governments should presume to impose taxes, duties or excises, on the same articles with Congress, the latter may abrogate and repeal the laws whereby they are imposed, upon the allegation that they interfere with the due collection of their taxes, duties or excises, by virtue of the following clause, part of section 8th, article 1st, viz., "To make all laws which shall be necessary and proper for carrying into execution the foregoing powers, and all other powers vested by this constitution in the government of the United States, or in any department or officer thereof."

The Congress might gloss over this conduct by construing every purpose for which the state legislatures now lay taxes, to be for the *"general welfare,"* and therefore as of their jurisdiction.

And the supremacy of the laws of the United States is established by article 6th, viz., "That this constitution and the laws of the United States, which shall be made in pursuance thereof, and *all treaties* made, or which shall be made, under the authority of the United States, shall be the *supreme law* of the *land; and the judges in every state shall be bound thereby; any thing in the constitution or laws of any state to the contrary notwithstanding.*" It has been alledged that the words "pursuant to the constitution," are a restriction upon the authority of Congress; but when it is considered that by other sections they are invested with every efficient power of government, and which may be exercised to the absolute destruction of the state governments, without any violation of even the forms of the constitution, this seeming restriction, as well as every other restriction in it, appears to us to be nugatory and delusive; and only introduced as a blind upon the real nature of the government. In our opinion, "pursuant to the constitution," will be co-extensive with the *will* and *pleasure* of Congress, which, indeed, will be the only limitation of their powers.

We apprehend that two co-ordinate sovereignties would be a solecism in politics. That therefore as there is no line of distinction drawn between the general, and state governments; as the sphere of their jurisdiction is undefined, it would be contrary to the nature of things, that both should exist together, one or the other would necessarily triumph in the fullness of dominion. However the contest could not be of long continuance, as the state governments are divested of every means of defence, and will be obliged by "the supreme law of the land" *to yield at discretion.*

It has been objected to this total destruction of the state governments, that the existence of their legislatures is made essential to the organization of Congress; that they must assemble for the appointment of the senators and president general of the United States. True, the state legislatures may be continued for some years, as boards of appointment, merely, after they are divested of every other function, but the framers of the constitution foreseeing that the people will soon be disgusted with this solemn mockery of a government without power and usefulness, have made a provision for relieving them from the imposition, in section 4th, of article 1st, viz., "The times, places, and manner of holding elections for senators and representatives, shall be prescribed in each state by the legislature thereof; *but the Congress may at any time, by law make or alter such regulations; except as to the place of chusing senators.*"

As Congress have the control over the time of the appointment of the president general, of the senators and of the representatives of the United States, they may prolong their existence in office, for life, by postponing the time of their election and appointment, from period to period, under various pretences, such as an apprehension of invasion, the factious disposition of the people, or any other plausible pretence that the occasion may suggest; and having thus obtained life-estates in the government, they may fill up the vacancies themselves, by their control over the mode of appointment; with this exception in regard to the senators, that as the place of appointment for them, must, by the constitution, be in the particular state, they may depute some body in the respective states, to fill up the vacancies in the senate, occasioned by death, until they can venture to assume it themselves. In this manner, may the only restriction in this clause be evaded. By virtue of the foregoing section, when the spirit of the people shall be gradually broken; when the general government shall be firmly established, and when a numerous standing army shall render opposition vain, the Congress may compleat the system of despotism, in renouncing all dependance on the people, by continuing themselves, and children in the government.

The celebrated *Montesquieu,* in his Spirit of Laws, vol. 1, page 12th, says, "That in a democracy there can be no exercise of sovereignty, but by the suffrages of the people, which are their will; now the sovereign's will is the sovereign himself; the laws therefore, which establish the right of suffrage, are fundamental to this government. In fact, it is as important to regulate in a republic in what manner, by whom, and concerning what suffrages are to be given, as it is in a monarchy to know who is the prince, and after what manner he ought to govern." The *time, mode* and *place* of the election of representatives, senators and president general of the United States, ought not to be under the control of Congress, but fundamentally ascertained and established.

The new constitution, consistently with the plan of consolidation, contains no reservation of the rights and privileges of the state governments, which was made in the confederation of the year 1778, by article the 2d, viz., "That each state retains its sovereignty, freedom and independence, and every power, jurisdiction and right, which is not by this confederation expressly delegated to the United States in Congress assembled."

The legislative power vested in Congress by the foregoing recited sections, is so unlimited in its nature; may be so comprehensive and boundless in its exercise, that this alone would be amply sufficient to annihilate the state governments, and swallow them up in the grand vortex of general empire.

The judicial powers vested in Congress are also so various

and extensive, that by legal ingenuity they may be extended to every case, and thus absorb the state judiciaries, and when we consider the decisive influence that a general judiciary would have over the civil polity of the several states, we do not hesitate to pronounce that this power, unaided by the legislative, would effect a consolidation of the states under one government.

The powers of a court of equity, vested by this constitution, in the tribunals of Congress; powers which do not exist in Pennsylvania, unless so far as they can be incorporated with jury trial, would, in this state, greatly contribute to this event. The rich and wealthy suitors would eagerly lay hold of the infinite mazes, perplexities and delays, which a court of chancery, with the appellate powers of the supreme court in fact as well as law would furnish him with, and thus the poor man being plunged in the bottomless pit of legal discussion, would drop his demand in despair.

In short, consolidation pervades the whole constitution. It begins with an annunciation that such was the intention. The main pillars of the fabric correspond with it, and the concluding paragraph is a confirmation of it. The preamble begins with the words, "We the people of the United States," which is the style of a compact between individuals entering into a state of society, and not that of a confederation of states. The other features of consolidation, we have before noticed.

Thus we have fully established the position, that the powers vested by this constitution in Congress, will effect a consolidation of the states under one government, which even the advocates of this constitution admit, could not be done without the sacrifice of all liberty.

3. We dissent, Thirdly, because if it were practicable to govern so extensive a territory as these United States includes, on the plan of a consolidated government, consistent with the principles of liberty and the happiness of the people, yet the construction of this constitution is not calculated to attain the object, for independent of the nature of the case, it would of itself, necessarily, produce a despotism, and that not by the usual gradations, but with the celerity that has hitherto only attended revolutions effected by the sword.

To establish the truth of this position, a cursory investigation of the principles and form of this constitution will suffice.

The first consideration that this review suggests, is the omission of a BILL of RIGHTS, ascertaining and fundamentally establishing those unalienable and personal rights of men, without the full, free, and secure enjoyment of which there can be no liberty, and over which it is not necessary for a good government to have the control. The principal of which are the rights of conscience, personal liberty by the clear and unequivocal establishment of the writ of *habeas corpus,* jury trial in criminal and civil cases, by an impartial jury of the vicinage or county, with the common-law proceedings, for the safety of the accused in criminal prosecutions; and the liberty of the press, that scourge of tyrants, and the grand bulwark of every other liberty and privilege; the stipulations heretofore made in favor of them in the state constitutions, are entirely superceded by this constitution.

The legislature of a free country should be so formed as to have a competent knowledge of its constituents, and enjoy their confidence. To produce these essential requisites, the representation ought to be fair, equal, and sufficiently numerous, to possess the same interests, feelings, opinions, and views, which the people themselves would possess, were they all assembled; and so numerous as to prevent bribery and undue influence, and so responsible to the people, by frequent and fair elections, as to prevent their neglecting or sacrificing the views and interests of their constituents, to their own pursuits.

We will now bring the legislature under this constitution to the test of the foregoing principles, which will demonstrate, that it is deficient in every essential quality of a just and safe representation.

The house of representatives is to consist of 65 members; that is one for about every 50,000 inhabitants, to be chosen every two years. Thirty-three members will form a quorum for doing business; and 17 of these, being the majority, determine the sense of the house.

The senate, the other constituent branch of the legislature, consists of 26 members being *two* from each state, appointed by their legislatures every six years—fourteen senators make a quorum; the majority of whom, eight, determines the sense of that body: except in judging on impeachments, or in making treaties, or in expelling a member, when two thirds of the senators present, must concur.

The president is to have the control over the enacting of laws, so far as to make the concurrence of *two* thirds of the representatives and senators present necessary, if he should object to the laws.

Thus it appears that the liberties, happiness, interests, and great concerns of the whole United States, may be dependent upon the integrity, virtue, wisdom, and knowledge of 25 or 26 men.—How unadequate and unsafe a representation! Inadequate, because the sense and views of 3 or 4 millions of people diffused over so extensive a territory comprising such various climates, products, habits, interests, and opinions, cannot be collected in so small a body; and besides, it is not a fair and equal representation of the people even in proportion to its number, for the smallest state has as much weight in the senate as the largest, and from the smallness of the number to be chosen for both branches of the legislature; and from the mode of election and appointment, which is under the control of Congress; and from the nature of the thing, men of the most elevated rank in life, will alone be chosen. The other orders in the society, such as farmers, traders, and mechanics, who all ought to have a competent number of their best informed men in the legislature, will be totally unrepresented.

The representation is unsafe, because in the exercise of such great powers and trusts, it is so exposed to corruption and undue influence, by the gift of the numerous places of honor and emoluments at the disposal of the executive; by the arts and address of the great and designing; and by direct bribery.

The representation is moreover inadequate and unsafe, because of the long terms for which it is appointed, and the mode of its appointment, by which Congress may not only control the choice of the people, but may so manage as to divest the people of this fundamental right, and become self-elected.

The number of members in the house of representatives *may* be encreased to one for every 30,000 inhabitants. But when we consider, that this cannot be done without the consent of the senate, who from their share in the legislative, in the executive, and judicial departments, and permanency of appointment, will be the great efficient body in this government, and whose weight and predominancy would be abridged by an increase of the representatives, we are persuaded that this is a circumstance that cannot be expected. On the contrary, the number of representatives will probably be continued at 65, although the population of the country may swell to treble what it now is; unless a revolution should effect a change.

We have before noticed the judicial power as it would effect a consolidation of the states into one government; we will now examine it, as it would affect the liberties and welfare of the people, supposing such a government were practicable and proper.

The judicial power, under the proposed constitution, is founded on the well-known principles of the *civil law,* by which the judge determines both on law and fact, and appeals are allowed from the inferior tribunals to the superior, upon the whole question; so that *facts* as well as *law,* would be re-examined, and even new facts brought forward in the court of appeals; and to use the words of a very eminent Civilian—"The cause is many times another thing before the court of appeals, than what it was at the time of the first sentence."

That this mode of proceeding is the one which must be adopted under this constitution, is evident from the following circumstances:—1st. That the trial by jury, which is the grand characteristic of the common law, is secured by the constitution, only in criminal cases.—2d. That the appeal from both *law* and *fact* is expressly established, which is utterly inconsistent with the principles of the common law, and trials by jury. The only mode in which an appeal from law and fact can be established, is, by adopting the principles and practice of the civil law; unless the United States should be drawn into the absurdity of calling and swearing juries, merely for the purpose of contradicting their verdicts, which would render juries contemptible and worse than useless.—3d. That the courts to be established would decide on all cases *of law and equity,* which is a well known

characteristic of the civil law, and these courts would have co-
nusance not only of the laws of the United States and of treaties,
and of cases affecting ambassadors, but of all cases of *admiralty
and maritime jurisdiction,* which last are matters belonging exclusively to the civil law, in every nation in Christendom.

Not to enlarge upon the loss of the invaluable right of trial by
an unbiassed jury, so dear to every friend of liberty, the monstrous expence and inconveniences of the mode of proceedings
to be adopted, are such as will prove intolerable to the people of
this country. The lengthy proceedings of the civil law courts in
the chancery of England, and in the courts of Scotland and
France, are such that few men of moderate fortune can endure
the expence of; the poor man must therefore submit to the
wealthy. Length of purse will too often prevail against right and
justice. For instance, we are told by the learned judge *Blackstone,* that a question only on the property of an ox, of the value
of *three* guineas, originating under the civil law proceedings in
Scotland, after many interlocutory orders and sentences below,
was carried at length from the court of sessions, the highest
court in that part of Great Britain, by way of *appeal* to the house
of lords, *where* the question of law and fact was finally determined. He adds, that no pique or spirit could in the court of
king's bench or common pleas at Westminster, have given continuance to such a cause for a tenth part of the time, nor have
cost a twentieth part of the expence. Yet the costs in the courts
of king's bench and common pleas in England, are infinitely
greater than those which the people of this country have ever
experienced. We abhor the idea of losing the transcendant privilege of trial by jury, with the loss of which, it is remarked by the
same learned author, that in Sweden, the liberties of the commons were extinguished by an aristocratic senate: and that *trial
by jury* and the liberty of the people went out together. At the
same time we regret the intolerable delay, the enormous expences and infinite vexation to which the people of this country
will be exposed from the voluminous proceedings of the courts
of civil law, and especially from the appellate jurisdiction, by
means of which a man may be drawn from the utmost boundaries of this extensive country to the seat of the supreme court of

the nation to contend, perhaps with a wealthy and powerful adversary. The consequence of this establishment will be an absolute confirmation of the power of aristocratical influence in the courts of justice: for the common people will not be able to contend or struggle against it.

Trial by jury in criminal cases may also be excluded by declaring that the libeller for instance shall be liable to an action of debt for a specified sum; thus evading the common law prosecution by indictment and trial by jury. And the common course of proceeding against a ship for breach of revenue laws by information (which will be classed among civil causes) will at the civil law be within the resort of a court, where no jury intervenes. Besides, the benefit of jury trial, in cases of a criminal nature, which cannot be evaded, will be rendered of little value, by calling the accused to answer far from home; there being no provision that the trial be by a jury of the neighbourhood or country. Thus an inhabitant of Pittsburgh, on a charge of crime committed on the banks of the Ohio, may be obliged to defend himself at the side of the Delaware, and so *vice versa.* To conclude this head: we observe that the judges of the courts of Congress would not be independent, as they are not debarred from holding other offices, during the pleasure of the president and senate, and as they may derive their support in part from fees, alterable by the legislature.

The next consideration that the constitution presents, is the undue and dangerous mixture of the powers of government; the same body possessing legislative, executive, and judicial powers. The senate is a constituent branch of the legislature, it has judicial power in judging on impeachments, and in this case unites in some measure the characters of judge and party, as all the principal officers are appointed by the president-general, with the concurrence of the senate and therefore they derive their offices in part from the senate. This may bias the judgments of the senators and tend to screen great delinquents from punishment. And the senate has, moreover, various and great executive powers, viz., in concurrence with the president-general, they form treaties with foreign nations, that may control and abrogate the constitutions and laws of the several states.

Indeed, there is no power, privilege or liberty of the state governments, or of the people, but what may be affected by virtue of this power. For all treaties, made by them, are to be the "supreme law of the land, any thing in the constitution or laws of any state, to the contrary notwithstanding."

And this great power may be exercised by the president and 10 senators (being two thirds of 14, which is a quorum of that body). What an inducement would this offer to the ministers of foreign powers to compass by bribery *such concessions* as could not otherwise be obtained. It is the unvaried usage of all free states, whenever treaties interfere with the positive laws of the land, to make the intervention of the legislature necessary to give them operation. This became necessary, and was afforded by the parliament of Great-Britain. In consequence of the late commercial treaty between that kingdom and France.—As the senate judges on impeachments, who is to try the members of the senate for the abuse of this power! And none of the great appointments to office can be made without the consent of the senate.

Such various, extensive, and important powers combined in one body of men, are inconsistent with all freedom; the celebrated Montesquieu tells us, that "when the legislative and executive powers are united in the same person, or in the same body of magistrates, there can be no liberty, because apprehensions may arise, lest the same monarch or *senate* should enact tyrannical laws, to execute them in a tyrannical manner.

"Again, there is no liberty, if the power of judging be not separated from the legislative and executive powers. Were it joined with the legislative, the life and liberty of the subject would be exposed to arbitrary control: for the judge would then be legislator. Were it joined to the executive power, the judge might behave with all the violence of an oppressor. There would be an end of every thing, were the same man, or the same body of the nobles, or of the people, to exercise those three powers; that of enacting laws; that of executing the public resolutions; and that of judging the crimes or differences of individuals."

The president-general is dangerously connected with the senate; his coincidence with the views of the ruling junto in that body, is made essential to his weight and importance in the government, which will destroy all independency and purity in the executive department, and having the power of pardoning without the concurrence of a council, he may screen from punishment the most treasonable attempts that may be made on the liberties of the people, when instigated by his coadjutors in the senate. Instead of this dangerous and improper mixture of the executive with the legislative and judicial, the supreme executive powers ought to have been placed in the president, with a small independent council, made personally responsible for every appointment to office or other act, by having their opinions recorded; and that without the concurrence of the majority of the quorum of this council, the president should not be capable of taking any step.

We have before considered internal taxation, as it would effect the destruction of the state governments, and produce one consolidated government. We will now consider that subject as it affects the personal concerns of the people.

The power of direct taxation applies to every individual, as congress, under this government, is expressly vested with the authority of laying a capitation or poll tax upon every person to any amount. This is a tax that, however oppressive in its nature, and unequal in its operation, is certain as to its produce and simple in its collection; it cannot be evaded like the objects of imposts or excise, and will be paid, because all that a man hath will he give for his head. This tax is so congenial to the nature of despotism, that it has ever been a favorite under such governments. Some of those who were in the late general convention from this state have long laboured to introduce a poll-tax among us.

The power of direct taxation will further apply to every individual, as Congress may tax land, cattle, trades, occupations, etc. in any amount, and every object of internal taxation is of that nature, that however oppressive, the people will have but this alternative, except to pay the tax, or let their property be taken, for all resistance will be in vain. The standing army and select militia would enforce the collection.

For the moderate exercise of this power, there is no control left in the state governments, whose intervention is destroyed. No relief, or redress of grievances can be extended, as heretofore by them. There is not even a declaration of RIGHTS to which the people may appeal for the vindication of their wrongs in the court of justice. They must therefore, implicitly obey the most arbitrary laws, as the worst of them will be pursuant to the principles and form of the constitution, and that strongest of all checks upon the conduct of administration, *responsibility to the people,* will not exist in this government. The permanency of the appointments of senators and representatives, and the control the Congress have over their election, will place them independent of the sentiments and resentment of the people, and the administration having a greater interest in the government than in the community, there will be no consideration to restrain them from oppression and tyranny. In the government of this state, under the old confederation, the members of the legislature are taken from among the people, and their interests and welfare are so inseparably connected with those of their constituents, that they can derive no advantage from oppressive laws and taxes, for they would suffer in common with their fellow citizens; would participate in the burdens they impose on the community, as they must return to the common level, after a short period; and notwithstanding every exertion of influence, every means of corruption, a necessary rotation excludes them from permanency in the legislature.

This large state is to have but ten members in that Congress which is to have the liberty, property and dearest concerns of every individual in this vast country at absolute command and even these ten persons, who are to be our only guardians; who are to supercede the legislature of Pennsylvania, will not be of the choice of the people, nor amenable to them. From the mode of their election and appointment they will consist of the lordly and high-minded; of men who will have no congenial feelings with the people, but a perfect indifference for, and contempt of them; they will consist of those harpies of power, that prey upon the very vitals; that riot on the miseries of the community. But we will suppose, although in all probability it may never be realized in fact, that our deputies in Congress have the welfare of their constituents at heart, and will exert themselves in their behalf, what security could even this afford; what relief could they extend to their oppressed constituents? To attain this, the majority of the deputies of the twelve other states in Congress must be alike well disposed; must alike forego the sweets of power, and relinquish the pursuits of ambition, which from the nature of things is not to be expected. If the people part with a responsible representation in the legislature, founded upon fair, certain and frequent elections, they have nothing left they can call their own. Miserable is the lot of that people whose every concern depends on the WILL and PLEASURE of their rulers. Our soldiers will become Janissaries, and our officers of government Bashaws; in short, the system of despotism will soon be completed.

From the foregoing investigation, it appears that the Congress under this constitution will not possess the confidence of the people, which is an essential requisite in a good government; for unless the laws command the confidence and respect of the great body of the people, so as to induce them to support them, when called on by the civil magistrate, they must be executed by the aid of a numerous standing army, which would be inconsistent with every idea of liberty; for the same force that may be employed to compel obedience to good laws, might and probably would be used to wrest from the people their constitutional liberties. The framers of this constitution appear to have been aware of this great deficiency; to have been sensible that no dependence could be placed on the people for their support: but on the contrary, that the government must be executed by force. They have therefore made a provision for this purpose in a permanent STANDING ARMY, and a MILITIA that may be subjected to as strict discipline and government.

A standing army in the hands of a government placed so independent of the people, may be made a fatal instrument to overturn the public liberties; it may be employed to enforce the collection of the most oppressive taxes, and to carry into execution the most arbitrary measures. An ambitious man who may have the army at his devotion, may step up into the throne, and seize upon absolute power.

The absolute unqualified command that Congress have over the militia may be made instrumental to the destruction of all liberty, both public and private; whether of a personal, civil or religious nature.

First, the personal liberty of every man probably from sixteen to sixty years of age, may be destroyed by the power Congress have in organizing and governing of the militia. As militia they may be subjected to fines to any amount, levied in a military manner; they may be subjected to corporal punishments of the most disgraceful and humiliating kind, and to death itself, by the sentence of a court martial: To this our young men will be more immediately subjected, as a select militia, composed of them, will best answer the purposes of government.

Secondly, the rights of conscience may be violated, as there is no exemption of those persons who are conscientiously scrupulous of bearing arms. These compose a respectable proportion of the community in the state. This is the more remarkable, because even when the distresses of the late war, and the evident disaffection of many citizens of that description, inflamed our passions, and when every person, who was obliged to risque his own life, must have been exasperated against such as on any account kept back from the common danger, yet even then, when outrage and violence might have been expected, the rights of conscience were held sacred.

At this momentous crisis, the framers of our state constitution made the most express and decided declaration and stipulations in favour of the rights of conscience: but now when no necessity exists, those dearest rights of men are left insecure.

Thirdly, the absolute command of Congress over the militia may be destructive of public liberty; for under the guidance of an arbitrary government, they may be made the unwilling instruments of tyranny. The militia of Pennsylvania may be marched to New England or Virginia to quell an insurrection occasioned by the most galling oppression, and aided by the standing army, they will no doubt be successful in subduing their liberty and independency; but in so doing, although the magnanimity of their minds will be extinguished, yet the meaner passions of resentment and revenge will be increased, and these in turn will be the ready and obedient instruments of despotism to enslave the others; and that with an irritated vengeance. Thus may the militia be made the instruments of crushing the last efforts of expiring liberty, of riveting the chains of despotism on their fellow citizens, and on one another. This power can be exercised not only without violating the constitution, but in strict conformity with it; it is calculated for this express purpose, and will doubtless be executed accordingly.

As this government will not enjoy the confidence of the people, but be executed by force, it will be a very expensive and burthensome government. The standing army must be numerous, and as a further support, it will be the policy of this government to multiply officers in every department: judges, collectors, tax-gatherers, excisemen and the whole host of revenue officers will swarm over the land, devouring the hard earnings of the industrious. Like the locusts of old, impoverishing and desolating all before them.

We have not noticed the smaller, nor many of the considerable blemishes, but have confined our objections to the great and essential defects; the main pillars of the constitution; which we have shewn to be inconsistent with the liberty and happiness of the people, as its establishment will annihilate the state governments, and produce one consolidated government that will eventually and speedily issue in the supremacy of despotism.

In this investigation, we have not confined our views to the interests or welfare of this state, in preference to the others. We have overlooked all local circumstances—we have considered this subject on the broad scale of the general good; we have asserted the cause of the present and future ages; the cause of liberty and mankind.

Letters from the Federal Farmer

*A systematic critique of the new Constitution, and a full elabora-
tion of anti-federalist thought was offered in a lengthy series of
articles usually entitled* Letters from the Federal Farmer, *published in the Poughkeepsie* Country Journal, *November 1787–
January 1788, but also issued and widely circulated in pamphlet
form in New York City and elsewhere. The full title of the pamphlet, printing five letters, was* Observations Leading to a Fair
Examination of the System of Government Proposed by the Late
Convention; and to Several Essential and Necessary Alterations
to It. In a Number of Letters from the Federal Farmer to the
Republican. *Besides this pamphlet, the author brought out* An
Additional Number of Letters, *thirteen more in all, that, as he put
it, illustrated and supported the principles laid down in the earlier letters. Though sometimes discursive and repetitious, the letters, skillfully written, moderate in tone, and thoughtful, were
perhaps the most eloquent and persuasive anti-federalist writings. The author, long thought to be Richard Henry Lee, a Virginia delegate to the Continental Congress then sitting in New
York, was in fact almost certainly not Lee, but more probably the
New York anti-federalist Melancton Smith. The first two letters,
dated October 8 and 9, 1787, printed below, convey "The Federal Farmer's" basic argument about the dangerous, consolidating, tyranny-tending nature of the new Constitution.*

I

October 8, 1787.

Dear Sir,

My letters to you last winter, on the subject of a well balanced national government for the United States, were the result

of free enquiry; when I passed from that subject to enquiries relative to our commerce, revenues, past administration, etc. I anticipated the anxieties I feel, on carefully examining the plan of government proposed by the convention. It appears to be a plan retaining some federal features; but to be the first important step, and to aim strongly to one consolidated government of the United States. It leaves the powers of government, and the representation of the people, so unnaturally divided between the general and state governments, that the operations of our system must be very uncertain. My uniform federal attachments, and the interest I have in the protection of property, and a steady execution of the laws, will convince you, that, if I am under any biass at all, it is in favor of any general system which shall promise those advantages. The instability of our laws increases my wishes for firm and steady government; but then, I can consent to no government, which, in my opinion, is not calculated equally to preserve the rights of all orders of men in the community. My object has been to join with those who have endeavoured to supply the defects in the forms of our governments by a steady and proper administration of them. Though I have long apprehended that fraudalent debtors, and embarrassed men, on the one hand, and men, on the other, unfriendly to republican equality, would produce an uneasiness among the people, and prepare the way, not for cool and deliberate reforms in the governments, but for changes calculated to promote the interests of particular orders of men. Acquit me, sir, of any agency in the formation of the new system; I shall be satisfied with seeing, if it shall be adopted, a prudent administration. Indeed I am so much convinced of the truth of Pope's maxim, that "That which is best administered is best," that I am much inclined to subscribe to it from experience. I am not disposed to unreasonably contend about forms. I know our situation is critical, and it behoves us to make the best of it. A federal government of some sort is necessary. We have suffered the present to languish; and whether the confederation was capable or not originally of answering any valuable purposes, it is now but of little importance. I will pass by the men, and states, who have been particularly instrumental in preparing the way for a change, and, perhaps, for governments not very favourable to the people at large. A constitution is now presented which we may reject, or which we may accept, with or without amendments; and to which point we ought to direct our exertions, is the question. To determine this question, with propriety, we must attentively examine the system itself, and the probable consequences of either step. This I shall endeavour to do, so far as I am able, with candor and fairness; and leave you to decide upon the propriety of my opinions, the weight of my reasons, and how far my conclusions are well drawn. Whatever may be the conduct of others, on the present occasion, I do not mean, hastily and positively to decide on the merits of the constitution proposed. I shall be open to conviction, and always disposed to adopt that which, all things considered, shall appear to me to be most for the happiness of the community. It must be granted, that if men hastily and blindly adopt a system of government, they will as hastily and as blindly be led to alter or abolish it; and changes must ensue, one after another, till the peaceable and better part of the community will grow weary with changes, tumults and disorders, and be disposed to accept any government, however despotic, that shall promise stability and firmness.

The first principal question that occurs, is, Whether, considering our situation, we ought to precipitate the adoption of the proposed constitution? If we remain cool and temperate, we are in no immediate danger of any commotions; we are in a state of perfect peace, and in no danger of invasions; the state governments are in the full exercise of their powers; and our governments answer all present exigencies, except the regulation of trade, securing credit, in some cases, and providing for the interest, in some instances, of the public debts; and whether we adopt a change, three or nine months hence, can make but little odds with the private circumstances of individuals; their happiness and prosperity, after all, depend principally upon their own exertions. We are hardly recovered from a long and distressing war: The farmers, fishmen etc. have not yet fully repaired the waste made by it. Industry and frugality are again assuming their proper station. Private debts are lessened, and public debts incurred by the war have been, by various ways, diminished; and

the public lands have now become a productive source for diminishing them much more. I know uneasy men, who wish very
much to precipitate, do not admit all these facts; but they are
facts well known to all men who are thoroughly informed in the
affairs of this country. It must, however, be admitted, that our
federal system is defective, and that some of the state governments are not well administered; but, then, we impute to the
defects in our governments many evils and embarrassments
which are most clearly the result of the late war. We must allow
men to conduct on the present occasion, as on all similar ones.
They will urge a thousand pretences to answer their purposes on
both sides. When we want a man to change his condition, we
describe it as miserable, wretched, and despised; and draw a
pleasing picture of that which we would have him assume. And
when we wish the contrary, we reverse our descriptions. Whenever a clamor is raised, and idle men get to work, it is highly
necessary to examine facts carefully, and without unreasonably
suspecting men of falshood, to examine, and enquire attentively,
under what impressions they act. It is too often the case in political concerns, that men state facts not as they are, but as they
wish them to be; and almost every man, by calling to mind past
scenes, will find this to be true.

Nothing but the passions of ambitious, impatient, or disorderly men, I conceive, will plunge us into commotions, if time
should be taken fully to examine and consider the system proposed. Men who feel easy in their circumstances, and such as
are not sanguine in their expectations relative to the consequences of the proposed change, will remain quiet under the
existing governments. Many commercial and monied men, who
are uneasy, not without just cause, ought to be respected; and,
by no means, unreasonably disappointed in their expectations
and hopes; but as to those who expect employments under the
new constitution; as to those weak and ardent men who always
expect to be gainers by revolutions, and whose lot it generally is
to get out of one difficulty into another, they are very little to be
regarded: and as to those who designedly avail themselves of
this weakness and ardor, they are to be despised. It is natural for
men, who wish to hasten the adoption of a measure, to tell us,

now is the crisis—now is the critical moment which must be seized, or all will be lost: and to shut the door against free enquiry, whenever conscious the thing presented has defects in it, which time and investigation will probably discover. This has been the custom of tyrants and their dependants in all ages. If it is true, what has been so often said, that the people of this country cannot change their condition for the worse, I presume it still behoves them to endeavour deliberately to change it for the better. The fickle and ardent, in any community, are the proper tools for establishing despotic government. But it is deliberate and thinking men, who must establish and secure governments on free principles. Before they decide on the plan proposed, they will enquire whether it will probably be a blessing or a curse to this people.

The present moment discovers a new face in our affairs. Our object has been all along, to reform our federal system, and to strengthen our governments—to establish peace, order and justice in the community—but a new object now presents. The plan of government now proposed is evidently calculated totally to change, in time, our condition as a people. Instead of being thirteen republics, under a federal head, it is clearly designed to make us one consolidated government. Of this, I think, I shall fully convince you, in my following letters on this subject. This consolidation of the states has been the object of several men in this country for some time past. Whether such a change can ever be effected in any manner; whether it can be effected without convulsions and civil wars; whether such a change will not totally destroy the liberties of this country—time only can determine.

To have a just idea of the government before us, and to shew that a consolidated one is the object in view, it is necessary not only to examine the plan, but also its history, and the politics of its particular friends.

The confederation was formed when great confidence was placed in the voluntary exertions of individuals, and of the respective states; and the framers of it, to guard against usurpation, so limited and checked the powers, that, in many respects, they are inadequate to the exigencies of the union. We find, therefore, members of congress urging alterations in the federal system almost as soon as it was adopted. It was early proposed to vest congress with powers to levy an impost, to regulate trade, etc., but such was known to be the caution of the states in parting with power, that the vestment, even of these, was proposed to be under several checks and limitations. During the war, the general confusion, and the introduction of paper money, infused in the minds of people vague ideas respecting government and credit. We expected too much from the return of peace, and of course we have been disappointed. Our governments have been new and unsettled; and several legislatures, by making tender, suspension, and paper money laws, have given just cause of uneasiness to creditors. By these and other causes, several orders of men in the community have been prepared, by degrees, for a change of government; and this very abuse of power in the legislatures, which, in some cases, has been charged upon the democratic part of the community, has furnished aristocratical men with those very weapons, and those very means, with which, in great measure, they are rapidly effecting their favourite object. And should an oppressive government be the consequence of the proposed change, posterity may reproach not only a few overbearing unprincipled men, but those parties in the states which have misused their powers.

The conduct of several legislatures, touching paper money, and tender laws, has prepared many honest men for changes in government, which otherwise they would not have thought of—when by the evils, on the one hand, and by the secret instigations of artful men, on the other, the minds of men were become sufficiently uneasy, a bold step was taken, which is usually followed by a revolution, or a civil war. A general convention for mere commercial purposes was moved for—the authors of this measure saw that the people's attention was turned solely to the amendment of the federal system; and that, had the idea of a total change been started, probably no state would have appointed members to the convention. The idea of destroying, ultimately, the state government, and forming one consolidated system, could not have been admitted—a convention, therefore, merely for vesting in congress power to regulate trade was proposed. This was pleasing to the commercial towns; and the landed people had little or no concern about it. September, 1786, a few men from the middle states met at Annapolis, and hastily proposed a convention to be held in May, 1787, for the purpose, generally, of amending the confederation—this was done before the delegates of Massachusetts, and of the other states arrived— still not a word was said about destroying the old constitution, and making a new one.—The states still unsuspecting, and not aware that they were passing the Rubicon, appointed members to the new convention, for the sole and express purpose of revising and amending the confederation—and, probably, not one man in ten thousand in the United States, till within these ten or twelve days, had an idea that the old ship was to be destroyed, and he put to the alternative of embarking in the new ship presented, or of being left in danger of sinking.—The States, I believe, universally supposed the convention would report alterations in the confederation, which would pass an examination in congress, and after being agreed to there, would be confirmed by all the legislatures, or be rejected. Virginia made a very respectable appointment, and placed at the head of it the first man in America: In this appointment there was a mixture of political characters; but Pennsylvania appointed principally those men who are esteemed aristocratical. Here the favourite moment for changing the government was evidently discerned by a few men, who seized it with address. Ten other states appointed, and though they chose men principally connected with commerce and the judicial department yet they appointed many good republican characters—had they all attended we should now see, I am persuaded a better system presented. The non-attendace of eight or nine men, who were appointed members of the convention, I shall ever consider as a very unfortunate event to the United States.—Had they attended, I am pretty clear, that the result of the convention would not have had that strong tendency to aristocracy now discernable in every part of the plan. There would not have been so great an accumulation of powers, especially as to the internal police of the country, in a few hands, as the constitution reported proposes to vest in them—the young visionary men, and the consolidating aristocracy, would have been more restrained than they have been. Eleven states met in the convention, and after four months' close attention presented the new constitution, to be adopted or rejected by the people. The uneasy and fickle part of the community may be prepared to receive any form of government; but, I presume, the enlightened and substantial part will give any constitution presented for their adoption, a candid and thorough examination; and silence those designing or empty men, who weakly and rashly attempt to precipitate the adoption of a system of so much importance.—We shall view the convention with proper respect—and, at the same time, that we reflect there were men of abilities and integrity in it, we must recollect how disproportionably the democratic and aristocratic parts of the community were represented.—Perhaps the judicious friends and opposers of the new constitution will agree, that it is best to let it rest solely on its own merits, or be condemned for its own defects.

In the first place, I shall premise, that the plan proposed is a plan of accommodation—and that it is in this way only, and by giving up a part of our opinions, that we can ever expect to obtain a government founded in freedom and compact. This circumstance candid men will always keep in view, in the discussion of this subject.

The plan proposed appears to be partly federal, but principally however, calculated ultimately to make the states one consolidated government.

The first interesting question, therefore suggested, is, how far the states can be consolidated into one entire government on free principles. In considering this question extensive objects are to be taken into view, and important changes in the forms of government to be carefully attended to in all their consequences. The happiness of the people at large must be the great object with every honest statesman, and he will direct every movement to this point. If we are so situated as a people, as not to be able to enjoy equal happiness and advantages under one government, the consolidation of the states cannot be admitted.

There are three different forms of free government under

which the United States may exist as one nation; and now is, perhaps, the time to determine to which we will direct our views. 1. Distinct republics connected under a federal head. In this case the respective state governments must be the principal guardians of the people's rights, and exclusively regulate their internal police; in them must rest the balance of government. The congress of the states, or federal head, must consist of delegates amenable to, and removeable by the respective states: This congress must have general directing powers; powers to require men and monies of the states; to make treaties, peace and war; to direct the operations of armies, etc. Under this federal modification of government, the powers of congress would be rather advisory or recommendatory than coercive. 2. We may do away the several state governments, and form or consolidate all the states into one entire government, with one executive, one judiciary, and one legislature, consisting of senators and representatives collected from all parts of the union: In this case there would be a compleat consolidation of the states. 3. We may consolidate the states as to certain national objects, and leave them severally distinct independent republics, as to internal police generally. Let the general government consist of an executive, a judiciary, and balanced legislature, and its powers extend exclusively to all foreign concerns, causes arising on the seas to commerce, imports, armies, navies, Indian affairs, peace and war, and to a few internal concerns of the community; to the coin, post-offices, weights and measures, a general plan for the militia, to naturalization, *and, perhaps to bankruptcies,* leaving the internal police of the community, in other respects, exclusively to the state governments; as the administration of justice in all causes arising internally, the laying and collecting of internal taxes, and the forming of the militia according to a general plan prescribed. In this case there would be a compleat consolidation, *quoad* certain objects only.

Touching the first, or federal plan, I do not think much can be said in its favor: The sovereignty of the nation, without coercive and efficient powers to collect the strength of it, cannot always be depended on to answer the purposes of government; and in a congress of representatives of sovereign states, there must necessarily be an unreasonable mixture of powers in the same hands.

As to the second, or compleat consolidating plan, it deserves to be carefully considered at this time, by every American: If it be impracticable, it is a fatal error to model our governments, directing our views ultimately to it.

The third plan, or partial consolidation, is, in my opinion, the only one that can secure the freedom and happiness of this people. I once had some general ideas that the second plan was practicable, but from long attention, and the proceedings of the convention, I am fully satisfied, that this third plan is the only one we can with safety and propriety proceed upon. Making this the standard to point out, with candor and fairness, the parts of the new constitution which appear to be improper, is my object. The convention appears to have proposed the partial consolidation evidently with a view to collect all powers ultimately, in the United States into one entire government; and from its views in this respect, and from the tenacity of the small states to have an equal vote in the senate, probably originated the greatest defects in the proposed plan.

Independent of the opinions of many great authors, that a free elective government cannot be extended over large territories, a few reflections must evince, that one government and general legislation alone, never can extend equal benefits to all parts of the United States: Different laws, customs, and opinions exist in the different states, which by a uniform system of laws would be unreasonably invaded. The United States contain about a million of square miles, and in half a century will, probably, contain ten millions of people; and from the center to the extremes is about 800 miles.

Before we do away the state governments, or adopt measures that will tend to abolish them, and to consolidate the states into one entire government, several principles should be considered and facts ascertained:—These, and my examination into the essential parts of the proposed plan, I shall pursue in my next.

II

October 9, 1787.

Dear Sir,

The essential parts of a free and good government are a full and equal representation of the people in the legislature, and the jury trial of the vicinage in the administration of justice—a full and equal representation, is that which possesses the same interests, feelings, opinions, and views the people themselves would were they all assembled—a fair representation, therefore, should be so regulated, that every order of men in the community, according to the common course of elections, can have a share in it—in order to allow professional men, merchants, traders, farmers, mechanics, etc. to bring a just proportion of their best informed men respectively into the legislature, the representation must be considerably numerous.—We have about 200 state senators in the United States, and a less number than that of federal representatives cannot, clearly, be a full representation of this people, in the affairs of internal taxation and police, were there but one legislature for the whole union. The representation cannot be equal, or the situation of the people proper for one government only—if the extreme parts of the society cannot be represented as fully as the central.—It is apparently impracticable that this should be the case in this extensive country—it would be impossible to collect a representation of the parts of the country five, six, and seven hundred miles from the seat of government.

Under one general government alone, there could be but one judiciary, one supreme and a proper number of inferior courts. I think it would be totally impracticable in this case to preserve a due administration of justice, and the real benefits of the jury trial of the vicinage—there are now supreme courts in each state in the union; and a great number of county and other courts subordinate to each supreme court—most of these supreme and inferior courts are itinerant, and hold their sessions in different parts every year of their respective states, counties and districts—with all these moving courts, our citizens, from the vast extent of the country must travel very considerable distances from home to find the place where justice is administered. I am not for bringing justice so near to individuals as to afford them any temptation to engage in law suits; though I think it one of the greatest benefits in a good government, that each citizen should find a court of justice within a reasonable distance, perhaps, within a day's travel of his home; so that, without great inconveniences ad enormous expences, he may have the advantages of his witnesses and jury—it would be impracticable to derive these advantages from one judiciary—the one supreme court at most could only set in the centre of the union, and move once a year into the centre of the eastern and southern extremes of it— and, in this case, each citizen, on an average, would travel 150 or 200 miles to find this court—that, however, inferior courts might be properly placed in the different counties, and districts of the union, the appellate jurisdiction would be intolerable and expensive.

If it were possible to consolidate the states, and preserve the features of a free government, still it is evident that the middle states, the parts of the union, about the seat of government, would enjoy great advantages, while the remote states would experience the many inconveniences of remote provinces. Wealth, offices, and the benefits of government would collect in the centre: and the extreme states and their principal towns, become much less important.

There are other considerations which tend to prove that the idea of one consolidated whole, on free principles, is ill-founded—the laws of a free government rest on the confidence of the people, and operate gently—and never can extend their influence very far—if they are executed on free principles, about the centre, where the benefits of the government induce the people to support it voluntarily; yet they must be executed on the principles of fear and force in the extremes.—This has been the case with every extensive republic of which we have any accurate account.

There are certain unalienable and fundamental rights, which in forming the social compact, ought to be explicitly ascertained and fixed—a free and enlightened people, in forming this compact, will not resign all their rights to those who govern, and they will fix limits to their legislators and rulers, which will soon be plainly seen by those who are governed, as well as by those who govern; and the latter will know they cannot be passed unperceived by the former, and without giving a general alarm.—These rights should be made the basis of every constitution: and if a people be so situated, or have such different opinions that they cannot agree in ascertaining and fixing them, it is a very strong argument against their attempting to form one entire society, to live under one system of laws only.—I confess, I never thought the people of these states differed essentially in these respects; they having derived all these rights from one common source, the British systems; and having in the formation of their state constitutions, discovered that their ideas relative to these rights are very similar. However, it is now said that the states differ so essentially in these respects, and even in the important article of the trial by jury, that when assembled in convention, they can agree to no words by which to establish that trial, or by which to ascertain and establish many other of these rights, as fundamental articles in the social compact. If so, we proceed to consolidate the states on no solid basis whatever.

But I do not pay much regard to the reasons given for not bottoming the new constitution on a better bill of rights. I still believe a complete federal bill of rights to be very practicable. Nevertheless I acknowledge the proceedings of the convention furnish my mind with many new and strong reasons, against a complete consolidation of the states. They tend to convince me, that it cannot be carried with propriety very far—that the convention have gone much farther in one respect than they found it practicable to go in another; that is, they propose to lodge in the general government very extensive powers—*powers* nearly, if not altogether, complete and unlimited, over the purse and the sword. But, in its organization, they furnish the strongest proof that the proper limbs, or parts of a government, to support and execute those powers on proper principles (or in which they can be safely lodged) cannot be formed. These powers must be lodged somewhere in every society; but then they should be lodged where the strength and guardians of the people are collected. They can be wielded, or safely used, in a free country only by an able executive and judiciary, a respectable senate, and a secure, full, and equal representation of the people. I think the principles I have premised or brought into view, are well founded—I think they will not be denied by any fair reasoner. It is in connection with these, and other solid principles, we are to examine the constitution. It is not a few democratic phrases, or a few well formed features, that will prove its merits; or a few small omissions that will produce its rejection among men of sense; they will enquire what are the essential powers in a community, and what are nominal ones; where and how the essential powers shall be lodged to secure government, and to secure true liberty.

In examining the proposed constitution carefully, we must clearly perceive an unnatural separation of these powers from the substantial representation of the people. The state governments will exist, with all their governors, senators, representatives, officers and expences; in these will be nineteen-twentieths of the representatives of the people; they will have a near connection, and their members an immediate intercourse with the people; and the probability is, that the state governments will possess the confidence of the people, and be considered generally as their immediate guardians.

The general government will consist of a new species of executive, a small senate, and a very small house of representatives. As many citizens will be more than three hundred miles from the seat of this government as will be nearer to it, its judges and officers cannot be very numerous, without making our governments very expensive. Thus will stand the state and the general governments, should the constitution be adopted without any alterations in their organization; but as to powers, the general government will possess all essential ones, at least on paper, and those of the states a mere shadow of power. And therefore, unless the people shall make some great exertions to restore to the state governments their powers in matters of internal police; as the powers to lay and collect, exclusively, internal taxes, to govern the militia, and to hold the decisions of their own judicial courts upon their own laws final, the balance cannot possibly continue long; but the state governments must be annihilated, or continue to exist for no purpose.

It is however to be observed, that many of the essential powers given the national government are not exclusively given; and the general government may have prudence enough to forbear the exercise of those which may still be exercised by the respective states. But this cannot justify the impropriety of giving powers, the exercise of which prudent men will not attempt, and imprudent men will, or probably can, exercise only in a manner destructive of free government. The general government, organized as it is, may be adequate to many valuable objects, and be able to carry its laws into execution on proper principles in several cases; but I think its warmest friends will not contend, that it can carry all the powers proposed to be lodged in it into effect, without calling to its aid a military force, which must very soon destroy all elective governments in the country, produce anarchy, or establish despotism. Though we cannot have now a complete idea of what will be the operations of the proposed system, we may, allowing things to have their common course, have a very tolerable one. The powers lodged in the general government, if exercised by it, must intimately effect the internal police of the states, as well as external concerns; and there is no reason to expect the numerous state governments, and their connections, will be very friendly to the execution of federal laws in those internal affairs, which hitherto have been under their own immediate management. There is more reason to believe, that the general government, far removed from the people, and none of its members elected oftener than once in two years, will be forgot or neglected, and its laws in many cases disregarded, unless a multitude of officers and military force be continually kept in view, and employed to enforce the execution of the laws, and to make the government feared and respected. No position can be truer than this, that in this country either neglected laws, or a military execution of them, must lead to a revolution, and to the destruction of freedom. Neglected laws must first lead to anarchy and confusion; and a military execution of laws is only a shorter way to the same point—despotic government.

"Brutus," Essays I, VI, X–XII, and XV

The anti-federalist writing which most nearly paralleled and confronted The Federalist, *undertaking a detailed, sometimes clause-by-clause, critique of the new Constitution, was a series of essays to "the Citizens of the Slate of New York," and signed "Brutus." (The pseudonym, of course, evoked images of the heroic Roman republican who killed the usurper-tyrant Caesar.) The sixteen essays appeared in the* New York Journal *between October 1787 and April 1788, the same months when* The Federalist *was appearing in New York newspapers. The essays of "Brutus" were widely reprinted and commented on, but were not reissued in pamphlet form. The author was probably Robert Yates, a New York judge, delegate to the Federal Convention, and a political ally of New York governor George Clinton.*

After an opening essay, Number I, where "Brutus" attacks the idea of a large, consolidated republic (see counterarguments in Federalist No. 10), he criticizes the parts of the Constitution he considers most dangerous to republican liberty. In Number VI he points out the danger in the taxing power (counter to Federalist Nos. 23 and 30–36), and in Number X he opposes the unlimited power to raise and support armies (counter to Federalist Nos. 24–29). "Brutus" takes particular pains, in Nos. XI–XV, to attack the wide powers and unrepublican tenure of the federal judiciary (counter to Federalist Nos. 78–83). Essay Nos. I, VI, X, XI, XII, and XV are printed here.

I
18 OCTOBER 1787

To the Citizens of the State of New York.

When the public is called to investigate and decide upon a question in which not only the present members of the community are deeply interested, but upon which the happiness and misery of generations yet unborn is in great measure suspended, the benevolent mind cannot help feeling itself peculiarly interested in the result.

In this situation, I trust the feeble efforts of an individual, to lead the minds of the people to a wise and prudent determination, cannot fail of being acceptable to the candid and dispassionate part of the community. Encouraged by this consideration, I have been induced to offer my thoughts upon the present important crisis of our public affairs.

Perhaps this country never saw so critical a period in their political concerns. We have felt the feebleness of the ties by which these United States are held together, and the want of sufficient energy in our present confederation, to manage, in some instances, our general concerns. Various expedients have been proposed to remedy these evils, but none have succeeded. At length a Convention of the states has been assembled, they have formed a constitution which will now, probably, be submitted to the people to ratify or reject, who are the fountain of all power, to whom alone it of right belongs to make or unmake constitutions, or forms of government, at their pleasure. The most important question that was ever proposed to your decision, or to the decision of any people under heaven, is before you, and you are to decide upon it by men of your own election, chosen specially for this purpose, if the constitution, offered to your acceptance, be a wise one, calculated to preserve the invaluable blessings of liberty, to secure the inestimable rights of mankind, and promote human happiness, then, if you accept it, you will lay a lasting foundation of happiness for millions yet unborn; generations to come will rise up and call you blessed.

You may rejoice in the prospects of this vast extended continent becoming filled with freemen, who will assert the dignity of human nature. You may solace yourselves with the idea, that society, in this favoured land, will fast advance to the highest point of perfection; the human mind will expand in knowledge and virtue, and the golden age be, in some measure, realised. But if, on the other hand, this form of government contains principles that will lead to the subversion of liberty—if it tends to establish a despotism, or, what is worse, a tyrannic aristocracy; then, if you adopt it, this only remaining assylum for liberty will be shut up, and posterity will execrate your memory.

Momentous then is the question you have to determine, and you are called upon by every motive which should influence a noble and virtuous mind, to examine it well, and to make up a wise judgment. It is insisted, indeed, that this constitution must be received, be it ever so imperfect. If it has its defects, it is said, they can be best amended when they are experienced. But remember, when the people once part with power, they can seldom or never resume it again but by force. Many instances can be produced in which the people have voluntarily increased the powers of their rulers; but few, if any, in which rulers have willingly abridged their authority. This is a sufficient reason to induce you to be careful, in the first instance, how you deposit the powers of government.

With these few introductory remarks, I shall proceed to a consideration of this constitution:

The first question that presents itself on the subject is, whether a confederated government be the best for the United States or not? Or in other words, whether the thirteen United States should be reduced to one great republic, governed by one legislature, and under the direction of one executive and judicial; or whether they should continue thirteen confederated republics, under the direction and control of a supreme federal head for certain defined national purposes only?

This enquiry is important, because, although the government reported by the convention does not go to a perfect and entire consolidation, yet it approaches so near to it, that it must, if executed, certainly and infallibly terminate in it.

This government is to possess absolute and uncontrolable power, legislative, executive and judicial, with respect to every object to which it extends, for by the last clause of section 8th, article 1st, it is declared "that the Congress shall have power to make all laws which shall be necessary and proper for carrying into execution the foregoing powers, and all other powers vested by this constitution, in the government of the United States; or in any department or office thereof." And by the 6th article, it is declared "that this constitution, and the laws of the United States, which shall be made in pursuance thereof, and the treaties made, or which shall be made, under the authority of the United States, shall be the supreme law of the land; and the judges in every state shall be bound thereby, any thing in the constitution, or law of any state to the contrary notwithstanding." It appears from these articles that there is no need of any intervention of the state governments, between the Congress and the people, to execute any one power vested in the general government, and that the constitution and laws of every state are nullified and declared void, so far as they are or shall be inconsistent with this constitution, or the laws made in pursuance of it, or with treaties made under the authority of the United States.—The government then, so far as it extends, is a complete one, and not a confederation. It is as much one complete government as that of New York or Massachusetts, has as absolute and perfect powers to make and execute all laws, to appoint officers, institute courts, declare offences, and annex penalties, with respect to every object to which it extends, as any other in the world. So far therefore as its powers reach, all ideas of confederation are given up and lost. It is true this government is limited to certain objects, or to speak more properly, some small degree of power is still left to the states, but a little attention to the powers vested in the general government, will convince every candid man, that if it is capable of being executed, all that is reserved for the individual states must very soon be annihilated, except so far as they are barely necessary to the organization of the general government. The powers of the general legislature extend to every case that is of the least importance—there is nothing valuable to human nature, nothing dear to free men, but what is within its power. It has authority to make laws which will affect the lives, the liberty, and property of every man in the United States; nor can the constitution or laws of any state, in any way prevent or impede the full and complete execution of every power given. The legislative power is competent to lay taxes, duties, imposts, and excises—there is no limitation to this power, unless it be said that the clause which directs the use to which those taxes, and duties shall be applied, may be said to be a limitation: but this is no restriction of the power at all, for by this clause they are to be applied to pay the debts and provide for the common defence and general welfare of the United States; but the legislature have authority to contract debts at their discretion; they are the sole judges of what is necessary to provide for the common defence, and they only are to determine what is for the general welfare; this power therefore is neither more nor less, than a power to lay and collect taxes, imposts, and excises, at their pleasure; not only [is] the power to lay taxes unlimited, as to the amount they may require, but it is perfect and absolute to raise them in any mode they please. No state legislature, or any power in the state governments, have any more to do in carrying this into effect, than the authority of one state has to do with that of another. In the business therefore of laying and collecting taxes, the idea of confederation is totally lost, and that of one entire republic is embraced. It is proper here to remark, that the authority to lay and collect taxes is the most important of any power that can be granted; it connects with it almost all other powers, or at least will in process of time draw all other after it; it is the great means of protection, security, and defence, in a good government, and the great engine of oppression and tyranny in a bad one. This cannot fail of being the case, if we consider the contracted limits which are set by this constitution, to the late [state?] governments, on this article of raising money. No state can emit paper money—lay any duties, or imposts, on imports, or exports, but by consent of the Congress; and then the net produce shall be for the benefit of the United States: the only mean therefore left, for any state to support its government and discharge its debts, is by direct taxation; and the United States have also power to lay and collect taxes, in any way they please. Every one who has thought on the subject, must be convinced that but small sums of money can be collected in any country, by direct taxes; when the federal government begins to exercise the right of taxation in all its parts, the legislatures of the several states will find it impossible to raise monies to support their governments. Without money they cannot be supported, and they must dwindle away, and, as before observed, their powers absorbed in that of the general government.

It might be here shown, that the power in the federal legislative, to raise and support armies at pleasure, as well in peace as in war, and their control over the militia, tend, not only to a consolidation of the government, but the destruction of liberty—I shall not, however, dwell upon these, as a few observations upon the judicial power of this government, in addition to the preceding, will fully evince the truth of the position.

The judicial power of the United States is to be vested in a supreme court, and in such inferior courts as Congress may from time to time ordain and establish. The powers of these courts are very extensive; their jurisdiction comprehends all civil causes, except such as arise between citizens of the same state; and it extends to all cases in law and equity arising under the constitution. One inferior court must be established, I presume, in each state, at least, with the necessary executive officers appendant thereto. It is easy to see, that in the common course of things, these courts will eclipse the dignity, and take away from the respectability, of the state courts. These courts will be, in themselves, totally independent of the states, deriving their authority from the United States, and receiving from them fixed salaries; and in the course of human events it is to be expected, that they will swallow up all the powers of the courts in the respective states.

How far the clause in the 8th section of the 1st article may operate to do away all idea of confederated states, and to effect an entire consolidation of the whole into one general government, it is impossible to say. The powers given by this article are very general and comprehensive, and it may receive a construction to justify the passing almost any law. A power to make all laws, which shall be *necessary and proper*, for carrying into execution, all powers vested by the constitution in the government of the United States, or any department or officer thereof, is a power very comprehensive and definite [indefinite?], and may, for ought I know, be exercised in a such manner as entirely to abolish the state legislature. Suppose the legislature of a state should pass a law to raise money to support their government and pay the state debt, may the Congress repeal this law, because it may prevent the collection of a tax which they may think proper and necessary to lay, to provide for the general welfare of the United States? For all laws made, in pursuance of this constitution, are the supreme law of the land, and the judges in every state shall be bound thereby, any thing in the constitution or laws of the different states to the contrary notwithstanding.— By such a law, the government of a particular state might be overturned at one stroke, and thereby be deprived of every means of its support.

It is not meant, by stating this case, to insinuate that the constitution would warrant a law of this kind; or unnecessarily to alarm the fears of the people, by suggesting, that the federal legislature would be more likely to pass the limits assigned them by the constitution, than that of an individual state, further than they are less responsible to the people. But what is meant is, that the legislature of the United States are vested with the great and uncontrolable powers, of laying and collecting taxes, duties, imposts, and excises; of regulating trade, raising and supporting armies, organizing, arming, and disciplining the militia, instituting courts, and other general powers. And are by this clause invested with the power of making all laws, *proper and necessary,* for carrying all these into execution; and they may so exercise this power as entirely to annihilate all the state governments, and reduce this country to one single government. And if they may do it, it is pretty certain they will; for it will be found that the power retained by individual states, small as it is, will be a clog upon the wheels of the government of the United States; the latter therefore will be naturally inclined to remove it out of the way. Besides, it is a truth confirmed by the unerring experience of ages, that every man, and every body of men, invested with power, are ever disposed to increase it, and to acquire a superiority over every thing that stands in their way. This disposition, which is implanted in human nature, will operate in the federal legislature to lessen and ultimately to subvert the state authority, and having such advantages, will most certainly succeed, if the federal government succeeds at all. It must be very evident then, that what this constitution wants of being a complete consolidation of the several parts of the union into one complete government, possessed of a perfect legislative, judicial, and executive powers, to all intents and purposes, it will necessarily acquire in its exercise and operation.

Let us now proceed to enquire, as I at first proposed, whether it be best the thirteen United States should be reduced to one great republic, or not? It is here taken for granted that all agree in this, that whatever government we adopt, it ought to be a free one; that it should be so framed as to secure the liberty of the citizens of America, and such an one as to admit of a full, fair, and equal representation of the people. The question then will be, whether a government thus constituted, and founded on such principles, is practicable, and can be exercised over the whole United States, reduced into one state?

If respect is to be paid to the opinion of the greatest and wisest men who have ever thought or wrote on the science of government, we shall be constrained to conclude, that a free republic cannot succeed over a country of such immense extent, containing such a number of inhabitants, and these encreasing in such rapid progression as that of the whole United States. Among the many illustrious authorities which might be produced to this point, I shall content myself with quoting only two. The one is the Baron de Montesquieu, *Spirit of Laws,* chap. xvi. vol. 1 [book VIII]. "It is natural to a republic to have only a small territory, otherwise it cannot long subsist. In a large republic there are men of larger fortunes, and consequently of less moderation; there are trusts too great to be placed in any single subject; he has interest of his own; he soon begins to think that he may be happy, great and glorious, by oppressing his fellow citizens; and that he may raise himself to grandeur on the ruins of his country. In a large republic, the public good is sacrificed to a thousand views; it is subordinate to exceptions, and depends on accidents. In a small one, the interest of the public is easier perceived, better understood, and more within the reach of every citizen; abuses are of less extent, and of course are less protected." Of the same opinion is the Marquis Beccaria.

History furnishes no example of a free republic, any thing like the extent of the United States. The Grecian republics were of small extent; so also was that of the Romans. Both of these, it is true, in process of time, extended their conquests over large territories of country; and the consequence was, that their governments were changed from that of free governments to those of the most tyrannical that ever existed in the world.

Not only the opinion of the greatest men, and the experience of mankind, are against the idea of an extensive republic, but a variety of reasons may be drawn from the reason and nature of things, against it, in every government, the will of the sovereign is the law. In despotic governments, the supreme authority being lodged in one, his will is law, and can be as easily expressed to a large extensive territory as to a small one. In a pure democracy the people are the sovereign, and their will is declared by themselves; for this purpose they must all come together to deliberate, and decide. This kind of government cannot be exercised, therefore, over a country of any considerable extent; it must be confined to a single city, or at least limited to such bounds as that the people can conveniently assemble, be able to debate, understand the subject submitted to them, and declare their opinion concerning it.

In a free republic, although all laws are derived from the consent of the people, yet the people do not declare their consent by themselves in person, but by representatives, chosen by them, who are supposed to know the minds of their constituents, and to be possessed of integrity to declare this mind.

In every free government, the people must give their assent to the laws by which they are governed. This is the true criterion between a free government and an arbitrary one. The former are ruled by the will of the whole, expressed in any manner they may agree upon; the latter by the will of one, or a few. If the people are to give their assent to the laws, by persons chosen and appointed by them, the manner of the choice and the number chosen, must be such, as to possess, be disposed, and consequently qualified to declare the sentiments of the people; for if they do not know, or are not disposed to speak the sentiments of the people, the people do not govern, but the sovereignty is in a few. Now, in a large extended country, it is impossible to have a representation, possessing the sentiments, and of integrity, to declare the minds of the people, without having it so numerous and unwieldly, as to be subject in great measure to the inconveniency of a democratic government.

The territory of the United States is of vast extent; it now contains near three millions of souls, and is capable of containing much more than ten times that number. Is it practicable for a country, so large and so numerous as they will soon become, to elect a representation, that will speak their sentiments, without their becoming so numerous as to be incapable of transacting public business? It certainly is not.

In a republic, the manners, sentiments, and interests of the people should be similar. If this be not the case, there will be a constant clashing of opinions; and the representatives of one part will be continually striving against those of the other. This will retard the operations of government, and prevent such conclusions as will promote the public good. If we apply this remark to the condition of the United States, we shall be convinced that it forbids that we should be one government. The United States includes a variety of climates. The productions of the different parts of the union are very variant, and their interests, of consequence, diverse. Their manners and habits differ as much as their climates and productions; and their sentiments are by no means coincident. The laws and customs of the several states are, in many respects, very diverse, and in some opposite; each would be in favor of its own interests and customs, and, of consequence, a legislature, formed of representatives from the respective parts, would not only be too numerous to act with any care or decision, but would be composed of such heterogenous and discordant principles, as would constantly be contending with each other.

The laws cannot be executed in a republic, of an extent equal to that of the United States, with promptitude.

The magistrates in every government must be supported in the execution of the laws, either by an armed force, maintained at the public expence for that purpose; or by the people turning out to aid the magistrate upon his command, in case of resistance.

In despotic governments, as well as in all the monarchies of Europe, standing armies are kept up to execute the commands of the prince or the magistrate, and are employed for this purpose when occasion requires: But they have always proved the destruction of liberty, and are abhorrent to the spirit of a free republic. In England, where they depend upon the parliament for their annual support, they have always been complained of as oppressive and unconstitutional, and are seldom employed in executing of the laws; never except on extraordinary occasions, and then under the direction of a civil magistrate.

A free republic will never keep a standing army to execute its laws. It must depend upon the support of its citizens. But when a government is to receive its support from the aid of the citizens, it must be so constructed as to have the confidence, respect, and affection of the people. Men who, upon the call of the magistrate, offer themselves to execute the laws, are influenced to do it either by affection to the government, or from fear; where a standing army is at hand to punish offenders, every man is actuated by the latter principle, and therefore, when the magistrate calls, will obey; but, where this is not the case, the government must rest for its support upon the confidence and respect which the people have for their government and laws. The body of the people being attached, the government will always be sufficient to support and execute its laws, and to operate upon the fears of any faction which may be opposed to it, not only to prevent an opposition to the execution of the laws themselves, but also to compel the most of them to aid the magistrate; but the people will not be likely to have such confidence in their rulers, in a republic so extensive as the United States, as necessary for these purposes. The confidence which the people have in their rulers, in a free republic, arises from their knowing them, from their being responsible to them for their conduct, and from the power they have of displacing them when they misbehave;

but in a republic of the extent of this continent, the people in general would be acquainted with very few of their rulers; the people at large would know little of their proceedings, and it would be extremely difficult to change them. The people in Georgia and New Hampshire would not know one another's mind, and therefore could not act in concert to enable them to effect a general change of representatives. The different parts of so extensive a country could not possibly be made acquainted with the conduct of their representatives, nor be informed of the reasons upon which measures were founded. The consequence will be, they will have no confidence in their legislature, suspect them of ambitious views, be jealous of every measure they adopt, and will not support the laws they pass. Hence the government will be nerveless and inefficient, and no way will be left to render it otherwise, but by establishing an armed force to execute the laws at the point of bayonet—a government of all others the most to be dreaded.

In a republic of such vast extent as the United States, the legislature cannot attend to the various concerns and wants of its different parts. It cannot be sufficiently numerous to be acquainted with the local condition and wants of the different districts, and if it could, it is impossible it should have sufficient time to attend to and provide for all the variety of cases of this nature, that would be continually arising.

In so extensive a republic, the great officers of government would soon become above the control of the people, and abuse their power to the purpose of aggrandizing themselves, and oppressing them. The trust committed to the executive offices, in a country of the extent of the United States, must be various and of magnitude. The command of all the troops and navy of the republic, the appointment of officers, the power of pardoning offences, the collecting of all the public revenues, and the power of expending them, with a number of other powers, must be lodged and exercised in every state, in the hands of a few. When these are attended with great honor and emolument, as they always will be in large states, so as greatly to interest men to pursue them, and to be proper objects for ambitious and designing men, such men will be ever restless in their pursuit after them. They will use the power, when they have acquired it, to the purposes of gratifying their own interest and ambition, and it is scarcely possible, in a very large republic, to call them to account for their misconduct, or to prevent their abuse of power.

These are some of the reasons by which it appears, that a free republic cannot long subsist over a country of the great extent of these states. If then this new constitution is calculated to consolidate the thirteen states into one, as it evidently is, it ought not to be adopted.

Though I am of opinion, that it is a sufficient objection to this government to reject it, that it creates the whole union into one government, under the form of a republic, yet if this objection was obviated, there are exceptions to it, which are so material and fundamental, that they ought to determine every man, who is a friend to the liberty and happiness of mankind, not to adopt it. I beg the candid and dispassionate attention of my countrymen while I state these objections—they are such as have obtruded themselves upon my mind upon a careful attention to the matter, and such as I sincerely believe are well founded. There are many objections, of small moment, of which I shall take no notice—perfection is not to be expected in any thing that is the production of man—and if I did not in my conscience believe that this scheme was defective in the fundamental principles—in the foundation upon which a free and equal government must rest—I would hold my peace.

Brutus.

VI
27 DECEMBER 1787

It is an important question, whether the general government of the United States should be so framed, as to absorb and swallow up the state governments? or whether on the contrary, the former ought not to be confined to certain defined national objects, while the latter should retain all the powers which concern the internal police of the state?

I have, in my former papers, offered a variety of arguments to prove, that a simple free government could not be exercised over this whole continent, and that therefore we must either give up our liberties and submit to an arbitrary one, or frame a constitution on the plan of confederation. Further reasons might be urged to prove this point—but it seems unnecessary, because the principal advocates of the new constitution admit of the position. The question therefore between us, this being admitted, is, whether or not this system is so formed as either directly to annihilate the state governments, or that in its operation it will certainly effect it. If this is answered in the affirmative, then the system ought not to be adopted, without such amendments as will avoid this consequence. If on the contrary it can be seen, that the state governments are secured in their rights to manage the internal police of the respective states, we must confine ourselves in our enquiries to the organization of the government and the guards and provisions it contains to prevent a misuse or abuse of power. To determine this question, it is requisite, that we fully investigate the nature, and the extent of the powers intended to be granted by this constitution to the rulers.

In my last number I called your attention to this subject, and proved, as I think, uncontrovertibly, that the powers given the legislature under the 8th section of the 1st article, had no other limitation than the discretion of the Congress. It was shown, that even if the most favorable construction was given to this paragraph, that the advocates for the new constitution could wish, it will convey a power to lay and collect taxes, imposts, duties, and excises, according to the discretion of the legislature, and to make all laws which they shall judge proper and necessary to carry this power into execution. This I showed would totally destroy all the power of the state governments. To confirm this, it is worth while to trace the operation of the government in some particular instances.

The general government is to be vested with authority to levy and collect taxes, duties, and excises; the separate states have also power to impose taxes, duties, and excises, except that they cannot lay duties on exports and imports without the consent of Congress. Here then the two governments have concurrent jurisdiction: both may lay impositions of this kind. But then the general government have supperadded to this power, authority to make all laws which shall be necessary and proper for carrying the foregoing power into execution. Suppose then that both governments should lay taxes, duties, and excises, and it should fall so heavy on the people that they would be unable, or be so burdensome that they would refuse to pay them both—would it not be necessary that the general legislature should suspend the collection of the state tax? It certainly would. For, if the people could not, or would not pay both, they must be discharged from the tax to the state, or the tax to the general government could not be collected.—The conclusion therefore is inevitable, that the respective state governments will not have the power to raise one shilling in any way, but by the permission of the Congress. I presume no one will pretend, that the states can exercise legislative authority, or administer justice among their citizens for any length of time, without being able to raise a sufficiency to pay those who administer their governments.

If this be true, and if the states can raise money only by permission of the general government, it follows that the state governments will be dependent on the will of the general government for their existence.

What will render this power in Congress effectual and sure in its operation is, that the government will have complete judicial and executive authority to carry all their laws into effect, which will be paramount to the judicial and executive authority of the individual states: in vain therefore will be all interference of the legislatures, courts, or magistrates of any of the states on the subject; for they will be subordinate to the general government, and engaged by oath to support it, and will be constitutionally bound to submit to their decisions.

The general legislature will be empowered to lay any tax they chuse, to annex any penalties they please to the breach of their revenue laws; and to appoint as many officers as they may think proper to collect the taxes. They will have authority to farm the revenues and to vest the farmer general, with his subalterns, with plenary powers to collect them, in any way which to them may appear eligible. And the courts of law, which they will be authorized to institute, will have cognizance of every case arising under the revenue laws, the conduct of all the officers employed in collecting them; and the officers of these courts will execute their judgments. There is no way, therefore, of avoiding the destruction of the state governments, whenever the Congress please to do it, unless the people rise up, and with a strong hand, resist and prevent the execution of constitutional laws. The fear of this, will, it is presumed, restrain the general government, for some time, within proper bounds; but it will not be many years before they will have a revenue, and force, at their command, which will place them above any apprehensions on the score.

How far the power to lay and collect duties and excises, may operate to dissolve the state governments, and oppress the people, it is impossible to say. It would assist us much in forming a just opinion on this head, to consider the various objects to which this kind of taxes extend, in European nations, and the infinity of laws they have passed respecting them. Perhaps, if leisure will permit, this may be essayed in some future paper.

It was observed in my last number, that the power to lay and collect duties and excises, would invest the Congress with authority to impose a duty and excise on every necessary and convenience of life. As the principal object of the government, in laying a duty or excise, will be, to raise money, it is obvious, that they will fix on such articles as are of the most general use and consumption; because, unless great quantities of the article, on which the duty is laid, is used, the revenue cannot be considerable. We may therefore presume, that the articles which will be the object of this species of taxes will be either the real necessaries of life; or if not these, such as from custom and habit are esteemed so. I will single out a few of the productions of our own country, which may, and probably will, be of the number.

Cider is an article that most probably will be one of those on which an excise will be laid, because it is one, which this country produces in great abundance, which is in very general use, is consumed in great quantities, and which may be said too not to be a real necessary of life. An excise on this would raise a large sum of money in the United States. How would the power, to lay and collect an excise on cider, and to pass all laws proper and necessary to carry it into execution, operate in its exercise? It might be necessary, in order to collect the excise on cider, to grant to one man, in each county, an exclusive right of building and keeping cider mills, and oblige him to give bounds and security for payment of the excise; or, if this was not done, it might be necessary to license the mills, which are to make this liquor, and to take from them security, to account for the excise; or, if otherwise, a great number of officers must be employed, to take account of the cider made, and to collect the duties on it.

Porter, ale, and all kinds of malt liquors, are the articles that would probably be subject also to an excise. It would be necessary, in order to collect such an excise, to regulate the manufactory of these, that the quantity made might be ascertained or otherwise security could not be had for the payment of the excise. Every brewery must then be licensed, and officers appointed, to take account of its product, and to secure the payment of the duty, or excise, before it is sold. Many other articles might be named, which would be objects of this species of taxation, but I refrain from enumerating them. It will probably be said, by those who advocate this system, that the observations already made on this head, are calculated only to inflame the minds of the people, with the apprehension of dangers merely imaginary. That there is not the least reason to apprehend, the general legislature will exercise their power in this manner. To this I would only say, that these kinds of taxes exist in Great Britain, and are severely felt. The excise on cider and perry, was imposed in that nation a few years ago, and it is in the memory of every one, who read the history of the transaction, what great tumults it occasioned.

This power, exercised without limitation, will introduce itself into every corner of the city, and country.—It will wait upon the ladies as their toilett, and will not leave them in any of their domestic concerns; it will accompany them to the ball, the play, and the assembly; it will go with them when they visit, and will, on all occasions, sit beside them in their carriages, nor will it desert them even at church; it will enter the house of every gentleman, watch over his cellar, wait upon his cook in the kitchen, follow the servants into the parlour, preside over the table, and note down all he eats or drinks; it will attend him to his bedchamber, and watch him while he sleeps; it will take cognizance of the professional man in his office, or his study; it will watch the merchant in the counting-house, or in his store; it will follow the mechanic to his shop, and in his work, and will haunt him in his family, and in his bed; it will be a constant companion of the industrious farmer in all his labour, it will be with him in the house, and in the field, observe the toil of his hands, and the sweat of his brow; it will penetrate into the most obscure cottage; and finally, it will light upon the head of every person in the United States. To all these different classes of people, and in all these circumstances, in which it will attend them, the language in which it will address them, will be GIVE! GIVE!

A power that has such latitude, which reaches every person in the community in every conceivable circumstance, and lays hold of every species of property they possess, and which has no bounds set to it, but the discretion of those who exercise it, I say, such a power must necessarily, from its very nature, swallow up all the power of the state governments.

I shall add but one other observation on this head, which is this—it appears to me a solecism, for two men, or bodies of men, to have unlimited power respecting the same object. It contradicts the scripture maxim, which saith "no man can serve two masters." The one power or the other must prevail, or else they will destroy each other, and neither of them effect their purpose. It may be compared to two mechanic powers, acting upon the same body in opposite directions; the consequence would be, if the powers were equal, the body would remain in a state of rest, or if the force of the one was superior to that of the other, the stronger would prevail, and overcome the resistance of the weaker.

But it is said, by some of the advocates of this system, "That the idea that Congress can levy taxes at pleasure, is false, and the suggestion wholly unsupported: that the preamble to the constitution is declaratory of the purposes of the union, and the assumption of any power not necessary to establish justice, etc. to provide for the common defence, etc. will be unconstitutional. Besides, in the very clause which gives the power of levying duties and taxes, the purposes to which the money shall be appropriated, are specified, viz., to pay the debts, and provide for the common defence and general welfare." I would ask those, who reason thus, to define what ideas are included under the terms, to provide for the common defence and general welfare? Are these terms definite, and will they be understood in the same manner, and to apply to the same cases by every one? No one will pretend they will. It will then be matter of opinion, what tends to the general welfare; and the Congress will be the only judges in the matter. To provide for the general welfare, is an abstract proposition, which mankind differ in the explanation of, as much as they do on any political or moral proposition that can be proposed; the most opposite measures may be pursued by different parties, and both may profess, that they have in view the general welfare; and both sides may be honest in their professions, or both may have sinister views. Those who advocate this new constitution declare, they are influenced by a regard to the general welfare; those who oppose it, declare they are moved by the same principle; and I have no doubt but a number on both sides are honest in their professions; and yet nothing is more certain than this, that to adopt this constitution, and not to adopt it, cannot both of them be promotive of the general welfare.

It is as absurd to say, that the power of Congress is limited by these general expressions, "to provide for the common safety, and general welfare," as it would be to say, that it would be limited, had the constitution said they should have power to lay taxes, etc. at will and pleasure. Were this authority given, it might be said, that under it the legislature could not do injustice, or pursue any measures, but such as were calculated to promote the public good, and happiness. For every man, rulers as well as others, are bound by the immutable laws of God and reason, always to will what is right. It is certainly right and fit, that the governors of every people should provide for the common defence and general welfare; every government, therefore, in the world, even the greatest despot, is limited in the exercise of his power. But however just this reasoning may be, it would be found, in practice, a most pitiful restriction. The government would always say, their measures were designed and calculated to promote the public good; and there being no judge between them and the people, the rulers themselves must, and would always, judge for themselves.

There are others of the favourers of this system, who admit, that the power of the Congress under it, with respect to revenue, will exist without limitation, and contend, that so it ought to be.

It is said, "The power to raise armies, to build and equip fleets, and to provide for their support, ought to exist without limitation, because it is impossible to foresee, or to define, the extent and variety of national exigencies, or the correspondent extent and variety of the means which may be necessary to satisfy them.["]

This, it is said, "is one of those truths which, to correct and unprejudiced minds, carries its own evidence along with it. It rests upon axioms as simple as they are universal: the means ought to be proportioned to the end; the person, from whose agency the attainment of any end is expected, ought to possess the means by which it is to be attained."*

This same writer insinuates, that the opponents to the plan promulgated by the convention, manifests a want of candor, in objecting to the extent of the powers proposed to be vested in this government; because he asserts, with an air of confidence, that the powers ought to be unlimited as to the object to which they extend; and that this position, if not self-evident, is at least clearly demonstrated by the foregoing mode of reasoning. But with submission to this author's better judgment, I humbly conceive his reasoning will appear, upon examination, more specious than solid. The means, says the gentleman, ought to be proportioned to the end: admit the proposition to be true it is then necessary to enquire, what is the end of the government of the United States, in order to draw any just conclusions from it. Is this end simply to preserve the general government, and to provide for the common defence and general welfare of the union only? certainly not: for beside this, the state government are to be supported, and provision made for the managing such of their internal concerns as are allotted to them. It is admitted, "that the circumstances of our country are such, as to demand a com-

*Vide Federalist No. 23.

pound, instead of a simple, a confederate, instead of a sole government," that the objects of each ought to be pointed out, and that each ought to possess ample authority to execute the powers committed to them. The government then, being complex in its nature, the end it has in view is so also; and it is as necessary, that the state governments should possess the means to attain the ends expected from them, as for the general government. Neither the general government, nor the state governments, ought to be vested with all the powers proper to be exercised for promoting the ends of government. The powers are divided between them—certain ends are to be attained by the one, and other certain ends by the other; and these, taken together, include all the ends of good government. This being the case, the conclusion follows, that each should be furnished with the means, to attain the ends, to which they are designed.

To apply this reasoning to the case of revenue; the general government is charged with the care of providing for the payment of the debts of the United States; supporting the general government, and providing for the defence of the union. To obtain these ends, they should be furnished with means. But does it thence follow, that they should command all the revenues of the United States! Most certainly it does not. For if so, it will follow, that no means will be left to attain other ends, as necessary to the happiness of the country, as those committed to their care. The individual states have debts to discharge; their legislatures and executives are to be supported, and provision is to be made for the administration of justice in the respective states. For these objects the general government has no authority to provide; nor is it proper it should. It is clear then, that the states should have the command of such revenues, as to answer the ends they have to obtain. To say, "that the circumstances that endanger the safety of nations are infinite," and from hence to infer, that all the sources of revenue in the states should be yielded to the general government, is not conclusive reasoning: for the Congress are authorized only to control in general concerns, and not regulate local and internal ones; and these are as essentially requisite to be provided for as those. The peace and happiness of a community is as intimately connected with the prudent direction of their domestic affairs, and the due administration of justice among themselves, as with a competent provision for their defence against foreign invaders, and indeed more so.

Upon the whole, I conceive, that there cannot be a clearer position than this, that the state governments ought to have an uncontrollable power to raise a revenue, adequate to the exigencies of their governments; and, I presume, no such power is left them by this constitution.

Brutus.

X
24 JANUARY 1788

The liberties of a people are in danger from a large standing army, not only because the rulers may employ them for the purposes of supporting themselves in any usurpations of power, which they may see proper to exercise, but there is great hazard, that an army will subvert the forms of the government, under whose authority they are raised, and establish one according to the pleasure of their leader.

We are informed, in the faithful pages of history, of such events frequently happening.—Two instances have been mentioned in a former paper. They are so remarkable, that they are worthy of the most careful attention of every lover of freedom.— They are taken from the history of the two most powerful nations that have ever existed in the world; and who are the most renowned, for the freedom they enjoyed, and the excellency of their constitutions:—I mean Rome and Britain.

In the first, the liberties of the commonwealth was destroyed, and the constitution overturned, by an army, lead by Julius Caesar, who was appointed to the command, by the constitutional authority of that commonwealth. He changed it from a free republic, whose fame had sounded, and is still celebrated by all the world, into that of the most absolute despotism. A standing army effected this change, and a standing army supported it through a succession of ages, which are marked in the annals of history, with the most horrid cruelties, bloodshed, and carnage;—

the most devilish, beastly, and unnatural vices, that ever punished or disgraced human nature.

The same army, that in Britain, vindicated the liberties of that people from the encroachments and despotism of a tyrant king, assisted Cromwell, their General, in wresting from the people, that liberty they had so dearly earned.

You may be told, these instances will not apply to our case:— But those who would persuade you to believe this, either mean to deceive you, or have not themselves considered the subject.

I firmly believe, no country in the world had ever a more patriotic army, than the one which so ably served this country, in the late war.

But had the General who commanded them, been possessed of the spirit of a Julius Caesar or a Cromwell, the liberties of this country, had in all probability, terminated with the war; or had they been maintained, might have cost more blood and treasure, than was expended in the conflict with Great Britain. When an anonymous writer addressed the officers of the army at the close of the war, advising them not to part with their arms, until justice was done them—the effect it had is well known. It affected them like an electric shock. He wrote like Caesar; and had the commander in chief, and a few more officers of rank, countenanced the measure, the desperate resolution had been taken, to refuse to disband. What the consequences of such a determination would have been, heaven only knows.—The army were in the full vigor of health and spirits, in the habit of discipline, and possessed of all our military stores and apparatus. They would have acquired great accessions of strength from the country.— Those who were disgusted at our republican forms of government (for such there then were, of high rank among us) would have lent them all their aid.—We should in all probability have seen a constitution and laws, dictated to us, at the head of an army, and at the point of a bayonet, and the liberties for which we had so severely struggled, snatched from us in a moment. It remains a secret, yet to be revealed, whether this measure was not suggested, or at least countenanced, by some, who have had great influence in producing the present system.—Fortunately indeed for this country, it had at the head of the army, a patriot as well as a general; and many of our principal officers, had not abandoned the characters of citizens, by assuming that of soldiers, and therefore, the scheme proved abortive. But are we to expect, that this will always be the case? Are we so much better than the people of other ages and of other countries, that the same allurements of power and greatness, which led them aside from their duty, will have no influence upon men in our country? Such an idea, is wild and extravagant.—Had we indulged such a delusion, enough has appeared in a little time past, to convince the most credulous, that the passion for pomp, power and greatness, works as powerfully in the hearts of many of our better sort, as it ever did in any country under heaven.—Were the same opportunity again to offer, we should very probably be grossly disappointed, if we made dependence, that all who then rejected the overture, would do it again.

From these remarks, it appears, that the evil to be feared from a large standing army in time of peace, does not arise solely from the apprehension, that the rulers may employ them for the purpose of promoting their own ambitious views, but that equal, and perhaps greater danger, is to be apprehended from their overturning the constitutional powers of the government, and assuming the power to dictate any form they please.

The advocates for power, in support of this right in the proposed government, urge that a restraint upon the discretion of the legislature, in respect to military establishments in time of peace, would be improper to be imposed, because they say, it will be necessary to maintain small garrisons on the frontiers, to guard against the depredations of the Indians, and to be prepared to repel any encroachments or invasions that may be made by Spain or Britain.

The amount of this argument stripped of the abundant verbiages with which the author has dressed it, is this:

It will probably be necessary to keep up a small body of troops to garrison a few posts, which it will be necessary to maintain, in order to guard against the sudden encroachments of the Indians, or of the Spaniards and British; and therefore, the general government ought to be invested with power to raise and keep up a standing army in time of peace, without restraint; at their discretion.

I confess, I cannot perceive that the conclusion follows from the premises. Logicians say, it is no good reasoning to infer a general conclusion from particular premises; though I am not much of a Logician, it seems to me, this argument is very like that species of reasoning.

When the patriots in the parliament in Great Britain, contended with such force of argument, and all the powers of eloquence, against keeping up standing armies in time of peace, it is obvious, they never entertained an idea, that small garrisons on their frontiers, or in the neighbourhood of powers, from whom they were in danger of encroachments, or guards, to take care of public arsenals would thereby be prohibited.

The advocates for this power farther urge that it is necessary, because it may, and probably will happen, that circumstances will render it requisite to raise an army to be prepared to repel attacks of an enemy, before a formal declaration of war, which in modern times has fallen into disuse. If the constitution prohibited the raising an army, until a war actually commenced, it would deprive the government of the power of providing for the defence of the country, until the enemy were within our territory. If the restriction is not to extend to the raising armies in case of emergency, but only to the keeping them up, this would leave the matter to the discretion of the legislature; and they might, under the pretence that there was danger of an invasion, keep up the army as long as they judged proper—and hence it is inferred, that the legislature should have authority to raise and keep up an army without any restriction. But from these premises nothing more will follow than this, that the legislature should not be so restrained, as to put it out of their power to raise an army, when such exigencies as are instanced shall arise. But it does not thence follow, that the government should be empowered to raise and maintain standing armies at their discretion as well in peace as in war. If indeed, it is impossible to vest the general government with the power of raising troops to garrison the frontier posts, to guard arsenals, or to be prepared to repel an attack, when we saw a power preparing to make one, without giving them a general and indefinite authority, to raise and keep up armies, without any restriction or qualification, then this reasoning might have weight; but this has not been proved nor can it be.

It is admitted that to prohibit the general government, from keeping up standing armies, while yet they were authorised to raise them in case of exigency, would be an insufficient guard against the danger. A discretion of such latitude would give room to elude the force of the provision.

It is also admitted that an absolute prohibition against raising troops, except in case of actual war, would be improper; because it will be requisite to raise and support a small number of troops to garrison the important frontier posts, and to guard arsenals; and it may happen, that the danger of an attack from a foreign power may be so imminent, as to render it highly proper we should raise an army, in order to be prepared to resist them. But to raise and keep up forces for such purposes and on such occasions, is not included in the idea, of keeping up standing armies in time of peace.

It is a thing very practicable to give the government sufficient authority to provide for these cases, and at the same time to provide a reasonable and competent security against the evil of a standing army—a clause to the following purpose would answer the end:

As standing armies in time of peace are dangerous to liberty, and have often been the means of overturning the best constitutions of government, no standing army, or troops of any description whatsoever, shall be raised or kept up by the legislature, except so many as shall be necessary for guards to the arsenals of the United States, or for garrisons to such posts on the frontiers, as it shall be deemed absolutely necessary to hold, to secure the inhabitants, and facilitate the trade with the Indians: unless when the United States are threatened with an attack or invasion from some foreign power, in which case the legislature shall be authorised to raise an army to be prepared to repel the attack; provided that no troops whatsoever shall be raised in time of peace, without the assent of two thirds of the members, composing both houses of the legislature.

A clause similar to this would afford sufficient latitude to the legislature to raise troops in all cases that were really necessary, and at the same time competent security against the establishment of that dangerous engine of despotism, a standing army.

The same writer who advances the arguments I have noticed, makes a number of other observations with a view to prove that the power to raise and keep up armies, ought to be discretionary in the general legislature; some of them are curious; he instances the raising of troops in Massachusetts and Pennsylvania, to show the necessity of keeping a standing army in time of peace; the least reflection must convince every candid mind that both these cases are totally foreign to his purpose—Massachusetts raised a body of troops for six months, at the expiration of which they were to disband of course; this looks very little like a standing army. But beside, was that commonwealth in a state of peace at that time? So far from it that they were in the most violent commotions and contents, and their legislature had formally declared that an unnatural rebellion existed within the state. The situation of Pennsylvania was similar; a number of armed men had levied war against the authority of the state, and openly avowed their intention of withdrawing their allegiance from it. To what purpose examples are brought, of states raising troops for short periods in times of war or insurrections, on a question concerning the propriety of keeping up standing armies in times of peace, the public must judge.

It is farther said, that no danger can arise from this power being lodged in the hands of the general government, because the legislatures will be a check upon them, to prevent their abusing it.

This is offered, as what force there is in it will hereafter receive a more particular examination. At present, I shall only remark, that it is difficult to conceive how the state legislatures can, in any case, hold a check over the general legislature, in a constitutional way. The latter has, in every instance to which their powers extend, complete control over the former. The state legislatures can, in no case, by law, resolution, or otherwise, of right, prevent or impede the general government, from enacting any law, or executing it, which this constitution authorizes them to enact or execute. If then the state legislatures check the general legislatures [*sic*], it must be by exciting the people to resist constitutional laws. In this way every individual, or every body of men, may check any government, in proportion to the influence they may have over the body of the people. But such kinds of checks as these, though they sometimes correct the abuses of government, oftner destroy all government.

It is further said, that no danger is to be apprehended from the exercise of this power, because it is lodged in the hands of representatives of the people; if they abuse it, it is in the power of the people to remove them, and chuse others who will pursue their interests. Not to repeat what has been said before, that it is unwise in any people, to authorize their rulers to do, what, if done, would prove injurious—I have, in some former numbers, shown, that the representation in the proposed government will be a mere shadow without the substance. I am so confident that I am well founded in this opinion, that I am persuaded, if it was to be adopted or rejected, upon a fair discussion of its merits, without taking into contemplation circumstances extraneous to it, as reasons for its adoption, nineteen twentieths of the sensible men in the union would reject it on this account alone: unless its powers were confined to much fewer objects than it embraces.

Brutus.

XI
31 JANUARY 1788

The nature and extent of the judicial power of the United States, proposed to be granted by this constitution, claims our particular attention.

Much has been said and written upon the subject of this new system on both sides, but I have not met with any writer, who has discussed the judicial powers with any degree of accuracy. And yet it is obvious, that we can form but very imperfect ideas of the manner in which this government will work, or the effect it will have in changing the internal police and mode of distributing justice at present subsisting in the respective states, without a thorough investigation of the powers of the judiciary and of the manner in which they will operate. This government is a complete system, not only for making, but for executing laws. And the courts of law, which will be constituted by it, are not only to decide upon the constitution and the laws made in pursuance of it, but by officers subordinate to them to execute, all their decisions. The real effect of this system of government, will therefore be brought home to the feelings of the people, through the medium of the judicial power. It is, moreover, of great importance, to examine with care the nature and extent of the judicial power, because those who are to be vested with it, are to be placed in a situation altogether unprecedented in a free country. They are to be rendered totally independent, both of the people and the legislature, both with respect to their offices and salaries. No errors they may commit can be corrected by any power above them, if any such power there be, nor can they be removed from office for making ever so many erroneous adjudications.

The only causes for which they can be displaced, is, conviction of treason, bribery, and high crimes and misdemeanors.

This part of the plan is so modelled, as to authorise the courts, not only to carry into execution the powers expressly given, but where these are wanting or ambiguously expressed, to supply what is wanting by their own decisions.

That we may be enabled to form a just opinion on this subject, I shall, in considering it,

1st. Examine the nature and extent of the judicial powers—and,

2d. Enquire, whether the courts who are to exercise them, are so constituted as to afford reasonable ground of confidence, that they will exercise them for the general good.

With a regard to the nature and extent of the judicial powers, I have to regret my want or capacity to give that full and minute explanation of them that the subject merits. To be able to do this, a man should be possessed of a degree of law knowledge far beyond what I pretend to. A number of hard words and technical phrases are used in this part of the system, about the meaning of which gentlemen learned in the law differ.

Its advocates know how to avail themselves of these phrases.

In a number of instances, where objections are made to the powers given to the judicial, they give such an explanation to the technical terms as to avoid them.

Though I am not competent, to give a perfect explanation of the powers granted to this department of the government, I shall yet attempt to trace some of the leading features of it, from which I presume it will appear, that they will operate to a total subversion of the state judiciaries, if not, to the legislative authority of the states.

In article 3d, sect. 2d, it is said, "The judicial power shall extend to all cases in law and equity arising under this constitution, the laws of the United States, and treaties made, or which shall be made, under their authority etc."

The first article to which this power extends, is, all cases in law and equity arising under this constitution.

What latitude of construction this clause should receive, it is not easy to say. At first view, one would suppose, that it meant no more than this, that the courts under the general government should exercise, not only the powers of courts of law, but also that of courts of equity, in the manner in which those powers are usually exercised in the different states. But this cannot be the meaning, because the next clause authorises the courts to take cognizance of all cases in law and equity arising under the laws of the United States; this last article, I conceive, conveys as much power to the general judicial as any of the state courts possess.

The cases arising under the constitution must be different from those arising under the laws, or else the two clauses mean exactly the same thing.

The cases arising under the constitution must include such, as bring into question its meaning, and will require an explanation of the nature and extent of the powers of the different departments under it.

This article, therefore, vests the judicial with a power to resolve all questions that may arise on any case on the construction of the constitution, either in law or in equity.

1st. They are authorised to determine all questions that may arise upon the meaning of the constitution in law. This article vests the courts with authority to give the constitution a legal construction, or to explain it according to the rules laid down for construing a law.—These rules give a certain degree of latitude of explanation. According to this mode of construction, the courts are to give such meaning to the constitution as comports best with the common, and generally received acceptation of the words in which it is expressed, regarding their ordinary and popular use, rather than their grammatical propriety. Where words are dubious, they will be explained by the context. The end of the clause will be attended to, and the words will be understood, as having a view to it; and the words will not be so understood as to bear no meaning or a very absurd one.

2d. The judicial are not only to decide questions arising upon the meaning of the constitution in law, but also in equity.

By this they are empowered, to explain the constitution according to the reasoning spirit of it, without being confined to the words or letter.

"From this method of interpreting laws," says Blackstone, "by the reason of them, arises what we call equity"; which is thus defined by Grotius, "the correction of that, wherein the law, by reason of its universality, is deficient"; for since in laws, all cases cannot be foreseen, or expressed, it is necessary, that when the decrees of the laws cannot be applied to particular cases, there should some where be a power vested of defining those circumstances, which had they been foreseen the legislator would have expressed; and these are the cases, which according to Grotius, "lex non exacte definit, sed arbitrio boni viri permittet."

The same learned author observes, "That equity, thus depending essentially upon each individual case, there can be no established rules and fixed principles of equity laid down, without destroying its very essence, and reducing it to a positive law."

From these remarks, the authority and business of the courts of law, under this clause, may be understood.

They will give the sense of every article of the constitution, that may from time to time come before them. And in their decisions they will not confine themselves to any fixed or established rules, but will determine, according to what appears to them, the reason and spirit of the constitution. The opinions of the supreme court, whatever they may be, will have the force of law; because there is no power provided in the constitution, that can correct their errors, or control their adjudications. From this court there is no appeal. And I conceive the legislature themselves, cannot set aside a judgment of this court, because they are authorised by the constitution to decide in the last resort. The legislature must be controled by the constitution, and not the constitution by them. They have therefore no more right to set aside any judgment pronounced upon the construction of the constitution, than they have to take from the president, the chief command of the army and navy, and commit it to some other person. The reason is plain; the judicial and executive derive their authority from the same source, that the legislature do theirs; and therefore in all cases, where the constitution does not make the one responsible to, or controlable by the other, they are altogether independent of each other.

The judicial power will operate to effect, in the most certain, but yet silent and imperceptible manner, what is evidently the tendency of the constitution—I mean, an entire subversion of the legislative, executive and judicial powers of the individual states. Every adjudication of the supreme court, on any question that may arise upon the nature and extent of the general government, will affect the limits of the state jurisdiction. In proportion as the former enlarge the exercise of their powers, will that of the latter be restricted.

That the judicial power of the United States, will lean strongly in favour of the general government, and will give such an explanation to the constitution, as will favour an extension of its jurisdiction, is very evident from a variety of considerations.

1st. The constitution itself strongly countenances such a mode of construction. Most of the articles in this system, which convey powers of any considerable importance, are conceived in general and indefinite terms, which are either equivocal, ambiguous, or which require long definitions to unfold the extent of their meaning. The two most important powers committed to any government, those of raising money, and of raising and keeping up troops, have already been considered, and shown to be unlimited by any thing but the discretion of the legislature. The clause which vests the power to pass all laws which are proper and necessary, to carry the powers given into execution, it has been shown, leaves the legislature at liberty, to do every thing, which in their judgment is best. It is said, I know, that this clause confers no power on the legislature, which they could not have had without it—though I believe this is not the fact, yet, admitting it to be, it implies that the constitution is not to receive an explanation strictly, according to its letter; but more power is implied than is expressed. And this clause, if it is to be considered, as explanatory of the extent of the powers given, rather than giving a new power, is to be understood as declaring, that in construing any of the articles conveying power, the spirit, intent and design of the clause, should be attended to, as well as the words in their common acceptation.

This constitution gives sufficient colour for adopting an equitable construction, if we consider the great end and design it professedly has in view—these appear from its preamble to be, "to form a more perfect union, establish justice, insure domestic tranquility, provide for the common defence, promote the general welfare, and secure the blessings of liberty to ourselves and posterity." The design of this system is here expressed, and it is proper to give such a meaning to the various parts, as will best promote the accomplishment of the end; this idea suggests itself naturally upon reading the preamble, and will countenance the court in giving the several articles such a sense, as will the most effectually promote the ends the constitution had in view—how this manner of explaining the constitution will operate in practice, shall be the subject of future enquiry.

2d. Not only will the constitution justify the courts in inclining to this mode of explaining it, but they will be interested in using this latitude of interpretation. Every body of men invested with office are tenacious of power; they feel interested, and hence it has become a kind of maxim, to hand down their offices, with all its rights and privileges, unimpared to their successors; the same principle will influence them to extend their power, and increase their rights; this of itself will operate strongly upon the courts to give such a meaning to the constitution in all cases where it can possibly be done, as will enlarge the sphere of their own authority. Every extension of the power of the general legislature, as well as of the judicial powers, will increase the powers of the courts; and the dignity and importance of the judges, will be in proportion to the extent and magnitude of the powers they exercise. I add, it is highly probable the emolument of the judges will be increased, with the increase of the business they will have to transact and its importance. From these considerations the judges will be interested to extend the powers of the courts, and to construe the constitution as much as possible, in such a way as to favour it; and that they will do it, appears probable.

3d. Because they will have precedent to plead, to justify them in it. It is well known, that the courts in England, have by their own authority, extended their jurisdiction far beyond the limits set them in their original institution, and by the laws of the land.

The court of exchequer is a remarkable instance of this. It was originally intended principally to recover the king's debts, and to order the revenues of the crown. It had a common law jurisdiction, which was established merely for the benefit of the king's accomptants. We learn from Blackstone, that the proceedings in this court are grounded on a writ called quo minus, in which the plaintiff suggests, that he is the king's farmer or debtor, and that the defendant hath done him the damage complained of, by which he is less able to pay the king. These suits, by the statute of Rutland, are expressly directed to be confined to such matters as specially concern the king, or his ministers in the exchequer. And by the *articuli super cartas,* it is enacted, that no common pleas be thenceforth held in the exchequer contrary to the form of the great charter: but now any person may sue in the exchequer. The surmise of being debtor to the king being matter of form, and mere words of course; and the court is open to all the nation.

When the courts will have a precedent before them of a court which extended its jurisdiction in opposition to an act of the legislature, is it not to be expected that they will extend theirs, especially when there is nothing in the constitution expressly against it? and they are authorised to construe its meaning, and are not under any control?

This power in the judicial, will enable them to mould the government, into almost any shape they please.—The manner in which this may be effected we will hereafter examine.

Brutus.

XII
7 FEBRUARY 1788

In my last, I showed, that the judicial power of the United States under the first clause of the second section of article eight, would be authorized to explain the constitution, not only according to its letter, but according to its spirit and intention; and having this power, they would strongly incline to give it such a construction as to extend the powers of the general government, as much as possible, to the diminution, and finally to the destruction, of that of the respective states.

I shall now proceed to show how this power will operate in its exercise to effect these purposes. In order to perceive the extent of its influence, I shall consider,

First. How it will tend to extend the legislative authority.

Second. In what manner it will increase the jurisdiction of the courts, and

Third. The way in which it will diminish, and destroy, both the legislative and judicial authority of the United States.

First. Let us enquire how the judicial power will effect an extension of the legislative authority.

Perhaps the judicial power will not be able, by direct and positive decrees, ever to direct the legislature, because it is not easy to conceive how a question can be brought before them in a course of legal discussion, in which they can give a decision, declaring, that the legislature have certain powers which they have not exercised, and which, in consequence of the determination of the judges, they will be bound to exercise. But it is easy to see, that in their adjudications they may establish certain principles, which being received by the legislature, will enlarge the sphere of their power beyond all bounds.

It is to be observed, that the supreme court has the power, in the last resort, to determine all questions that may arise in the course of legal discussion, on the meaning and construction of the constitution. This power they will hold under the constitution, and independent of the legislature. The latter can no more deprive the former of this right, than either of them, or both of them together, can take from the president, with the advice of the senate, the power of making treaties, or appointing ambassadors.

In determining these questions, the court must and will assume certain principles, from which they will reason, in forming their decisions. These principles, whatever they may be, when they become fixed, by a course of decisions, will be adopted by the legislature, and will be the rule by which they will explain their own powers. This appears evident from this consideration, that if the legislature pass laws, which, in the judgment of the court, they are not authorised to do by the constitution, the court will not take notice of them; for it will not be denied, that the constitution is the highest or supreme law. And the courts are vested with the supreme and uncontrollable power, to determine, in all cases that come before them, what the constitution means; they cannot, therefore, execute a law, which, in their judgment, opposes the constitution, unless we can suppose they can make a superior law give way to an inferior. The legislature, therefore, will not go over the limits by which the courts may adjudge they are confined. And there is little room to doubt but that they will come up to those bounds, as often as occasion and opportunity may offer, and they may judge it proper to do it. For as on the one hand, they will not readily pass laws which they know the courts will not execute, so on the other, we may be sure they will not scruple to pass such as they know will give effect, as often as they may judge it proper.

From these observations it appears, that the judgment of the judicial, on the constitution, will become the rule to guide the legislature in their construction of their powers.

What the principles are, which the courts will adopt, it is impossible for us to say; but taking up the powers as I have explained them in my last number, which they will possess under this clause, it is not difficult to see, that they may, and probably will, be very liberal ones.

We have seen, that they will be authorized to give the constitution a construction according to its spirit and reason, and not to confine themselves to its letter.

To discover the spirit of the constitution, it is of the first importance to attend to the principal ends and designs it has in view. These are expressed in the preamble, in the following words, viz, "We, the people of the United States, in order to form a more perfect union, establish justice, insure domestic tranquility, provide for the common defence, promote the general welfare, and secure the blessings of liberty to ourselves and our posterity, do ordain and establish this constitution," etc. If the end of the government is to be learned from these words, which are clearly designed to declare it, it is obvious it has in view every object which is embraced by any government. The preservation of internal peace—the due administration of justice—and to provide for the defence of the community, seems to include all the objects of government; but if they do not, they are certainly comprehended in the words, "to provide for the general welfare." If it be further considered, that this constitution, if it is ratified, will not be a compact entered into by states, in their corporate capacities, but an agreement of the people of the United States, as one great body politic, no doubt can remain, but that the great end of the constitution, if it is to be collected from the preamble, in which its end is declared, is to constitute a government which is to extend to every case for which any government is instituted, whether external or internal. The courts, therefore, will establish this as a principle in expounding the constitution, and will give every part of it such an explanation, as will give latitude to every department under it, to take cognizance of every matter, not only that affects the general and national concerns of the union, but also of such as relate to the administration of private justice, and to regulating the internal and local affairs of the different parts.

Such a rule of exposition is not only consistent with the general spirit of the preamble, but it will stand confirmed by considering more minutely the different clauses of it.

The first object declared to be in view is "To form a perfect union." It is to be observed, it is not an union of states or bodies corporate; had this been the case the existence of the state governments, might have been secured. But it is a union of the people of the United States considered as one body, who are to ratify this constitution, if it is adopted. Now to make a union of this kind perfect, it is necessary to abolish all inferior governments, and to give the general one compleat legislative, executive and judicial powers to every purpose. The courts therefore will establish it as a rule in explaining the constitution to give it such a construction as will best tend to perfect the union or take from the state governments every power of either making or executing laws. The second object is "to establish justice." This must include not only the idea of instituting the rule of justice, or of making laws which shall be the measure or rule of right, but also of providing for the application of this rule or of administering justice under it. And under this the courts will in their decisions extend the power of the governments to all cases they possibly can, or otherwise they will be restricted in doing what appears to be the intent of the constitution they should do, to wit, pass laws and provide for the execution of them, for the general distribution of justice between man and man. Another end declared is "to insure domestic tranquility." This comprehends a provision against all private breaches of the peace, as well as against all public commotions or general insurrections; and to attain the object of this clause fully, the government must exercise the power of passing laws on these subjects, as well as of appointing magistrates with authority to execute them. And the courts will adopt these ideas in their expositions. I might proceed to the other clause, in the preamble, and it would appear by a consideration of all of them separately, as it does by taking them together, that if the spirit of this system is to be known from its declared end and design in the preamble, its spirit is to subvert and abolish all the powers of the state government, and to embrace every object to which any government extends.

As it sets out in the preamble with this declared intention, so it proceeds in the different parts with the same idea. Any person, who will peruse the 8th section with attention, in which most of the powers are enumerated, will perceive that they either expressly or by implication extend to almost every thing about which any legislative power can be employed. But if this equitable mode of construction is applied to this part of the constitution, nothing can stand before it.

This will certainly give the first clause in that article a construction which I confess I think the most natural and grammatical one, to authorise the Congress to do any thing which in their judgment will tend to provide for the general welfare, and this amounts to the same thing as general and unlimited powers of legislation in all cases.

XII (PART II)
14 FEBRUARY 1788

This same manner of explaining the constitution, will fix a meaning, and a very important one too, to the 18th clause of the same section, which authorises the Congress to make all laws which shall be proper and necessary for carrying into effect the foregoing powers, etc. A voluminous writer in favor of this system, has taken great pains to convince the public, that this clause means nothing; for that the same powers expressed in this, are implied in other parts of the constitution. Perhaps it is so, but still this will undoubtedly be an excellent auxilliary to assist the courts to discover the spirit and reason of the constitution, and when applied to any and every of the other clauses granting power, will operate powerfully in extracting the spirit from them.

I might instance a number of clauses in the constitution, which, if explained in an *equitable* manner, would extend the powers of the government to every case, and reduce the state legislatures to nothing; but, I should draw out my remarks to an undue length, and I presume enough has been said to show, that the courts have sufficient ground in the exercise of this power, to determine, that the legislature have no bounds set to them by this constitution, by any supposed right the legislatures of the respective states may have, to regulate any of their local concerns.

I proceed, 2d, to inquire, in what manner this power will increase the jurisdiction of the courts.

I would here observe, that the judicial power extends, expressly, to all civil cases that may arise save such as arise between citizens of the same state, with this exception to those of that description, that the judicial of the United States have cognizance of cases between citizens of the same state, claiming lands under grants of different states. Nothing more, therefore, is necessary to give the courts of law, under this constitution, complete jurisdiction of all civil causes, but to comprehend cases between citizens of the same state not included in the foregoing exception.

I presume there will be no difficulty in accomplishing this. Nothing more is necessary than to set forth, in the process, that the party who brings the suit is a citizen of a different state from the one against whom the suit is brought, and there can be little doubt but that the court will take cognizance of the matter, and if they do, who is to restrain them? Indeed, I will freely confess, that it is my decided opinion, that the courts ought to take cognizance of such causes, under the powers of the constitution. For one of the great ends of the constitution is, "to establish justice." This supposes that this cannot be done under the existing governments of the states; and there is certainly as good reason why individuals, living in the same state, should have justice, as those who live in different states. Moreover, the constitution expressly declares, that "the citizens of each state shall be entitled to all the privileges and immunities of citizens in the several states." It will therefore be no fiction, for a citizen of one state to set forth, in a suit, that he is a citizen of another; for he that is entitled to all the privileges and immunities of a country, is a citizen of that country. And in truth, the citizen of one state will, under this constitution, be a citizen of every state.

But supposing that the party, who alledges that he is a citizen of another state, has recourse to fiction in bringing in his suit, it is well known, that the courts have high authority to plead, to justify them in suffering actions to be brought before them by such fictions. In my last number I stated, that the court of exchequer tried all causes in virtue of such a fiction. The court of king's bench, in England, extended their jurisdiction in the same way. Originally, this court held pleas, in civil cases, only of trespasses and other injuries alleged to be committed *vi et armis.* They might likewise, says Blackstone, upon the division of the *aula regia,* have originally held pleas of any other civil action whatsoever (except in real actions which are now very seldom in use) provided the defendant was an officer of the court, or in the custody of the marshall or prison-keeper of this court, for breach of the peace, etc. In process of time, by a fiction, this court began to hold pleas of any personal action whatsoever; it being surmised, that the defendant has been arrested for a supposed trespass that "he has never committed, and being thus in the custody of the marshall of the court, the plaintiff is at liberty to proceed against him, for any other personal injury; which surmise of being in the marshall's custody, the defendant is not at liberty to dispute." By a much less fiction, may the pleas of the courts of the United States extend to cases between citizens of the same state. I shall add no more on this head, but proceed briefly to remark, in what way this power will diminish and destroy both the legislative and judicial authority of the states.

It is obvious that these courts will have authority to decide upon the validity of the laws of any of the states, in all cases where they come in question before them. Where the constitution gives the general government exclusive jurisdiction, they will adjudge all laws made by the states, in such cases, void *ab initio.* Where the constitution gives them concurrent jurisdiction, the laws of the United States must prevail, because they are the supreme law. In such cases, therefore, the laws of the state legislatures must be repealed, restricted, or so construed, as to give full effect to the laws of the union on the same subject. From these remarks it is easy to see, that in proportion as the general government acquires power and jurisdiction, by the liberal construction which the judges may give the constitution, will those of the states lose its rights, until they become so trifling and unimportant, as not to be worth having. I am much mistaken, if this system will not operate to effect this with as much celerity, as those who have the administration of it will think prudent to suffer it. The remaining objections to the judicial power shall be considered in a future paper.

Brutus.

XV
20 MARCH 1788

I said in my last number, that the supreme court under this constitution would be exalted above all other power in the government, and subject to no control. The business of this paper will be to illustrate this, and to show the danger that will result from it. I question whether the world ever saw, in any period of it, a court of justice invested with such immense powers, and yet placed in a situation so little responsible. Certain it is, that in England, and in the several states, where we have been taught to believe, the courts of law are put upon the most prudent establishment, they are on a very different footing.

The judges in England, it is true, hold their offices during their good behaviour, but then their determinations are subject to correction by the house of lords; and their power is by no means so extensive as that of the proposed supreme court of the union.—I believe they in no instance assume the authority to set aside an act of parliament under the idea that it is inconsistent with their constitution. They consider themselves bound to decide according to the existing laws of the land, and never undertake to control them by adjudging that they are inconsistent with the constitution—much less are they vested with the power of giving an *equitable* construction to the constitution.

The judges in England are under the control of the legislature, for they are bound to determine according to the laws passed by them. But the judges under this constitution will control the legislature, for the supreme court are authorised in the last resort, to determine what is the extent of the powers of the Congress; they are to give the constitution an explanation, and there is no power above them to set aside their judgment. The framers of this constitution appear to have followed that of the British, in rendering the judges independent, by granting them their offices during good behaviour, without following the constitution of England, in instituting a tribunal in which their errors may be corrected; and without averting to this, that the judicial under this system have a power which is above the legislative, and which indeed transcends any power before given to a judicial by any free government under heaven.

I do not object to the judges holding their commissions during good behaviour. I suppose it a proper provision provided they were made properly responsible. But I say, this system has followed the English government in this, while it has departed from almost every other principle of their jurisprudence, under the idea, of rendering the judges independent; which, in the British constitution, means no more than that they hold their places during good behaviour, and have fixed salaries, they have made the judges *independent,* in the fullest sense of the word. There is no power above them, to control any of their decisions. There is no authority that can remove them, and they cannot be controlled by the laws of the legislature. In short, they are independent of the people, of the legislature, and of every power under heaven. Men placed in this situation will generally soon feel themselves independent of heaven itself. Before I proceed to illustrate the truth of these assertions, I beg liberty to make one remark—Though in my opinion the judges ought to hold their offices during good behaviour, yet I think it is clear, that the reasons in favour of this establishment of the judges in England, do by no means apply to this country.

The great reason assigned, why the judges in Britain ought to be commissioned during good behaviour, is this, that they may be placed in a situation, not to be influenced by the crown, to give such decisions, as would tend to increase its powers and prerogatives. While the judges held their places at the will and pleasure of the king, on whom they depended not only for their offices, but also for their salaries, they were subject to every undue influence. If the crown wished to carry a favorite point, to accomplish which the aid of the courts of law was necessary, the pleasure of the king would be signified to the judges. And it required the spirit of a martyr, for the judges to determine contrary to the king's will.—They were absolutely dependent upon him both for their offices and livings. The king, holding his office during life, and transmitting it to his posterity as an inheritance, has much stronger inducements to increase the prerogatives of his office than those who hold their offices for stated periods, or even for life. Hence the English nation gained a great point, in favour of liberty. When they obtained the appointment of the judges, during good behaviour, they got from the crown a concession, which deprived it of one of the most powerful engines with which it might enlarge the boundaries of the royal prerogative and encroach on the liberties of the people. But these reasons do not apply to this country, we have no hereditary monarch; those who appoint the judges do not hold their offices for life, nor do they descend to their children. The same arguments, therefore, which will conclude in favor of the tenor of the judge's offices for good behaviour, lose a considerable part of their weight when applied to the state and condition of America. But much less can it be shown, that the nature of our government requires that the courts should be placed beyond all account more independent, so much so as to be above control.

I have said that the judges under this system will be *independent* in the strict sense of the word: To prove this I will show— that there is no power above them that can control their decisions, or correct their errors. There is no authority that can remove them from office for any errors or want of capacity, or lower their salaries, and in many cases their power is superior to that of the legislature.

1st. There is no power above them that can correct their errors or control their decisions.—The adjudications of this court are final and irreversible, for there is no court above them to which appeals can lie, either in error or on the merits.—In this respect it differs from the courts in England, for there the house of lords is the highest court, to whom appeals, in error, are carried from the highest of the courts of law.

2d. They cannot be removed from office or suffer a diminution of their salaries, for any error in judgment or want of capacity.

It is expressly declared by the constitution, "That they shall at stated times receive a compensation for their services which shall not be diminished during their continuance in office."

The only clause in the constitution which provides for the removal of the judges from office, is that which declares, that "the president, vice-president, and all civil officers of the United States, shall be removed from office, on impeachment for, and conviction of treason, bribery, or other high crimes and misdemeanors." By this paragraph, civil officers, in which the judges are included, are removable only for crimes. Treason and bribery are named, and the rest are included under the general terms of high crimes and misdemeanors.—Errors in judgment, or want of capacity to discharge the duties of the office, can never be supposed to be included in these words, *high crimes and misdemeanors.* A man may mistake a case in giving judgment, or manifest that he is incompetent to the discharge of the duties of a judge, and yet give no evidence of corruption or want of integrity. To support the charge, it will be necessary to give in evidence some facts that will show, that the judges commited the error from wicked and corrupt motives.

3d. The power of this court is in many cases superior to that of the legislature. I have showed, in a former paper, that this court will be authorised to decide upon the meaning of the constitution, and that, not only according to the natural and ob[vious] meaning of the words, but also according to the spirit and intention of it. In the exercise of this power they will not be subordinate to, but above the legislature. For all the departments of this government will receive their powers, so far as they are expressed in the constitution, from the people immediately, who are the source of power. The legislature can only exercise such powers as are given them by the constitution, they cannot assume any of the rights annexed to the judicial, for this plain reason, that the same authority which vested the legislature with their powers, vested the judicial with theirs—both are derived from the same source, both therefore are equally valid, and the judicial hold their powers independently of the legislature, as the legislature do of the judicial.—The supreme court then have a right, independent of the legislature, to give a construction to the constitution and every part of it, and there is no power provided in this system to correct their construction or do it away. If, therefore, the legislature pass any laws, inconsistent with the sense the judges put upon the constitution, they will declare it void; and therefore in this respect their power is superior to that of the legislature. In England the judges are not only subject to have their decisions set aside by the house of lords, for error, but in cases where they give an explanation to the laws or constitution of the country, contrary to the sense of the parliament, though the parliament will not set aside the judgment of the court, yet, they have authority, by a new law, to explain a former one, and by this means to prevent a reception of such decisions. But no such power is in the legislature. The judges are supreme— and no law, explanatory of the constitution, will be binding on them.

From the preceding remarks, which have been made on the judicial powers proposed in this system, the policy of it may be fully developed.

I have, in the course of my observation on this constitution, affirmed and endeavored to shew, that it was calculated to abolish entirely the state governments, and to melt down the states into one entire government, for every purpose as well internal and local, as external and national. In this opinion the opposers of the system have generally agreed—and this has been uniformly denied by its advocates in public. Some individuals, indeed, among them, will confess, that it has this tendency, and scruple not to say, it is what they wish; and I will venture to predict, without the spirit of prophecy, that if it is adopted without amendments, or some such precautions as will ensure amendments immediately after its adoption, that the same gentlemen who have employed their talents and abilities with such success to influence the public mind to adopt this plan, will employ the same to persuade the people, that it will be for their good to abolish the state governments as useless and burdensome.

Perhaps nothing could have been better conceived to facilitate the abolition of the state governments than the constitution of the judicial. They will be able to extend the limits of the general government gradually, and by insensible degrees, and to accommodate themselves to the temper of the people. Their decisions on the meaning of the constitution will commonly take place in cases which arise between individuals, with which the public will not be generally acquainted; one adjudication will form a precedent to the next, and this to a following one. These cases will immediately affect individuals only; so that a series of determinations will probably take place before even the people will be informed of them. In the mean time all the art and address of those who wish for the change will be employed to make converts to their opinion. The people will be told, that their state officers, and state legislatures are a burden and expence without affording any solid advantage, for that all the laws passed by them, might be equally well made by the general legislature. If to those who will be interested in the change, be added, those who will be under their influence, and such who will submit to almost any change of government, which they can be persuaded to believe will ease them of taxes, it is easy to see, the party who will favor the abolition of the state governments would be far from being inconsiderable.—In this situation, the general legislature, might pass one law after another, extending the general and abridging the state jurisdictions, and to sanction their proceedings would have a course of decisions of the judicial to whom the constitution has committed the power of explaining the constitution.—If the states remonstrated, the constitutional mode of deciding upon the validity of the law, is with the supreme court, and neither people, nor state legislatures, nor the general legislature can remove them or reverse their decrees.

Had the construction of the constitution been left with the legislature, they would have explained it at their peril; if they exceed their powers, or sought to find, in the spirit of the constitution, more than was expressed in the letter, the people from whom they derived their power could remove them, and do themselves right; and indeed I can see no other remedy that the people can have against their rulers for encroachments of this nature. A constitution is a compact of a people with their rulers; if the rulers break the compact, the people have a right and ought to remove them and do themselves justice; but in order to enable them to do this with the greater facility, those whom the people choose at stated periods, should have the power in the last resort to determine the sense of the compact; if they determine contrary to the understanding of the people, an appeal will lie to the people at the period when the rulers are to be elected, and they will have it in their power to remedy the evil; but when this power is lodged in the hands of men independent of the people, and of their representatives, and who are not, constitutionally, accountable for their opinions, no way is left to control them but *with a high hand and an outstretched arm.*

Brutus.

THE MEANING OF GOVERNMENT BY CONSENT

Explained in Federalist Numbers 52–72 (Nos. 52, 53, 57, 62, 67, 68, and 70 are most important).

Generally speaking, the debates over the need for a stronger national government and over the tendencies toward tyranny under the new Constitution resulted in a standoff. The federalists thought their case for a more "energetic" government had been established firmly, while the anti-federalists were satisfied that affairs could be managed under the Articles of Confederation, with perhaps some strengthening amendments. Likewise, the federalists regarded their defense of the freedom-preserving character of the new Constitution, especially the clever argument for the "extended republic" in Federalist No. 10 and the explanation of checks and balances in No. 51, as strong and forthright. The antifederalists, though, continued to insist on the dangers from the taxing power, the linkages of the Senate and the president, the power to raise armies, and the federal judiciary.

Each side, confident in its own position, also began to probe the relatively new, creative, and intriguing question beneath all their debates: what did it really mean to rest government on the consent of the governed and what were the most efficacious devices for making that agreed-upon goal a reality? Slowly, as the federalists began to explain the nature of the House of Representatives and the Senate, and the mode of election of the President, their ideas of the link between the people and the officers of government took clearer form. Publius' explanation of the House of

Representatives (Federalist Nos. 52–61), of the Senate (Nos. 62–66), and of the election and "character" of the executive (Nos. 67–72), revealed his conception of representation and consent. The anti-federalists, at first rather generally in the essays of "John DeWitt," "Cato," and "Brutus," and then profoundly and in careful distinction from the federalists in the speeches of Melancton Smith at the New York Ratifying Convention, developed a more radical, and to them more genuinely republican idea of what it meant to "give consent" to one's governors.

The documents in this section by "John DeWitt," by "Cato," by "Brutus," and by Melancton Smith are reprinted from Herbert J. Storing, ed., The Complete Anti-Federalist *(7 vols., Chicago, 1981), with the generous permission of the University of Chicago Press: vol. IV, pp. 24–28; vol. II, pp. 116–119, 123–125, 382–387, 442–446; vol. VI, pp. 149–169, 171–173.*

"John DeWitt," Essay III
(November 5, 1787)

The same Massachusetts anti-federalist, "John DeWitt," who had warned of the dangers of consolidated government in essays printed in pp. 188–199, explained his idea of representation in the next essay of his series, Number 3, which first appeared in the Boston American Herald *on November 5, 1787.*

III

*To the Free Citizens
of the Commonwealth of Massachusetts.*

Civil liberty, in all countries, hath been promoted by a free discussion of publick measures, and the conduct of publick men.

The FREEDOM OF THE PRESS hath, in consequence thereof, been esteemed one of its safe guards. That freedom gives the right, at all times, to every citizen to lay his sentiments, in a decent manner, before the people. If he will take that trouble upon himself, whether they are in point or not, his countrymen are obliged to him for so doing; for, at least, they lead to an examination of the subject upon which he writes.—If any possible situation makes it a duty, it is our present important one, for in the course of sixty or ninety days you are to approve of or reject the present proceedings of your Convention, which, if established, will certainly effect, in a greater or less degree, during the remainder of your lives, those privileges which you esteem dear to you, and not improbably those of your children for succeeding ages. Now therefore is unquestionably the proper time to examine it, and see if it really is what, upon paper, it appears to be. If with your eyes open, you deliberately accept it, however different it may prove in practice from what it appears in theory, you will have nobody to blame but yourselves; and what is infinitely worse, as I have before endeavoured to observe to you, you will be wholly without a remedy. It has many zealous advocates, and they have attempted, at least as far as their modesty would permit, to monopolize our gazettes, with their encomiums upon it. With the people they have to manage, I would hint to them, their zeal is not their best weapon, and exertions of such a kind, artful attempts to seize the moment, do seldom tend either to elucidate and explain principles, or ensure success. Such conduct ought to be an additional stimulus for those persons who are not its professed admirers, to speak their sentiments with freedom however unpopular.—Such conduct ought to inspire caution, for as a man is invariably known by his company, so is the tendency of principles known by their advocates.—Nay, it ought to lead you to enquire who are its advocates? Whether ambitious men throughout America, waiting with impatience to make it a stepping stone to posts of honour and emolument, are not of this class? Whether men who openly profess to be tired of republican governments, and sick to the heart of republican measures; who daily ridicule a government of choice, and pray ardently for one of force, are not of the same class? And, whether there are not men among us, who disapprove of it only because it is not an absolute monarchy, but who, upon the whole, are among its advocates?—In such examinations as these, you cannot mispend a proportion of the sixty days.

All contracts are to be construed according to the meaning of the parties at the time of making them. By which is meant, that mutual communications shall take place, and each shall explain to the other their ideas of the contract before them.—If any unfair practices are made use of, if its real tendency is concealed by either party, or any advantage taken in the execution of it, it is in itself fraudulent and may be avoided. There is no difference in the constitution of government.—Consent it is allowed is the spring.—The form is the mode in which the people choose to direct their affairs, and the magistrates are but trustees to put that mode in force.—It will not be denied, that this people, of any under Heaven, have a right of living under a government of their own choosing.—That government, originally consented to, which is in practice, what it purports to be in theory, is a government of choice; on the contrary, that which is essentially different in practice, from its appearance in theory, however it may be in letter a government of choice, it never can be so in spirit. Of this latter kind appear to me to be the proceedings of the Federal Convention.—They are presented as a Frame of Government purely Republican, and perfectly consistent with the individual governments in the Union. It is declared to be constructed for national purposes only, and not calculated to interfere with domestic concerns. You are told, that the rights of the people are very amply secured, and when the wheels of it are put in motion, it will wear a milder aspect than its present one. Whereas the very contrary of all this doctrine appears to be true. Upon an attentive examination you can pronounce it nothing less, than a government which, in a few years, will degenerate to a complete Aristocracy, armed with powers unnecessary in any case to bestow, and which in its vortex swallows up every other Government upon the Continent. In short, my fellow-citizens, it can be said to be nothing less than a hasty stride to Universal Empire in this Western World, flattering, very flattering to young ambitious minds, but fatal to the liberties of the people. The cord is strained to the very utmost.—There is every spice of the SIC JUBEO possible in the composition. Your consent is requested, because it is essential to the introduction of it; after having received confirmation, your complaints may increase the whistling of the wind, and they will be equally regarded.

It cannot be doubted at this day by any men of common sense, that there is a charm in politicks. That persons who enter reluctantly into office become habitated, grow fond of it, and are loath to resign it.—They feel themselves flattered and elevated, and are apt to forget their constituents, until the time returns that they again feel the want of them.—They uniformly exercise all the powers granted to them, and ninety-nine in a hundred are for grasping at more. It is this passionate thirst for power, which has produced different branches to exercise different departments and mutual checks upon those branches. The aristocratical hath ever been found to have the most influence, and the people in most countries have been particularly attentive in providing checks against it. Let us see if it is the case here.—A President, a Senate, and a House of Representatives are proposed. The Judicial Department is at present out of the question, being separated excepting in impeachments. The Legislative is divided between the People who are the Democratical, and the Senate who are the Aristocratical part, and the Executive between the same Senate and the President who represents the Monarchial Branch.—In the construction of this System, their interests are put in opposite scales. If they are exactly balanced, the Government will remain perfect; if there is a prepondency, it will firmly prevail. After the first four years, each Senator will hold his seat for the term of six years. This length of time will be amply sufficient of itself to remove any checks that he may have upon his independency, from the fear of a future election. He will consider that it is a serious portion of his life after the age of thirty; that places of honour and trust are not generally obtained unsolicited. The same means that placed him there may be again made use of; his influence and his abilities arising from his opportunities, will, during the whole term increase those means; he will have a complete negative upon all laws that shall be general, or that shall favor individuals, and a voice in the appointment of all officers in the United States.—Thus habituated to power, and living in the daily practice of granting favors and receiving solicitations, he may hold himself completely independent of the people, and at the same time ensure his election. If there remains even a risque, the blessed assistance of a little well-distributed money, will remove it.

With respect to the Executive, the Senate excepting in nomination, have a negative upon the President, and if we but a moment attended to their situation and to his, and to the power of persuasion over the human mind, especially when employed in behalf of friends and favorites, we cannot hesitate to say, that he will be infinitely less apt to disoblige them, than they to refuse him. It is far easier for twenty to gain over one, than one twenty; besides, in the one case, we can ascertain where the denial comes from, and the other we cannot. It is also highly improbable but some of the members, perhaps a major part, will hold their seats during their lives. We see it daily in our own Government, and we see it in every Government we are acquainted with, however many the cautions, and however frequent the elections.

These considerations, added to their share above mentioned in the Executive department must give them a decided superiority over the House of Representatives.—But that superiority is greatly enhanced, when we consider the difference of time for which they are chosen. They will have become adepts in the mystery of administration, while the House of Representatives may be composed perhaps two thirds of members, just entering into office, little used to the course of business, and totally unacquainted with the means made use of to accomplish it.—Very possible also in a country where they are total strangers.—But, my fellow-citizens, the important question here arises, who are this House of Representatives? "A representative Assembly, says the celebrated Mr. Adams, is the sense of the people, and the perfection of the portrait, consists in the likeness."—Can this Assembly be said to contain the sense of the people?—Do they resemble the people in any one single feature?—Do you represent your wants, your grievances, your wishes, in person? If that is impracticable, have you a right to send one of your townsmen for that purpose?—Have you a right to send one from your county? Have you a right to send more than one for every thirty thousand of you? Can he be presumed knowing to your different, peculiar situations—your abilities to pay publick taxes, when they ought to be abated, and when increased? Or is there any possibility of giving him information? All these questions must be answered in the negative. But how are these men to be chosen? Is there any other way than by dividing the Senate into districts? May not you as well at once invest your annual Assemblies with the power of choosing them—where is the essential difference? The nature of the thing will admit of none. Nay, you give them the power to prescribe the mode. They may invest it in themselves.—If you choose them yourselves, you must take them upon credit, and elect those persons you know only by common fame. Even this privilege is denied you annually, through fear that you might withhold the shadow of control over them. In this view of the System, let me sincerely ask you, where is the people in this House of Representatives?—Where is the boasted popular part of this much admired System?—Are they not cousins-german in every sense to the Senate? May they not with propriety be termed an Assistant Aristocratical Branch, who will be infinitely more inclined to co-operate and compromise with each other, than to be the careful guardians of the rights of their constituents? Who is there among you would not start at being told, that instead of your present House of Representatives, consisting of members chosen from every town, your future Houses were to consist of but ten in number, and these to be chosen by districts?—What man among you would betray his country and approve of it? And yet how infinitely preferable to the plan proposed?—In the one case the elections would be annual, the persons elected would reside in the center of you, their interests would be yours, they would be subject to your immediate control, and nobody to consult in their deliberations.—But in the other, they are chosen for double the time, during which, however well disposed, they become strangers to the very people choosing them, they reside at a distance from you, you have no control over them, you cannot observe their conduct, and they have to consult and finally be guided by twelve other States, whose interests are, in all material points, directly opposed to yours. Let me again ask you, What citizen is there in the Commonwealth of Massachusetts, that would deliberately consent laying aside the mode proposed, that the several Senates of the several States, should be the popular Branch, and together, form one National House of Representatives?—And yet one moment's attention will evince to you, that this blessed proposed Representation of the People, this apparent faithful Mirror, this striking Likeness, is to be still further refined, and more Aristocratical four times told.—Where now is the exact balance which has been so diligently attended to? Where lies the security of the people? What assurances have they that either their taxes will not be exacted but in the greatest emergencies, and then sparingly, or that standing armies will be raised and supported for the very plausible purpose only of cantoning them upon their frontiers? There is but one answer to these questions.—They have none. Nor was it intended by the makers they should have, for meaning to make a different use of the latter, they never will be at a loss for ways and means to expend the former. They do not design to beg a second time. Knowing the danger of frequent applications to the people, they ask for the whole at once, and are now by their conduct, teazing and absolutely haunting of you into a compliance.—If you choose all these things should take place, by all means gratify them. Go, and establish this Government, which is unanimously confessed imperfect, yet incapable of alteration. Intrust it to men, subject to the same unbounded passions and infirmities as yourselves, possessed with an insatiable thirst for power, and many of them, carrying in them vices, tho' tinsel'd and concealed, yet, in themselves, not less dangerous than those more naked and exposed. But in the mean time, add an additional weight to the stone that now covers the remains of the Great WARREN and MONTGOMERY; prepare an apology for the blood and treasure, profusely spent to obtain those rights which you now so timely part with. Conceal yourselves from the ridicule of your enemies, and bring your New England spirits to a level with the contempt of mankind. Henceforth you may sit yourselves down with propriety, and say, Blessed are they that never expect, for they shall not be disappointed.

John DeWitt.

"Cato," Letters V and VII
(November 22, 1787; January 3, 1788)

Another early entry in the debate over the new Constitution, "Cato," also criticized the provisions for representation of the people in the choice of the House of Representatives, the Senate, and the executive. Though his arguments are not as searching as those of "Brutus" and Melancton Smith below, "Cato" does re-iterate common anti-federalist arguments about representation, and expresses unusually explicit anti-federalist suspicions that the new Constitution provided insufficient guards against the greed and ambitions in human nature. "Cato" was the heroic defender of Roman republican virtue and liberty against the usurpations of the tyrant Caesar, familiar to eighteenth-century Americans not only from Plutarch's classic account of his life, but also from Joseph Addison's immensely popular play, "Cato" (1713). He has often been identified as New York Governor George Clinton, but there is no solid evidence of that. Cato's Letters Nos. V (which particularly meets the arguments of Federalist No. 67) and VII, first printed in the New York Journal, *November 22, 1787 and January 3, 1788, respectively, are reprinted here.*

V

To the Citizens of the State of New York.

In my last number I endeavored to prove that the language of the article relative to the establishment of the executive of this new government was vague and inexplicit, that the great powers of the president, connected with his duration in office would lead

to oppression and ruin. That he would be governed by favorites
and flatterers, or that a dangerous council would be collected
from the great officers of state;—that the ten miles square, if the
remarks of one of the wisest men, drawn from the experience of
mankind, may be credited, would be the asylum of the base,
idle, avaricious and ambitious, and that the court would possess
a language and manners different from yours; that a vice president is as unnecessary, as he is dangerous in his influence—that
the president cannot represent you because he is not of your own
immediate choice, that if you adopt this government, you will
incline to an arbitrary and odious aristocracy or monarchy—that
the president possessed of the power, given him by this frame of
government differs but very immaterially from the establishment of monarchy in Great Britain, and I warned you to beware
of the fallacious resemblance that is held out to you by the advocates of this new system between it and your own state governments.

And here I cannot help remarking, that inexplicitness seems
to pervade this whole political fabric: certainty in political compacts, which Mr. Coke calls *the mother and nurse of repose and
quietness,* the want of which induced men to engage in political
society, has ever been held by a wise and free people as essential
to their security; as, on the one hand it fixes barriers which the
ambitious and tyrannically disposed magistrate dare not overleap,
and on the other, becomes a wall of safety to the community—
otherwise stipulations between the governors and governed are
nugatory; and you might as well deposit the important powers of
legislation and execution in one or a few and permit them to
govern according to their disposition and will; but the world is
too full of examples, which prove that *to live by one man's will
became the cause of all men's misery.* Before the existence of
express political compacts it was reasonably implied that the
magistrate should govern with wisdom and justice, but mere
implication was too feeble to restrain the unbridled ambition of
a bad man, or afford security against negligence, cruelty, or any
other defect of mind. It is alledged that the opinions and manners of the people of America, are capable to resist and prevent
an extension of prerogative or oppression; but you must recol-

lect that opinion and manners are mutable, and may not always be a permanent obstruction against the encroachments of government; that the progress of a commercial society begets luxury, the parent of inequality, the foe to virtue, and the enemy to restraint; and that ambition and voluptuousness aided by flattery, will teach magistrates, where limits are not explicitly fixed to have separate and distinct interests from the people, besides it will not be denied that government assimilates the manners and opinions of the community to it. Therefore, a general presumption that rulers will govern well is not a sufficient security.—You are then under a sacred obligation to provide for the safety of your posterity, and would you now basely desert their interests, when by a small share of prudence you may transmit to them a beautiful political patrimony, that will prevent the necessity of their travelling through seas of blood to obtain that, which your wisdom might have secured:—It is a duty you owe likewise to your own reputation, for you have a great name to lose; you are characterised as cautious, prudent and jealous in politics; whence is it therefore, that you are about to precipitate yourselves into a sea of uncertainty, and adopt a system so vague, and which has discarded so many of your valuable rights:—Is it because you do not believe that an American can be a tyrant? If this be the case you rest on a weak basis; Americans are like other men in similar situations, when the manners and opinions of the community are changed by the causes I mentioned before, and your political compact inexplicit, your posterity will find that great power connected with ambition, luxury, and flattery, will as readily produce a Caesar, Caligula, Nero, and Domitian in America, as the same causes did in the Roman empire.

But the next thing to be considered in conformity to my plan, is the first article of this new government, which comprises the erection of the house of representatives and senate, and prescribes their various powers and objects of legislation. The most general objections to the first article, are that biennial elections for representatives are a departure from the safe democratical principles of annual ones—that the number of representatives are too few; that the apportionment and principles of increase are unjust; that no attention has been paid to either the numbers or property in each state in forming the senate; that the mode in which they are appointed and their duration, will lead to the establishment of an aristocracy; that the senate and president are improperly connected, both as to appointments, and the making of treaties, which are to become the supreme law of the land; that the judicial in some measure, to wit, as to the trial of impeachments, is placed in the senate, a branch of the legislative, and some times a branch of the executive: that Congress have the improper power of making or altering the regulations prescribed by the different legislatures, respecting the time, place, and manner of holding elections for representatives, and the time and manner of choosing senators; that standing armies may be established, and appropriation of money made for their support for two years; that the militia of the most remote state may be marched into those states situated at the opposite extreme of this continent; that the slave trade is, to all intents and purposes permanently established; and a slavish capitation, or poll-tax, may at any time be levied—these are some of the many evils that will attend the adoption of this government.

But with respect to the first objection, it may be remarked that a well digested democracy has this advantage over all others, to wit, that it affords to many the opportunity to be advanced to the supreme command, and the honors they thereby enjoy fill them with a desire of rendering themselves worthy of them; hence this desire becomes part of their education, is matured in manhood, and produces an ardent affection for their country, and it is the opinion of the great Sidney, and Montesquieu that this is in a great measure produced by annual election of magistrates.

If annual elections were to exist in this government, and learning and information to become more prevalent, you never will want men to execute whatever you could design.—Sidney observes "that a well governed state is as fruitful to all good purposes as the seven headed serpent is said to have been in evil; when one head is cut off, many rise up in the place of it." He remarks further, that "it was also thought, that free cities by frequent elections of magistrates became nurseries of great and able men, every man endeavoring to excel others, that he might be advanced to the honor he had no other title to, than what might arise from his merit, or reputation," but the framers of this *perfect government,* as it is called, have departed from this democratical principle, and established bi-ennial elections for the house of representatives, who are to be chosen by the people, and sextennial for the senate, who are to be chosen by the legislatures of the different states, and have given to the executive the unprecedented power of making temporary senators, in case of vacancies, by resignation or otherwise; and so far forth establishing a precedent for virtual representation (though in fact, their original appointment is virtual) thereby influencing the choice of the legislatures, or if they should not be so complaisant as to conform to his appointment—offence will be given to the executive and the temporary members will appear ridiculous by rejection; this temporary member, during his time of appointment, will of course act by a power derived from the executive, and for, and under his immediate influence.

It is a very important objection to this government, that the representation consists of so few; too few to resist the influence of corruption, and the temptation to treachery, against which all governments ought to take precautions—how guarded you have been on this head, in your own state constitution, and yet the number of senators and representatives proposed for this vast continent, does not equal those of your own state; how great the disparity, if you compare them with the aggregate numbers in the United States. The history of representation in England, from which we have taken our model of legislation, is briefly this: before the institution of legislating by deputies, the whole free part of the community usually met for that purpose; when this became impossible, by the increase of numbers the community was divided into districts, from each of which was sent such a number of deputies as was a complete representation of the various numbers and orders of citizens within them; but can it be asserted with truth, that six men can be a complete and full representation of the numbers and various orders of the people in this state? Another thing [that] may be suggested against the small number of representatives is, that but few of you will have the chance of sharing even in this branch of the legislature; and that the choice will be confined to a very few; the more complete it is, the better will your interests be preserved, and the greater the opportunity you will have to participate in government, one of the principal securities of a free people; but this subject has been so ably and fully treated by a writer under the signature of Brutus, that I shall content myself with referring you to him thereon, reserving further observations on the other objections I have mentioned, for my future numbers.

Cato.

VII

To the Citizens of the State of New York.

That the senate and president are further improperly connected, will appear, if it is considered, that their dependence on each other will prevent either from being a check upon the other; they must act in concert, and whether the power and influence of the one or the other is to prevail, will depend on the character and abilities of the men who hold those offices at the time. The senate is vested with such a proportion of the executive, that it would be found necessary that they should be constantly sitting. This circumstance did not escape the convention, and they have provided for the event, in the 2d article, which declares, that the executive may, on extraordinary occasions, *convene both houses or either of them.* No occasion can exist for calling the assembly without the senate; the words *or either of them,* must have been intended to apply only to the senate. Their wages are already provided for; and it will be therefore readily observed, that the partition between a perpetuation of their sessions and a perpetuation of their offices, in the progress of the government, will be found to be but thin and feeble. Besides, the senate, who have the sole power to try all impeachments, in case of the impeachment of the president, are to determine, as judges, the propriety of the advice they gave him, as senators. Can the senate in this, therefore, be an impartial judicature? And will they not rather serve as a screen to great public defaulters?

Among the many evils that are incorporated in this new system of government, is that of congress having the power of making or altering the regulations prescribed by the different legislatures, respecting the time, place, and manner of holding elections for representatives, and the time, and manner of choosing senators. If it is enquired, in what manner this regulation may be exercised to your injury—the answer is easy.

By the first article the house of representatives shall consist of members, chosen every second year by the people of the several states, who are qualified to vote for members of their several state assemblies; it can therefore readily be believed, that the different state legislatures, provided such can exist after the adoption of this government, will continue those easy and convenient modes for the election of representatives for the national legislature, that are in use, for the election of members of assembly for their own states; but the congress have, by the constitution, a power to make other regulations, or alter those in practice, prescribed by your own state legislature; hence, instead of having the places of elections in the precincts, and brought home almost to your own doors, congress may establish a place, or places, at either the extremes, center, or outer parts of the states; at a time and season too, when it may be very inconvenient to attend; and by these means destroy the rights of election; but in opposition to this reasoning, it is asserted, that it is a necessary power because the states might omit making rules for the purpose, and thereby defeat the existence of that branch of the government; this is what logicians call *argumentum absurdum,* for the different states, if they will have any security at all in this government, will find it in the house of representatives, and they, therefore, would not be very ready to eradicate a principle in which it dwells, or involve their country in an instantaneous revolution. Besides, if this was the apprehension of the framers, and the ground of that provision, why did not they extend this controlling power to the other duties of the several state legislatures. To exemplify this the states are to appoint senators and electors for choosing of a president; but the time is to be under the direction of congress. Now, suppose they were to omit the appointment of senators and electors, though congress was to appoint the time, which might [as] well be apprehended as the omission of regulations for the election of members of the house of representatives, provided they had that power; or suppose they were not to meet at all: of course, the government cannot proceed in its exercise. And from this motive, or apprehension, congress ought to have taken these duties entirely in their own hands, and, by a decisive declaration, annihilated them, which they in fact have done by leaving them without the means of support, or at least resting on their bounty. To this, the advocates for this system oppose the common, empty declamation, that there is no danger that congress will abuse this power; but such language, as relative to so important a subject, is mere vapour, and sound without sense. Is it not in their power, however, to make such regulations as may be inconvenient to you? It must be admitted, because the words are unlimited in their sense. It is a good rule, in the construction of a contract, to support, that what may be done will be; therefore, in considering this subject, you are to suppose, that in the exercise of this government, a regulation of congress will be made, for holding an election for the whole state at Poughkeepsie, at New York, or, perhaps, at Fort Stanwix: who will then be the actual electors for the house of representatives? Very few more than those who may live in the vicinity of these places. Could any others afford the expense and time of attending? And would not the government by this means have it in their power to put whom they pleased in the house of representatives? You ought certainly to have as much or more distrust with respect to the exercise of these powers by congress, than congress ought to have with respect to the exercise of those duties which ought to be entrusted to the several states, because over them congress can have a legislative controlling power.

Hitherto we have tied up our rulers in the exercise of their duties by positive restrictions—if the cord has been drawn too tight, loosen it to the necessary extent, but do not entirely unbind them.—I am no enemy to placing a reasonable confidence in them; but such an unbounded one as the advocates and framers of this new system advise you to, would be dangerous to your liberties; it has been the ruin of other governments, and will be yours, if you adopt with all its latitudinal powers—unlimited confidence in governors as well as individuals is frequently the parent of deception [despotism?].—What facilitated the corrupt designs of Philip of Macedon, and caused the ruin of Athens, but the unbounded confidence in their statesmen and rulers? Such improper confidence Demosthenes was so well convinced had ruined his country, that in his second Philippic oration he remarks—"that there is one common bulwark with which men of prudence are naturally provided, the guard and security of all people, particularly of free states, against the assaults of tyrants—What is this? Distrust. Of this be mindful; to this adhere; preserve this carefully, and no calamity can affect you."— Montesquieu observes, that "the course of government is attended with an insensible descent to evil, and there is no reascending to good without very great efforts." The plain inference from this doctrine is, that rulers in all governments will erect an interest separate from the ruled, which will have a tendency to enslave them. There is therefore no other way of interrupting this insensible descent and warding off the evil as long as possible, than by establishing principles of distrust in your constituents, and cultivating the sentiment among yourselves. But let me enquire of you, my countrymen, whether the freedom and independence of elections is a point of magnitude? If it is, what kind of a spirit of amity, deference and concession, is that which has put in the power of congress at one stroke to prevent your interference in government, and do away your liberties forever? Does either the situation or circumstances of things warrant it?

Cato.

"Brutus," Essays IV and XVI
(November 29, 1787 ; April 10, 1788)

"Brutus," who had expounded on the tyrannical tendencies of the judiciary in the new Constitution (see pp. 308–328), also denied that representation could be effective under the provisions for the House of Representatives and the Senate. "Brutus'" Essays No. 4 and No. 16, which meet the arguments in Federalist Nos. 52–57 on the House of Representatives, and Nos. 62 and 63 on the Senate, are printed below. These essays were first published in the New York Journal *on November 29, 1787, and April 10, 1788, respectively.*

IV
29 NOVEMBER 1787

To the People of the State of New York.

There can be no free government where the people are not possessed of the power of making the laws by which they are governed, either in their own persons, or by others substituted in their stead.

Experience has taught mankind, that legislation by representatives is the most eligible, and the only practicable mode in which the people of any country can exercise the right, either prudently or beneficially. But then, it is a matter of the highest importance, in forming this representation, that it be so constituted as to be capable of understanding the true interests of the society for which it acts, and so disposed as to pursue the good and happiness of the people as its ultimate end. The object of every free government is the public good, and all lesser interests yield to it. That of every tyrannical government, is the happiness and aggrandisement of one, or a few, and to this the public felicity, and every other interest must submit.—The reason of this difference in these governments is obvious. The first is so constituted as to collect the views and wishes of the whole people in that of their rulers, while the latter is so framed as to separate the interests of the governors from that of the governed. The principle of self love, therefore, that will influence the one to promote the good of the whole, will prompt the other to follow its own private advantage. The great art, therefore, in forming a good constitution, appears to be this, so to frame it, as that those to whom the power is committed shall be subject to the same feelings, and aim at the same objects as the people do, who transfer to them their authority. There is no possible way to effect this but by an equal, full and fair representation; this, therefore, is the great desideratum in politics. However fair an appearance any government may make, though it may possess a thousand plausible articles and be decorated with ever so many ornaments, yet if it is deficient in this essential principle of a full and just representation of the people, it will be only like a painted sepulcher.—For, without this it cannot be a free government; let the administration of it be good or ill, it still will be a government, not according to the will of the people, but according to the will of a few.

To test this new constitution then, by this principle, is of the last importance.—It is to bring the touch-stone of national liberty, and I hope I shall be excused, if, in this paper, I pursue the subject commenced in my last number, to wit, the necessity of an equal and full representation in the legislature.—In that, I showed that it was not equal, because the smallest states are to send the same number of members to the senate as the largest, and, because the slaves, who afford neither aid or defence to the government, are to encrease the proportion of members. To prove that it was not a just or adequate representation, it was urged, that so small a number could not resemble the people, or possess their sentiments and dispositions. That the choice of members would commonly fall upon the rich and great, while the middling class of the community would be excluded. That in so small a representation there was no security against bribery and corruption.

The small number which is to compose this legislature, will not only expose it to the danger of that kind of corruption, and undue influence, which will arise from the gift of places of honour and emolument, or the more direct one of bribery, but it will also subject it to another kind of influence no less fatal to the liberties of the people, though it be not so flagrantly repugnant to the principles of rectitude. It is not to be expected that a legislature will be found in any country that will not have some of its members, who will pursue their private ends, and for which they will sacrifice the public good. Men of this character are, generally, artful and designing, and frequently possess brilliant talents and abilities; they commonly act in concert, and agree to share the spoils of their country among them; they will keep their object ever in view, and follow it with constancy. To effect their purpose, they will assume any shape, and, Proteus like, mould themselves into any form—where they find members proof against direct bribery or gifts of offices, they will endeavor to mislead their minds by specious and false reasoning, to impose upon their unsuspecting honesty by an affectation of zeal for the public good; they will form juntos, and hold out-door meetings; they will operate upon the good nature of their opponents, by a thousand little attentions, and teaze them into compliance by the earnestness of solicitation. Those who are acquainted with the manner of conducting business in public assemblies, know how prevalent art and address are in carrying a measure, even over men of the best intentions, and of good understanding. The firmest security against this kind of improper and dangerous influence, as well as all other, is a strong and numerous representation: in such a house of assembly, so great a number must be gained over, before the private views of individuals could be gratified that there could be scarce a hope of success. But in the federal assembly, seventeen men are all that is necessary to pass a law. It is probable, it will seldom happen that more than twenty-five will be requisite to form a majority, when it is considered what a number of places of honor and emolument will be in the gift of the executive, the powerful influence that great and designing men have over the honest and unsuspecting, by their art and address, their soothing manners and civilities, and their cringing flattery, joined with their affected patriotism; when these different species of influence are combined, it is scarcely to be hoped that a legislature, composed of so small a number, as the one proposed by the new constitution, will long resist their force.

A farther objection against the feebleness of the representation is, that it will not possess the confidence of the people. The execution of the laws in a free government must rest on this confidence, and this must be founded on the good opinion they entertain of the framers of the laws. Every government must be supported, either by the people having such an attachment to it, as to be ready, when called upon, to support it, or by a force at the command of the government, to compel obedience. The latter mode destroys every idea of a free government; for the same force that may be employed to compel obedience to good laws, might, and probably would be used to wrest from the people their constitutional liberties.—Whether it is practicable to have a representation for the whole union sufficiently numerous to obtain that confidence which is necessary for the purpose of internal taxation, and other powers to which this proposed government extends, is an important question. I am clearly of opinion, it is not, and therefore I have stated this in my first number, as one of the reasons against going into an entire consolidation of the states.—One of the most capital errors in the system, is that of extending the powers of the federal government to objects to which it is not adequate, which it cannot exercise without endangering public liberty, and which it is not necessary they should possess, in order to preserve the union and manage our national concerns; of this, however, I shall treat more fully in some future paper.—But, however this may be, certain it is, that the representation in the legislature is not so formed as to give reasonable ground for public trust.

In order for the people safely to repose themselves on their rulers, they should not only be of their own choice. But it is requisite they should be acquainted with their abilities to manage the public concerns with wisdom. They should be satisfied that those who represent them are men of integrity, who will pursue the good of the community with fidelity; and will not be turned aside from their duty by private interest, or corrupted by undue influence; and that they will have such a zeal for the good of those whom they represent, as to excite them to be diligent in their service; but it is impossible the people of the United States should have sufficient knowledge of their representatives, when the numbers are so few, to acquire any rational satisfaction on either of these points. The people of this state will have very little acquaintance with those who may be chosen to represent them; a great part of them will, probably, not know the characters of their own members, much less that of a majority of those who will compose the federal assembly; they will consist of men, whose names they have never heard, and whose talents and regard for the public good, they are total strangers to; and they will have no persons so immediately of their choice so near them, of their neighbours and of their own rank in life, that they can feel themselves secure in trusting their interests in their hands. The representatives of the people cannot, as they now do, after they have passed laws, mix with the people, and explain to them the motives which induced the adoption of any measure, point out its utility, and remove objections or silence unreasonable clamours against it.—The number will be so small that but a very few of the most sensible and respectable yeomanry of the country can ever have any knowledge of them: being so far removed from the people, their station will be elevated and important, and they will be considered as ambitious and designing. They will not be viewed by the people as part of themselves, but as a body distinct from them, and having separate interests to pursue; the consequence will be, that a perpetual jealousy will exist in the minds of the people against them; their conduct will be narrowly watched; their measures scrutinized; and their laws opposed, evaded, or reluctantly obeyed. This is natural, and exactly corresponds with the conduct of individuals towards those in whose hands they intrust important concerns. If the person confided in, be a neighbour with whom his employer is intimately acquainted, whose talents, he knows, are sufficient to manage the business with which he is charged, his honesty and fidelity unsuspected, and his friendship and zeal for the service of the principal unquestionable, he will commit his affairs into his hands with unreserved confidence, and feel himself secure; all the transactions of the agent will meet with the most favorable construction, and the measures he takes will give satisfaction. But, if the person employed be a stranger, whom he has never seen, and whose character for ability or fidelity he cannot fully learn—if he is constrained to choose him, because it was not in his power to procure one more agreeable to his wishes, he will trust him with caution, and be suspicious of all his conduct.

If then this government should not derive support from the good will of the people, it must be executed by force, or not executed at all; either case would lead to the total destruction of liberty.—The convention seemed aware of this, and have therefore provided for calling out the militia to execute the laws of the union. If this system was so framed as to command that respect from the people, which every good free government will obtain, this provision was unnecessary—the people would support the civil magistrate. This power is a novel one, in free governments—these have depended for the execution of the laws on the Posse Comitatus, and never raised an idea, that the people would refuse to aid the civil magistrate in executing those laws they themselves had made. I shall now dismiss the subject of the incompetency of the representation, and proceed, as I promised, to shew, that, impotent as it is, the people have no security that they will enjoy the exercise of the right of electing this assembly, which, at best, can be considered but as the shadow of representation.

By section 4, article I, the Congress are authorized, at any time, by law, to make, or alter, regulations respecting the time, place, and manner of holding elections for senators and representatives, except as to the places of choosing senators. By this clause the right of election itself, is, in a great measure, transferred from the people to their rulers.—One would think, that if any thing was necessary to be made a fundamental article of the original compact, it would be, that of fixing the branches of the legislature, so as to put it out of its power to alter itself by modifying the election of its own members at will and pleasure.

When a people once resign the privilege of a fair election, they clearly have none left worth contending for.

It is clear that, under this article, the federal legislature may institute such rules respecting elections as to lead to the choice of one description of men. The weakness of the representation, tends but too certainly to confer on the rich and well-born, all honours; but the power granted in this article, may be so exercised, as to secure it almost beyond a possibility of control. The proposed Congress may make the whole state one district, and direct, that the capital (the city of New York, for instance) shall be the place for holding the election; the consequence would be, that none but men of the most elevated rank in society would attend, and they would as certainly choose men of their own class; as it is true what the Apostle Paul saith, that "no man ever yet hated his own flesh, but nourisheth and cherisheth it."—They may declare that those members who have the greatest number of votes, shall be considered as duly elected; the consequence would be that the people, who are dispersed in the interior parts of the state, would give their votes for a variety of candidates, while any order, or profession, residing in populous places, by uniting their interests, might procure whom they pleased to be chosen—and by this means the representatives of the states may be elected by one tenth part of the people who actually vote. This may be effected constitutionally, and by one of those silent operations which frequently takes place without being noticed, but which often produces such changes as entirely to alter a government, subvert a free constitution, and rivet the chains on a free people before they perceive they are forged. Had the power of regulating elections been left under the direction of the state legislature, where the people are not only nominally but substantially represented, it would have been secure; but if it was taken out of their hands, it surely ought to have been fixed on such a basis as to have put it out of the power of the federal legislature to deprive the people of it by law. Provision should have been made for marking out the states into districts, and for choosing, by a majority of votes, a person out of each of them of permanent property and residence in the district which he was to represent.

If the people of America will submit to a constitution that will vest in the hands of any body of men a right to deprive them by law of the privilege of a fair election, they will submit to almost any thing. Reasoning with them will be in vain, they must be left until they are brought to reflection by feeling oppression—they will then have to wrest from their oppressors, by a strong hand, that which they now possess, and which they may retain if they will exercise but a moderate share of prudence and firmness.

I know it is said that the dangers apprehended from this clause are merely imaginary, that the proposed general legislature will be disposed to regulate elections upon proper principles, and to use their power with discretion, and to promote the public good. On this, I would observe, that constitutions are not so necessary to regulate the conduct of good rulers as to restrain that of bad ones.—Wise and good men will exercise power so as to promote the public happiness under any form of government. If we are to take it for granted, that those who administer the government under this system, will always pay proper attention to the rights and interests of the people, nothing more was necessary than to say who should be invested with the powers of government, and leave them to exercise it at will and pleasure. Men are apt to be deceived both with respect to their own dispositions and those of others. Though this truth is proved by almost every page of the history of nations, to wit, that power lodged in the hands of rulers to be used at discretion, is almost always exercised to the oppression of the people, and the aggrandizement of themselves; yet most men think if it was lodged in their hands they would not employ it in this manner.—Thus when the prophet Elisha told Hazael, "I know the evil that thou wilt do unto the children of Israel; their strong holds wilt thou set on fire, and their young men, wilt thou slay with the sword, and wilt dash their children, and rip up their women with child." Hazael had no idea that he ever should be guilty of such horrid cruelty, and said to the prophet, "Is thy servant a dog that he should do this great thing." Elisha answered, "The Lord hath shewed me that thou shalt be king of Syria." The event proved, that Hazael only wanted an opportunity to perpetrate these enormities without restraint, and he had a disposition to do them, though he himself knew it not.

Brutus.

XVI
10 APRIL 1788

When great and extraordinary powers are vested in any man, or body of men, which in their exercise, may operate to the oppression of the people, it is of high importance that powerful checks should be formed to prevent the abuse of it.

Perhaps no restraints are more forcible, than such as arise from responsibility to some superior power.—Hence it is that the true policy of a republican government is, to frame it in such manner, that all persons who are concerned in the government, are made accountable to some superior for their conduct in office.—This responsibility should ultimately rest with the People. To have a government well administered in all its parts, it is requisite the different departments of it should be separated and lodged as much as may be in different hands. The legislative power should be in one body, the executive in another, and the judicial in one different from either—but still each of these bodies should be accountable for their conduct. Hence it is impracticable, perhaps, to maintain a perfect distinction between these several departments—for it is difficult, if not impossible, to call to account the several officers in government, without in some degree mixing the legislative and judicial. The legislature in a free republic are chosen by the people at stated periods, and their responsibility consists, in their being amenable to the people. When the term, for which they are chosen, shall expire, who will then have opportunity to displace them if they disapprove of their conduct—but it would be improper that the judicial should be elective, because their business requires that they should possess a degree of law knowledge, which is acquired only by a regular education, and besides it is fit that they should be placed, in a certain degree in an independent situation, that they may maintain firmness and steadiness in their decisions. As the people therefore ought not to elect the judges, they cannot be amenable to them immediately, some other mode of amenability must therefore be devised for these, as well as for all other officers which do not spring from the immediate choice of the people: this is to be effected by making one court subordinate to another, and by giving them cognizance of the behaviour of all officers; but on this plan we at last arrive at some supreme, over whom there is no power to control but the people themselves. This supreme controlling power should be in the choice of the people, or else you establish an authority independent, and not amenable at all, which is repugnant to the principles of a free government. Agreeable to these principles I suppose the supreme judicial ought to be liable to be called to account, for any misconduct, by some body of men, who depend upon the people for their places; and so also should all other great officers in the state, who are not made amenable to some superior officers. This policy seems in some measure to have been in view of the framers of the new system, and to have given rise to the institution of a court of impeachments.—How far this Court will be properly qualified to execute the trust which will be reposed in them, will be the business of a future paper to investigate. To prepare the way to do this, it shall be the business of this, to make some remarks upon the constitution and powers of the senate, with whom the power of trying impeachments is lodged.

The following things may be observed with respect to the constitution of the senate.

1st. They are to be elected by the legislatures of the states and not by the people, and each state is to be represented by an equal number.

2d. They are to serve for six years, except that one third of those first chosen are to go out of office at the expiration of two years, one third at the expiration of four years, and one third at the expiration of six years, after which this rotation is to be preserved, but still every member will serve for the term of six years.

3d. If vacancies happen by resignation or otherwise, during the recess of the legislature of any state, the executive is authorised to make temporary appointments until the next meeting of the legislature.

4. No person can be a senator who has not arrived to the age of thirty years, been nine years a citizen of the United States, and who is not at the time he is elected an inhabitant of the state for which he is elected.

The apportionment of members of senate among the states is not according to numbers, or the importance of the states; but is equal. This, on the plan of a consolidated government, is unequal and improper; but is proper on the system of confederation—on this principle I approve of it. It is indeed the only feature of any importance in the constitution of a confederated government. It was obtained after a vigorous struggle of that part of the Convention who were in favor of preserving the state governments. It is to be regretted, that they were not able to have infused other principles into the plan, to have secured the government of the respective states, and to have marked with sufficient precision the line between them and the general government.

The term for which the senate are to be chosen, is in my judgment too long, and no provision being made for a rotation will, I conceive, be of dangerous consequence.

It is difficult to fix the precise period for which the senate should be chosen. It is a matter of opinion, and our sentiments on the matter must be formed, by attending to certain principles. Some of the duties which are to be performed by the senate, seem evidently to point out the propriety of their term of service being extended beyond the period of that of the assembly. Besides as they are designed to represent the aristocracy of the country, it seems fit they should possess more stability, and so continue a longer period than that branch who represent the democracy. The business of making treaties and some other which it will be proper to commit to the senate, requires that they should have experience, and therefore that they should remain some time in office to acquire it.—But still it is of equal importance that they should not be so long in office as to be likely to forget the hand that formed them, or be insensible of their interests. Men long in office are very apt to feel themselves independent and to form and pursue interests separate from those who appointed them. And this is more likely to be the case with the

senate, as they will for the most part of the time be absent from
the state they represent, and associate with such company as will
possess very little of the feelings of the middling class of people.
For it is to be remembered that there is to be a *federal city,* and
the inhabitants of it will be the great and the mighty of the earth.
For these reasons I would shorten the term of their service to
four years. Six years is a long period for a man to be absent from
his home, it would have a tendency to wean him from his constituents.

   A rotation in the senate, would also in my opinion be of great
use. It is probable that senators once chosen for a state will, as
the system now stands, continue in office for life. The office will
be honorable if not lucrative. The persons who occupy it will
probably wish to continue in it, and therefore use all their influence and that of their friends to continue in office.—Their
friends will be numerous and powerful, for they will have it in
their power to confer great favors; besides it will before long be
considered as disgraceful not to be re-elected. It will therefore
be considered as a matter of delicacy to the character of the
senator not to return him again.—Every body acquainted with
public affairs knows how difficult it is to remove from office a
person who is [has?] long been in it. It is seldom done except in
cases of gross misconduct. It is rare that want of competent ability procures it. To prevent this inconvenience I conceive it would
be wise to determine, that a senator should not be eligible after
he had served for the period assigned by the constitution for a
certain number of years; perhaps three would be sufficient. A
farther benefit would be derived from such an arrangement; it
would give opportunity to bring forward a greater number of
men to serve their country, and would return those, who had
served, to their state, and afford them the advantage of becoming
better acquainted with the condition and politics of their constituents. It farther appears to me proper, that the legislatures
should retain the right which they now hold under the confederation, of recalling their members. It seems an evident dictate
of reason, that when a person authorises another to do a piece of
business for him, he should retain the power to displace him,

when he does not conduct according to his pleasure. This power in the state legislatures, under confederation, has not been exercised to the injury of the government, nor do I see any danger of its being so exercised under the new system. It may operate much to the public benefit.

These brief remarks are all I shall make on the organization of the senate. The powers with which they are invested will require a more minute investigation.

This body will possess a strange mixture of legislative, executive and judicial powers, which in my opinion will in some cases clash with each other.

1. They are one branch of the legislature, and in this respect will possess equal powers in all cases with the house of representatives; for I consider the clause which gives the house of representatives the right of originating bills for raising a revenue as merely nominal, seeing the senate be authorised to propose or concur with amendments.

2. They are a branch of the executive in the appointment of ambassadors and public ministers, and in the appointment of all other officers, not otherwise provided for; whether the forming of treaties, in which they are joined with the president, appertains to the legislative or the executive part of the government, or to neither, is not material.

3. They are part of the judicial, for they form the court of impeachments.

It has been a long established maxim, that the legislative, executive and judicial departments in government should be kept distinct. It is said, I know, that this cannot be done. And therefore that this maxim is not just, or at least that it should only extend to certain leading features in a government. I admit that this distinction cannot be perfectly preserved. In a due balanced government, it is perhaps absolutely necessary to give the executive qualified legislative powers, and the legislative or a branch of them judicial powers in the last resort. It may possibly also, in some special cases, be advisable to associate the legislature, or a branch of it, with the executive, in the exercise of acts of great national importance. But still the maxim is a good one, and a separation of these powers should be sought as far as is practicable. I can scarcely imagine that any of the advocates of the system will pretend, that it was necessary to accumulate all these powers in the senate. . . .

                                                                Brutus.

Speeches of Melancton Smith
(June 20–27, 1788)

The last important part of the debate over the Constitution took place in New York State, where opposition to it had been strong ever since two New York delegates to the Federal Convention, Robert Yates and John Lansing, had departed in July 1787 because they objected to the shape being taken by the proposed new government. A dominant party in New York, headed by Governor George Clinton, opposed ratification and elected a solid anti-federal majority (46 to 19) to the New York convention, which met in June 1788. As the convention opened, however, news of the New Hampshire and Virginia ratifications arrived, the ninth and tenth states to do so, insuring that the new Constitution would go into effect. New York, then, had the choice of joining or refusing to join the new union. The latter prospect was unwelcome in many ways, so the delegates, despite their predelections, felt strong pressure to ratify. Alexander Hamilton, Robert R. Livingston, and other skilled federalist advocates took the lead in the debates. The anti-federalists engaged Hamilton and his colleagues vigorously, and produced searching arguments opposing the new Constitution and its theoretical justifications. The most profound of the anti-federalist speakers was Melancton Smith who rose repeatedly to challenge Hamilton and the other now-confident federalists. In a series of debates on June 20–27, Smith criticized the construction of the House of Representatives and the Senate with arguments that developed

*fully a conception of government by consent consistent with
Smith's republican principles. His position in many ways differs
from the ideas of representation and legislative conduct offered
in Federalist Nos. 52–57 on the House of Representatives, and
Nos. 62 and 63 on the Senate. Smith began his speeches in direct
opposition to remarks by Hamilton on Article I, Section 2, on the
composition and election of the House of Representatives, They
were first printed in* The Debates and Proceedings of the Convention of the State of New York *(New York, Francis Childs,
1788).*

. . . He [Smith] was as strongly impressed with the necessity of
a Union, as any one could be: He would seek it with as much
ardor. In the discussion of this subject, he was disposed to make
every reasonable concession, and indeed to sacrifice every thing
for a Union, except the liberties of his country, than which he
could contemplate no greater misfortune. But he hoped we were
not reduced to the necessity of sacrificing or even endangering
our liberties to preserve the Union. If that was the case, the alternative was dreadful. But he would not now say that the adoption of the Constitution would endanger our liberties; because
that was the point to be debated, and the premises should be laid
down previously to the drawing of any conclusion. He wished
that all observations might be confined to this point; and that
declamation and appeals to the passions might be omitted.

Why, said he, are we told of our weakness? Of the defence-
less condition of the southern parts of our state? Or the exposed
situation of our capital? Of Long Island surrounded by water,
and exposed to the incursions of our neighbours in Connecticut?
Of Vermont having separated from us and assumed the powers
of a distinct government; and of the North-West part of our state
being in the hands of a foreign enemy?—Why are we to be
alarmed with apprehensions that the Eastern states are inimical,
and disinclined to form alliances with us? He was sorry to find
that such suspicions were entertained. He believed that no such
disposition existed in the Eastern states. Surely it could not be
supposed that those states would make war upon us for exercising the rights of freemen, deliberating and judging for ourselves,

on a subject the most interesting that ever came before any assembly. If a war with our neighbour was to be the result of not acceding, there was no use in debating here; we had better receive their dictates, if we were unable to resist them. The defects of the Old Confederation needed as little proof as the necessity of an Union: But there was no proof in all this, that the proposed Constitution was a good one. Defective as the Old Confederation is, he said, no one could deny but it was possible we might have a worse government. But the question was not whether the present Confederation be a bad one; but whether the proposed Constitution be a good one.

It had been observed, that no examples of Federal Republics had succeeded. It was true that the ancient confederated Republics were all destroyed—so were those which were not confederated; and all ancient Governments of every form had shared the same fate. Holland had undoubtedly experienced many evils from the defects in her government; but with all these defects, she yet existed; she had under her Confederacy made a principal figure among the nations of Europe, and he believed few countries had experienced a greater share of internal peace and prosperity. The Germanic Confederacy was not the most pertinent example to produce on this occasion:—Among a number of absolute Princes who consider their subjects as their property, whose will is law, and to whose ambition there are no bounds, it was no difficult task to discover other causes from which the convulsions in that country rose, than the defects of their Confederation. Whether a Confederacy of States under any form be a practicable Government, was a question to be discussed in the course of investigating this Constitution.

He was pleased that thus early in the debate, the honorable gentleman had himself shown, that the intent of the Constitution was not a Confederacy, but a reduction of all the states into a consolidated government. He hoped the gentleman would be complaisant enough to exchange names with those who disliked the Constitution, as it appeared from his own concession that they were Federalists, and those who advocated it Anti-Federalists. He begged leave, however, to remind the gentleman, that Montesquieu, with all the examples of modern and ancient Republics in view, gives it as his opinion, that a confederated Republic has all the internal advantages of a Republic, with the external force of a Monarchical Government. He was happy to find an officer of such high rank recommending to the other officers of Government, and to those who are members of the Legislature, to be unbiassed by any motives of interest or state importance. Fortunately for himself, he was out of the verge of temptations of this kind, not having the honor to hold any office under the state. But then he was exposed, in common with other gentlemen of the Convention, to another temptation, against which he thought it necessary that we should be equally guarded:—If, said he, this Constitution is adopted, there will be a number of honorable and lucrative offices to be filled, and we ought to be cautious lest an expectancy of some of them should influence us to adopt without due consideration.

We may wander, said he, in the fields of fancy without end, and gather flowers as we go: It may be entertaining—but it is of little service to the discovery of truth:—We may on one side compare the scheme advocated by our opponents to golden images, with feet part of iron and part of clay; and on the other, to a beast dreadful and terrible, and strong exceedingly, having great iron teeth, which devours, breaks in pieces, and stamps the residue with his feet: And after all, said he, we shall find that both these allusions are taken from the same vision; and their true meaning must be discovered by sober reasoning.

He would agree with the honorable gentleman, that perfection in any system of government was not to be looked for. If that was the object, the debates on the one before them might soon be closed.—But he would observe that this observation applied with equal force against changing any systems—especially against material and radical changes.—Fickleness and inconstancy, he said, was characteristic of a free people; and in framing a Constitution for them, it was, perhaps the most difficult thing to correct this spirit, and guard against the evil effects of it—he was persuaded it could not be altogether prevented without destroying their freedom—it would be like attempting to correct a small indisposition in the habit of the body, by fixing the patient in a confirmed consumption.—This fickle and inconstant spirit was the more dangerous in bringing about changes in the government. The instance that had been adduced by the gentleman from sacred history, was an example in point to prove this: The nation of Israel having received a form of civil government from Heaven, enjoyed it for a considerable period; but at length labouring under pressures, which were brought upon them by their own misconduct and imprudence, instead of imputing their misfortunes to their true causes, and making a proper improvement of their calamities, by a correction of their errors, they imputed them to a defect in their constitution; they rejected their Divine Ruler, and asked Samuel to make them a King to judge them, like other nations. Samuel was grieved at their folly; but still, by the command of God, he hearkened to their voice; tho' not until he had solemnly declared unto them the manner in which the King should reign over them. "This, (says Samuel) shall be the manner of the King that shall reign over you. He will take your sons and appoint them for himself, for his chariots, and for his horsemen, and some shall run before his chariots; and he will appoint him captains over thousands, and captains over fifties, and will set them to ear his ground, and to reap his harvest, and to make his instruments of war, and instruments of his chariots. And he will take your daughters to be confectionaries, and to be cooks, and to be bakers. And he will take your fields, and your vine yards, and your olive yards, even the best of them, and give them to his servants. And he will take the tenth of your seed, and of your vineyards, and give to his officers and to his servants. And he will take your men servants and your maid servants, and your goodliest young men, and your asses, and put them to his work. He will take the tenth of your sheep: And ye shall be his servants. And ye shall cry out in that day, because of your King which ye have chosen you; and the Lord will not hear you in that day."—How far this was applicable to the subject he would not now say; it could be better judged of when they had gone through it.—On the whole he wished to take up this matter with candor and deliberation.

He would now proceed to state his objections to the clause just read (section 2 of article I, clause 3). His objections were comprised under three heads: 1st, the rule of appointment is unjust; 2d, there is no precise number fixed on below which the house shall not be reduced; 3d, it is inadequate. In the first place the rule of apportionment of the representatives is to be according to the whole number of the white inhabitants, with three fifths of all others; that is in plain English, each state is to send Representatives in proportion to the number of freemen, and three fifths of the slaves it contains. He could not see any rule by which slaves are to be included in the ratio of representation: The principle of a representation, being that every free agent should be concerned in governing himself, it was absurd to give that power to a man who could not exercise it—slaves have no will of their own: The very operation of it was to give certain privileges to those people who were so wicked as to keep slaves. He knew it would be admitted that this rule of apportionment was founded on unjust principles, but that it was the result of accommodation; which he supposed we should be under the necessity of admitting, if we meant to be in union with the Southern States, though utterly repugnant to his feelings. In the second place, the number was not fixed by the Constitution, but left at the discretion of the Legislature; perhaps he was mistaken; it was his wish to be informed. He understood from the Constitution, that sixty-five Members were to compose the House of Representatives for three years; that after that time a census was to be taken, and the numbers to be ascertained by the Legislature on the following principles: 1st, they shall be apportioned to the respective States according to numbers; 2d, each State shall have one at least; 3d, they shall never exceed one to every thirty thousand. If this was the case, the first Congress that met might reduce the number below what it now is; a power inconsistent with every principle of a free government, to leave it to the discretion of the rulers to determine the number of the representatives of the people. There was no kind of security except in the integrity of the men who were entrusted; and if you have no other security, it is idle to contend about Constitutions. In the third place, supposing Congress should declare that there should be one representative for every thirty thousand of the people, in his opinion it would be incompetent to the great purposes of representation. It was, he said, the fundamental principle of a free government, that the people should make the laws by which they were to be governed: He who is controlled by another is a slave; and that government which is directed by the will of any one or a few, or any number less than is the will of the community, is a government for slaves.

The next point was, how was the will of the community to be expressed? It was not possible for them to come together; the multitude would be too great: In order, therefore to provide against this inconvenience, the scheme of representation had been adopted, by which the people deputed others to represent them. Individuals entering into society became one body, and that body ought to be animated by one mind; and he conceived that every form of government should have that complexion. It was true that notwithstanding all the experience we had from others, it had not appeared that the experiment of representation had been fairly tried: there was something like it in the ancient republics, in which, being of small extent, the people could easily meet together, though instead of deliberating, they only considered of those things which were submitted to them by their magistrates. In Great Britain representation had been carried much farther than in any government we knew of, except our own; but in that country it now had only a name. America was the only country, in which the first fair opportunity had been offered. When we were Colonies, our representation was better than any that was then known: Since the revolution we had advanced still nearer to perfection. He considered it as an object, of all others the most important, to have it fixed on its true principle; yet he was convinced that it was impracticable to have such a representation in a consolidated government. However, said he, we may approach a great way towards perfection by encreasing the representation and limiting the powers of Congress. He considered that the great interest and liberties of the people could only be secured by the State Governments. He admitted, that if the new government was only confined to great national objects, it would be less exceptionable; but it extended to every thing dear to human nature. That this was the case could be proved without any long chain of reasoning:—for that power which had both the purse and the sword, had the government of the whole country, and might extend its powers to any and to every object. He had already observed, that by the true doctrine of representation, this principle was established—that the representative must be chosen by the free will of the majority of his constituents: It therefore followed that the representative should be chosen from small districts. This being admitted, he would ask, could 65 men for 3,000,000, or 1 for 30,000, be chosen in this manner? Would they be possessed of the requisite information to make happy the great number of souls that were spread over this extensive country?—There was another objection to the clause: If great affairs of government were trusted to a few men, they would be more liable to corruption. Corruption, he knew, was unfashionable amongst us, but he supposed that Americans were like other men; and though they had hitherto displayed great virtues, still they were men; and therefore such steps should be taken as to prevent the possibility of corruption. We were now in that stage of society, in which we could deliberate with freedom;—how long it might continue, God only knew! Twenty years hence, perhaps, these maxims might become unfashionable; we already hear, said he, in all parts of the country, gentlemen ridiculing that spirit of patriotism and love of liberty, which carried us through all our difficulties in times of danger.—When patriotism was already nearly hooted out of society, ought we not to take some precautions against the progress of corruption? . . .

21 JUNE 1788

To determine whether the number of representatives proposed by this Constitution is sufficient, it is proper to examine the qualifications which this house ought to possess, in order to exercise their powers discreetly for the happiness of the people. The idea that naturally suggests itself to our minds, when we speak of representatives is, that they resemble those they represent; they should be a true picture of the people; possess the knowledge of their circumstances and their wants; sympathize in all their distresses, and be disposed to seek their true interests. The knowledge necessary for the representatives of a free people, not only comprehends extensive political and commercial information, such as is acquired by men of refined education, who have leisure to attain to high degrees of improvement, but it should also comprehend that kind of acquaintance with the common concerns and occupations of the people, which men of the middling class of life are in general much better competent to, than those of a superior class. To understand the true commercial interests of a country, not only requires just ideas of the general commerce of the world, but also, and principally, a knowledge of the productions of your own country and their value, what your soil is capable of producing, the nature of your manufacturers, and the capacity of the country to increase both. To exercise the power of laying taxes, duties and excises with discretion, requires something more than an acquaintance with the abstruse parts of the system of finance. It calls for a knowledge of the circumstances and ability of the people in general, a discernment how the burdens imposed will bear upon the different classes.

From these observations results this conclusion that the number of representatives should be so large, as that while it embraces men of the first class, it should admit those of the middling class of life. I am convinced that this Government is so constituted, that the representatives will generally be composed of the first class in the community, which I shall distinguish by the name of the natural aristocracy of the country. I do not mean to give offence by using this term. I am sensible this idea is treated by many gentlemen as chimerical. I shall be asked what is meant by the natural aristocracy—and told that no such distinction of classes of men exists among us. It is true it is our singular felicity that we have no legal or hereditary distinctions of this kind; but still there are real differences: Every society naturally divides itself into classes. The author of nature has bestowed on some greater capacities than on others—birth, education, talents and wealth, create distinctions among men as visible and of as much influence as titles, stars and garters. In every society, men of this class will command a superior degree of respect—and if the government is so constituted as to admit but few to exercise the power of it, it will, according to the natural course of things, be in their hands. Men in the middling class, who are qualified as representatives, will not be so anxious to be chosen as those of the first. When the number is so small the office will be highly elevated and distinguished—the stile in which the members live will probably be high—circumstances of this kind, will render the place of a representative not a desirable one to sensible, substantial men, who have been used to walk in the plain and frugal paths of life.

Besides, the influence of the great will generally enable them to succeed in elections—it will be difficult to combine a district of country containing 30 or 40,000 inhabitants, frame your election laws as you please, in any one character; unless it be in one of conspicuous, military, popular, civil or legal talents. The great easily form associations; the poor and middling class form them with difficulty. If the elections be by plurality, as probably will be the case in this state, it is almost certain, none but the great will be chosen—for they easily unite their interest.—The common people will divide, and their divisions will be promoted by the others. There will be scarcely a chance of their uniting, in any other but some great man, unless in some popular demagogue, who will probably be destitute of principle. A substantial yeoman of sense and discernment, will hardly ever be chosen. From these remarks it appears that the government will fall into the hands of the few and the great. This will be a government of oppression. I do not mean to declaim against the great, and charge them indiscriminately with want of principle and honesty.—The same passions and prejudices govern all men. The circumstances in which men are placed in a great measure give a cast to the human character. Those in middling circumstances, have less temptation—they are inclined by habit and the company with whom they associate, to set bounds to their passions and appetites—if this is not sufficient, the want of means to gratify them will be a restraint—they are obliged to employ their time in their respective callings—hence the substantial yeomanry of the country are more temperate, of better morals and less ambition than the great. The latter do not feel for the poor and middling class; the reasons are obvious—they are not obliged to use the pains and labour to procure property as the other.—They feel not the inconveniences arising from the payment of small sums. The great consider themselves above the common people—entitled to more respect—do not associate with them—they fancy themselves to have a right of preeminence in every thing. In short, they possess the same feelings, and are under the influence of the same motives, as an hereditary nobility. I know the idea that such a distinction exists in this country is ridiculed by some—but I am not the less apprehensive of anger from their influence on this account.—Such distinctions exist all the world over—have been taken notice of by all writers on free government—and are founded in the nature of things. It has been the principal care of free governments to guard against the encroachments of the great. Common observation and experience prove the existence of such distinctions. Will any one say, that there does not exist in this country the pride of family, of wealth, of talents; and that they do not command influence and respect among the common people? Congress, in their address to the habitants of the province of Quebec, in 1775, state this distinction in the following forcible words quoted from the Marquis Beccaria. "In every human society, there is an essay continually tending to confer on one part of the height of power and happiness, and to reduce the other to the extreme of weakness and misery. The intent of good laws is to oppose this effort, and to diffuse their influence universally and equally." We ought to guard against the government being placed in the hands of this class.—They cannot have that sympathy with their constituents which is necessary to connect them closely to their interest: Being in the habit of profuse living, they will be profuse in the public expenses. They find no difficulty in paying their taxes, and therefore do not feel public burdens: Besides if they govern, they will enjoy the emoluments of the government. The middling class, from their frugal habits, and feeling themselves the public burdens, will be careful how they increase them.

But I may be asked, would you exclude the first class in the community, from any share in legislation? I answer by no means—they would be more dangerous out of power than in it—they would be factious—discontented and constantly dis-

turbing the government—it would also be unjust—they have
their liberties to protect as well as others—and the largest share
of property. But my idea is, that the Constitution should be so
framed as to admit this class, together with a sufficient number
of the middling class to control them. You will then combine the
abilities and honesty of the community—a proper degree of information, and a disposition to pursue the public good. A representative body, composed principally of respectable yeomanry
is the best possible security to liberty.—When the interest of this
part of the community is pursued, the public good is pursued;
because the body of every nation consists of this class. And because the interest of both the rich and the poor are involved in
that of the middling class. No burden can be laid on the poor, but
what will sensibly affect the middling class. Any law rendering
property insecure, would be injurious to them.—When therefore
this class in society pursue their own interest, they promote that
of the public, for it is involved in it.

In so small a number of representatives, there is great danger
from corruption and combination. A great politician has said
that every man has his price: I hope this is not true in all its extent—but I ask the gentlemen to inform, what government there
is, in which it has not been practised? Notwithstanding all that
has been said of the defects in the Constitution of the ancient
Confederacies of the Grecian Republics, their destruction is to
be imputed more to this cause than to any imperfection in their
forms of government. This was the deadly poison that effected
their dissolution. This is an extensive country, increasing in
population and growing in consequence. Very many lucrative
offices will be in grant of the government, which will be the
object of avarice and ambition. How easy will it be to gain over
a sufficient number, in the bestowment of these offices, to promote the views and purposes of those who grant them! Foreign
corruption is also to be guarded against. A system of corruption
is known to be the system of government in Europe. It is practised without blushing. And we may lay it to our account it will
be attempted amongst us. The most effectual as well as natural
security against this, is a strong democratic branch in the legislature frequently chosen, including in it a number of the sub-

stantial, sensible yeomanry of the country. Does the house of representatives answer this description? I confess, to me they hardly wear the complexion of a democratic branch—they appear the mere shadow of representation. The whole number in both houses amounts to 91—of these 46 make a quorum; and 24 of those being secured, may carry any point. Can the liberties of three millions of people be securely trusted in the hands of 24 men? Is it prudent to commit to so small a number the decision of the great questions which will come before them? Reason revolts at the idea.

The honorable gentleman from New York has said that 65 members in the house of representatives are sufficient for the present situation of the country, and taking it for granted that they will increase as one for 30,000, in 25 years they will amount to 200. It is admitted by this observation that the number fixed in the Constitution, is not sufficient without it is augmented. It is not declared that an increase shall be made, but is left at the discretion of the legislature, by the gentleman's own concession; therefore the Constitution is imperfect. We certainly ought to fix in the Constitution those things which are essential to liberty. If anything falls under this description, it is the number of the legislature. To say, as this gentleman does, that our security is to depend upon the spirit of the people, who will be watchful of their liberties, and not suffer them to be infringed, is absurd. It would equally prove that we might adopt any form of government. I believe were we to create a despot, he would not immediately dare to act the tyrant; but it would not be long before he would destroy the spirit of the people, or the people would destroy him. If our people have a high sense of liberty, the government should be congenial to this spirit—calculated to cherish the love of liberty, while yet it had sufficient force to restrain licentiousness. Government operates upon the spirit of the people, as well as the spirit of the people operates upon it—and if they are not conformable to each other, the one or the other will prevail. In a less time than 25 years, the government will receive its tone. What the spirit of the country may be at the end of that period, it is impossible to foretell: Our duty is to frame a government friendly to liberty and the rights of mankind, which will tend to cherish and cultivate a love of liberty among our citizens. If this government becomes oppressive it will be by degrees: It will aim at its end by disseminating sentiments of government opposite to republicanism; and proceed from step to step in depriving the people of a share in the government. A recollection of the change that has taken place in the minds of many in this country in the course of a few years, ought to put us upon our guard. Many who are ardent advocates for the new system, reprobate republican principles as chimerical and such as ought to be expelled from society. Who would have thought ten years ago, that the very men who risqued their lives and fortunes in support of republican principles, would now treat them as the fictions of fancy?—A few years ago we fought for liberty.—We framed a general government on free principles.—We placed the state legislatures, in whom the people have a full and fair representation, between Congress and the people. We were then, it is true, too cautious; and too much restricted the powers of the general government. But now it is proposed to go into the contrary, and a more dangerous extreme; to remove all barriers; to give the New Government free access to our pockets, and ample command of our persons; and that without providing for a genuine and fair representation of the people. No one can say what the progress of the change of sentiment may be in 25 years. The same men who now cry up the necessity of an energetic government, to induce a compliance with this system, may in much less time reprobate this in as severe terms as they now do the Confederation, and may as strongly urge the necessity of going as far beyond this, as this beyond the Confederation.—Men of this class are increasing—they have influence, talents and industry.—It is time to form a barrier against them. And while we are willing to establish a government adequate to the purposes of the union, let us be careful to establish it on the broad basis of equal liberty.

23 JUNE 1788

Honorable Mr. *Smith.* I did not intend to make any more observations on this article. Indeed, I have heard nothing to day, which has not been suggested before, except the polite reprimand I have received for my declamation. I should not have risen again, but to examine who has proved himself the greatest declaimer. The gentleman wishes me to describe what I meant, by representing the feelings of the people. If I recollect right, I said the representative ought to understand, and govern his conduct by the true interest of the people.—I believe I stated this idea precisely. When he attempts to explain my ideas, he explains them away to nothing; and instead of answering, he distorts, and then sports with them. But he may rest assured, that in the present spirit of the Convention, to irritate is not the way to conciliate. The gentleman, by the false gloss he has given to my argument, makes me an enemy to the rich: This is not true. All I said, was, that mankind were influenced, in a great degree, by interests and prejudices:—That men, in different ranks of life, were exposed to different temptations—and that ambition was more peculiarly the passion of the rich and great. The gentleman supposes the poor have less sympathy with the sufferings of their fellow creatures; for that those who feel most distress themselves, have the least regard to the misfortunes of others:—Whether this be reasoning or declamation, let all who hear us determine. I observed that the rich were more exposed to those temptations, which rank and power hold out to view; that they were more luxurious and intemperate, because they had more fully the means of enjoyment; that they were more ambitious, because more in the hope of success. The gentleman says my principle is not true; for that a poor man will be as ambitious to be a constable, as a rich man to be a governor:—But he will not injure his country so much by the party he creates to support his ambition.

The next object of the gentleman's ridicule is my idea of an aristocracy; and he indeed has done me the honor, to rank me in the order. If then I am an aristocrat, and yet publicly caution my countrymen against the encroachments of the aristocrats, they will surely consider me as one of their most disinterested friends. My idea of aristocracy is not new:—It is embraced by many writers on government:—I would refer the gentleman for a definition of it to the honorable John Adams, one of our natural aristocrats. This writer will give him a description the most ample and satisfactory. But I by no means intended to carry my idea of it to such a ridiculous length as the gentleman would have me; nor will any of my expressions warrant the construction he imposes on them. My argument was, that in order to have a true and genuine representation, you must receive the middling class of people into your government—such as compose the body of this assembly. I observed, that a representation from the United States could not be so constituted, as to represent completely the feelings and interests of the people; but that we ought to come as near this object as possible. The gentlemen say, that the exactly proper number of representatives is so indeterminate and vague, that it is impossible for them to ascertain it with any precision. But surely, they are able to see the distinction between twenty and thirty. I acknowledged that a complete representation would make the legislature too numerous; and therefore, it is our duty to limit the powers, and form checks on the government, in proportion to the smallness of the number.

The honorable gentleman next animadverts on my apprehensions of corruption, and instances the present Congress, to prove an absurdity in my argument. But is this fair reasoning? There are many material checks to the operations of that body, which the future Congress will not have. In the first place, they are chosen annually:—What more powerful check! They are subject to recall: Nine states must agree to any important resolution, which will not be carried into execution, till it meets the approbation of the people in the state legislatures. Admitting what he says, that they have pledged their faith to support the acts of Congress; yet, if these be contrary to the essential interests of the people, they ought not to be acceded to; for they are not bound to obey any law, which tends to destroy them.

It appears to me, that had economy been a motive for making the representation small, it might have operated more properly in leaving out some of the offices which this constitution requires. I am sensible that a great many of the common people, who do not reflect, imagine that a numerous representation involves a great expence:—But they are not aware of the real security it gives to an economical management in all the departments of government.

The gentleman further declared, that as far his acquaintance extended, the people thought sixty-five a number fully large enough for our State Assembly; and hence inferred, that sixty-five is to two hundred and forty thousand, as sixty five is to three millions.—This is curious reasoning.

I feel that I have troubled the committee too long. I should not indeed have risen again upon this subject, had not my ideas been grossly misrepresented.

[*On 24 June George Livingston moved "That no person shall be eligible as a senator for more than six years in any term of twelve years, and that it shall be in the power of the legislatures of the several states to recall their senators, or either of them, and to elect others in their stead, to serve for the remainder of the time for which such senator or senators, so recalled, were appointed."*]

25 JUNE 1788

Mr. *Smith* . . . argued as follows. The amendment embraces two objects: First, that the senators shall be eligible for only six years in any term of twelve years: Second, that they shall be subject to the recall of the legislatures of their several states. It is proper that we take up these points separately. I concur with the honorable gentleman, that there is a necessity for giving this branch a greater stability than the house of representatives. I think his reasons are conclusive on this point. But, sir, it does not follow from this position that the senators ought to hold their places during life. Declaring them ineligible during a certain term after six years, is far from rendering them less stable than is necessary. We think the amendment will place the senate in a proper medium between a fluctuating and a perpetual body. As the clause now stands, there is no doubt that the senators will hold their office perpetually; and in this situation, they must of necessity lose their dependence and attachment to the people. It is certainly inconsistent with the established principles of republicanism, that the senate should be a fixed and unchangeable body of men. There should be then some constitutional provision against this evil. A rotation I consider as the best possible mode of affecting a remedy. The amendment will not only have a tendency to defeat any plots, which may be formed against the liberty and authority of the state governments, but will be the best means to extinguish the factions which often prevail, and which are sometimes so fatal in legislative bodies. This appears to me an important consideration. We have generally found, that perpetual bodies have either combined in some scheme of usurpation, or have been torn and distracted with cabals.—Both have been the source of misfortunes to the state. Most people acquainted with history will acknowledge these facts. Our Congress would have been a fine field for party spirit to act in.—That body would undoubtedly have suffered all the evils of faction, had it not been secured by the rotation established by the articles of the confederation. I think a rotation in the government is a very important and truly republican institution. All good republicans, I presume to say, will treat it with respect.

It is a circumstance strongly in favor of rotation, that it will have a tendency to diffuse a more general spirit of emulation, and to bring forward into office the genius and abilities of the continent.—The ambition of gaining the qualifications necessary to govern, will be in some proportion to the chance of success. If the office is to be perpetually confined to a few, other men of equal talents and virtue, but not possessed of so extensive an influence, may be discouraged from aspiring to it. The more perfectly we are versed in the political science, the more firmly will the happy principles of republicanism be supported. The true policy of constitutions will be to increase the information of the country, and disseminate the knowledge of government as universally as possible. If this be done, we shall have, in any dangerous emergency, a numerous body of enlightened citizens, ready for the call of their country. As the constitution now is, you only give an opportunity to two men to be acquainted with the public affairs. It is a maxim with me, that every man employed in a high office by the people, should from time to time return to them, that he may be in a situation to satisfy them with respect to his conduct and the measures of administration. If I recollect right, it was observed by an honorable member from New York, that this amendment would be an infringement of the natural rights of the people. I humbly conceive, if the gentleman reflects maturely on the nature of his argument, he will acknowledge its weakness. What is government itself, but a restraint upon the natural rights of the people? What constitution was ever devised, that did not operate as a restraint on their original liberties? What is the whole system of qualifications, which take place in all free governments, but a restraint? Why is a certain age made necessary? Why a certain term of citizenship? This constitution itself, sir, has restraints innumerable.—The amendment, it is true, may exclude two of the best men; but it can rarely happen, that the state will sustain any material loss by this. I hope and believe that we shall always have more than two men, who are capable of discharging the duty of a senator. But if it should so happen that the state possessed only two capable men, it will be necessary that they should return home, from time to time, to inspect and regulate our domestic affairs. I do not conceive the state can suffer any inconvenience. The argument indeed might have some weight were the representation very large: But as the power is to be exercised upon only two men, the apprehensions of the gentlemen are entirely without foundation.

With respect to the second part of the amendment, I would observe that as the senators are the representatives of the state legislatures, it is reasonable and proper that they should be under their control. When a state sends an agent commissioned to transact any business, or perform any service, it certainly ought to have a power to recall him. These are plain principles, and so far as they apply to the case under examination, they ought to be adopted by us. Form this government as you please, you must at all events lodge in it very important powers: These powers must be in the hands of a few men, so situated as to produce a small degree of responsibility. These circumstances ought to put us upon our guard; and the inconvenience of this necessary delegation of power should be corrected, by providing some suitable checks.

Against this part of the amendment a great deal of argument has been used, and with considerable plausibility. It is said if the amendment takes place, the senators will hold their office only during the pleasure of the state legislatures, and consequently will not possess the necessary firmness and stability. I conceive, sir, there is a fallacy in this argument, founded upon the suspicion that the legislature of a state will possess the qualities of a mob, and be incapable of any regular conduct. I know that the impulses of the multitude are inconsistent with systematic government. The people are frequently incompetent to deliberate discussion, and subject to errors and imprudencies. Is this the complexion of the state legislatures? I presume it is not. I presume that they are never actuated by blind impulses—that they rarely do things hastily and without consideration. The state legislatures were select bodies of men, chosen for their superior wisdom, and so organized as to be capable of calm and regular conduct. My apprehension is, that the power of recall would not be exercised as often as it ought. It is highly improbable that a man, in whom the state has confided, and who has an established influence, will be recalled, unless his conduct has been notoriously wicked.—The arguments of the gentleman therefore, do not apply in this case. It is further observed, that it would be improper to give the legislatures this power, because the local interests and prejudices of the states ought not to be admitted into the general government; and that if the senator is rendered too independent of his constituents, he will sacrifice the interests of the Union to the policy of his state. Sir, the senate has been generally held up by all parties as a safe guard to the rights of the several states. In this view, the closest connection between them has been considered as necessary. But now it seems we speak a different language.—We now look upon the least attachment to their state as dangerous.—We are now for separating them, and rendering them entirely independent, that we may root out the last vestige of state sovereignty.

An honorable gentleman from New York observed yesterday, that the states would always maintain their importance and authority, on account of their superior influence over the people. To prove this influence, he mentioned the aggregate number of the state representatives throughout the continent. But I ask him, how long the people will retain their confidence for two thousand representatives, who shall meet once in a year to make laws for regulating the heighth of your fences and the repairing of your roads? Will they not by and by be saying—Here, we are paying a great number of men for doing nothing: We had better give up all the civil business of our state with its powers to congress, who are sitting all the year round: We had better get rid of the useless burden. That matters will come to this at last, I have no more doubt than I have of my existence. The state governments, without object or authority, will soon dwindle into insignificance, and be despised by the people themselves. I am, sir, at a loss to know how the state legislatures will spend their time. Will they make laws to regulate agriculture? I imagine this will be best regulated by the sagacity and industry of those who practise it. Another reason offered by the gentleman is, that the states will have a greater number of officers than the general government. I doubt this. Let us make a comparison. In the first place, the federal government must have a complete set of judicial officers of different ranks throughout the continent: Then, a numerous train of executive officers, in all the branches of the revenue, both internal and external, and all the civil and military departments. Add to this, their salaries will probably be larger and better secured than those of any state officers. If these numerous offices are not at once established, they are in the power of congress, and will all in time be created. Very few offices will be objects of ambition in the states. They will have no establishments at all to correspond with some of those I have mentioned.—In other branches, they will have the same as congress. But I ask, what will be their comparative influence and importance? I will leave it, sir, to any man of candour, to determine whether there will not probably be more lucrative and honorable places in the gift of congress than in the disposal of the states all together. But the whole reasoning of the gentlemen rests upon the principle that the states will be able to check the general government, by exciting the people to opposition: It only goes to prove, that the state officers will have such an influence over the people, as to impel them to hostility and rebellion. This kind of check, I contend, would be a pernicious one; and certainly ought to be prevented. Checks in government ought to act silently, and without public commotion. I think that the harmony of the two powers should by all means be maintained: If it be not, the operation of government will be baneful—one or the other of the parties must finally be destroyed in the conflict. The constitutional line between the authority of each should be so obvious, as to leave no room for jealous apprehensions or violent contests.

It is further said, that the operation of local interests should be counteracted; for which purpose, the senate should be rendered permanent. I conceive that the true interest of every state is the interest of the whole; and that if we should have a well regulated government, this idea will prevail. We shall indeed have few local interests to pursue, under the new constitution; because it limits the claims of the states by so close a line, that on their part there can be little dispute, and little worth disputing about. But, sir, I conceive that partial interests will grow continually weaker, because there are not those fundamental differences between the real interests of the several states, which will long prevent their coming together and becoming uniform.

Another argument advanced by the gentlemen is, that our amendment would be the means of producing factions among the electors: That aspiring men would misrepresent the conduct of a faithful senator; and by intrigue, procure a recall, upon false grounds, in order to make room for themselves. But, sir, men who are ambitious for places will rarely be disposed to render those places unstable. A truly ambitious man will never do this, unless he is mad. It is not to be supposed that a state will recall a man once in twenty years, to make way for another. Dangers of this kind are very remote: I think they ought not to be brought seriously into view.

More than one of the gentlemen have ridiculed my apprehensions of corruption. How, say they, are the people to be corrupted? By their own money? Sir, in many countries, the people pay money to corrupt themselves: why should it not happen in this? Certainly, the congress will be as liable to corruption as other bodies of men. Have they not the same frailties, and the same temptations? With respect to the corruption arising from the disposal of offices, the gentlemen have treated the argument as insignificant. But let any one make a calculation, and see whether there will not be good offices enough, to dispose of to every man who goes there, who will then freely resign his seat; for, can any one suppose, that a member of congress would not go out and relinquish his four dollars a day, for two or three thousand pounds a year? It is here objected that no man can hold an office created during the time he is in congress—but it will be easy for a man of influence, who has in his eye a favorite office previously created and already filled, to say to his friend, who holds it—Here—I will procure you another place of more emolument, provided you will relinquish yours in favor of me. The constitution appears to be a restraint, when in fact it is none at all. I presume, sir, there is not a government in the world in which there is greater scope for influence and corruption in the disposal of offices. Sir, I will not declaim, and say all men are dishonest; but I think that, in forming a constitution, if we presume this, we shall be on the safest side. The extreme is certainly less dangerous than the other. It is wise to multiply checks to a greater degree than the present state of things requires. It is said that corruption has never taken place under the old government—I believe, gentlemen hazard this assertion without proofs. That it has taken place in some degree is very probable. Many millions of money have been put into the hands of government, which have never yet been accounted for: The accounts are not yet settled, and Heaven only knows when they will be.

I have frequently observed a restraint upon the state governments, which congress never can be under, construct that body as you please. It is a truth, capable of demonstration, that the nearer the representative is to his constituent, the more attached and dependent he will be.—In the states, the elections are frequent, and the representatives numerous: They transact business in the midst of their constituents, and every man may be called upon to account for his conduct. In this state the council of appointment are elected for one year.—The proposed constitution establishes a council of appointment who will be perpetual.—Is there any comparison between the two governments in point of security? It is said that the governor of this state is limited in his powers—indeed his authority is small and insignificant, compared to that of the senate of the United States.

27 JUNE 1788

[*After some comments about taxation, Smith returned to the idea of representation.*]

Another idea is in my mind, which I think conclusive against a simple government for the United States. It is not possible to collect a set of representatives, who are acquainted with all parts of the continent. Can you find men in Georgia who are acquainted with the situation of New Hampshire? who know what taxes will best suit the inhabitants; and how much they are able to bear? Can the best men make laws for a people of whom they are entirely ignorant? Sir, we have no reason to hold our state governments in contempt, or to suppose them incapable of acting wisely. I believe they have operated more beneficially than most people expected, who considered that those governments were erected in a time of war and confusion, when they were very liable to errors in their structure. It will be a matter of astonishment to all unprejudiced men hereafter, who shall reflect upon our situation, to observe to what a great degree good government has prevailed. It is true some bad laws have been passed in most of the states; but they arose more from the difficulty of the times, than from any want of honesty or wisdom. Perhaps there never was a government, which in the course of ten years did not do something to be repented of. As for Rhode Island, I do not mean to justify her—she deserves to be condemned.—If there were in the world but one example of political depravity, it would be hers: And no nation ever merited or suffered a more genuine infamy, than a wicked administration has attached to her character. Massachusetts also has been guilty of errors: and has lately been distracted by an internal convulsion. Great Britain, notwithstanding her boasted constitution, has been a perpetual scene of revolutions and civil war.—Her parliaments have been abolished; her kings have been banished and murdered. I assert that the majority of the governments in the union have operated better than any body had reason to expect: and that nothing but experience and habit is wanting, to give the state laws all the stability and wisdom necessary to make them respectable. If these things be true, I think we ought not to exchange our condition, with a hazard of losing our state constitutions. We all agree that a general government is necessary: But it ought not to go so far, as to destroy the authority of the members. We shall be unwise, to make a new experiment in so important a matter, without some known and sure grounds to go upon. The state constitutions should be the guardians of our domestic rights and interests; and should be both the support and the check of the federal government. . . .

Sir, has any country which has suffered distresses like ours, exhibited within a few years, more striking marks of improvement and prosperity? How its population has grown; how its agriculture, commerce and manufactures have been extended and improved! How many forests have been cut down; how many wastes have been cleared and cultivated; how many additions have been made to the extent and beauty of our towns and cities! I think our advancement has been rapid. In a few years, it is to be hoped, that we shall be relieved from our embarrassments; and unless new calamities come upon us, shall be flourishing and happy. . . .

Appendix I

The Articles of Confederation*
1777 (1781)

Articles of Confederation and perpetual Union between the states of New Hampshire, Massachusetts-Bay, Rhode Island and Providence Plantations, Connecticut, New York, New Jersey, Pennsylvania, Delaware, Maryland, Virginia, North Carolina, South Carolina, and Georgia.

I. The stile of this Confederacy shall be "The United States of America."

II. Each state retains its sovereignty, freedom, and independence, and every power, jurisdiction, and right, which is not by this Confederation expressly delegated to the United States, in Congress assembled.

III. The said states hereby severally enter into a firm league of friendship with each other, for their common defence, the security of their liberties, and their mutual and general welfare, binding themselves to assist each other, against all force offered to, or attacks made upon them, or any of them, on account of religion, sovereignty, trade, or any other pretence whatever.

IV. The better to secure and perpetuate mutual friendship and intercourse among the people of the different states in this union, the free inhabitants of each of these states, paupers, vagabonds, and fugitives from justice excepted, shall be entitled to

---

*The Articles of Confederation were drafted by a committee of Congress appointed 11 June 1776, and agreed to by Congress 15 November 1777. They did not go into force until ratified by the last of the thirteen states, Maryland, on 1 March 1781.

all privileges and immunities of free citizens in the several states; and the people of each state shall have free ingress and regress to and from any other state, and shall enjoy therein all the privileges of trade and commerce, subject to the same duties, impositions and restrictions as the inhabitants thereof respectively, provided that such restriction shall not extend so far as to prevent the removal of property imported into any state, to any other state, of which the owner is an inhabitant; provided also that no imposition, duties or restriction shall be laid by any state, on the property of the United States, or either of them.

If any person guilty of, or charged with treason, felony, or other high misdemeanor in any state, shall flee from justice, and be found in any of the United States, he shall, upon demand of the Governor or executive power of the state from which he fled, be delivered up and removed to the state having jurisdiction of his offence.

Full faith and credit shall be given in each of these states to the records, acts and judicial proceedings of the courts and magistrates of every other state.

V. For the most convenient management of the general interests of the United States, delegates shall be annually appointed in such manner as the legislature of each state shall direct, to meet in Congress on the first Monday in November, in every year, with a power reserved to each state to recall its delegates, or any of them, at any time within the year, and to send others in their stead for the remainder of the year.

No state shall be represented in Congress by less than two, nor by more than seven members; and no person shall be capable of being a delegate for more than three years in any term of six years; nor shall any person, being a delegate, be capable of holding any office under the United States, for which he, or another for his benefit receives any salary, fees or emolument of any kind.

Each state shall maintain its own delegates in a meeting of the states, and while they act as members of the committee of the states.

In determining questions in the United States in Congress assembled, each state shall have one vote.

Freedom of speech and debate in Congress shall not be impeached or questioned in any court or place out of Congress, and the members of Congress shall be protected in their persons from arrests and imprisonments, during the time of their going to and from, and attendance on Congress, except for treason, felony, or breach of the peace.

VI. No state, without the consent of the United States in Congress assembled, shall send any embassy to, or receive any embassy from, or enter into any conference, agreement, alliance or treaty with any king, prince or state; nor shall any person holding any office of profit or trust under the United States, or any of them, accept of any present, emolument, office or title of any kind whatever from any king, prince or foreign state; nor shall the United States in Congress assembled, or any of them, grant any title of nobility.

No two or more states shall enter into any treaty, confederation or alliance whatever between them, without the consent of the United States in Congress assembled, specifying accurately the purposes for which the same is to be entered into, and how long it shall continue.

No state shall lay any imposts or duties, which may interfere with any stipulations in treaties, entered into by the United States in Congress assembled, with any king, prince or state, in pursuance of any treaties already proposed by Congress, to the courts of France and Spain.

No vessels of war shall be kept up in time of peace by any state, except such number only, as shall be deemed necessary by the United States in Congress assembled, for the defence of such state, or its trade; nor shall any body of forces be kept up by any state in time of peace, except such number only, as in the judgment of the United States in Congress assembled, shall be deemed requisite to garrison the forts necessary for the defence of such state; but every state shall always keep up a well regulated and disciplined militia, sufficiently armed and accoutred, and shall provide and constantly have ready for use, in public stores, a due number of field pieces and tents, and a proper quantity of arms, ammunition, and camp equipage.

No state shall engage in any war without the consent of the

United States in Congress assembled, unless such state be actually invaded by enemies, or shall have received certain advice of a resolution being formed by some nation of Indians to invade such state, and the danger is so imminent as not to admit of a delay till the United States in Congress assembled can be consulted: nor shall any state grant commissions to any ships or vessels of war, nor letters of marque or reprisal, except it be after a declaration of war by the United States in Congress assembled, and then only against the kingdom or state and the subjects thereof, against which war has been so declared, and under such regulations as shall be established by the United States in Congress assembled, unless such state be infested by pirates, in which case vessels of war may be fitted out for that occasion, and kept so long as the danger shall continue, or until the United States in Congress assembled, shall determine otherwise.

VII. When land forces are raised by any state for the common defence, all officers of or under the rank of colonel, shall be appointed by the legislature of each state respectively, by whom such forces shall be raised, or in such manner as such state shall direct, and all vacancies shall be filled up by the state which first made the appointment.

VIII. All charges of war, and all other expenses that shall be incurred for the common defence or general welfare, and allowed by the United States in Congress assembled, shall be defrayed out of a common treasury, which shall be supplied by the several states in proportion to the value of all land within each state, granted to or surveyed for any person, as such land and the buildings and improvements thereon shall be estimated according to such mode as the United States in Congress assembled, shall from time to time direct and appoint.

The taxes for paying that proportion shall be laid and levied by the authority and direction of the legislatures of the several states within the time agreed upon by the United States in Congress assembled.

IX. The United States in Congress assembled, shall have the sole and exclusive right and power of determining on peace and war, except in the cases mentioned in the sixth article—of sending and receiving ambassadors—entering into treaties and alliances, provided that no treaty of commerce shall be made whereby the legislative power of the respective states shall be restrained from imposing such imposts and duties on foreigners, as their own people are subjected to, or from prohibiting the exportation or importation of any species of goods or commodities whatsoever—of establishing rules for deciding in all cases, what captures on land or water shall be legal, and in what manner prizes taken by land or naval forces in the service of the United States shall be divided or appropriated—of granting letters of marque and reprisal in times of peace—appointing courts for the trial of piracies and felonies committed on the high seas and establishing courts for receiving and determining finally appeals in all cases of captures, provided that no member of Congress shall be appointed a judge of any of the said courts.

The United States in Congress assembled shall also be the last resort on appeal in all disputes and differences now subsisting or that hereafter may arise between two or more states concerning boundary, jurisdiction or any other causes whatever; which authority shall always be exercised in the manner following. Whenever the legislative or executive authority or lawful agent of any state in controversy with another shall present a petition to Congress stating the matter in question and praying for a hearing, notice thereof shall be given by order of Congress to the legislative or executive authority of the other state in controversy, and a day assigned for the appearance of the parties by their lawful agents, who shall then be directed to appoint by joint consent, commissioners or judges to constitute a court for hearing and determining the matter in question: but if they cannot agree, Congress shall name three persons out of each of the United States, and from the list of such persons each party shall alternately strike out one, the petitioners beginning, until the number shall be reduced to thirteen; and from that number not less than seven, nor more than nine names as Congress shall direct, shall in the presence of Congress be drawn out by lot, and the persons whose names shall be so drawn or any five of them, shall be commissioners or judges, to hear and finally determine the controversy, so always as a major part of the judges who shall hear the cause shall agree in the determination: and if either party shall neglect to attend at the day appointed, without showing reasons, which Congress shall judge sufficient, or being present shall refuse to strike, the Congress shall proceed to nominate three persons out of each state, and the secretary of Congress shall strike in behalf of such party absent or refusing; and the judgement and sentence of the court to be appointed, in the manner before prescribed, shall be final and conclusive; and if any of the parties shall refuse to submit to the authority of such court, or to appear or defend their claim or cause, the court shall nevertheless proceed to pronounce sentence, or judgment, which shall in like manner be final and decisive, the judgment or sentence and other proceedings being in either case transmitted to Congress, and lodged among the acts of Congress for the security of the parties concerned: provided that every commissioner, before he sits in judgment, shall take an oath to be administered by one of the judges of the supreme or superior court of the state, where the cause shall be tried, "well and truly to hear and determine the matter in question, according to the best of his judgment, without favour, affection or hope of reward": provided also, that no state shall be deprived of territory for the benefit of the United States.

All controversies concerning the private right of soil claimed under different grants of two or more states, whose jurisdictions as they may respect such lands, and the states which passed such grants are adjusted, the said grants or either of them being at the same time claimed to have originated antecedent to such settlement of jurisdiction, shall on the petition of either party to the Congress of the United States, be finally determined as near as may be in the same manner as is before prescribed for deciding disputes respecting territorial jurisdiction between different states.

The United States in Congress assembled shall also have the sole and exclusive right and power of regulating the alloy and value of coin struck by their own authority, or by that of the respective states—fixing the standard of weights and measures throughout the United States—regulating the trade and managing all affairs with the Indians, not members of any of the states, provided that the legislative right of any state within its own limits be not infringed or violated—establishing or regulating post-offices from one state to another, throughout all the United States, and exacting such postage on the papers passing through the same as may be requisite to defray the expenses of the said office—appointing all officers of the land forces, in the service of the United States, excepting regimental officers—appointing all the officers of the naval forces, and commissioning all officers whatever in the service of the United States—making rules for the government and regulation of the said land and naval forces, and directing their operations.

The United States in Congress assembled shall have authority to appoint a committee, to sit in the recess of Congress, to be denominated "A Committee of the States," and to consist of one delegate from each state; and to appoint such other committees and civil officers as may be necessary for managing the general affairs of the United States under their direction—to appoint one of their number to preside, provided that no person be allowed to serve in the office of president more than one year in any term of three years; to ascertain the necessary sums of money to be raised for the service of the United States, and to appropriate and apply the same for defraying the public expenses—to borrow money, or emit bills on the credit of the United States, transmitting every half-year to the respective states an account of the sums of money so borrowed or emitted—to build and equip a navy—to agree upon the number of land forces, and to make requisitions from each state for its quota, in proportion to the number of white inhabitants in such state; which requisition shall be binding, and thereupon the legislature of each state shall appoint the regimental officers, raise the men and cloath, arm and equip them in a solid-like manner, at the expence of the United States; and the officers and men so cloathed, armed, and equipped shall march to the place appointed, and within the time agreed on by the United States in Congress assembled. But if the United States in Congress assembled shall, on consideration of circumstances judge proper that any state should not raise men, or should raise a smaller number than its quota, and that any other state should raise a greater number of men than the quota thereof, such extra number shall be raised, officered, cloathed, armed, and equipped in the same manner as the quota of such state, unless the legislature of such state shall judge that such extra number cannot be safely spared out of the same, in which case they shall raise, officer, cloath, arm, and equip as many of such extra number as they judge can be safely spared. And the officers and men so cloathed, armed, and equipped, shall march to the place appointed, and within the time agreed on by the United States in Congress assembled.

The United States in Congress assembled shall never engage in a war, nor grant letters of marque and reprisal in time of peace, nor enter into any treaties or alliances, nor coin money, nor regulate the value thereof, nor ascertain the sums and expenses necessary for the defence and welfare of the United States, or any of them, nor emit bills, nor borrow money on the credit of the United States, nor appropriate money, nor agree upon the number of vessels of war, to be built or purchased, or the number of land or sea forces to be raised, nor appoint a commander in chief of the army or navy, unless nine states assent to the same: nor shall a question on any other point, except for adjourning from day to day be determined, unless by the votes of a majority of the United States in Congress assembled.

The Congress of the United States shall have power to adjourn to any time within the year, and to any place within the United States, so that no period of adjournment be for a longer duration than the space of six months, and shall publish the journal of their proceedings monthly, except such parts thereof relating to treaties, alliances or military operations, as in their judgment require secrecy; and the yeas and nays of the delegates of each state on any question shall be entered on the journal, when it is desired by any delegate; and the delegates of a state, or any of them, at his or their request shall be furnished with a transcript of the said journal, except such parts as are above excepted, to lay before the legislatures of the several states.

X. The Committee of the States, or any nine of them, shall be authorized to execute, in the recess of Congress, such of the powers of Congress as the United States in Congress assembled, by the consent of nine states, shall from time to time think expedient to vest them with; provided that no power be delegated to the said Committee, for the exercise of which, by the Articles of Confederation, the voice of nine states in the Congress of the United States assembled is requisite.

XI. Canada acceding to this confederation, and joining in the measures of the United States, shall be admitted into, and entitled to all the advantages of this union; but no other colony shall be admitted into the same, unless such admission be agreed to by nine states.

XII. All bills of credit emitted, monies borrowed, and debts contracted by, or under the authority of Congress, before the assembling of the United States, in pursuance of the present confederation, shall be deemed and considered as a charge against the United States, for payment and satisfaction whereof the said United States, and the public faith are hereby solemnly pledged.

XIII. Every state shall abide by the determinations of the United States in Congress assembled, on all questions which by this confederation are submitted to them. And the Articles of this Confederation shall be inviolably observed by every state, and the union shall be perpetual; nor shall any alteration at any time hereafter be made in any of them; unless such alteration be agreed to in a Congress of the United States, and be afterwards confirmed by the legislatures of every state.

And Whereas it hath pleased the Great Governor of the World to incline the hearts of the legislatures we respectively represent in Congress, to approve of, and to authorize us to ratify the said articles of confederation and perpetual union. Know Ye that we the undersigned delegates, by virtue of the power and authority to us given for that purpose, do by these presents, in the name and in behalf of our respective constituents, fully and entirely ratify and confirm each and every of the said articles of confederation and perpetual union, and all and singular the matters and things therein contained: And we do further solemnly plight and engage the faith of our respective constituents, that they shall abide by the determinations of the United States in Congress assembled, on all questions, which by the said confederation are submitted to them. And that the articles thereof shall be inviolably observed by the states we respectively represent, and that the union shall be perpetual.

Appendix II

The Constitution of the United States of America

We the people of the United States, in order to form a more perfect union, establish justice, insure domestic tranquility, provide for the common defense, promote the general welfare, and secure the blessings of liberty to ourselves and our posterity, do ordain and establish this Constitution for the United States of America.

ARTICLE I.

SECTION 1. All legislative powers herein granted shall be vested in a Congress of the United States, which shall consist of a Senate and House of Representatives.

SECTION 2. The House of Representatives shall be composed of members chosen every second year by the people of the several states, and the electors in each state shall have the qualifications requisite for electors of the most numerous branch of the state legislature.

No person shall be a representative who shall not have attained to the age of 25 years, and been seven years a citizen of the United States, and who shall not, when elected, be an inhabitant of that state in which he shall be chosen.

Representatives and direct taxes shall be apportioned among the several states which may be included within this union, according to their respective numbers, which shall be determined by adding to the whole number of free persons, including those bound to service for a term of years, and excluding Indians not taxed, three-fifths of all other persons. The actual enumeration shall be made within three years after the first meeting of the Congress of the United States, and within every subsequent term of ten years, in such manner as they shall by law direct. The number of representatives shall not exceed one for every 30,000, but each state shall have at least one representative; and until such enumeration shall be made, the state of New Hampshire shall be entitled to choose three, Massachusetts eight, Rhode Island and Providence Plantations one, Connecticut five, New York six, New Jersey four, Pennsylvania eight, Delaware one, Maryland six, Virginia ten, North Carolina five, South Carolina five, and Georgia three.

When vacancies happen in the representation from any state, the executive authority thereof shall issue writs of election to fill such vacancies.

The House of Representatives shall choose their speaker and other officers; and shall have the sole power of impeachment.

SECTION 3. The Senate of the United States shall be composed of two senators from each state, chosen by the legislature thereof, for six years; and each senator shall have one vote.

Immediately after they shall be assembled in consequence of the first election, they shall be divided as equally as may be into three classes. The seats of the senators of the first class shall be vacated at the expiration of the second year, of the second class at the expiration of the fourth year, and of the third class at the expiration of the sixth year, so that one-third may be chosen every second year; and if vacancies happen by resignation, or otherwise, during the recess of the legislature of any state, the executive thereof may make temporary appointments until the next meeting of the legislature, which shall then fill such vacancies.

No person shall be a senator who shall not have attained to the age of 30 years, and been nine years a citizen of the United

States, and who shall not, when elected, be an inhabitant of that state for which he shall be chosen.

The vice president of the United States shall be president of the Senate, but shall have no vote, unless they be equally divided.

The Senate shall choose their other officers, and also a president pro tempore, in the absence of the vice president, or when he shall exercise the office of president of the United States.

The Senate shall have the sole power to try all impeachments. When sitting for that purpose, they shall be on oath or affirmation. When the president of the United States is tried, the chief justice shall preside: And no person shall be convicted without the concurrence of two-thirds of the members present.

Judgment in cases of impeachment shall not extend further than to removal from office, and disqualification to hold and enjoy any office of honour, trust or profit under the United States; but the party convicted shall nevertheless be liable and subject to indictment, trial, judgment and punishment, according to law.

SECTION 4. The times, places and manner of holding elections, for senators and representatives, shall be prescribed in each state by the legislature thereof; but Congress may at any time by law make or alter such regulations, except as to the places of choosing senators.

The Congress shall assemble at least once in every year, and such meeting shall be on the first Monday in December, unless they shall by law appoint a different day.

SECTION 5. Each house shall be the judge of the elections, returns and qualifications of its own members, and a majority of each shall constitute a quorum to do business; but a smaller number may adjourn from day to day, and may be authorized to compel the attendance of absent members, in such manner, and under such penalties as each house may provide.

Each house may determine the rules of its proceedings, punish its members for disorderly behaviour, and, with the concurrence of two-thirds, expel a member.

Each house shall keep a journal of its proceedings, and from time to time publish the same, excepting such parts as may in their judgment require secrecy; and the yeas and nays of the members of either house on any question shall, at the desire of one-fifth of those present, be entered on the journal.

Neither house, during the session of Congress, shall, without the consent of the other, adjourn for more than three days, nor to any other place than that in which the two houses shall be sitting.

SECTION 6. The senators and representatives shall receive a compensation for their services, to be ascertained by law, and paid out of the treasury of the United States. They shall in all cases, except treason, felony and breach of the peace, be privileged from arrest during their attendance at the session of their respective houses, and in going to and returning from the same; and for any speech or debate in either house, they shall not be questioned in any other place.

No senator or representative shall, during the time for which he was elected, be appointed to any civil office under the authority of the United States, which shall have been created, or the emoluments whereof shall have been increased during such time; and no person holding any office under the United States, shall be a member of either house during his continuance in office.

SECTION 7. All bills for raising revenue shall originate in the House of Representatives; but the Senate may propose or concur with amendments as on other bills.

Every bill which shall have passed the House of Representatives and the Senate, shall, before it becomes a law, be presented to the president of the United States; if he approve, he shall sign it, but if not, he shall return it, with his objections, to that house in which it shall have originated, who shall enter the objections at large on their journal, and proceed to reconsider it. If after such reconsideration, two-thirds of that house shall agree to pass the bill, it shall be sent together with the objections, to the other house, by which it shall likewise be reconsidered, and if approved by two-thirds of that house, it shall become a law. But in all cases the votes of both houses shall be determined by yeas and nays, and the names of the persons voting for and against the bill shall be entered on the journal of each house respectively. If any bill shall not be returned by the president within ten days (Sundays excepted) after it shall have been presented to him, the same shall be a law, in like manner as if he had signed it, unless the Congress by their adjournment prevent its return, in which case it shall not be a law.

Every order, resolution, or vote to which the concurrence of the Senate and House of Representatives may be necessary (except on a question of adjournment) shall be presented to the president of the United States; and before the same shall take effect, shall be approved by him, or, being disapproved by him, shall be re-passed by two-thirds of the Senate and House of Representatives, according to the rules and limitations prescribed in the case of a bill.

SECTION 8. The Congress shall have the power to lay and collect taxes, duties, imposts and excises, to pay the debts and provide for the common defence and general welfare of the United States; but all duties, imposts and excises shall be uniform throughout the United States:

To borrow money on the credit of the United States:

To regulate commerce with foreign nations, and among the several states, and with the Indian tribes:

To establish an uniform rule of naturalization, and uniform laws on the subject of bankruptcies throughout the United States:

To coin money, regulate the value thereof, and of foreign coin, and fix the standard of weights and measures:

To provide for the punishment of counterfeiting the securities and current coin of the United States:

To establish post-offices and post-roads:

To promote the progress of science and useful arts, by securing for limited times to authors and inventors the exclusive rights to their respective writings and discoveries:

To constitute tribunals inferior to the supreme court:

To define and punish piracies and felonies committed on the high seas, and offences against the law of nations:

To declare war, grant letters of marque and reprisal, and make rules concerning captures on land and water:

To raise and support armies, but no appropriation of money to that use shall be for a longer term than two years:

To provide and maintain a navy:

To make rules for the government and regulation of the land and naval forces:

To provide for calling forth the militia to execute the laws of the union, suppress insurrections and repel invasions:

To provide for organizing, arming and disciplining the militia, and for governing such part of them as may be employed in the service of the United States, reserving to the states respectively, the appointment of the officers, and the authority of training the militia according to the discipline prescribed by Congress:

To exercise exclusive legislation in all cases whatsoever, over such district (not exceeding ten miles square) as may, by cession of particular states, and the acceptance of Congress, become the seat of the government of the United States, and to exercise like authority over all places purchased by the consent of the legislature of the state in which the same shall be, for the erection of forts, magazines, arsenals, dock-yards, and other needful buildings:

And,

To make all laws which shall be necessary and proper for carrying into execution the foregoing powers, and all other powers vested by this constitution in the government of the United States, or in any department or officer thereof.

SECTION 9. The migration or importation of such persons as any of the states now existing shall think proper to admit, shall not be prohibited by the Congress prior to the year 1808, but a tax or duty may be imposed on such importation, not exceeding 10 dollars for each person.

The privilege of the writ of *habeas corpus* shall not be suspended, unless when in cases of rebellion or invasion the public safety may require it.

No bill of attainder or *ex post facto* law shall be passed.

No capitation, or other direct tax shall be laid unless in proportion to the census or enumeration herein before directed to be taken.

No tax or duty shall be laid on articles exported from any state.

No preference shall be given by any regulation of commerce or revenue to the ports of one state over those of another; nor shall vessels bound to, or from, one state, be obliged to enter, clear, or pay duties in another.

No money shall be drawn from the treasury, but in consequence of appropriations made by law; and a regular statement and account of the receipts and expenditures of all public money shall be published from time to time.

No title of nobility shall be granted by the United States: And no person holding any office of profit or trust under them, shall, without the consent of Congress, accept of any present, emolument, office, or title, of any kind whatever, from any king, prince or foreign state.

SECTION 10. No state shall enter into any treaty, alliance, or confederation; grant letters of marque and reprisal; coin money;

emit bills of credit; make any thing but gold and silver coin a tender in payment of debts; pass any bill of attainder, *ex post facto* law, or law impairing the obligation of contracts, or grant any title of nobility.

No state shall, without the consent of Congress, lay any imposts or duties on imports or exports, except what may be absolutely necessary for executing its inspection laws; and the net produce of all duties and imposts, laid by any state on imports or exports, shall be for the use of the treasury of the United States; and all such laws shall be subject to the revision and control of the Congress.

No state shall, without the consent of Congress, lay any duty on tonnage, keep troops, or ships of war in time of peace, enter into any agreement or compact with another state, or with a foreign power, or engage in war, unless actually invaded, or in such imminent danger as will not admit of delay.

ARTICLE II.

SECTION 1. The executive power shall be vested in a president of the United States of America. He shall hold his office during the term of four years, and, together with the vice president, chosen for the same term, be elected as follows:

Each state shall appoint, in such manner as the legislature thereof may direct, a number of electors, equal to the whole number of senators and representatives to which the state may be entitled in the Congress; but no senator or representative, or person holding an office of trust or profit under the United States, shall be appointed an elector.

The electors shall meet in their respective states, and vote by ballot for two persons, of whom one at least shall not be an inhabitant of the same state with themselves. And they shall make a list of all the persons voted for, and of the number of votes for each; which list they shall sign and certify, and transmit sealed to the seat of the government of the United States, directed to the president of the Senate. The president of the

Senate shall, in the presence of the Senate and House of Representatives, open all the certificates and the votes shall then be counted. The person having the greatest number of votes shall be president, if such number be a majority of the whole number of electors appointed; and if there be more than one who have such majority, and have an equal number of votes, then the House of Representatives shall immediately choose by ballot one of them for president; and if no person have a majority, then from the five highest on the list, the said House shall, in like manner, choose the president. But in choosing the president, the votes shall be taken by states, the representation from each state having one vote; a quorum for this purpose shall consist of a member or members from two-thirds of the states, and a majority of all the states shall be necessary to a choice. In every case, after the choice of the president, the person having the greatest number of votes of the electors shall be the vice president. But if there should remain two or more who have equal votes, the Senate shall choose from them by ballot the vice president.

The Congress may determine the time of choosing the electors, and the day on which they shall give their votes; which day shall be the same throughout the United States.

No person except a natural born citizen, or a citizen of the United States, at the time of the adoption of this constitution, shall be eligible to the office of president; neither shall any person be eligible to that office, who shall not have attained to the age of 35 years, and been 14 years a resident within the United States.

In case of the removal of the president from office, or of his death, resignation, or inability to discharge the powers and duties of the said office, the same shall devolve on the vice president, and the Congress may by law provide for the case of removal, death, resignation, or inability, both of the president and vice president, declaring what officer shall then act as president, and such officer shall act accordingly, until the disability be removed, or a president shall be elected.

The president shall, at stated times, receive for his services, a compensation, which shall neither be increased nor diminished during the period for which he shall have been elected, and he shall not receive within that period any other emolument from the United States, or any of them.

Before he enter on the execution of his office, he shall take the following oath or affirmation:

"I do solemnly swear (or affirm) that I will faithfully execute the office of president of the United States, and will to the best of my ability, preserve, protect and defend the constitution of the United States."

SECTION 2. The president shall be commander in chief of the army and navy of the United States, and of the militia of the several states, when called into actual service of the United States; he may require the opinion, in writing, or the principal officer in each of the executive departments, upon any subject relating to the duties of their respective offices, and he shall have power to grant reprieves and pardons for offences against the United States, except in cases of impeachment.

He shall have power, by and with the advice and consent of the Senate, to make treaties, provided two-thirds of the senators present concur; and he shall nominate, and by and with the advice and consent of the Senate, shall appoint ambassadors, other public ministers and consuls, judges of the supreme court, and all other officers of the United States, whose appointments are not herein otherwise provided for, and which shall be established by law. But the Congress may by law vest the appointment of such inferior officers, as they think proper, in the president alone, in the courts of law, or in the heads of departments.

The president shall have power to fill up all vacancies that may happen during the recess of the Senate, by granting commissions, which shall expire at the end of their next session.

SECTION 3. He shall, from time to time, give to the Congress information of the state of the union, and recommend to their consideration, such measures as he shall judge necessary and expedient; he may, on extraordinary occasions, convene both houses, or either of them, and in case of disagreement between them, with respect to the time of adjournment, he may adjourn them to such time as he shall think proper; he shall receive ambassadors and other public ministers; he shall take care that the laws be faithfully executed, and shall commission all the officers of the United States.

SECTION 4. The president, vice president, and all civil officers of the United States shall be removed from office on impeachment for, and conviction of, treason, bribery, or other high crimes and misdemeanors.

ARTICLE III.

SECTION 1. The judicial power of the United States, shall be vested in one supreme court, and in such inferior courts as the Congress may, from time to time, ordain and establish. The judges, both of the supreme and inferior courts, shall hold their offices during good behaviour, and shall, at stated times, receive for their services a compensation, which shall not be diminished during their continuance in office.

SECTION 2. The judicial power shall extend to all cases, in law and equity, arising under this constitution, the laws of the United States, and treaties made, or which shall be made under their authority; to all cases affecting ambassadors, other public ministers and consuls; to all cases of admiralty and maritime jurisdiction; to controversies to which the United States shall be a party: to controversies between two or more states, between a state and citizens of another state, between citizens of different states, between citizens of the same state, claiming lands under grants of different states, and between a state, or citizens thereof, and foreign states, citizens or subjects.

In all cases affecting ambassadors, other public ministers and consuls, and those in which a state shall be party, the supreme court shall have original jurisdiction. In all the other cases beforementioned, the supreme court shall have appellate jurisdiction, both as to law and fact, with such exceptions, and under such regulations as the Congress shall make.

The trial of all crimes, except in cases of impeachment, shall be by jury; and such trial shall be held in the state where the said crimes shall have been committed; but when not committed within any state, the trial shall be at such place or places as the Congress may by law have directed.

SECTION 3. Treason against the United States shall consist only in levying war against them, or in adhering to their enemies, giving them aid and comfort. No person shall be convicted of treason unless on the testimony of two witnesses to the same overt act, or on confession in open court.

The Congress shall have power to declare the punishment of treason, but no attainder of treason shall work corruption of blood, or forfeiture, except during the life of the person attained.

ARTICLE IV

SECTION 1. Full faith and credit shall be given in each state to the public acts, records and judicial proceedings of every other state. And the Congress may by general laws prescribe the manner in which such acts, records, and proceedings shall be proved, and the effect thereof.

SECTION 2. The citizens of each state shall be entitled to all privileges and immunities of citizens in the several states.

A person charged in any state with treason, felony, or other crime, who shall flee from justice, and be found in another state, shall, on demand of the executive authority of the state from which he fled, be delivered up, to be removed to the state having jurisdiction of the crime.

No person held to service or labour in one state, under the laws thereof, escaping into another, shall, in consequence of any law or regulation therein, be discharged from such service or labour, but shall be delivered up on claim of the party to whom such service or labour may be due.

SECTION 3. New states may be admitted by Congress into this union; but no new state shall be formed or erected within the jurisdiction of any other state, nor any state be formed by the junction of two or more states, or parts of states, without the consent of the legislatures of the states concerned, as well as of the Congress.

The Congress shall have power to dispose of and make all needful rules and regulations respecting the territory or other property belonging to the United States; and nothing in this constitution shall be so construed as to prejudice any claims of the United States, or of any particular state.

SECTION 4. The United States shall guarantee to every state in this union, a republican form of government, and shall protect each of them against invasion; and on application of the legislature, or of the executive (when the legislature cannot be convened), against domestic violence.

ARTICLE V.

The Congress, whenever two-thirds of both houses shall deem it necessary, shall propose amendments to this constitution, or on the application of the legislatures of two-thirds of the several states, shall call a convention for proposing amendments, which, in either case, shall be valid to all intents and purposes, as part of this constitution, when ratified by the legislatures of three-fourths of the several states, or by conventions in three-fourths thereof, as the one or the other mode of ratification may be proposed by the Congress: Provided, that no amendment which may be made prior to the year 1808, shall in any manner affect the first and fourth clauses in the ninth section of the first article; and that no state, without its consent, shall be deprived of its equal suffrage in the Senate.

ARTICLE VI.

All debts contracted and engagements entered into, before the adoption of this constitution, shall be as valid against the United States under this constitution, as under the confederation.

This constitution, and the laws of the United States which shall be made in pursuance thereof; and all treaties made, or which shall be made, under the authority of the United States shall be the supreme law of the land; and the judges in every state shall be bound thereby, any thing in the constitution or laws of any state to the contrary notwithstanding.

The senators and representatives before-mentioned, and the members of the several state legislatures, and all executive and judicial officers, both of the United States and of the several states, shall be bound by oath or affirmation, to support this constitution; but no religious test shall ever be required as a qualification to any office or public trust under the United States.

ARTICLE VII.

The ratification of the conventions of nine states, shall be sufficient for the establishment of this constitution between the states so ratifying the same.

Done in convention, by the unanimous consent of the States present, the 17th day of September, in the year of our Lord 1787, and of the independence of the United States of America the 12th. In witness whereof we have hereunto subscribed our names.

[Names omitted]

Articles of Amendment

AMENDMENT 1.

Congress shall make no law respecting an establishment of religion, or prohibiting the free exercise thereof; or abridging the freedom of speech or of the press; or the right of the people peaceably to assemble, and to petition the government for a redress of grievances.

AMENDMENT 2.

A well-regulated militia being necessary to the security of a free state, the right of the people to keep and bear arms shall not be infringed.

AMENDMENT 3.

No soldier shall, in time of peace, be quartered in any house without the consent of the owner, nor in time of war but in a manner to be prescribed by law.

AMENDMENT 4.

The right of the people to be secure in their persons, houses, papers, and effects, against unreasonable searches and seizures, shall not be violated, and no warrants shall issue but upon probable cause, supported by oath or affirmation, and particularly describing the place to be searched, and the persons or things to be seized.

AMENDMENT 5.

No person shall be held to answer for a capital or other infamous crime unless on a presentment or indictment of a grand jury, except in cases arising in the land or naval forces, or in the militia, when in actual service, in time of war or public danger; nor shall any person be subject for the same offence to be twice put in jeopardy of life or limb; nor shall be compelled in any criminal case to be a witness against himself, nor be deprived of life, liberty, or property, without due process of law; nor shall private property be taken for public use without just compensation.

AMENDMENT 6.

In all criminal prosecutions, the accused shall enjoy the right to a speedy and public trial, by an impartial jury of the state and district wherein the crime shall have been committed, which district shall have been previously ascertained by law, and to be informed of the nature and cause of the accusation; to be confronted with the witnesses against him; to have compulsory process for obtaining witnesses in his favor, and to have the assistance of counsel for his defense.

AMENDMENT 7.

In suits at common law, where the value in controversy shall exceed twenty dollars, the right of trial by jury shall be preserved, and no fact tried by a jury shall be otherwise re-examined in any court of the United States than according to the rules of the common law.

AMENDMENT 8.

Excessive bail shall not be required, nor excessive fines imposed, nor cruel and unusual punishments inflicted.

AMENDMENT 9.

The enumeration in the constitution of certain rights shall not be construed to deny or disparage others retained by the people.

AMENDMENT 10.

The powers not delegated to the United States by the constitution, nor prohibited by it to the states, are reserved to the states respectively, or to the people.

AMENDMENT 11 (1798).

The judicial power of the United States shall not be construed to extend to any suit in law or equity, commenced or prosecuted against one of the United States, by citizens of another state, or by citizens or subjects of any foreign state.

AMENDMENT 12 (1804).

The electors shall meet in their respective states, and vote by ballot for President and vice president, one of whom at least shall not be an inhabitant of the same state with themselves; they shall name in their ballots the person voted for as President, and in distinct ballots the person voted for as vice president; and they shall make distinct lists of all persons voted for as President, and of all persons voted for as vice president, and of the number of votes for each, which lists they shall sign and certify, and transmit, sealed, to the seat of the government of the United States directed to the president of the Senate; the president of the Senate shall, in the presence of the Senate and House of Representatives, open all the certificates, and the votes shall then be counted; the person having the greatest number of votes for President shall be the President, if such number be a majority of the whole number of electors appointed; and if no person have such majority, then from the persons having the highest numbers not exceeding three, on the list of those voted for as President, the House of Representatives shall choose immediately, by ballot, the President. But in choosing the President, the votes shall be taken by states, the representation from each state having one vote; a quorum for this purpose shall consist of a member or members from two-thirds of the states, and a majority of all the states shall be necessary to a choice. And if the House of Representatives shall not choose a President, whenever the right of choice shall devolve upon them, before the fourth day of March next following, then the vice president shall act as President, as in the case of the death or other constitutional disability of the President. The person having the greatest number of votes as vice president shall be the vice president, if such number be a majority of the whole number of electors appointed, and if no person have a majority, then from the two highest numbers on the list the Senate shall choose the vice president; a quorum for the purpose shall consist of two-thirds of the whole number of senators, and a majority of the whole number shall be necessary to a choice. But no person constitutionally ineligible to the office of President shall be eligible to that of vice president of the United States.

AMENDMENT 13 (1865).

SECTION 1. Neither slavery nor involuntary servitude, except as a punishment for crime whereof the party shall have been duly convicted, shall exist within the United States, or any place subject to their jurisdiction.

SECTION 2. Congress shall have power to enforce this article by appropriate legislation.

AMENDMENT 14 (1868).

SECTION 1. All persons born or naturalized in the United States, and subject to the jurisdiction thereof, are citizens of the United States and of the state wherein they reside. No state shall make or enforce any law which shall abridge the privileges or immunities of citizens of the United States; nor shall any state deprive any person of life, liberty, or property without due process of law; nor deny to any person within its jurisdiction the equal protection of the law.

SECTION 2. Representatives shall be apportioned among the several States according to their respective numbers, counting the whole number of persons in each state, excluding Indians not taxed. But when the right to vote at any election for the choice of electors for President and vice president of the United States, representatives in Congress, the executive and judicial officers of a State, or the members of the legislature thereof, is denied to any of the male members of such state being of twenty-one years of age, and citizens of the United States, or in any way abridged, except for participation in rebellion or other crime, the basis of representation therein shall be reduced in the proportion which the number of such male citizens shall bear to the whole number of male citizens twenty-one years of age in such state.

SECTION 3. No person shall be a senator or representative in Congress, or elector of President and vice president, or hold any office, civil or military, under the United States, or under any state, who, having previously taken an oath, as a member of Congress, or as an officer of the United States, or as a member of any state legislature, or as an executive or judicial officer of any state, to support the Constitution of the United States, shall have engaged in insurrection or rebellion against the same, or given aid and comfort to the enemies thereof. But Congress may, by a vote of two-thirds of each house, remove such disability.

SECTION 4. The validity of the public debt of the United States, authorized by law, including debts incurred for payment of pensions and bounties for services in suppressing insurrection or rebellion, shall not be questioned. But neither the United States nor any state shall assume or pay any debt or obligation incurred in aid of insurrection or rebellion against the United States, or any claim for the loss or emancipation of any slave; but all such debts, obligations, and claims shall be held illegal and void.

SECTION 5. The Congress shall have power to enforce, by appropriate legislation, the provisions of this article.

AMENDMENT 15 (1870).

SECTION 1. The right of citizens of the United States to vote shall not be denied or abridged by the United States or by any state, on account of race, color, or previous condition of servitude.

SECTION 2. The Congress shall have power to enforce this article by appropriate legislation.

AMENDMENT 16 (1913).

The Congress shall have power to lay and collect taxes on income, from whatever source derived, without apportionment among the several States, and without regard to any census or enumeration.

AMENDMENT 17 (1913).

The Senate of the United States shall be composed of two senators from each state, elected by the people thereof for six years; and each senator shall have one vote. The electors in each state shall have the qualifications requisite for electors of the most numerous branch of the state legislatures.

When vacancies happen in the representation of any state in the Senate, the executive authority of such state shall issue writs of election to fill such vacancies; provided, that the legislature of any state may empower the executive thereof to make temporary appointments until the people fill the vacancies by election as the legislature may direct.

This amendment shall not be so construed as to affect the election or term of any senator chosen before it becomes valid as part of the Constitution.

AMENDMENT 18 (1919).

SECTION 1. After one year from the ratification of this article the manufacture, sale, or transportation of intoxicating liquors within, the importation thereof into, or exportation thereof from the United States and all territory subject to the jurisdiction thereof, for beverage purposes is hereby prohibited.

SECTION 2. The Congress and the several states shall have concurrent power to enforce this article by appropriate legislation.

SECTION 3. This article shall be inoperative unless it shall have been ratified as an amendment to the Constitution by the legislatures of the several states, as provided in the Constitution, within seven years from the date of submission hereof to the states by the Congress.

AMENDMENT 19 (1920).

The right of the citizens of the United States to vote shall not be denied or abridged by the United States or by any state on account of sex.

Congress shall have power to enforce this article by appropriate legislation.

AMENDMENT 20 (1933).

SECTION 1. The terms of the President and vice president shall end at noon on the 20th day of January, and the terms of senators and representatives at noon on the 3rd day of January, of the year in which such terms would have ended if this article had not been ratified; and the terms of their successors shall then begin.

SECTION 2. The Congress shall assemble at least once in every year, and such meeting shall begin at noon on the 3rd day of January, unless they shall by law appoint a different day.

SECTION 3. If, at the time fixed for the beginning of the term of President, the President elect shall have died, the vice president elect shall become President. If a President shall not have been chosen before the time fixed for the beginning of his term, or if the President elect shall have failed to qualify, then the vice president elect shall act as President until a President shall have qualified; and the Congress may by law provide for the case wherein neither a President elect nor a vice president elect shall have qualified, declaring who shall then act as President, or the manner in which one who is to act shall be selected, and such person shall act accordingly until a President or vice president shall have qualified.

SECTION 4. The Congress may by law provide for the case of the death of any of the persons from whom the House of Representatives may choose a President, whenever the right of choice shall have devolved upon them, and for the case of the death of any of the persons from whom the Senate may choose a vice president, whenever the right of choice shall have devolved upon them.

SECTION 5. Sections 1 and 2 shall take effect on the 15th day of October following the ratification of this article.

SECTION 6. This article shall be inoperative unless it shall have been ratified as an amendment to the Constitution by the legislatures of three-fourths of the several states within seven years from the date of its submission.

AMENDMENT 21 (1933).

SECTION 1. The eighteenth article of amendment to the Constitution of the United States is hereby repealed.

SECTION 2. The transportation or importation into any state, territory, or possession of the United States, for delivery or use therein of intoxicating liquors, in violation of the laws thereof, is hereby prohibited.

SECTION 3. This article shall be inoperative unless it shall have been ratified as an amendment to the Constitution by conventions in the several states, as provided in the Constitution, within seven years from the date of the submission hereof to the states by the Congress.

AMENDMENT 22 (1951).

No person shall be elected to the office of the President more than twice, and no person who has held the office of President, or acted as President, for more than two years of a term to which some other person was elected President shall be elected to the office of the President more than once. But this Article shall not apply to any person holding the office of President when this Article was proposed by the Congress, and shall not prevent any person who may be holding the office of President, or acting as President, during the term within which this Article becomes operative from holding the office of President or acting as President during the remainder of such term.

AMENDMENT 23 (1961).

SECTION 1. The District constituting the seat of Government of the United States shall appoint in such manner as the Congress may direct:

A number of electors of President and vice president equal to the whole number of Senators and Representatives in Congress to which the District would be entitled if it were a State, but in no event more than the least populous State; they shall be in addition to those appointed by the States, but they shall be considered, for the purpose of the election of President and vice president, to be electors appointed by a State; and they shall meet in the District and perform such duties as provided by the twelfth article of amendment.

SECTION 2. The Congress shall have power to enforce this article by appropriate legislation.

AMENDMENT 24 (1964).

SECTION 1. The right of citizens of the United States to vote in any primary or other election for President or vice president, for electors for President or vice president, or for Senator or Representative in Congress, shall not be denied or abridged by the United States or any State by reason of failure to pay any poll tax or other tax.

SECTION 2. The Congress shall have power to enforce this article by appropriate legislation.

AMENDMENT 25 (1967).

SECTION 1. In case of the removal of the President from office or of his death or resignation, the vice president shall become President.

SECTION 2. Whenever there is a vacancy in the office of the vice president, the President shall nominate a vice president who shall take office upon confirmation by a majority of vote of both Houses of Congress.

SECTION 3. Whenever the President transmits to the President pro tempore of the Senate and the Speaker of the House of Representatives his written declaration that he is unable to discharge the powers and duties of his office, and until he transmits to them a written declaration to the contrary, such powers and duties shall be discharged by the vice president as Acting President.

SECTION 4. Whenever the vice president and a majority of either the principal officers of the executive departments or of such other body as Congress may by law provide, transmit to the President pro tempore of the Senate and the Speaker of the House of Representatives their written declaration that the President is unable to discharge the powers and duties of his office, the vice president shall immediately assume the powers and duties of the office as Acting President.

Thereafter, when the President transmits to the President pro tempore of the Senate and the Speaker of the House of Representatives his written declaration that no inability exists, he shall resume the powers and duties of his office unless the vice president and a majority of either the principal officers of the executive departments or of such other body as Congress may by law provide, transmit within four days to the President pro tempore of the Senate and the Speaker of the House of Representatives their written declaration that the President is unable to discharge the powers and duties of his office. Thereupon Congress shall decide the issue, assembling within forty-eight hours for that purpose if not in session. If the Congress, within twenty-one days after receipt of the latter written declaration, or, if Congress is not in session, within twenty-one days after Congress is required to assemble, determines by two-thirds vote of both Houses that the President is unable to discharge the powers and duties of his office, the vice president shall continue to discharge the same as Acting President; otherwise, the President shall resume the powers and duties of his office.

AMENDMENT 26 (1971).

SECTION 1. The right of citizens of the United States, who are eighteen years or older, to vote shall not be denied or abridged by the United States or any State on account of age.

SECTION 2. The Congress shall have the power to enforce this article by appropriate legislation.

Appendix III

Principal Speakers at the Federal Convention of 1787

Abraham Baldwin (1754–1807), Georgia; lawyer, educator

Gunning Bedford, Jr. (1747–1812), Delaware; lawyer, politician

William Blount (1749–1800), North Carolina; politician, land speculator

Pierce Butler (1744–1822), South Carolina; soldier, planter

George Clymer (1739–1813), Pennsylvania; merchant, politician

John Dickinson (1732–1808), Delaware; lawyer, author, politician

Oliver Ellsworth (1745–1807), Connecticut; lawyer, judge, scholar, politician

Benjamin Franklin (1706–1790), Pennsylvania; printer, author, scientist, diplomat

Elbridge Gerry (1744–1814), Massachusetts; merchant, politician

Nathaniel Gorham (1738–1796), Massachusetts; merchant, politician, land speculator

Alexander Hamilton (1755–1804), New York; lawyer, politician

William Samuel Johnson (1727–1819), Connecticut; lawyer, judge, scholar

Rufus King (1755–1827), Massachusetts; lawyer, politician, diplomat

John Langdon (1741–1819), New Hampshire; merchant, politician

James Madison (1751–1836), Virginia; author, politician

Luther Martin (1748–1826), Maryland; lawyer, politician

George Mason (1725–1792), Virginia; planter, scholar

John Francis Mercer (1759–1821), Maryland; lawyer, politician

Gouverneur Morris (1752–1816), Pennsylvania; lawyer, politician, diplomat

William Paterson (1745–1806), New Jersey; lawyer, judge, politician

Charles Pinckney (1757–1824), South Carolina; lawyer, politician

Charles C. Pinckney (1746–1825), South Carolina; soldier, planter, politician

Edmund Randolph (1753–1813), Virginia; lawyer, politician

George Read (1733–1798), Delaware; lawyer, judge

John Rutledge (1739–1800), South Carolina; lawyer, politician, planter, judge

Roger Sherman (1721–1793), Connecticut; shoemaker, politician

Caleb Strong (1745–1819), Massachusetts; lawyer, politician

George Washington (1732–1799), Virginia; soldier, planter, politician

Hugh Williamson (1735–1819), North Carolina; scholar, doctor

James Wilson (1742–1798), Pennsylvania; lawyer, scholar, politician, land speculator, judge

Annotated
Bibliography

Documents

The Records of the Federal Convention (4 vols., New Haven, 1937), ed. by Max Farrand; fifth volume supplement ed. by James Hutson, New Haven, 1987; the fullest record of the proceedings of the Convention.

Documentary History of the Ratification of the Constitution of the United States (24 vols., Madison, WI, 1976), ed. by Merrill Jensen and John Kaminski; the complete documentary source for the ratification contest, including debates in all the states.

The Complete Anti-Federalist (7 vols., Chicago, 1981), ed. by Herbert J. Storing; the full, authoritative source for antifederalist writings.

Essays on the Constitution of the United States (Brooklyn, NY, 1892), ed. by Paul L. Ford; incomplete but still useful as a source for additional federalist writings.

The Federalist Papers (New York, Signet Classics, 1961), ed. by Clinton Rossiter; full reprinting; inexpensive; useful introduction; excellent index; for students.

The Papers of Alexander Hamilton (24 vols., New York, 1961), ed. by Harold C. Syrett and others; the full record of Hamilton's thought, especially useful for his speeches at the New York ratifying convention of 1788.

The Selected Writings and Speeches of Alexander Hamilton (Washington, DC, 1985), ed. by Morton Frisch; best single volume of Hamilton's important works, with an introduction.

The Papers of James Madison Congressional Series (17 vols., Chicago and Charlottesville, VA, 1962), ed. by W. T. Hutchinson, Robert Rutland, and others; excellent source for Madison's correspondence, writings, and speeches during 1787 and 1788.

The Selected Writings of James Madison (Indianapolis, 2006), ed. by Ralph Ketcham; Madison's major writings on politics and government, with an introduction.

The Papers of George Mason (3 vols., Chapel Hill, NC, 1970), ed. by Robert Rutland; best full collection of the papers of an important anti-federalist.

Secondary Sources

Adair, Douglass, *Fame and the Founding Fathers* (New York, 1974); graceful, penetrating essays on the thought of Madison, Hamilton, and others.

Adams, Willi P., *The First American Constitutions: Republican Ideology and the Making of the State Constitutions in the Revolutionary Era* (Chapel Hill, NC, 1980); explains the contributions of the state constitution makers to the political thought of the era.

Amar, Akhil, *America's Constitution: A Biography* (New York, 2005); interesting account of the forming and life of the Constitution.

Bailyn, Bernard, *The Ideological Origins of the American Revolution* (Cambridge, MA, 1967); the best account of its subject.

Banning, Lance, *The Sacred Fire of Liberty: James Madison and the Founding of the Federal Republic* (New York,

1995); incisive account of Madison's intellectual and political leadership, ca. 1785–1792.

Berkin, Carol, *A Brilliant Solution: Inventing the American Constitution* (New York, 2002); interesting story of the people and debates at the Federal Convention of 1787.

Cornell, Saul, *Other Founders: Antifederalism, 1788–1828* (Chapel Hill, NC, 1999); best study of anti-federalism and its continuing influence in American history.

Diamond, Martin, "Democracy and the *Federalist*: A Reconsideration of the Framers' Intent," *American Political Science Review,* vol. 53 (1959), pp. 52–68; a pathbreaking study linking the ideas of the Declaration of Independence with those of the Constitution.

Diamond, Martin, "The *Federalist*'s View of Federalism," in *Essays in Federalism* (Claremont, CA, 1961); the best explanation of the concept of federalism.

Epstein, David, *The Political Theory of the Federalist* (Chicago, 1984); a searching, sometimes overelaborate analysis showing that "Publius" was both a Lockean defender of natural rights and an Aristotelian promoter of the public interest through good government.

Gibson, Alan, *Interpreting the Founding: Guide to the Enduring Debates over the Origins and Foundations of the American Republic* (Lawrence, KS, 2010); an incisive and comprehensive analysis of federalist and anti-federalist thought.

Ketcham, Ralph, *Framed for Posterity: The Enduring Philosophy of the Constitution* (Lawrence, KS, 1993); an overview of the ideals of republicanism, liberty, the public good, and federalism in the Constitution, 1787 to the present.

Ketcham, Ralph, *James Madison, A Biography* (New York, 1971); a full biography of "The Father of the Constitution."

Main, Jackson Turner, *The Antfederalists, Critics of the Constitution, 1781–1788* (Chapel Hill, NC, 1961); best scholarly account of the political opposition to the new Constitution.

McDonald, Forrest, *We the People: The Economic Origins of the Constitution* (Chicago, 1958); detailed, enlightening study of the economic status of members of the Federal Convention, and of the delegates to the state ratifying conventions.

Meade, Robert D., *Patrick Henry, Practical Revolutionary* (Philadelphia, 1969); detailed biography of the foremost anti-federalist orator.

Mitchell, Broadus, *Alexander Hamilton* (2 vols., New York, 1957, 1962); detailed, scholarly, sympathetic biography of the most nationally-oriented federalist.

Onuf, Peter, *The Origins of the Federal Republic: Jurisdictional Controversies in the United States, 1775–1787* (Philadelphia, 1983); explains the influence of relations among the states on the nature of the federal Constitution.

Rahe, Paul, *Republics Ancient and Modern: Classical Republicanism and the American Revolution* (Chapel Hill, NC, 1992); thorough study of the political ideas of the Founding Era.

Rakove, Jack, *Original Meanings: Politics and Ideas in the Making of the Constitution* (New York, 1996); brilliant on that subject.

Reardon, John, *Edmund Randolph: A Biography* (New York, 1975); thorough, thoughtful biography of an anti-federalist of 1787 who became a federalist in 1788.

Rossiter, Clinton, *Alexander Hamilton and the Constitution* (New York, 1964); a lucid explanation of Hamilton's "energetic" approach to government.

Rossiter, Clinton, *1787: The Grand Convention* (New York, 1966); interesting, well-informed account of the Convention and of its members.

Seed, Geoffrey, *James Wilson* (Millwood, NY, 1978); a searching analysis of Wilson's thought based on a close study of his writings.

Storing, Herbert, *What the Anti-Federalists Were For* (Chicago, 1981); the best study of anti-federalist thought by an outstanding political theorist.

Stourzh, Gerald, *Alexander Hamilton and the Idea of Republican Government* (Stanford, CA, 1979); the best explanation of Hamilton's political thought.

Van Doren, Carl, *Benjamin Franklin* (New York, 1937); detailed, interesting biography of the Convention's foremost revolutionary and conciliator.

Wills, Garry, *Explaining America: The Federalist* (New York, 1981); thoughtful analysis of the *Federalist* emphasizing the influence of Hume and other Scottish thinkers.

Wood, Gordon, *The Creation of the American Republic, 1776–1787* (Chapel Hill, NC, 1969); the best study of the world of political ideas from which the Constitution arose, showing its relationship to revolutionary ideals.

Index of Ideas